D0612821

973.
7   Taylor, John M.
Tay   Confederate raider

c1994 $24.95
519003 HA

CASS COUNTY PUBLIC LIBRARY
400 E. MECHANIC
HARRISONVILLE, MO 64701

H

CASS COUNTY PUBLIC LIBRARY
Harrisonville, MO   64701

PRESENTED BY

Mr. & Mrs. David McKee
Mr. & Mrs. Richard McLain
Mrs. Davie Anderson
In memory of
Rita Jones

CONFEDERATE RAIDER

Also by John M. Taylor

William Henry Seward: Lincoln's Right Hand

General Maxwell Taylor: The Sword and the Pen

Garfield of Ohio

From the White House Inkwell

Korea's Syngman Rhee

(writing as Richard C. Allen)

CONFEDERATE RAIDER

RAPHAEL SEMMES
OF THE *ALABAMA*

John M. Taylor

0 0022 0070218 7

Brassey's

Washington · London

CASS COUNTY PUBLIC LIBRARY
300 E. MECHANIC
HARRISONVILLE, MO 64701

519003

Copyright © 1994 by Brassey's, Inc.

All rights reserved. No part of this book may be reproduced, stored in a retrieval system, or transmitted in any form or by any means—electronic, electrostatic, magnetic tape, mechanical, photocopying, recording, or otherwise—without permission in writing from the publisher.

Brassey's Inc.

Editorial Offices	*Order Department*
Brassey's Inc.	Brassey's Book Orders
8000 Westpark Drive	c/o Macmillan Publishing Co.
First Floor	100 Front Street, Box 500
McLean, Virginia 22102	Riverside, New Jersey 08075

Brassey's books are available at special discounts for bulk purchases for sales promotions, premiums, fund-raising, or educational use.

Library of Congress Cataloging-in-Publication Data

Taylor, John M.
  Confederate raider: Raphael Semmes of the Alabama/John M. Taylor.
    p. cm.
  Includes index.
  ISBN 0-02-881086-4
  1. Semmes, Raphael, 1809–1877. 2. Admirals—Confederate States of America—
Biography. 3. Confederate States of America. Navy—Biography. 4. United States—History—
Civil War, 1861–1865—Naval operations. I. Title.
E467.1.S47T39   1994
973.7'57'092—dc20
[B]   94-4382
                                                                                       CIP

10 9 8 7 6 5 4 3 2 1

Printed in the United States of America

A military or naval man cannot go very far astray who abides by the point of honor.

—*Raphael Semmes*

Contents

Preface   ix

1. "We Fired No Gun of Triumph"   1

2. The Old Navy   12

3. Mexico   22

4. Through the Burning Woods   35

5. "Give Me That Ship"   49

6. "Doing a Pretty Fair Business"   58

7. "Semmes Was Too Clever"   70

8. Farewell to the *Sumter*   84

9. The Mysterious *290*   98

10. The Pirate Semmes   109

11. Off the Grand Banks   121

12. "Give It to the Rascals"   135

13. The Trail of Fire   146

14. Ruling the Waves   157

15. "Daar Kom die *Alabama*"   170

16. In Asian Waters   181

17. Showdown off Cherbourg   195

18. Defeated but Not Conquered   210

19. "As Hard and Determined as Flint"   224

20. "A Flagrant Violation of Faith"   235

21. Defiance   248

22. Sunset   261

23. Semmes of the *Alabama*   270

Epilogue   279

Appendix: Semmes's Victims   283

Notes   287

Index   309

Preface

To a considerable extent, the story of the Confederacy at sea is the story of Raphael Semmes, who was the most successful practitioner of the naval strategy of commerce raiding. The more famous of his two commands, the *Alabama,* traveled some 75,000 miles without ever touching a Confederate port, and accounted for sixty-four of the two-hundred-odd Northern merchantmen destroyed by Confederate raiders. In the South, Semmes was lionized for his attacks on Northern shipping and for his courage in challenging the U.S.S. *Kearsarge* off Cherbourg in 1864. North of the Mason-Dixon line he was denounced as a pirate. By any standard, he was one of the most interesting and controversial figures to come out of the war.

Why, then, has there been no biography of Semmes since an uncritical and unsatisfying volume published in 1938? I can offer at least three reasons. First, the Civil War has been perceived as a land war, one in which naval developments were of relatively little importance. Most histories recognize the significance of the Northern blockade, but otherwise focus on the land war. Indeed, not until the publication, in 1960, of Virgil Carrington Jones's three-volume *The Civil War at Sea* did the maritime dimension of the war receive adequate treatment.

Second, the Civil War produced so many notable commanders on both sides that the handful of gifted Confederate naval leaders headed by Semmes were eclipsed by giants such as Robert E. Lee, "Stonewall" Jackson, and William T. Sherman. Their battlefields were preserved and carefully mapped; where the *Alabama* once sailed, the "dark illimitable ocean" closed in behind.

In Semmes's case a third factor is pertinent, for Semmes did nothing to facilitate the task of a modern biographer. In the preface to his eight-hundred-page Civil War reminiscences, *Memoirs of Service*

Afloat, Semmes wrote that "the career of the author was a sealed book to all but himself." He gives few clues to the reasoning behind his key decisions, including that of challenging the *Kearsarge*. In none of his writings does he discuss his upbringing or his early years in the U.S. Navy. And because he was at that time an unknown naval officer, there are periods in these pre–Civil War years when Semmes all but disappears from sight.

In writing my biography of a contemporary of Semmes's, Secretary of State William Henry Seward, I was inundated with material, most of it from Seward's own pen. Semmes, in contrast, seems almost to have erased any paper trail. I estimate that there are no more than a few hundred of Semmes's letters extant, many of them of little consequence. I have been unable to locate a photograph of his wife that I could label as such with any degree of confidence.

Although Semmes's memoir is one of the most interesting and readable of Civil War reminiscences, it is a legal brief for the Confederate cause rather than an autobiography. Even so, any study of Semmes depends to a considerable degree on his own accounts. His journals—rescued at the last moment from the sinking *Alabama*—are to be found in the multivolume *Official Records* of the Civil War. These narratives, however biased, are generally accurate in matters of fact; in some cases they can be checked against Federal and other accounts. At the same time they are notable for certain omissions, and postwar accounts by men of the *Alabama* were colored by a reluctance to relate any incident that might reflect unfavorably on their famous ship.

Notwithstanding the problems he poses to a biographer, the Civil War produced no more remarkable figure than Raphael Semmes. He led the near destruction of the U.S. merchant marine and was the only naval officer on either side to fight two battles at sea. He helped defend Richmond in the final year of the war and was the only officer in Confederate service to hold the dual rank of admiral and general. He was, moreover, one of the premier intellects of the naval service. He was not only an oceanographer and an expert on marine law, but also a skillful writer and a devotee of English poetry.

Although Semmes was a hard-bitten sea warrior, he had the soul of a romantic. The climactic duel off Cherbourg between the *Alabama* and the *Kearsarge* was the last naval battle to be initiated by a formal challenge. But Semmes was also a zealot—a true believer who went to his grave convinced of the legality of secession and the justice of the Confederate cause. He was as capable of taunting a Yankee skipper whose ship he had captured as he was careful to give his prisoners the best care that his crowded ships could afford.

A number of persons assisted in the writing of this book. Anderson Humphrey, coauthor of the definitive Semmes genealogy, put me in touch with several of the admiral's descendants. Manuscript collectors Lewis Leigh Jr., Michael Masters, and Philip H. Jones provided copies of several unusual Semmes letters. Cameron Moseley allowed me to quote his grandmother's description of Raphael Semmes in Paris. At the Museum of the City of Mobile, curator Charles Torrey assisted in locating material relating to Semmes's homes in Mobile. Civil War bibliophile Elden "Josh" Billings lent me a number of scarce volumes from his extensive library. At the National Defense University, the chief of special collections, Susan Lemke, and her assistant, Tina Lavato, helped locate books in other institutions. Autograph dealer Gary Hendershott provided an unusual war-date photograph. John Haskell of the Swem Libary, College of William and Mary, provided a computer run on institutional holdings of Semmes material. General Luke Finlay, Admiral Semmes's great-grandson, provided genealogical data, including new information on the admiral's marriage.

Two American historians, Norman C. Delaney and Frank Merli, have shared with me their vast knowledge of the Civil War at sea. Professor Delaney's extensive writings on the *Alabama* are cited repeatedly in the pages that follow. Both of these scholars called my attention to little-known source materials, and both read selected chapters in draft. They bear no responsibility for my conclusions, however, which in some instances may be at variance with their own.

This book, like its predecessors, has benefited immensely from repeated readings by my wife, Priscilla, a professional editor whose publications include the Phi Beta Kappa quarterly newsletter. My daughter, Kathy Shaibani, also an editorial professional, offered additional suggestions concerning the manuscript. Quotations from Semmes's own writings have required little editing, but in quoting the admiral I have at times deleted the commas that he occasionally employed to excess.

John M. Taylor
McLean, Virginia

CONFEDERATE RAIDER

CHAPTER 1

"We Fired No Gun of Triumph"

I n June 1861, two months after Confederate forces had fired on Fort Sumter, North and South alike were taking the first, tentative steps toward all-out war. From Washington, President Lincoln had announced that a portion of the United States was in a state of insurrection and issued a call for volunteers. This act, in turn, prompted Virginia—the border state being most assiduously wooed by both sides—to throw in her lot with the Confederacy. With positions hardening on both sides, Lincoln had proclaimed a naval blockade against the seceded states.

The task facing Lincoln's Navy Department was formidable, for at the outset of the war it had only forty-two ships with which to monitor some 3,500 miles of Confederate coastline. But the department set to chartering ships for blockade duty; by the end of 1861 it would have 260 warships in service.[1] Both sides were preparing for a land war, but how long such a war would last would depend in part on who controlled the sea.

The Confederacy, meanwhile, had a rapidly expanding army but no navy to speak of. At the time of Fort Sumter, the Confederate "navy" consisted of ten river craft mounting, in aggregate, fifteen guns.[2] The Confederates had subsequently added a few coastal vessels to their inventory, but had not a single ship on the high seas. The South's military mobilization was devoted almost entirely to ground forces.

One man was determined to change all this—to make the Confederacy as feared at sea as it was soon to become on land. Commander Raphael Semmes, late of the U.S. Navy, arrived at the interim Confederate capital of Montgomery, Alabama, in February. There he met with a longtime acquaintance, Jefferson Davis, the newly inaugurated president of the Confederacy. To Davis, and then to Secretary of the Navy Stephen R. Mallory, Semmes spelled out his plan to take the war to the enemy. Not to the Federal navy, which greatly outnumbered any naval force that the Confederacy could expect to muster, but to the U.S. merchant fleet.

In 1861 the U.S. merchant marine was the largest in the world. No one surpassed the skill and ingenuity of Yankee shipwrights in the design and construction of wooden ships. America's carrying trade had steadily increased in the 1840s and 1850s, fueled by the discovery of gold in California, the opening of treaty ports in Japan and China, and a whaling fleet that operated from the North Atlantic to the Bering Strait.

Semmes viewed the U.S. merchant marine as the North's Achilles' heel. If Confederate cruisers were to threaten the very existence of the merchant marine, would not the North's powerful shipping interests force the Lincoln government to sue for peace? In the course of thirty-five years in the U.S. Navy, Semmes had read extensively in naval history. He had studied especially the exploits of John Paul Jones in the American Revolution and the bold frigate captains of the War of 1812. He concluded that, under certain circumstances, a weak naval power could hold hostage the merchant marine of a more powerful adversary.

At the outset of the Civil War, Raphael Semmes was almost fifty-two years old and was beginning to gray around the temples. He was of average height for men of his day—about five feet eight inches—and in later life claimed never to have weighed more than 130 pounds. But he was spare and taut and carried himself with an erect military bearing. In an era when full beards were the fashion, Semmes sported instead an imperious, pointed mustache that would lead his crewmen to call him "Old Beeswax." Semmes's appearance was an accurate reflection of the man. The tightset mouth, flashing gray eyes, and flamboyant mustache announced that here was a man accustomed to being obeyed.

Some thought Semmes too old to command a cruiser in wartime, but the high-strung Alabamian was eager to go to war. He had a firm grasp of naval tactics, an encyclopedic knowledge of winds and currents, and an immense capacity for work. Above all, he had a deep-seated hostility toward the vulgarity and commercialism that he associated with the North, and his commitment to the cause of Southern independence was total.

After convincing President Davis of the merits of commerce raiding, Semmes had pressed Secretary of the Navy Stephen Mallory to find him a suitable vessel to take to sea. There were few seagoing vessels of any kind in the Confederacy, but in a list of ships requisitioned for the navy Semmes had spotted a small screw steamer, of about 500 tons, capable of mounting four or five cannon. At that time, she was the best the South had to offer.

With Mallory's blessing, Semmes traveled to New Orleans to look her over. New Orleans was then the largest city in the South, one long associated with cotton and sin. Semmes was saddened by what he saw of the Crescent City; her cotton wharves were deserted and the harbor all but empty. Writer George W. Cable would recall, "The brave, steady fellows . . . had laid down the pen, taken up the sword and musket, and followed after the earlier and more eager volunteers."[3] Semmes, for his part, identified with this martial spirit. Always the cavalier, he noted with approval that the balconies were crowded with brightly dressed belles, cheering their men on to battle.[4]

Semmes was very much at home in New Orleans. His own home, in Mobile, Alabama, was only 150 miles to the east. A cousin, Thomas J. Semmes, was a prominent New Orleans attorney; he was pleased to make room for Raphael in his Charles Street offices. Raphael also had the company of his oldest son, for Spencer Semmes had joined the First Regiment of Louisiana Infantry and was camped just outside the city.[5]

Even as he looked for a sea command, Semmes had domestic problems that defied resolution. His wife, Anne, who deplored secession, had gone to live with her family in Cincinnati. She was devoted to her husband and uncomfortable with her Unionist family, yet where else was she to go? The war was dividing even close families. Raphael's only brother, Samuel, was a Unionist in Maryland. A cousin, Alexander Semmes, would become a flag officer in the Federal navy.

In New Orleans, however, Semmes was pleased with the ship that he had come to inspect. She was small—only 184 feet long, with a thirty-foot beam—but new and staunchly built, having been constructed in Philadelphia in 1859. Semmes saw possibilities in the little steamer despite the fact that she had been designed strictly for passenger service. "Her lines were easy and graceful," he later wrote, "and she had a sort of saucy air about her, which seemed to say that she was not averse to the service on which she was about to be employed."[6] Semmes reported favorably to Mallory and was authorized to commission her in the Confederate service. On June 3, 1861, he presided over a brief ceremony. A Confederate flag, the gift of some New Orleans ladies, was raised before a small group of invited guests. Cannons boomed in salute, and a three-man band played "Dixie." Then, with the guests still on board, the *Sumter* made a short speed trial up the river.

Semmes set about converting his command into a warship—a daunting task. Passenger accommodations were cleared away, a new suit of sails purchased, the main deck reinforced, magazines installed, and coal bunkers enlarged. The Alabamian went about his task with energy and imagination: To allow the *Sumter* to alter her appearance, he equipped her with a hinged funnel, which, when not in use, made her indistinguishable from any other bark. But would he be able to put to sea before New Orleans was totally blockaded? He wrote in his journal,

> A month has elapsed since I began the preparation of the *Sumter* for sea, and yet we are not ready. . . . The river is not yet blockaded, but expected to be tomorrow. . . . Whilst penning the last paragraph news reaches us that the Lincoln Government has crossed the Potomac and invaded Virginia. Thus commences a bloody and a bitter war.[7]

Work on the *Sumter* continued. Materials and skilled workmen were hard to come by, but Semmes had an ally in Captain Lawrence Rousseau, commanding the New Orleans naval district. Rousseau provided all the assistance he could, but the work nevertheless proceeded slowly. Where were the guns that had been ordered from Norfolk? Semmes sent one of his officers, Robert Chapman, to search for them, and found that they had been thrown off a train to make room for other goods.[8]

Semmes could hardly conceal his impatience. He wrote in his journal,

Saturday, June 1 finds us not yet ready for sea! The tanks have all been taken on board and stowed; the gun carriages for the 32s will be finished on Monday. The circles for the 8-inch gun have been laid down, and the fighting-bolts are ready for placing. On Monday I shall throw the crew on board, and by Thursday next I shall *without doubt* be ready for sea. We are losing a great deal of precious time. The enemy's flag is being flaunted in our faces . . . and, as yet, we have not struck a blow.[9]

Not the next week, as Semmes had promised, but the week after, the *Sumter* was ready for sea. Her armament consisted of four thirty-two-pound howitzers in broadside, plus an eight-inch pivot gun between her first and second masts. Semmes had taken a special interest in the pivot gun, which traversed on an iron track of his own design. The *Sumter*'s speed had proved disappointing, however—a maximum of ten knots, he informed Mallory, slower than any of the Federal warships patrolling off New Orleans. Moreover, even with enlarged coal bunkers she carried fuel for only a week under steam.

In contrast to these difficulties, manning the ship proved easy. Semmes had requested as his executive officer John McIntosh Kell, a bluff, thirty-eight-year-old Georgian whom Semmes had once defended in a court-martial. Kell would serve Semmes loyally and efficiently throughout the war. Because the Confederacy had far more naval officers than it had ships, Semmes was able to handpick his other officers as well, and for his crew he had his choice among the many seamen stranded in New Orleans by the blockade. Semmes wrote to Mallory on June 14,

I have an excellent set of men on board, though they are nearly all green, and it will require some little practice and drilling at the guns to enable them to handle them creditably. Shall I be fortunate [enough] to reach the high seas, you may rely upon my implicit obedience of your instructions to "do the enemy's commerce the greatest injury in the shortest time."[10]

Semmes wondered how he might communicate with the Navy Department through the enemy blockade. He could attempt to send multiple copies of his reports on blockade runners, but these would always be subject to capture. For sensitive material he worked out a code with Mallory based on *Reid's English Dictionary*. "If I wish to use the word 'prisoner,'" Semmes wrote the secretary, "my reference to it would be as follows: 323, B, 15; the first number referring to the page, the letter to the column, and the second number to the number of the word from the top of the column."[11]

Getting to sea, however, was Semmes's immediate challenge. Already the activity of a few Confederate privateers was attracting the attention of the Federal navy. By June 18, when the *Sumter* was truly ready, the channels from New Orleans into the Gulf of Mexico were blocked by four of the fastest and most powerful Federal steamers: the 3,765-ton *Powhatan,* the 4,582-ton *Niagara,* the 3,307-ton *Minnesota,* and the 2,070-ton *Brooklyn.* None mounted fewer than twenty-one guns, and any one of the four was capable of turning the *Sumter* into kindling in a stand-up fight.

Fortunately for Semmes, there were several routes by which the *Sumter* might reach the Gulf of Mexico. The eastern route through Lake Pontchartrain was the most direct, but also the most dangerous. Not only was it riddled with shoals, but in any except the poorest visibility a blockader would have a clear view of any vessel attempting to leave the port. The other routes all required a departing vessel to take the main channel of the Mississippi through the southernmost extension of the delta. South of New Orleans, before emptying into the Gulf, the river divided like a great chicken foot into four channels: Pass à l'Outre, Northeast Pass, South Pass, and Southwest Pass. While this abundance of routes was troublesome to any blockader— the first and last passes were thirty-five miles apart—the two middle passes were too shallow for even small vessels.

On the night of June 18 the *Sumter* cast off her moorings and slipped down the river. Semmes anchored for three days south of New Orleans to drill his crew and complete his plans. Rather than confront the powerful *Powhatan*, he wanted to take the *Sumter* out the easternmost exit, Pass à l'Outre, and attempt to outrun the *Brooklyn.* Any escape attempt would require an experienced river pilot, however, and obtaining the right one could be a problem. Mississippi pilots were a law unto themselves. Theirs was a seller's market, for the risks associated with navigating the sandbars around a port such as New Orleans made their services indispensable. Moreover, the New Orleans pilots were an unhappy group, for the war-imposed collapse of the city's maritime trade theatened their livelihood. Their attachment to the Confederate cause was fragile and occasionally suspect.

On the night of June 21 Semmes received word that the *Powhatan* had left her station off the Southwest Pass. Under the circumstances, he abandoned his plan to exit to the east. Instead, he immediately raised steam and prepared to depart via the Southwest Pass. Arriving at the lighthouse at 10:30 P.M., he signaled for a pilot only to have the keeper ignore his request. Semmes anchored in the channel and fumed for the rest of the night. Sure enough, by dawn the *Powhatan* was back at her station.

Semmes did not intend to suffer such treatment again. The *Sumter*'s commander, furious, sent one of his officers, Lieutenant John Stribling, to the chief of the Pilots Association with a message:

> This is to command you to repair on board this ship with three or four of the most experienced pilots of the bar. . . . If any man disobeys this summons, I will not only have his [license] taken away from him, but I will send an armed force and arrest and bring him on board.[12]

Stribling returned on the afternoon of June 22 with several unhappy pilots. After listening to "some stammering excuses," Semmes ordered that one of them must stay on board the *Sumter*, to be relieved if necessary at the end of a week. On June 23 he wrote Mallory that he was at the Head of Passes, awaiting an opportunity to break out. Although only Pass à l'Outre or the Southwest Pass could accommodate the *Sumter*, the Federals did not necessarily know this. And while at the Head of Passes, Semmes had the use of a small gunboat, the *Ivy*, for reconnaissance.

In the course of several days at his anchorage, Semmes fought the ubiquitous mosquitoes and considered his options. There were four Federal blockaders operating just outside the sandbars that posed navigational obstacles to any departing ship. Indeed, the senior Federal officer on station was an Old Navy acquaintance of Semmes, Lieutenant David D. Porter, commanding the *Powhatan*. Porter, for his part, knew that something was brewing, in part because he could see the *Ivy* scouting the passes. He used his pivot gun to keep the *Ivy* at a distance and felt sure that he had the *Sumter* under control. In one message to the Navy Department he threw in some doggerel:

> Bombs bursting in air
> And the rockets' red glare
> Show the *Ivy* and *Sumter*
> That our ship is still here.[13]

Eager to take some initiative, Porter, on June 27, sent a landing party to Pilottown, on the Southwest Pass, where they destroyed the telegraph link with New Orleans.[14] Semmes, not to be outdone, extinguished the lighthouses at Pass à l'Outre and South Point, an action that obliged Federal blockaders to stand farther offshore in bad weather.

The next week brought another false alarm. On the morning of June 29 *Sumter*'s lookout reported that the *Brooklyn* was nowhere to be seen. Semmes ordered steam, and in a few minutes the raider was running toward Pass à l'Outre, the muddy river gurgling past her sides. Alas, after a run of four miles came bad news: The *Brooklyn* was at her usual station. The *Sumter* apparently had dragged her anchor during the night, moving just enough for the *Brooklyn* to be obscured by a clump of trees. Semmes banked his fires, and his crew returned to their losing battle against the heat and mosquitoes. On June 30 Semmes wrote Mallory that he was still at the Head of Passes, with several enemy ships blockading the exits. "I am only surprised that the *Brooklyn* does not come up to this anchorage, which she might easily do, as there is water enough and no military precautions whatever have been taken to hold it."[15]

On the night of June 29 Semmes sent the *Ivy* and another craft to watch the two deep-water passes, but they found nothing to report on enemy movements. Semmes had now been at the Head of Passes for ten days, and his patience was wearing thin. Twisting his mustache tips in a characteristic manner, he reflected once again on the odds for a successful dash to the Gulf. He feared the firepower of the *Powhatan* but thought that the *Sumter* might have an edge on her in speed. The *Brooklyn*, however, was much more heavily armed than Semmes's raider, and faster as well.

The morning of Sunday, June 30, dawned much like those that had preceded it. The sun was hot, but the shipboard routine included muster, and Semmes required that his crew be in proper uniform. More than the usual cleanup would be required, for the *Sumter* had received fresh provisions the previous night, and coal dust was everywhere. Semmes ordered the *Sumter* down Pass à l'Outre for a training exercise, halting west of the lighthouse. There, as the anchor chain ran out and the mosquitoes moved in, a solitary oysterman rowed to the *Sumter* and hailed the officer of the deck. The *Brooklyn*, he said, had left her station to chase a sail and was nowhere in sight.

Was this yet another false alarm? Semmes thought not. In his words, "The crew, who had been 'cleaning themselves' for Sunday muster, at once stowed away their bags; the swinging-booms were gotten alongside, the boats run up, and in ten minutes the steam was again hissing, as if impatient of control."[16] The ship's head swung into the Mississippi current, and the *Sumter* began her run for Pass à l'Outre.

But Semmes was not yet done with the mischievous river pilots. Very little escaped the *Sumter*'s skipper, and he noticed on the run downriver that his pilot looked uneasy. What was the matter? Ashen, the pilot replied that he knew nothing of Pass à l'Outre; his work had been entirely on the Southwest Pass. Semmes, outraged, ordered the pilot to carry on anyhow, "and if he ran us ashore or put us in the hands of the enemy he would swing him to the yardarm as a traitor."[17] Fortunately, the *Sumter* had not yet passed the lighthouse, and Kell ran up the "Pilot Wanted" signal. By then the pilots were treating Semmes with considerable respect, and as the *Sumter* approached the lighthouse a whaleboat bearing a second pilot came promptly to her side. Semmes managed to imbue the scene with an air of romance:

> In the balcony of the pilot's house, which had been built in the very marsh . . . there stood a beautiful woman, the pilot's young wife, waving him on to his duty, with her handkerchief. . . . I uncovered my head gallantly to my fair countrywoman. A few moments more and a tow-line had been thrown to the boat, and the gallant young fellow stood on the horse-block beside me.[18]

The *Sumter* steamed on and within fifteen minutes was across the bar. "Now, Captain, you are all clear," the pilot told him, preparing to jump into his own boat alongside. "Give her hell and let her go!"[19]

As the *Sumter* emerged into the Gulf, Semmes faced a critical decision. The *Brooklyn* was no longer out of sight but was hurrying back to her station and was no more than four miles away. A hasty consultation aboard the *Sumter* was not reassuring; one of Semmes's officers who had served aboard the Federal vessel insisted that the *Brooklyn* could make fourteen knots and that there was no chance that the *Sumter* could escape her.

Semmes himself was uneasy, but having come this far he would not turn back. He sent for his chief engineer, Miles Freeman, and asked for a report. The engines were performing well, said Freeman, and he might even be able to coax another half knot out of them. The *Sumter* put on full sail and increased steam pressure from eighteen to twenty-five pounds. To lighten ship, Semmes jettisoned a small howitzer and fifteen hundred gallons of water.[20]

Semmes was far from giving up. He knew his ship, and he was convinced that the *Sumter,* with her large fore-and-aft sail, could sail "closer to the wind"—that is, make greater headway in a breeze off her bow—than could her pursuer. He steered a northeasterly course, making a gradual arc toward the Gulf of Mexico, followed by the *Brooklyn* under full sail and spewing black smoke. Semmes could not help admiring the majesty of her appearance, with her broad, flaring bow, and with masts and yards "as taut and square as those of an old time sailing frigate."[21]

Then a rain squall broke between the two ships, effectively concealing each from the other. Some time later the *Brooklyn* emerged from the squall with her twenty-one guns run out, looming much larger than she had just minutes before. The *Sumter* was making a good nine and a half knots, but it appeared for a time that her cruise would be over before it began. *Brooklyn*'s flag was clearly discernible at her peak, and it was disconcerting to the Confederates to see blue-clad Federal officers studying the little *Sumter* through their glasses. Semmes called for the paymaster, Henry Myers, and directed him to bring the cash box and ship's papers topside, to be cast overboard if necessary. Semmes had with him $10,000 in gold, provided by the Navy Department, and he did not intend for it to fall into Yankee hands.

The breeze freshened, to Semmes's advantage. Not only was the *Sumter* better close to the wind than her antagonist, but she was "stealing the wind" from the *Brooklyn*—sailing on a tack between the breeze and the Yankee vessel. The *Sumter* now began to pull away from her pursuer, and after a three-and-a-half-hour chase the frustrated *Brooklyn* returned to her station off Pass à l'Outre.

The *Sumter* was free—as free as the seagulls that circled in her wake. Fortune had favored the brave. A more cautious commander, seeing the powerful *Brooklyn* on an interception course, might have returned to the safety of the Head of Passes, to try another day. Not Raphael Semmes. He was prudent, but he was also willing to take risks. Future admiral David D. Porter, commanding the blockading squadron, conceded that the *Sumter*'s escape was "a bold and dashing adventure" and "perhaps one of the most exciting chases of the war."[22]

Semmes realized, of course, that he had enjoyed the advantage of surprise. He was also aware that his real work had scarcely begun. In his own words,

> We fired no gun of triumph in the face of the enemy—my powder was too precious for that—but I sent the crew aloft, to man the rigging, and three such cheers were given for the Confederate flag . . . that had waved from the *Sumter*'s peak during the exciting chase, as could proceed only from the throats of American seamen, in the act of defying a tyrant.[23]

"*Dies memorabilis,*" Semmes began, as he recounted in his journal the developments that had seen the *Sumter* gain the open sea. "What an eventful career we have before us! May the Almighty smile upon us and our cause, and may we show ourselves worthy servants of Him and it."[24] The first Confederate cruiser was loose on the high seas, and Raphael Semmes would make the Yankees howl!

CHAPTER 2

The Old Navy

In the early decades of the nineteenth century, Washington, D.C., was a scattered collection of boardinghouses, bars, and shacks, interspersed with a handful of public buildings. Living conditions were primitive; there was no police department or fire department, and pigs and cattle freely roamed the streets. Alternately choking in dust or drowning in mud, the young capital was widely perceived as wasteland that had been cunningly consigned to the federal government by two neighboring states, Maryland and Virginia.

Not all was desolation along the banks of the Potomac, however. A few miles north of the capital, on the Maryland side of the river, lay Georgetown. Incorporated in 1789, the little river town had prospered as a shipping center for tobacco. The tobacco trade waned with the new century, but for many people Georgetown remained a far more civilized habitat than the shabby capital next door. Whereas Washington was the rude product of a political compromise, Georgetown had churches, cobblestone streets, taverns, and even a Roman Catholic seminary. Rock Creek, which was a common border for the two municipalities, separated two ways of life.

There had been Semmeses in Maryland for as long as anyone could remember. A Benedict Semmes had been part of Leonard Baltimore's

1634 expedition to the New World. In Charles County they grew tobacco; in Georgetown, they were typical of the growing commercial middle class.

The Semmeses were Catholics, with a large philosophical stake in the success of Lord Baltimore's colony. The proprietor had obtained his charter from Charles I, and the colony that he established had religious toleration as a cornerstone. The period of the English Civil War had been a trying one in Maryland, however, for not even an official policy of toleration could entirely paper over the differences between Catholic Cavaliers and Protestant Roundheads that had brought war to the motherland.

Raphael Semmes's father, Richard Thompson Semmes, was born in Charles County, Maryland, in 1784. He became a tobacco farmer and in 1808 married a Maryland girl, Catherine Middleton, whose forebears included Arthur Middleton, a signer of the Declaration of Independence. She bore Richard Semmes three children, one of whom died in infancy, before her own death after less than three years of marriage.

Raphael, the older of the two boys, was born in Charles County, Maryland, on September 27, 1809. He and his brother grew up as part of the extended Semmes clan. Young Raphael is known to have worked at one time in a lumberyard owned by an uncle, and he probably assisted in other family enterprises as well. The death of Richard Semmes in 1823, at the age of thirty-nine, prompted consultation between two of his surviving brothers, Benedict and Raphael. What was to be done with Richard's two boys? Legal custody went to Benedict Semmes, a prominent physician who had just been elected to the state House of Delegates, but the boys spent much of their time with their uncle Raphael in Georgetown.[1]

Born in 1786, the elder Raphael Semmes was a man of wide business interests, ranging from liquor to banking. After entering the wholesale grocery business, he joined an export-import house for which he made several trips across the Atlantic. Starting his own trading company in 1819, he stocked his Georgetown warehouse with goods from abroad. At various times the senior Raphael Semmes was also a director of the Farmers and Mechanics Bank and proprietor of a distillery near Mount Vernon, Virginia.[2]

In 1816 the senior Raphael Semmes had married another Maryland native, Mary Jenkins, by whom he would eventually have thirteen children. There were already five when, in 1823, he became the de facto guardian for his brother Richard's two sons. Perhaps because of Benedict Semmes's frequent absences, or perhaps because of schooling considerations, Raphael and Samuel grew up with the family of the senior Raphael Semmes in a red-brick house at 3257 N Street.[3] But they spent much of their time in Charles County as well, visiting their uncle Benedict and enjoying life on the banks of the Chesapeake Bay.

Although the younger Raphael Semmes was to tell little of his childhood, it appears to have been a pleasant one. His education was sporadic, however, marked by periods of tutoring and occasional attendance at private schools; he appears to have spent several years at a military school, Charlotte Hall Military Academy, in St. Mary's County.[4] When not studying or helping with the various family enterprises, he swam in the Potomac and watched slaves bring in the tobacco crop in southern Maryland.

Despite his limited formal schooling, young Raphael appears to have had a good education by the standards of his day. He studied Latin, read widely in the classics, and developed an interest in science that he would retain all his life. He was particularly interested in history. Political luminaries such as Henry Clay, Franklin Pierce, and Alexander Stephens occasionally visited the Semmes residence, and Raphael could hardly avoid absorbing some of the political atmosphere that surrounded the nation's capital. He came to look upon the house on N Street as embodying the best in cosmopolitan America: prosperity without greed, and culture without affectation. The warmth that he came to feel for his foster family was fully reciprocated. A foster brother, "B. J." Semmes, would call Raphael "the dearest love of my boyhood."[5]

The Semmes family were communicants at Georgetown's Holy Trinity Church, the oldest Catholic church in the Washington area. Young Raphael came to view Catholicism as an important part of his cultural heritage and to regard his Catholic forebears as a driving force behind the growth of political liberty in both Britain and America.

At sixteen, young Raphael was slim and small-boned. His dark hair and olive complexion lent plausibility to those who believed that the Semmes family had its roots in France. As for his temperament, acquaintances remembered him as cool and reserved, but these recollections came after the subject had matured into a cool and reserved adult. Given his interest in history, young Semmes was tempted by the prospect of a career in law. But the family to which he now belonged had a military as well as a commercial tradition. The elder

Raphael Semmes had served in the War of 1812, and his wife's father had commanded a warship in the American Revolution. In addition, young Raphael was constantly exposed to the lure of the sea. Vessels from many parts of the world called at the Georgetown wharves, and the senior Raphael Semmes regaled the family with tales of his many voyages. Ultimately, young Semmes decided to try his luck in the navy.

The U.S. Navy had fallen on hard times since its glory days in the War of 1812. Although it comprised some 272 officers and five thousand men, the navy of 1826 had no vessel larger than a frigate, and only four of these. Most of its vessels were tied up in East Coast ports.[6] Officers spent much of their time "awaiting orders," and because they were paid only while on active duty, most were obliged to find a second profession. Congress, fearful of encouraging a naval aristocracy, refused to authorize any rank higher than that of captain.

Until the establishment of the naval academy at Annapolis in 1845, the navy obtained its officers through what amounted to an apprentice system. A young man, usually from a family with political connections, was appointed a midshipman and placed aboard a ship. After several hard years at sea, in which he learned not only ship handling but subjects like navigation and astronomy, a midshipman went before a board of examiners. If he survived this test he became a "passed midshipman" and could pursue a career in the navy—if there were any commissioned billets available.

Raphael Semmes had the requisite political connections to obtain a midshipman's warrant. Benedict Semmes was by then speaker of the Maryland House of Delegates, and although nominally a Democrat he had good connections with the administration of President John Quincy Adams. Through his uncle's good offices, Semmes was appointed a midshipman by President Adams on April 1, 1826. Raphael must have felt particularly close to Benedict Semmes, for when he published his first book—a narrative of the Mexican War—in 1851, he dedicated it not to his wife or to the elder Raphael, but to Benedict J. Semmes, "as a slight return for the many kindnesses received at his hands."[7]

When Raphael Semmes reported to the sloop *Lexington* in the spring of 1826, he was making a sharp break from the salons of Georgetown. Few occupations were more dangerous than service in the navy, where death from enemy action was rare but death from accidents and disease was commonplace. "Like pears closely packed," novelist Herman Melville wrote, "the crowded crew mutually decay through close contact, and every plague spot is contagious."[8] The food in all navies—generally based on salt beef and biscuits—was notorious. Water, most often carried in wooden casks, sometimes became undrinkable.

For the sailors in the forecastle, danger aloft and squalor below were not the only threats to health. Death or injury might come from a drunken brawl in some liberty port or from punishment administered aboard their own ship. A sailor was as much at the mercy of his captain as a slave was in the power of his overseer. A navy court-martial could prescribe the death penalty for some twenty-two offenses, including the unlawful destruction of public property, sleeping on watch, and failing to clear for action.[9] Flogging was the standard punishment in the U.S. Navy and would remain so until 1850.

Midshipmen stood somewhere between the sailors in the forecastle and the officers aft; hence the term. They were berthed in their own quarters, most often in the gun room. They were subordinate to the ship's officers but exempt from the corporal punishments visited upon the crew. The "young gentlemen" were often teenagers, patronized by the officers and profanely denounced by veteran crewmen. Their life was not easy. For forty dollars a month, from which a mess bill was deducted, each midshipman was expected to stand watch, assist at gun drill, supervise the endless scouring of decks, and climb aloft in all weather.

Midshipmen ate, slept, and studied in cramped quarters below deck. The tough bullied the small, yet most of them coped. Midshipmen were rarely assigned permanent duties, but there were two requirements. First, each was to do whatever he was told, and do it quickly. Second, he was expected to keep a diary. The purpose of the diary, which was examined each week by the ship's commander, was to ensure that America's naval officers knew how to spell. Most U.S. Navy ships carried a civilian schoolmaster who attempted to give the midshipmen lessons in mathematics and navigation.[10] Through some alchemy, they were expected to learn how to handle a cumbersome vessel whose motor power—the wind—was constantly in flux, and to do so with a hard-bitten crew working scores of mysterious ropes.

For all its hardships, however, the navy retained an allure for young men of good family. There was much to see: Old World cities like Málaga, Tripoli, and Naples; legendary fortresses like Gibraltar; and places with exotic names like Algiers, Singapore, and Zanzibar.

Young Semmes was a good prospect for the navy, for he was bright, interested in navigation, and fascinated by the currents of wind and water. The deeds of men like John Paul Jones and Stephen Decatur nourished dreams of naval glory.

Semmes's first cruise on the *Lexington* was to the island of Trinidad, to bring home the body of one of the heroes of the War of 1812, Commodore Oliver H. Perry. For two years young Raphael cruised the Caribbean and the Mediterranean, on vessels variously engaged in showing the flag and in tracking down the last of the Caribbean pirates. He took some law books with him aboard the *Lexington,* but mostly he learned of the sea:

> In time he was to know almost by heart the glassy, steaming mazes of [the Caribbean]—the reefs, shoals and bars, the river mouths and shallow, tortuous channels, the islets and white beaches, the winds and the currents. He poked into harbors reeking with villainous smells and centuries of romance; intercepted slavers and scores of sail suspected of carrying black ivory; lay becalmed for days or rode out tropical hurricanes and mountainous seas.[11]

Semmes served on board the *Lexington* until September 1826, when he was placed on leave for reasons of ill health. After a comparatively short convalescence he served on the U.S.S. *Erie* for part of 1829 and on the U.S.S. *Brandywine* for the rest of 1829 and the first nine months of the following year. On September 29, 1830, he was posted to the U.S.S. *Porpoise* of the West Indies squadron, which was attempting to suppress piracy in the Caribbean.[12]

Semmes returned from this succession of cruises in 1831 and spent several months in Norfolk, Virginia, boning up for his pass examination. Subjects on which midshipmen were to be examined included rigging and stowing a ship, the handling of artillery, arithmetic, navigation, and astronomical calculations. The examination was by no means pro forma; in one year, only thirty-nine of eighty-nine midshipmen passed.[13] Semmes not only passed but ranked second in his class. He became a passed midshipman on April 28, 1832.

It was one thing to be a passed midshipman; it was another to find a billet. From May to October 1832, Semmes was involved in surveying Narragansett Bay in Rhode Island. (This assignment is of interest in that it represented Semmes's only extended posting north of the Mason-Dixon line.) He was on leave for five months over the winter of 1832–33, after which he was posted to Norfolk and given responsibility for maintaining the navy's chronometers, precision timepieces used in determining a ship's position.[14] For many young men, such an assignment might have killed off interest in the navy once and for all. On Semmes, it had the opposite effect. He developed an interest in chronometers that he carried through life.

Passed midshipman or not, Semmes had not yet made a final decision as to his profession. During extended leaves of absence he read law with his brother, Samuel, in Maryland, and with friends in Ohio. He was admitted to the Maryland bar in April 1834, but rather than practice law with his brother he moved to Cincinnati in July of that year. There he boarded at the home of Oliver and Electra Spencer, and became smitten with their daughter, Anne Elizabeth. While courting his future wife, he defended several young Ohioans who were charged with having destroyed the presses of an abolitionist journal. The prosecuting attorney was a politically ambitious Ohioan, Salmon P. Chase, who would later serve as Lincoln's secretary of the treasury. Semmes won an acquittal in what appears to have been his first brush with the volatile issue of slavery.[15]

Semmes might have devoted the rest of his life to the law had not fate intervened in the form of a communication from the Navy Department. In March 1835 he was directed to report for duty on one of the navy's famous frigates, the *Constellation*. The thirty-eight-gun *Constellation* was one of the most venerable ships of the U.S. Navy; her four decades of service had included days of glory in the War of 1812 and the campaigns against the Barbary pirates. Repeatedly rebuilt, the frigate was now on one uneventful cruise after another, this time to the Caribbean. There, Semmes had a chance to observe Britain's colonies just after the Emancipation Act of 1833 had freed all slaves. The midshipman had heretofore had little occasion to reflect on slavery as an institution; now, in colonies like Antigua and Jamaica, he saw emancipation as an act of questionable wisdom—one that was destroying the plantation economies and crippling trade.

In 1836 Semmes served briefly and without special distinction in the Second Seminole War. During the campaign in Florida, he was detached from the *Constellation,* placed in command of a small steamer, the *Lieutenant Izard,* and ordered to transport supplies and 150 Florida militiamen to an army force, under the command of General Richard Call, deployed upstream along the Withlacoochee River.

In early October, Semmes was told to find out whether his ship, towing a bargeload of supplies, could navigate far enough upstream to supply Call's force. In carrying out a reconnaissance on October 11, Semmes ran his ship aground and was unable to free her. Although crewmen were able to row the barge to Call's headquarters, the *Izard* was a total loss. Semmes and his crew, many of them enfeebled by disease, returned by boat to Pensacola on October 18.[16]

Even as a junior officer, Semmes was not one to suffer fools gladly. When a local paper, the Pensacola *Gazette,* criticized him for losing his ship, the twenty-seven-year-old midshipman penned a pungent retort. "If there is blame to be attached to myself or my officers," he wrote the *Gazette,* "this will be a proper subject for a *court of inquiry* and not for newspaper discussion."[17] There appears to have been no formal inquiry, and Semmes was not penalized for losing his ship. At a comparatively early age, however, he had demonstrated two qualities that would mark his later career: a willingness to meet criticism head-on and an insistence on correct legal procedures.

Semmes's posting aboard the *Constellation* ended in 1837, and on his return to Norfolk he found that, after eleven years as a midshipman, he had at long last been promoted to lieutenant. Good billets remained scarce, however, and his promotion—as of February 9, 1837—marked the beginning of a six-year period of shore duty.

At about this time, on May 2, 1837, Semmes married Anne Elizabeth Spencer. Hers was a prominent Cincinnati family; her grandfather had been an officer in the Continental Army, and her father, Oliver M. Spencer, was a prominent Ohio businessman. The eighteen-year-old bride was described by one acquaintance as "a stately, handsome girl with regular chiseled features, brilliant brunette complexion and hazel eyes."[18] Her family was Protestant, and it may have required all of Semmes's eloquence to gain their consent to the marriage. Although Anne soon became a convert to Catholicism, the wedding took place at Cincinnati's Christ Church (Episcopal).*

For the next five years, Semmes alternated between a sporadic law practice and postings to naval stations along the Florida coast and the Gulf of Mexico. While stationed at Pensacola in 1841 he purchased a

---

*The accepted date for Semmes's marriage has been May 5, 1937. However, the parish records of Christ Church record the ceremony three days earlier. (Affidavit in the Semmes family collection of General Luke Finlay, Annapolis, Maryland.)

plot of land in Baldwin County, Alabama, on the west bank of the Perdido River, which separates Alabama from the Florida panhandle. Perdido Beach was convenient to Pensacola, and there were other navy families there. The move was an important one for Semmes, for in moving to the house that he called Prospect Hill, he was putting down roots in the Deep South. From that time on he regarded himself as a citizen of Alabama.

From May 1841 to April 1845 Semmes served as a surveyor of the Gulf Coast, with his base at Pensacola. For the most part this was a happy period: The work was undemanding, and Raphael had time for his family. The Semmeses were parents of young sons, Samuel Spencer and Oliver, when Raphael was first posted to Pensacola. There, Anne gave birth to two girls, Electra and Katherine, in 1843 and 1845.

Even in Pensacola, however, there were signs that Semmes could be "difficult"—that even in a navy noted for its feuds and protocol, his was a prickly, sea-lawyer personality. In 1843, Semmes attempted unsuccessfully to have his brother-in-law, Francis Spencer, appointed chief clerk of the Pensacola Navy Yard. Commodore Alexander Dallas, commandant of the yard, ignored Semmes's recommendation and appointed one of his own friends, Edwin Vanbaun, to the post.

From here the feud escalated. Semmes claimed that Dallas spoke to him in a humiliating manner in the presence of others. He wrote to the Navy Department, accusing Dallas of submitting false musters and his chief clerk of absenteeism. Dallas, in turn, placed Semmes under house arrest, and when Semmes left his quarters to deliver a protest, threatened him with the guardhouse. Semmes made a second protest to the Navy Department; this one resulted in Dallas's court-martial for his treatment of Semmes and for the conduct of Vanbaun. The principal charge was that involving Vanbaun. Dallas explained that although his clerk was seldom at the yard, his duties were carried out by someone. Because no money was missing, Dallas was acquitted.[19] Fortunately for Semmes, Dallas was also reassigned.

If Semmes had a hero in the Old Navy, it may have been Matthew Maury. Although not yet renowned as an oceanographer, Maury was a leader in the campaign for naval reform. In 1840 and 1841 he wrote a series of articles in the *Southern Literary Messenger* in which he attacked the powerful Board of Navy Commissioners for virtually all the navy's ills: delays in the introduction of steamers, slow promotions, insufficient training.[20] In part in reaction to Maury's criticism, the Tyler administration abolished the board and replaced it with five functional bureaus that would be the basis for navy administration well into the twentieth century.

Nevertheless, Semmes was wearying of the navy. As the years passed he had become disillusioned with a service in which only seniority mattered—in which "a man's years, and not his brains, should be the test of promotion and employment." Once commissioned, an officer could only hope to outlive his peers. Semmes later wrote,

> A more perfect system could not have been invented, by our worst enemies, if their object had been to destroy us. It dampens hope, it stifles talent, it cripples energy. . . . If there are clever and intelligent officers in the navy, it is . . . despite . . . the system under which they live, and not by reason of it.[21]

Remarkably, Semmes's feud with Commodore Dallas had no career-threatening implications. In the fall of 1843, he was given his first seagoing command, the U.S.S. *Poinsett,* one of the navy's first steamers. One of his assignments the following year was to transport a State Department representative to Veracruz, the first leg of a mission to Mexico City. Not content with providing transport, Semmes requested and received permission to accompany the envoy to Mexico City. Never one to idle away his time, he studied the flora and fauna and made notes on wind patterns on the journey from Veracruz. Two years later, when the United States was at war with Mexico, Semmes would again find himself on the road to Mexico City, and his knowledge of the topography would be very much in demand.

In 1845, following a leave of several months, Semmes returned to the Home Squadron as first officer on a ten-gun brig, the *Porpoise*. The *Porpoise* was in the Caribbean when the war with Mexico erupted. The brig, under the command of Lieutenant William E. Hunt, made brief stops at Cap Haitien and Port-au-Prince before returning to Pensacola on about July 1, 1846. After taking on provisions, the *Porpoise* hastened, "with all the speed of a dull vessel," to join the U.S. naval squadron off Veracruz.[22]

CHAPTER 3

Mexico

Semmes was an expansionist. Along with a great many of his countrymen, he believed that America's destiny was to span the continent from the Atlantic to the Pacific. In the 1840s, Mexico's tenuous hold on California, and the apparent desire of Texas to join the United States, made this dream seem attainable.

Strained relations between the United States and Mexico, growing out of the U.S. annexation of Texas and President Polk's stated desire to acquire California, brought the prospect of hostilities closer. Mexico was unwilling to sell its territory, and so Polk chose to force the issue. In March 1846 he ordered General Zachary Taylor to advance his four-thousand-man army across the Nueces River—long accepted as Texas's southern boundary—into disputed territory north of the Rio Grande. The incident that Polk doubtless expected took place on April 25, 1846, when Taylor's soldiers clashed with Mexican cavalry.

The American strategy, once war was a fact, called for the occupation of California and the capture of Mexico City. The Mexican capital would be the goal of the largest U.S. force, some ten thousand men commanded by the gifted but vain General Winfield Scott. In November 1846, the War and Navy departments implemented

Scott's ambitious plan for capturing the fortress town of Veracruz, some 220 miles east of Mexico City. Once Veracruz was captured, Scott would have a base from which to undertake a campaign against the enemy capital.

Commanding the navy's Home Squadron, and responsible for operations in the Gulf, was fifty-four-year-old Commodore David Conner, an able veteran of the War of 1812. His squadron initially consisted of two heavy frigates, three sloops, five brigs, and two new steamers, the *Mississippi* and the *Princeton*. His orders in the event of hostilities were to blockade the Mexican coast and protect American shipping.[1]

For the first nine months of the war, Conner's primary responsibility was the blockade. He had no concern for Mexico's tiny navy, but blockade work posed problems of its own. To be recognized in terms of international law, a blockade had to be demonstrably effective— that is, more than a "paper" blockade. To avoid antagonizing other marine powers, such as Britain, it had to interfere as little as possible with neutral commerce. The U.S. Navy was free to capture Mexican vessels, but ships flying neutral flags were to be allowed to pass unless carrying contraband.

Conner's flotilla was responsible for watching seven Mexican ports under conditions that offered no protection from the fickle weather of the Gulf. It was tiresome, unrewarding duty that afforded few opportunities for glory. Semmes, then attached to Conner's staff on the flagship, *Raritan,* would write, "We looked forward from our ship, as from a prison . . . without [variation] other than the occasional arrival of one of the blockading squadron, to fill up with water and provisions."[2]

Although Pensacola was the main naval base in the Mexican War, the navy also maintained an advanced position at Anton Lizardo, a group of small islands about twelve miles southeast of Veracruz. The blockade conducted from there required vessels of sufficiently shallow draft to operate on Mexican rivers, but it depended especially on ships capable of holding station offshore during the stormy winter months. Despite the implicit challenge to their seamanship, Semmes and his fellow officers chafed at their relative inactivity, especially after Zachary Taylor's victories in northern Mexico.

On October 23, Semmes—to his relief—was transferred from Conner's staff to command one of the blockaders, the brig *Somers.* The *Somers* was small—only 133 feet long, displacing 266 tons—but she mounted ten thirty-two-pounders and was built for speed. Alas, the *Somers* also had a checkered past. In 1842 she had been the scene of the only documented mutiny on a U.S. Navy vessel, an episode that had resulted in the execution of three mutineers, one of whom, Midshipman Philip Spencer, was the son of President John Tyler's secretary of war. The incident had given the brig a bad name—sailors knew that on certain nights she was visited by the spirits of the three mutineers—but Raphael Semmes loved her lines. Never mind that she was poorly designed and dangerously top-heavy.

Semmes was satisfied with the officers and midshipmen he inherited and receptive to any ideas on how to break the monotony of blockade duty. In mid-November a Mexican brig, the *Creole*, eluded the *Somers* and to Semmes's embarrassment ran safely into the harbor at Veracruz. In the absence of both Conner and his deputy, Semmes approved a daring plan to destroy the *Creole*, proposed to him by his first officer, James Parker. On the night of November 26 Semmes took the *Somers* to just outside Veracruz. Parker, accompanied by midshipmen Clay Rogers and John Hynson and five sailors, rowed into the harbor, burned the *Creole*, and escaped safely in the ensuing confusion.[3]

Conner's deputy as squadron commander was Commodore Matthew C. Perry, later to achieve fame for opening Japan to the Western world. In December 1846 Perry thought it time to relieve the *Somers*, which had been on blockade duty for several months without a respite. But relief was slow in coming, and in the end did not come at all. The *Somers* was anchored off Green Island on the morning of December 8 when the lookout spotted a suspicious sail. Semmes got his ship under way and was beating up the coast when the officer of the deck called his attention to a black patch of water ahead. Semmes ordered a shortening of sail, but before much could be done the *Somers* was struck by a squall that Semmes would later compare to a whirlwind.

The brig was riding light—low on provisions and carrying only six tons of ballast—and the unexpected storm threw her almost immediately on her starboard side. Water poured through the hatches and scuttles. Semmes ordered the masts cut away, but *Somers*'s yards were in the water and the ship now past saving. Two of the ship's three boats were smashed as the brig went over. Amid the chaos, Semmes helped pile men into the one remaining boat and gave the order to abandon ship. Stripping to his shirt and undershorts, he plunged into the sea. A strong swimmer, he made his way to a piece of wooden grating, which he shared with his first officer, Parker.[4]

Semmes and Parker were only about a mile offshore, but a strong current was taking them down the coast. Fortunately, the *Somers*'s surviving boat, commanded by Midshipman Francis Clarke, had discharged her first load on Green Island and had come out looking for additional survivors. In Semmes's recollection, he and Parker were hauled into the boat more dead than alive and taken to a nearby British man-of-war, *Endymion*.[5] Casualties from the wreck were heavy. The ill-fated *Somers* had gone down in less than ten minutes, taking with her thirty-nine of her complement of seventy-six.[6]

In any nineteenth-century navy the loss of a ship could mean the end of her skipper's career, and no one realized this better than Raphael Semmes. He requested a court of inquiry, which was convened on the flagship within weeks of the disaster. Semmes painted the storm as an act of God for which the *Somers* had been as prepared as any vessel could be; the surviving officers supported his testimony. Semmes's defense must have been eloquent, for the court exonerated him even though some on the panel were of the view that if the *Somers* had been better ballasted she would not have capsized.[7]

Exonerated or not, Semmes found himself back on the *Raritan*, where he shared a cabin with another hard-luck officer, Lieutenant John A. Winslow. Two years younger than Semmes, Winslow had been born in North Carolina but brought up in New England. Just days after the loss of the *Somers*, Winslow, commanding the brig *Morris*, had lost his ship on a reef off the Mexican coast. Winslow wrote his wife of the *Somers* disaster:

> Think what an awful experience [it was], a ship struck over in a squall and sinking under you and you obliged to trust to an oar or something such for life. However it is a joke now. . . . Semmes, the Captain that was, I am very intimate with, so I frequently say, "Captain Semmes, they are going to send you out to learn to take care of ships in blockade," to which he replies, "Captain Winslow, they are going to send you to learn the bearing of reefs."[8]

On March 9, 1847, Scott's ten-thousand-man army landed near Veracruz, which at that time was the most powerful fortress in the Western Hemisphere. No amphibious operation of such magnitude had ever been attempted by U.S. forces, but Scott and Conner cooperated closely, and the Mexicans chose not to defend the beaches. Thanks in part to the availability of specially built landing craft, the

Americans were able to land the bulk of Scott's army in a single day without the loss of a boat or a life.[9]

Scott's next step was to capture Veracruz. Unfortunately for the Americans, his plans to capture the city were on hold because of delays in the delivery of heavy artillery to Scott's army. The navy was in a position to help, but each service was a law unto itself, and any cooperation depended on the relations between commanders in the field. By this time Commodore Conner had been succeeded by his deputy, Perry. When Scott asked Perry if he could borrow some naval artillery, the commodore acquiesced, but with one proviso: Navy guns must be manned by navy men.

The upshot was that Perry landed six of his heaviest guns—some weighing more than three tons—to support the siege of Veracruz. Each piece had to be landed by boat and dragged some three miles across sand and inlets to sites south of the city, a task that required two hundred sailors for each gun. But the seamen bent to their task with a will; while on blockade duty they had been confined to their ships, eating salt pork and hardtack and attempting to sleep in steaming, unventilated quarters. Land war seemed a welcome respite.

One of the navy's thirty-two-pounders was commanded by Semmes, who was instructed as to its placement by Scott's chief engineer, Captain Robert E. Lee. The navy guns opened fire on March 24, to the consternation of Veracruz's defenders, who thought that the Americans still lacked heavy artillery. Perry's sailors were enthusiastic cannoneers, and Semmes enjoyed his somewhat incongruous role on land:

> We bivouacked our men in a clump of bushes on the southern, or off-slope of the sand hill on the brow of which the battery was placed; cooked an excellent supper, with plenty of hot coffee; smoked a cigar, and went to bed. This is to say, each of us made a hole in the sand to conform to the angularity of his figure, and pulled a blanket over his head.

Sleep did not come easily to Semmes, who could hear his sailors talking—with many a "damn your eyes"—through the night.[10]

Veracruz capitulated on March 25, after a twenty-four-hour bombardment, prompting Lieutenant Thomas J. Jackson, the Stonewall Jackson of later years, to call Scott's victory the equal of any military operation in U.S. history.[11] The U.S. forces had suffered only seventy-three casualties. Naval artillery had played a crucial role, for without it Scott would probably have been obliged to assault the city with infantry, at far greater cost. The commanding general acknowledged his indebtedness to the Home Squadron for its "prompt, cheerful and able assistance."[12] Semmes, however, regretted that the American bombardment had damaged so many of the homes of poor people in the city; Scott's nearly bloodless victory was "an awful tragedy to the enemy."[13]

Semmes was reconciling himself to a return to Perry's flagship when fate intervened. Just before the *Somers* disaster Semmes had approved a raid not unlike the one that had resulted in the destruction of the *Creole*. Having heard from a British vessel that the Mexicans had a powder magazine almost within sight of the *Somers*'s anchorage, two of Semmes's officers—the brig's physician, John H. Wright, and the intrepid Clay Rogers—had proposed an attempt to destroy it. After two night forays in which the men from the *Somers* succeeded only in getting lost, the two set out a third time on the night of December 5–6. By this time the Mexicans were aware that something was up, and one of the Americans, Rogers, was captured by a Mexican patrol. Semmes had insisted at the outset that the mission be undertaken in uniform, so that neither American could be accused of spying. Nevertheless, reports reached Scott's lines that the Mexicans planned to try Rogers as a spy.

Weeks passed, as the matter was referred to Washington. Eventually the Navy Department authorized a protest to the Mexican president, Antonio López de Santa Anna, concerning the treatment being accorded Rogers, and Perry chose Semmes as his messenger. Semmes drew $300 for expenses and selected a sailor, Francis Seymour, to accompany him. The two navy men, accompanied by a slightly incongruous cavalry escort, set out in early April on a sixty-mile trek to catch up with General Scott's army. Semmes considered the march something of a lark; his description of their stop in the village of Las Vigas reads like a travel feature:

> The night was clear, and the stars bright, and the keen mountain air caused me to wrap my blanket closely around me. . . . Before we retired, Auguste [a French-trained cook who had joined Semmes's party in Jalapa] . . . prepared us an excellent supper; to which we did ample justice, after our long and toilsome ride amongst the mountains. With the aid of my friendly pile of straw, I should have passed a capital night, but for the fleas, which assaulted me without mercy.[14]

With his keen eye for exotic flora, Semmes was fascinated by the pulque plant and its intoxicating brew. Each plant, Semmes was told, could yield up to a gallon of liquid per day; this extract was then allowed to ferment for three to ten days. Semmes thought that the resulting product tasted a bit like buttermilk, but noted that it was intoxicating if drunk in quantity.

The navy party caught up with Scott just after the American victory at Cerro Gordo on April 18, 1847. Even in the flush of victory, "Old Fuss and Feathers" was not pleased at the arrival of a navy emissary with orders from Washington that appeared to take precedence over his own. After first indicating that he had no objection to Semmes's joining his army, Scott had second thoughts and informed Semmes through an aide that he would not be permitted to have any dealings with the enemy. Indeed, Scott claimed to have information that Rogers already had been accorded prisoner-of-war status. Semmes's mission was clearly in jeopardy, and he immediately penned a letter to Scott:

> Commodore Perry has been charged by the President of the United States to make a communication to the government of Mexico. . . . He has selected me as his agent to carry out the views of the President, & has directed me to apply to you for the means of executing his orders. With regard to the question as to who is the proper channel through which this communication is to be made, I can, of course, have nothing to say . . . but the President has thought proper to judge of this for himself, & I am here by authority of one of the Departments of the government.

Semmes then asked Scott, if he still refused to permit Semmes to carry out his mission, to put his position in writing, "in order that I may exhibit it to my commander in chief as a sufficient reason for failing to execute his orders."[15]

Scott reconsidered. Without specifically reversing his position, he wrote Semmes on May 9 that he could remain with the army or return to the coast as he thought best.[16] Subsequently, he appears to have informed the naval officer that he would be allowed to communicate with Mexican authorities on Rogers's behalf if a suitable opportunity presented itself. Semmes had no difficulty with the decision whether to return to the coast or continue with Scott's army. He was impatient, however, with the pace of the American advance.

Whereas Scott felt obliged to await replacements for the four thousand volunteers whose terms were about to expire, Semmes thought
the Mexican resistance ready to crumble.[17]

On July 11 Scott proposed a prisoner exchange to the Mexicans,
employing Semmes as his emissary. Bearing a flag of truce, Semmes
met a Mexican general along a dusty road and passed on to him
papers that spelled out the U.S. position with respect to Rogers. The
affair took on a comic-opera aspect when Rogers—who had never
been under more than house arrest—escaped from his captors and
made his way from Mexico City to Scott's headquarters. Semmes had
been persistent and articulate, but the success of his mission owed
much to good fortune.

Scott's army was by that time camped at Puebla, some eighty miles
southeast of Mexico City. The city provided a good base for the
Americans: Its altitude was sufficient to alleviate the summer heat,
and its population was largely opposed to the Santa Anna regime.
American officers were frequently invited into Mexican homes;
Semmes found the Mexican women attractive. He also warmed
somewhat toward General Scott, writing that the commanding general "could be as agreeable and fascinating a social companion as he
was a distinguished military leader."[18]

But, with the Rogers mission complete, what was Semmes to do
next? He was far more interested in seeing the war to its close than in
returning to the coast, and events worked in his favor. Communications with Veracruz were sporadic; during one period when the army
was out of touch with Perry's flotilla Semmes wrangled an invitation
from Scott's deputy, General William J. Worth, to join his staff.
Worth was a tough combat soldier who had served under Scott in the
War of 1812 as well as in the Mexican conflict. He had distinguished
himself at Cerro Gordo and in the capture of Puebla.

By August 7 Scott had been at Puebla three months, filling his
ranks. With an army restored to about ten thousand, he resumed his
march on Mexico City and on August 10 reached Popocatepetl and
the great mountain range overlooking the valley of Mexico. All this
time, Semmes was proving of considerable assistance to General
Worth. Not only was he a trained artilleryman but he was fluent in
Spanish and had a retentive mind for topography. He may have been
the only person on Worth's staff with prior knowledge of Mexico.
When the American army reached Ayutla, ten miles southeast of
Mexico City, Semmes was one of several of Worth's staff officers sent

forward to locate the most practical route into the enemy capital. They found a little-used and virtually undefended route around Lake Chalco, and Scott abandoned his plan for a frontal assault in favor of a flanking movement that proved successful.[19] As a troubleshooter for Worth, Semmes had a number of dealings with Robert E. Lee, whom he would later praise as having a mind "which has no superior" in the Corps of Engineers.[20]

Santa Anna now faced Taylor's invading army to the north and Scott's army to the east. In August, Scott won brisk battles at Contreras and Churubusco and marched to within sight of Mexico City. Semmes was in Worth's tent on August 20 when the British consul general and a Mexican official arrived to propose a truce. Worth sent them on to Scott, under escort, and the result was an agreement to discuss an armistice at the home of the British diplomat. Three of Scott's generals—Franklin Pierce, John A. Quitman, and Persifor F. Smith—served as U.S. representatives; Semmes acted as their interpreter. "We sat up the whole night," he wrote, "disputing with our opponents about the *wording* of a few articles, to the phraseology of which Señor Mora, who did all the talking on the Mexican side, attached great importance."[21] Semmes, who was convinced that the Mexicans were stalling, was opposed to any armistice, but negotiations continued from late August until September 5. Finally, Scott broke off the talks.

The Americans defeated yet another Mexican force at Molino del Rey and, on September 13, stormed the fortified hill of Chapultepec at the Mexican capital. There, Semmes and Army Lieutenant Ulysses S. Grant supervised the mounting of howitzers on belfries and roofs. But there were to be no more battles. On the morning of September 14 the soldiers of Scott's army stood wearily at attention as the Stars and Stripes was raised over the Plaza de Armas in Mexico City. The war was over.

Because of Raphael Semmes's conspicuous and controversial service in the Civil War, his actions in the earlier conflict with Mexico have attracted little attention. Nevertheless, Semmes played as useful a role in that conflict as did any naval officer in what was essentially a land war. Once the *Somers* disaster was behind him, he distinguished himself not only as a staff officer to Worth but as an artilleryman at Veracruz and Mexico City. He demonstrated both initiative and tact in converting his mission on behalf of a captured midshipman into a full-time role in the land campaign. On three occasions he was mentioned in dispatches by Worth, who lauded his "intelligence and bravery" and his "habitual gallantry, intelligence and devotion." At the close of the war Worth wrote to Scott,

> To Lieutenant Semmes of the Navy, volunteer aide-de-camp, the most cordial thanks of the general of the division are tendered for his uniform gallantry and assistance; and the general-in-chief is respectfully requested to present the conduct of this accomplished and gallant officer to the special notice of the chief of . . . our glorious Navy.[22]

Such commendations from a sister service might or might not prove helpful to Semmes professionally. Nevertheless, the Mexican War had been a learning experience. He had survived the loss of the *Somers*. He had commanded artillery in combat. He had successfully handled some very delicate negotiations with no less a figure than General Scott. And while on that monotonous blockade duty, he had watched Commodore Conner deal with ships intercepted while trading with the enemy. Semmes himself took pride in what had been a scrupulously legal blockade; from David Conner, Semmes had learned much that he would put to use in the American civil war.

In personal terms, the Raphael Semmes who emerged from the Mexican War showed many of the traits that would mark his later career. These were reflected in his first book of memoirs, written in Mobile in 1850 and 1851, at a time when Semmes probably expected to see no more service with the U.S. Navy, and certainly no further combat service.

Semmes's clumsy title—*Service Afloat and Ashore During the Mexican War*—does a disservice to a book that is crisply written, informative, and in a few places even eloquent. With characteristic thoroughness, Semmes began his book with an extended section on the history of Mexico in the first half of the nineteenth century. Of the country's population of eight million, Semmes estimated that some 85 percent lived in abject poverty, owning no property and condemned to perform the most menial of tasks to earn their livelihood. In the author's view, the Mexican underclass was far worse off than slaves were in the American South:

> The closer relation which exists between master and slave with us begets more or less of mutual regard; the master

bestowing upon his slave the kindly feeling which is naturally inspired by those who are dependent upon us, and the slave, in return, regarding himself as a member of his master's family, and more or less identified with his interests.[23]

The abolitionist movement in the United States was gaining strength even as Semmes wrote, and his insistence that slaves in the South were better off than most Mexicans already has a defensive tone. Semmes, as a naval officer, had little firsthand knowledge of slavery. But the life of a slave on a well-run plantation may have seemed relatively placid compared with life belowdecks in the U.S. Navy, where the lash was the standard means of punishment.

As a sojourner, Semmes attempted to approach the Latin culture with an open mind. Noting that upper-class Mexican women generally rode astride, like men, Semmes thought this far more sensible than jeopardizing their safety by riding sidesaddle, as women did in the United States. He noted that many Mexican women smoked, with the younger ones favoring small cigars "which they hold with grace between their thumb and forefinger."[24] But when it came to sexual behavior, he was quite judgmental:

> Among the upper classes of Mexican females, I am inclined to think there is less virtue than with us. Among the lower classes, with rare exceptions, there is none. Women of all classes are very prolific, and begin to bear children at a very early age. I have frequently been pained to see a girl of thirteen or fourteen, lugging her own child through the streets. . . . These poor creatures, being thus early reduced to a life of toil and hardship, are in an infinitely worse condition than the female slaves on our southern plantations, who have masters to feed and take care of their infants.[25]

His own Catholicism notwithstanding, Semmes found little to admire in the Mexican clergy. He saw it as divided into three strata, largely along class lines, with each jealous of the other. Senior clergy had little sympathy for the mass of the populace, but indulged themselves in lives of indolence and ease. Semmes believed that even the "regular" clergy, with whom the people had most contact, were held in low esteem.

And what did Semmes think of his country's conquest of Mexico? Not all Americans had supported President Polk's war. Henry Clay, one of the country's most respected statesmen, had opposed it. Semmes's army counterpart, Ulysses S. Grant, thought it an aggressive and unnecessary conflict. Semmes, in contrast, had no misgivings. He had favored the annexation of Texas without regard to any consequences.[26] He was in this period a firm believer in America's "manifest destiny":

> The Mexican War had its origins in causes far above and beyond the petty theater of events. . . . The passage of our race into Texas, New Mexico, and California was but the first step in that great movement southward, which forms a part of our destiny. An all-wise Providence has placed us in juxtaposition with an inferior people, in order, without doubt, that we may sweep over them, and remove them (as a people) and their worn-out institutions from the face of the earth.[27]

Semmes's attitude was blatantly chauvinistic, but it contained an element of altruism as well. When he deplored Mexico's feudal society, he had the interests of the peasantry in mind. How could Mexico progress when virtually all political and financial power was in the hands of a selfish oligarchy? In a dig at the discredited warlord, General Santa Anna, Semmes concluded that the first step for Mexico must be a return to civilian government. Military men "are all dangerous, for the reason that they are military men; . . . their habits, their love of power, their education, all unfit them for the discharge of civil duties."[28]

Some of Semmes's other political musings have an air of unreality. For instance, he felt that territorial expansion on the part of the United States somehow provided a means of isolating and containing fundamental political differences among his countrymen. At such time as the United States stretched from the Atlantic to the Pacific, why should it matter that a meeting might be held in Boston to denounce some law of the Union? In Semmes's strange vision—one that made no allowance for improved communications—"the individual states will become less and less important, and local jealousies and heart-burnings will [have negligible] effect upon the nation at large."[29]

Semmes would prove to be a better naval officer than political prophet. But his comments on the Mexican War show him to have been a strong nationalist at this time. He also had a global perspective, prophesying that the United States would in time become the preeminent commercial power in the Western Hemisphere. Twenty years hence, according to Semmes, it would be not Britannia but America who "rules the waves."[30]

CHAPTER 4

Through the Burning Woods

T he Mexican War was an impor-
tant professional milestone for Semmes. He had seen as much action
in that conflict as any naval officer and had gained the respect of his
seniors in two services. He had enjoyed a taste of glory. He was in no
mood to return to the peacetime navy, which, in any case, had no
immediate need for his services. In November 1847 he returned to
his home at Prospect Hill, "awaiting orders."

In January 1848 they came. Semmes was given command of the
340-ton storeship *Electra*, based in nearby Pensacola. It was a good
assignment, in that it restored him to active duty with a command
based close to his home. Even so, once at sea Semmes was homesick.
On March 4 he noted in his journal that his oldest son, Spencer, had
turned ten that day, adding that he felt sad at the prospect of a long
separation from his family.[1]

Homesick or not, Semmes maintained strict discipline aboard ship.
His log on the *Electra* included these entries:

> —Punished George McGowan with one dozen of the cats for
> disorderly conduct on shore and James Sergeant with the
> same for drunkenness.

35

—Punished John Travers with nine lashes with the cats for refusing to obey the surgeon's steward when ordered to assist a sick messmate.

In one forty-two-day period Semmes ordered sixteen floggings, ranging in severity from two lashes to twelve. Inasmuch as Navy Department statistics indicate that the "average" ship saw some fifty floggings per year, Semmes was clearly a tough disciplinarian.[2]

In June 1848, while offloading supplies near Veracruz, Semmes borrowed some seamen from another U.S. vessel, the *Iris*. The conduct of one of the borrowed hands resulted in what Semmes considered an egregious instance of disobedience to orders. He reported the incident to the captain of the *Iris*, who, in Semmes's view, failed to take appropriate action. Semmes then appealed to his squadron commander, writing, "I have persisted in prosecuting the offender, in the present instance, from a stern sense of duty—not only to my individual authority, but to the discipline of the service."[3] The details of this incident are obscure, but Semmes's zeal in pursuing the matter suggests that he was a man not easily crossed.

Whatever his sailors thought of Semmes—and they probably regarded him as a martinet—he was a puzzle to his officers. Even as a midshipman he seems to have felt little need for companionship outside his family. Robert Rogers, one of his officers aboard the *Somers*, recalled Semmes as brave, well instructed, and observant. But he also recognized an enigmatic quality in his skipper: "Indeed he was a silent man. I have seen him, almost daily, standing aft, clinging to a back-stay, looking in a fixed direction . . . as if in reflection or introspection. He would remain [thus] for hours."[4]

Semmes appears to have been torn between a desire for professional advancement—that is, sea command—and longing for his family. In June 1848 he asked for shore duty; the request was promptly granted. Two years after he had entered Mexico City with Scott's victorious army, Semmes found himself inspector of provisions and clothing for the Pensacola Navy Yard. For many, this would have been an enviable assignment. The Gulf waters provided some of the finest fish and oysters to be found anywhere, and the duties were hardly onerous.

On February 20, 1849, he was given command of a schooner, the *Flirt*, of the Home Squadron. Semmes's knowledge of Spanish may have led to this assignment, for the *Flirt* was sent to patrol off Yucatán, where an ongoing insurgency was contributing to the endemic political instability in Mexico. On March 9 Semmes wrote a dispatch to the secretary of the navy that indicated that he had developed some intelligence sources in the area around Campeche:

> There is no longer any doubt that this Indian war, if it was not originally instigated by the British inhabitants of the Belize [Honduras], has been favored and kept in activity by them. There is a constant traffic in arms & other munitions of war carried on between the Indians and these [British] people.[5]

In October, however, Semmes once again requested shore duty, stating that he desired to move his family to Mobile for the sake of his children's schooling. He and Anne were now the parents of six children, three boys and three girls. Life in rural Alabama was pleasant, but schools were probably rudimentary in that sparsely populated area. In any case, in October 1849 Semmes moved his family from their home on the Perdido River to Mobile, where he hoped to develop a law practice.

Before going on inactive status with the navy, Semmes seized on an opportunity to confront his service in court. In June 1849 four passed midshipmen were about to be court-martialed at Pensacola for refusal to obey orders aboard the *Albany*. In a case that reflected the autocratic aspect of all navy service, midshipmen Francis Clarke, John Kell, Charles Hopkins, and Francis Roe were charged with disobeying orders aboard the *Albany* while on a peacetime cruise in the Caribbean.

At Pensacola, Clarke ran into Semmes, and it was a warm reunion. Clarke had been a midshipman on board the *Somers* when that ship had capsized, and his behavior then had been heroic. After landing one boatload of survivors he had returned to the scene of the wreck, near which he had rescued Semmes, his first officer, and a seaman.

Semmes owed much to Francis Clarke, but he was convinced in any case that Clarke and his fellow midshipmen had acted correctly in disobeying the "illegal" orders to perform menial tasks such as lighting the candles in officers' cabins. When the four accused men asked Semmes to serve as their counsel, he quickly agreed. In the course of a two-week trial, Semmes elicited testimony that the *Albany*'s skipper, Commander Victor Randolph, was a harsh disciplinarian and made the case that any navy officer had the right to disobey "illegal" orders. But did the fact that an order was demeaning make it illegal? On the base there was strong sympathy for the four midshipmen, but when the court announced its verdict on August 4, all were found guilty and dismissed from the service.[6]* To Semmes, the verdict was one more bit of evidence that the U.S. Navy was run by a collection of mossbacks.

Although it was Semmes's sense of obligation toward Francis Clarke that had initially led him to participate in the case, during the trial he had come to appreciate another of the defendants, John Kell. Semmes would later write,

> The relation of counsel and client . . . brought us close togeth-
> er, and I discovered that young Kell had in him the making of
> a man. So far from being a mutineer, he had a high respect for
> discipline, and had only resisted obedience to the order in
> question from a refined sense of gentlemanly propriety.[7]

More than a decade later, John Kell became Semmes's able executive officer, first on the *Sumter* and then on the *Alabama*.

Semmes's move to Mobile in the fall of 1849 began an interlude that would last more than six years. Initially, he divided his time between the law and his book on the Mexican War. In the spring of 1851 he received permission to go to Cincinnati to arrange for the publication of his memoir, *Service Afloat and Ashore During the Mexican War,* whose appearance at the end of the year brought him a degree of literary prestige. The *New York Tribune* wrote that Semmes's descriptions were "drawn with great felicity," while the Charleston, South Carolina, *Standard* said that Semmes "has given to the public a very attractive work upon Mexico itself, as well as upon the Mexican War."[8] Sales appear to have justified publication of an abridged version in 1852 under the title *The Campaign of General Scott in the Valley of Mexico.* Because the book was friendly to Scott, it was effectively a campaign biography in the year that Scott ran unsuccessfully for the presidency.

The record does not show whether Semmes was able to establish himself as a lawyer in Mobile, but the navy frequently called on him

---

*Semmes's labor on behalf of the four midshipmen was not entirely in vain, for in 1851, after considerable political pressure on behalf of the defendants, the sentences were overturned and the midshipmen reinstated.

to serve on court-martial boards. Any court-martial required at least five officers, and the navy employed officers on the inactive list to staff them. Semmes served on six courts between 1849 and 1851, excusing himself from at least one other on the grounds of illness in his family. The pay was poor, but the court sessions gave Semmes and his peers an intimate knowledge of the navy's justice system.[9]

Soon, for either financial or personal reasons, Semmes was once again petitioning for sea duty. On August 15, 1850, he asked to be returned to command of the *Flirt,* only to be informed that her next commander had already been selected.[10] In October 1851 he again requested active service, to no avail. These rebuffs were not Semmes's only complaints against the navy. He believed that he was due extra compensation for certain survey work he had done along the Gulf Coast, but his appeals were denied.[11]

By 1853 the Semmeses' oldest son, Spencer, was fifteen years old and hoping to go to West Point. Semmes, with no strong political connections, had little chance of getting an appointment from any member of the Alabama congressional delegation. Desperate, he wrote an obsequious letter to President Pierce, recalling their brief association when Pierce was an armistice commissioner in Mexico and asking whether he would consider Spencer for a presidential appointment. Semmes may have forgotten that his Mexico memoir had been turned into a campaign biography for Pierce's election opponent, General Winfield Scott, but Pierce had not. The president did not reply to Semmes directly, but sent word that presidential appointments were reserved for sons of persons who had died in battle.[12]

In 1855 the navy discovered a vacancy in the ranks of commanders, and by the inscrutable workings of the seniority system that he despised, Semmes was promoted to commander, with rank dating from September 14, 1855. Would his new status bring a return to active service? Not necessarily, for there were far more commanders than command billets. In February 1856 Semmes again wrote the secretary of the navy to request sea duty. This time he was successful in his appeal, and for part of 1856 he commanded the mail steamer *Illinois.* She would be the last U.S. ship that he would command.[13]

Semmes was gratified by the promotion, but he was no more satisfied with the U.S. Navy as an institution than he had been before. At the root of the problem was the absence of any retirement system. The officers who had fought the War of 1812 were remarkably long-lived, and there was no incentive for them to leave the service. Yet the government continued to appoint new midshipmen, even as the number of ships in service declined.

Such laurels as the navy gathered in the decades between the War of 1812 and the Civil War were largely in the area of exploration. In 1838, Lieutenant Charles Wilkes, commanding a flotilla of six ships, embarked on a voyage to chart the southern polar seas. The expedition, which lasted nearly four years, was the most important scientific expedition undertaken by the navy in the nineteenth century. Equally important were Commodore Perry's voyages to Japan in 1852 and 1853, part of a diplomatic initiative from Washington that opened Japan to Western trade.

But morale in the professional navy remained poor. Semmes, secure in his new rank, wrote to the secretary of the navy in 1856 deploring the limited opportunities for officers to go to sea. Not only was there a gross oversupply of lieutenants and commanders, he wrote, but the Navy Department exacerbated the problem by failing to employ commanders at sea except as skippers of sloops. Because the navy had only a dozen or so sloops, but had some ninety-seven commanders, "years will elapse before [junior commanders] will have an opportunity for sea service." Semmes had a proposal: "I would therefore respectfully suggest to you the policy of employing Commanders as executive officers on board the six new steamers," he wrote, adding that a commander might also be assigned to the flagships of the navy's six squadrons.[14]

In due course Semmes received a reply from Secretary of the Navy James C. Dobbin. "The Department is at all times gratified to receive from the Officers of the Navy any suggestions for the improvement of the Service," the secretary replied. He commended the interest "so clearly evinced" in Semmes's letter.[15]

In November 1856, Semmes was assigned to the Lighthouse Service as an inspector of stations. Congress, in 1852, had become sufficiently concerned over the maintenance of the country's lighthouses that it had created a nine-member Lighthouse Board in the Treasury Department to oversee them. The board had divided the country's coastline into twelve districts, each with an inspector responsible for constructing lighthouses as approved by the board and for keeping existing lights in good repair. The inspectors were naval officers and were expected to visit the lights in their districts every three months.[16]

For most of 1857, Semmes combined his private law practice with trips to inspect lighthouses along the Gulf of Mexico. He appears to have discharged this mundane function efficiently, for in September 1858 he was called to Washington to serve as secretary to the board. For the next two and a half years he worked in a small office in the basement of the Treasury Department, handling the day-to-day business of the board. He enjoyed his new responsibilities, telling his son Spencer that his position was an important one, "involving as it does the annual expenditure of about a million dollars & the lighting of three thousand miles of Coast."[17]

The nation's capital had grown considerably since Semmes's days as a teenager in Georgetown. In the 1850s it numbered some forty thousand inhabitants, of whom a quarter were black. Householders still dumped refuse into the streets, and in the summer months mosquitoes still bred by the million in stagnant ponds across the city. But there were signs of progress as well. By the 1850s the city boasted gas lights along Pennsylvania Avenue and in many government buildings. Horse-drawn omnibuses had improved commuting within the city.[18]

The part of Washington that mattered was bounded on the east by the Capitol and on the west by the White House. Strolling eastward on Pennsylvania Avenue from the President's House, a visitor encountered the massive Treasury Department, which dwarfed the unpretentious offices of the Department of State on the corner of 15th and F streets. Such hotels as the capital boasted—the National, the Kirkwood, and the Willard—were along the north side of Pennsylvania Avenue; the south side was the "wrong" side. Although the slave trade in the capital had been nominally abolished as part of the Compromise of 1850, Washington remained a Southern town. There was a brisk business in the kidnaping of free Negroes, and no black, slave or free, could testify in court against a white.[19]

Like many of his army and navy colleagues, Semmes viewed the civilian world of commerce and politics with a certain distaste. Nevertheless, the glacial pace of navy promotions had long made it advisable for officers to develop political connections, and Washington was a place where officers of any rank could mix with the politicians. Within the navy the saying was that a cruise in Washington was worth two around Cape Horn.[20] Such politicking did not come easily to one of Semmes's reserve, nor did he have the money necessary to entertain on a grand scale. The family lived frugally. Records for the District of Columbia do not show Semmes as a property owner, but do show that his household at one time included two boarders.[21]

Meanwhile, the Compromise of 1850 was collapsing, in part because of the North's unwillingness to enforce the provision that called for the return of fugitive slaves. The opening of Kansas to rival groups of proslavery and antislavery settlers led to the establishment of contending territorial governments and to a breakdown of order. Soon, John Brown's raid against Harpers Ferry, Virginia, with the avowed aim of instigating a slave uprising, would spread alarm throughout the South.

Since the Mexican War, Semmes had come to identify more with the South and less with the United States. His was much more than the sectional loyalty of a newcomer to Alabama; rather, it grew out of his study of economic trends and constitutional doctrine. An avid reader, Semmes was convinced that the South was a victim of economic oppression by the North—that policies determined in Washington had resulted in a transfer of wealth from the South to the North. He placed much of the blame on the recently departed Henry Clay. Clay's "American System" had provided for tariffs to protect fledgling New England industries. Yet the effect of tariff legislation, Semmes concluded, was to stifle foreign competition and compel the Southern consumer to pay artificially high prices for manufactured goods.

In Semmes's view the problem went beyond economic policy. He saw the North and the South as inherently antagonistic. Thinking in the North was dominated by the New England intelligentsia, which in turn was drawn from intolerant descendants of the Puritans. From religious intolerance it was but a short step to constitutional obstructionism. Recalling New England's opposition to the War of 1812, Semmes concluded, "As long as they were in a minority . . . [the New England states] stood strictly on their state rights, in resisting such measures as were unpalatable to them, even to the extremity of threatening secession." It was only when they found themselves in the majority that New Englanders had abandoned their states' rights doctrine.[22]

Thus Semmes saw the United States as composed of incompatible societies. The result could only be disastrous for the Southern minority. He quoted with approval the French writer Alexis de Tocqueville, who two decades earlier had compared the states to hostile nations under one government. The tyranny of the majority, of which Tocqueville had warned, was at hand.[23] One of Semmes's heroes was Patrick Henry, who had opposed ratification of the Constitution on the ground that the more populous North would eventually come to dominate the South.

Semmes moved from the realm of political science to that of sociology. As he read America's history, most Americans could trace their roots to either New England or Virginia—colonies with sharply different values and societies. Those who had settled around the Chesapeake "were the gay and dashing cavaliers, who, as a class, afterward adhered to the fortunes of [Charles I], whilst the first settlers of Massachusetts were composed of the same materials that formed the . . . parliament of Cromwell."[24] The Cavalier and the Puritan colonies had since evolved into very different cultures. Their societies had come to reflect their environments, being in one case cold and inhospitable, in the other, generous and fruitful. In part because of its more congenial climate, the South had begun to outstrip the North. "Whilst the civilization of the North was coarse and practical, that of the South was more intellectual and refined."[25]

Semmes's perception of cultures in conflict was not unique; it was echoed in much of the South. An article in the *Southern Literary Messenger* in 1860 concluded, "The Southern people come of that race . . . recognized as Cavaliers . . . directly descended from the Norman Barons of William the Conqueror, a race distinguished in its earliest history for its warlike and fearless character."[26] Many Southerners believed in the inherent virtue of their agricultural society. "That the North does our trading and manufacturing mostly is true," wrote one Alabamian in 1858, "and we are willing that they should. Ours is an agricultural people, and God grant that we may continue so."[27]

As for the volatile issue of slavery, Semmes dismissed antislavery agitation as a red herring, an issue that Northern politicians exploited in order to isolate and weaken the South. Those who opposed the spread of slavery were not humanitarians; rather, they feared the political repercussions from the formation of new slave states. "The fat Southern goose could not resist being plucked as things stood, but it was feared that if slavery was permitted to go into the Territories, the goose might become strong enough to resist being plucked."[28]

Semmes himself appears to have owned slaves only occasionally—servants were not a luxury he could regularly afford—but he probably had two or three at Prospect Hill. When the family moved to Washington, one of these slaves, "Jake," had been left behind to be hired out to neighbors. To Semmes's chagrin, Jake was convicted of burglary in February 1859 and sentenced to death.

Semmes took a paternal interest in the case. He wrote his lawyer in Alabama that if he thought that Jake merited the death penalty he would not raise a hand in his behalf. But he knew his man to be gentle, and he insisted that it would be "an outrage upon humanity" to execute such a person: "As you describe the case, I have not the least doubt that he has been corrupted & seduced into the commission of crime, by the low, unprincipled whites—particularly the women—with whom, it appears, he was permitted to deal."[29]

Because the jury had recommended clemency, Semmes felt certain that the governor would pardon Jake.

Semmes was convinced that the North and South were incompatible as societies and that the South was the injured party. But what of secession? He had read extensively in the area of constitutional law, and he was convinced that the Union was a voluntary compact from which any state could withdraw. To be sure, the original thirteen states had accepted some restraints on their sovereignty—giving up, for example, the rights to wage war and to print money—when they formed the United States. But the Constitution, in contrast to the earlier Articles of Confederation, said nothing about the new union's being *perpetual*. Semmes chose to ignore a succession of Supreme Court decisions that had assumed the existence of a single, sovereign American people. He now looked for the cotton kingdom to extend from the Gulf to the Pacific; whether it was desirable to have Northerners settling the Plains States was less clear.

If Semmes's views were close to those of the Southern fire-eaters in Congress, his style was not. He kept his political opinions largely to himself and worked regular hours in his little office in the basement of the Treasury Department. The Lighthouse Board met infrequently; as secretary, Semmes handled much of the routine business himself. Complaints about the maintenance of various lighthouses went to him, and often it was he who arranged for necessary repairs. Nevertheless, he found time to indulge his scientific interests at the Smithsonian Institution and the Library of Congress. In 1860, he assured the director of the Smithsonian that no one had been authorized to collect bird eggs in Florida, but that lighthouse keepers would be pleased to assist the Smithsonian in the collection of scientific data.[30]

Semmes gave few indications at this time of the dynamism that he would bring to the Confederate navy. He projected no charisma or martial presence. Future admiral David D. Porter, who was later among Semmes's sterner critics, wrote of this period that the Alabamian "had no particular taste for his profession, but had a fondness for literature and was a good talker and writer." Others were more observant. Another Federal officer recalled Semmes as "brave, well instructed, scholarly, and a keen observer and thought-ful analyst."[31]

In Semmes's view, much depended on the outcome of the presidential election of 1860. He watched with concern as the Democrats, meeting in Charleston, split over the party platform. When Southern delegates judged the plank guaranteeing slavery in the territories too weak, eight state delegations walked out and the convention adjourned. The election was ultimately contested by four parties: the Republicans, with Lincoln their candidate; the "regular" Democrats, led by Stephen A. Douglas; and two splinter parties based in the South and the border states. Although Semmes was a Southerner to the core, his presidential preference was Douglas, whom he saw as the one candidate who would allow the slave states the same access to the territories as the free states got.

Confederate general James Longstreet remarked after the war that virtually no army officers were overt secessionists in 1861 and that many Southerners who followed their states did not believe there was sufficient cause for revolution.[32] Such was not the case with Raphael Semmes. He later recalled his attitude in the crucial winter of 1860–61:

> I approved the secession movement of the Southern states, though I had no agency in it. . . . Although I cared very little about the institution of slavery, I thought that the subordinate position of the inferior race was its proper position. I believed that the doctrine of States' Rights was the only doctrine which would save our Republic from the fate of all other Republics that had gone before us.[33]

On January 11, 1861, Alabama seceded from the Union, following the example of South Carolina, Mississippi, and Florida. Batteries at Charleston, South Carolina, had already fired on a U.S. ship bringing supplies to Fort Sumter, and war seemed close. On the evening of January 13, Semmes called upon Clement C. Clay, one of Alabama's two U.S. senators. In Mrs. Clay's recollection, Semmes's call coincided with that of another—unnamed—navy officer:

> The surprise . . . of our visitors when they beheld each other was great, but Senator Clay's and my own was greater, as hour after hour was consumed in obvious restraint. . . . Midnight had arrived ere our now forgotten guest rose and

bade us "good night." Then Commander Semmes hastened to
unburden himself. He had resolved to out-sit the other gentleman if it took all night. "As my Senator, Mr. Clay," he said,
"I want to report to you my decision on an important matter.
I have resolved to hand in my resignation to the United States
Government, and tender my services to that of the
Confederate States. I don't know what the intention of my
brother officer is, but I could take no risk with him," he
added.[34]

For all of Semmes's later zeal for the Confederate cause, he did not
immediately resign his Federal commission. Although he was convinced both of the legality of secession and of the South's justification
in exercising that right, his personal situation was difficult. The
seniority that he had built up in the service of the United States was
his principal economic asset. It was not something that he could
lightly discard. Anne Semmes, for her part, was distraught. Her own
family in Cincinnati were Unionists, and she urged her husband to
remain with the Old Navy. Some of Semmes's own family were
Unionists as well, including his brother, Samuel, to whom he was
devoted.[35]

The month that followed was an uneasy one. "I am still at my post
at the Light-House Board," Semmes wrote one Southern legislator,
"performing my routine duties but listening with an aching ear and
beating heart for the first sounds of the great disruption which is at
hand."[36] On January 21 he joined the crowd that packed the Senate
galleries to hear the valedictory speeches of five senators from seceding states, including Jefferson Davis and Stephen R. Mallory.

Not until February 14 did he receive a telegram from the interim
Confederate capital at Montgomery, Alabama, asking him to report
there at his earliest convenience. Semmes no longer hesitated. On
February 15 he submitted a brief letter of resignation to Secretary of
the Navy Isaac Toucey. Ironically, only weeks earlier Semmes had
been named to fill a vacancy on the Lighthouse Board caused by the
death of one of its members. This "promotion" brought from
Semmes a second letter of resignation.

Forty-eight hours after receiving his summons from Montgomery,
Semmes took emotional leave of his family. There had been previous
leave-takings, of course, but this one was different. Whatever the outcome of Alabama's secession, Semmes could never return to a quiet
hearth in Washington. His six children now ranged in age from twen-

ty-two to twelve. Spencer, the oldest, was living in Georgia and about to become engaged. Oliver, the second son, was in his third year as a cadet at West Point. The three girls, Electra, Anne Elizabeth, and Katherine, were still at home, as was twelve-year-old Raphael.

Anne Semmes came close to the era's womanly ideal in submerging her own preferences in deference to her husband's wishes. She was now sorely tested. Semmes decided that she and the children should initially move to Samuel Semmes's home near Baltimore. Then, depending on developments, they might choose to move south or to Cincinnati. Semmes did not expect a war, but he did not rule out the possibility.

On February 16 he boarded a coastal steamer for Fredericksburg, Virginia. There he caught a train for the trip to Montgomery by way of Richmond. Neither Virginia nor North Carolina had yet seceded, and for much of the two-day trip Semmes was besieged by people eager for the latest news from Washington.

As his train rattled south, Semmes considered what he should tell Jefferson Davis and his advisers in Montgomery. At the close of the Mexican War he had gone on record with some harsh words for the ages-old naval practice of privateering. He had conceded that, because commerce raiders could usually evade slower, heavier war-ships, they represented a means of equalizing the strength of nations on the high seas. But his judgment on them had been strongly negative:

> There is a growing disposition among civilized nations to put an end to this disreputable mode of warfare under any cir-cumstances. It had its origin in remote and barbarous ages, and has for its object rather the plunder of the bandit than honorable warfare. . . . The crews of these vessels . . . are lit-tle better than licensed pirates; and it behooves all civilized nations . . . to suppress the practice altogether.[37]

Well, times change. If there *were* to be war between the North and the South, might not the former's merchant marine prove its most vulnerable point? Months earlier Semmes had written to a Southern legislator, "If you are warred upon at all, it will be by a commercial people. . . . It is at ships and shipping, therefore, that you must strike."[38]

Semmes's train rolled through the Carolinas, across Georgia, and into his adopted state of Alabama. Semmes was a romantic, and his emotions were easily stirred. Near Montgomery, the train passed a forest fire, "the flames now and then running up a lightwood tree, and throwing a weird and fitful glare upon the passing train." Was there not a symbol in the fire?

This night-ride, through the burning pine woods of Alabama, afterward stood as a great gulf in my memory, forming an impassable barrier, as it were, between my past and my future life. It had cost me pain to cross the gulf, but once crossed, I never turned to look back. When I washed and dressed in Montgomery the next morning . . . the labors and associations of a lifetime had been inscribed in a volume that had been closed, and a new book, whose pages were as yet all blank, had been opened.[39]

CHAPTER 5

"Give Me That Ship"

Situated on bluffs overlooking a bend in the Alabama River, the town of Montgomery was reckoned one of the most attractive in the South. It boasted shaded streets of fine residences, with lawns and gardens "arranged in such order as to impress the beholder that these are [places] of wealth, taste and refinement."[1] Named for a hero of the Revolutionary War, General Richard Montgomery, the town numbered about eight thousand inhabitants, half of them slaves. It had served as the state capital since 1847.[2]

Now, Montgomery was assuming a role never foreseen for the town, that of interim capital of the Confederacy. On February 4, 1861, representatives of six states that had left the Union met there and established the Confederate States of America. At the state capitol—modeled, in the style of the day, after a Greek temple—Jefferson Davis took the oath as provisional president before a festive crowd. Montgomery's three hotels—the Exchange, Montgomery Hall, and the Madison—were overflowing with officials, office seekers, and soldiers.

When Semmes arrived in Montgomery on February 18, he was fortunate in being able to find lodgings at the palatial residence of a prominent local banker, William Knox, who was the father-in-law of

one of Semmes's many cousins, New Orleans attorney Thomas
Semmes. Raphael's first official call was on Charles M. Conrad,
chairman of the Committee on Naval Affairs, whose telegram had
brought him to Montgomery. (Such a summons might appropriately
have come from the secretary of the navy, but Jefferson Davis had
not yet filled this position.) Meeting with Conrad, Semmes confirmed
that he was not the only Old Navy veteran who had changed his allegiance. Others present included Captain Lawrence Rousseau, one of
the senior officers of the U.S. Navy, and Captain Victor Randolph,
recently commander of the Pensacola Navy Yard. There were already
more than a hundred ex–U.S. Navy officers in town, many well past
their prime. Semmes would *not* be lumped with these mossbacks!

In the euphoria of the moment, any senior officer of the Federal
forces who had thrown in his lot with the South was an instant
celebrity. After meeting with Conrad, Semmes went to the capitol,
where the erstwhile secretary of the Lighthouse Board was given the
honor of admission to the floor. Semmes knew many of the legisla-
tors from his years in Washington, including Howell Cobb and
Robert Toombs of Georgia, both destined for senior positions in the
Confederacy. Semmes was impressed with what he saw. Writing many
years later, after internal bickering had contributed to the
Confederacy's defeat, Semmes judged this first legislature "by far the
best Congress that ever assembled under the new government."[3]

That afternoon Semmes met with President Davis in his rooms at
the Exchange Hotel. They had known each other in Washington, and
Davis quickly got down to business, asking Semmes if he had
resigned his Federal commissions. When Semmes replied affirmative-
ly, Davis launched into a discussion of the problems that beset the
South in preparing its defenses. Most facilities for the manufacture of
arms and ammunition were located in the North; the South did not
even have percussion caps for its rifles. Because the Confederate
Congress had not yet provided for a navy, Davis wanted to use
Semmes in a special capacity, as a one-man purchasing expedition for
the Confederacy.

It is a commentary on the relations between the U.S. government
and the seceded states that, until the attack on Fort Sumter,
Southerners were free to make arms purchases from Northern facto-
ries. There was no restriction on North-South trade, any more than
on postal deliveries, and the fledgling Confederacy made good use of
the freedom accorded it. In his letter of instructions for Semmes,
Davis identified one Northern manufacturer who could supply

Semmes with gunpowder and might be open to a proposal to build a factory in the South. The president provided a list of cannon to be purchased if available. In addition, he authorized Semmes to offer good wages to any skilled laborers he might encounter, for Davis was acutely aware of the South's poor manufacturing base.[4]

On February 21, Semmes returned to the despised North on his secret mission. He was not the only Confederate representative on a shopping expedition. At almost the same time, Captain Louis Zimmer went to New York City with an order for one million percussion caps. He was able to purchase 800,000 at a Manhattan shop and thus to ensure that they would reach the South in time for the first Battle of Manassas.[5]

Semmes wrote little about his own mission, even after the war, because he wished to protect those with whom he met and concluded contracts. He stopped first in Richmond, where he visited the state arsenal and the Tredegar Iron Works. Although Virginia had not yet seceded, Davis had asked Semmes to ascertain what might be expected from the Tredegar works, and Semmes was favorably impressed. He had planned to contract with the Tredegars for some heavy cannon, but when he learned that one of the partners had gone to Montgomery to negotiate directly with Confederate authorities, he moved on.[6]

In Washington, Semmes was allowed not only to visit the government arsenal but also to inspect a new machine for the manufacture of percussion caps. He spoke with some of the machinists, and attempted to talk them into going south. By a nice coincidence, he was in Washington on the day of Lincoln's inauguration. The Alabamian was too contemptuous of "Black Republicans" to attend the festivities, but had he done so he might have reflected on certain similarities between himself and the new president. Both men had been born in 1809, within a few months of one another. Each had lost his mother at an early age. Each was largely self-taught, and had become a keen reader of history. Each had practiced law, and each had an instinctive sympathy for the underdog.

But there were sharp differences as well, so sharp as to make any comparison largely meaningless. Lincoln was sociable and gregarious, a man who delighted in the company of others. Semmes was reserved and made few close friends. Lincoln saw people in terms of their potential; Semmes was inclined to view them as impediments to God's grand design. Lincoln considered slavery a great moral evil, while Semmes thought it irrelevant to the current constitutional crisis. Lincoln considered the Union permanent and secession therefore illegal; he was opposed to any concessions to the South beyond his vow not to interfere with slavery where it existed. Semmes believed that secession was not only legal but essential if the South and its culture were to survive. Lincoln the politican had been elected to preserve the Union; Semmes the warrior was now sworn to destroy it.

Not surprisingly, the Alabamian was deaf to Lincoln's protestations of friendship for the South; in his memoirs he would dismiss the inauguration with sarcastic references to the heavy security around the president. To Semmes, Lincoln was a clone of the ineffectual James Buchanan. "He would not coerce the states, but he would hold on to the ceded places within their limits, and collect the public revenue."[7]

While in Washington, Semmes was able to visit with his family for the last time in more than three years. Anne was preparing to move to Cincinnati with her daughters and twelve-year-old Raphael. After a poignant farewell, Semmes caught the train to New York City on March 5.

Semmes spent the next three weeks in "enemy country," dividing his time between New York City and industrial sites in Connecticut and Massachusetts. March 8 found him in Springfield, Massachusetts, an important industrial center and the site of a government arsenal. He wrote Alexander H. Stephens, the Confederate vice president, that Northern munitions brokers were very cautious and unwilling to deliver arms until certain that funds were in hand with which to pay for them.[8] Nevertheless, Semmes was able to contract for a variety of war matériel, including a line of machinery for the rifling of cannon. Doing business with the despised Yankees amused Semmes; it also confirmed him in his prejudices:

> Some of these men, who would thus have sold body and soul to me for a sufficient consideration, occupied high social positions, and were men of wealth. I dined with them, at their comfortable residences near their factories, where the music of boring out cannon accompanied the clatter of the dishes, and the popping of champagne-corks. . . . Many of these gentlemen, being unable to carry out their contracts with the Confederate States because of the prompt breaking out of the war, afterwards obtained lucrative contracts from the Federal Government, and became, in consequence, intensely loyal.[9]

In mid-March, Semmes boarded a Hudson River steamer and traveled to West Point. Oliver, twenty-one, was in his third year at the military academy. He had not resigned when Alabama seceded, for like many of his peers he was reluctant to throw away the prospect of a Federal commission if there was to be no war. In this respect his attitude was not much different from that of the opportunistic industrialists with whom his father had been dealing, but no such comparison would have occurred to Semmes. Neither father nor son left a record of their conversations at this time. Ultimately, the younger Semmes resigned from West Point and served with distinction in the Confederate army.

Returning to New York City, Raphael Semmes found a letter from Stephen Mallory, recently named secretary of the navy in the Confederate cabinet. Mallory directed him to locate and to purchase, if possible, fast, light-draft vessels suitable for coastal defense. Semmes made this task a priority, combing the harbors in and around New York City in search of acceptable vessels. Alas, there was nothing to be had except aging hulks of no military value.[10]

By the end of March, Semmes realized that his mission was at an end. Some of the people on whom he called were receiving him coolly, and he believed that he was under some form of surveillance by Federal authorities. Nonetheless, returning to the South was no problem. Steamers were still running between New York City and Savannah, flying the Federal flag at the peak and the Confederate flag below. Semmes himself did not expect a war; he wrote to Vice President Stephens: "I still maintain my opinion, notwithstanding the inaugural & the tune of the Republican papers, that we shall have no war. The mass of the Northern people, [outside] the Republican party, are opposed to it. Every intelligent man with whom I have conversed here scouts the idea."[11]

Semmes caught a Savannah-bound steamer in late March, and on April 4 he was back in Montgomery reporting to Mallory, who by then had been confirmed as secretary of the navy. In the few days of peace that remained, Semmes was put in charge of the Confederate Lighthouse Bureau—in effect, handling the same bureaucratic functions he had left behind in Washington. But he would have none of this; he appointed a couple of clerks to look after the lighthouses and made clear to Mallory—perhaps to President Davis as well—that he had in mind a more active role in the event of hostilities.

These came soon enough. Confederate batteries fired on Fort Sumter on April 12, and the outnumbered Federal garrison surrendered the following day. Semmes had no misgivings about the act, or about the Confederates' having been maneuvered into firing the first shot. For him, the meaning of Fort Sumter was that the Confederates had succeeded in driving an insolent enemy out of one of the strongest forts in the South.[12]

Most people in Montgomery shared this view. In front of Government House, the red-brick cotton warehouse that had been converted into government offices, cannons fired salutes to General Pierre G. T. Beauregard, the "victor of Sumter"; to the Confederacy; and to President Davis. Bands in the streets played "Dixie" and "Bonnie Blue Flag." Crowds serenaded Davis and other officials, demanding speeches.

Semmes had no time for celebration, for he had an important appointment with Secretary Mallory:

> I had already passed the prime of life, and was going gently down that declivity, at whose base we shall all arrive sooner or later, but *I thanked God* that I had still a few years before me, and vigor enough of constitution, to strike in defense of the right. I at once sought an interview with the Secretary of the Navy, and explained to him my desire to go afloat.[13]

Among the various Confederate department heads, few had a less enviable position than Stephen R. Mallory. The burly navy secretary had been appointed to the cabinet primarily because of geographical considerations. His native state of Florida was entitled to a cabinet seat, and if one were to be granted, the navy portfolio seemed appropriate for a state that was largely surrounded by water. It hardly mattered who was appointed, for the Confederacy was gearing up for a land war.

Almost offhandedly, Davis made an excellent choice. Mallory, forty-eight, had been brought up in Key West, where the sea touched nearly every aspect of life. Like Semmes, he was largely self-educated. He had gone into Democratic politics and become a power in the state. In 1850 he was elected to the U.S. Senate, where he became first a member, and then chairman, of the Naval Affairs Committee.

Mallory kept a low profile in Washington. He had little to say on the divisive issue of slavery, and if he was noted for anything it was his fondness for food and wine. In the secession winter of 1860–61, he followed his home state out of the Union with some reluctance. But Mallory's appearance—he was inclined to stoutness, and had one eyelid that drooped—disguised an incisive mind that now considered how the South could make the best use of its limited naval resources.[14]

Limited they were. The Confederacy had virtually no navy with which to confront an enemy that began the war with forty warships and the facilities for constructing hundreds more. The South, in contrast, had little in the way of a shipbuilding industry of any kind:

> There was not, in the whole Confederacy, the means of turning out a complete steam engine of a size suitable for ships. The timber for the potential Confederate ships still stood in the forests; the iron required was still in the mines. . . . There was not a rolling mill capable of turning out two-and-a-half-inch plate.[15]

If these handicaps were not enough, Mallory had to contend with the Confederate government's massive indifference to naval matters. Whereas Lincoln readily allotted the resources necessary for a naval blockade of the South, Jefferson Davis had little interest in anything related to the navy.

Balanced against these liabilities were a few pluses, one of which was the personality of the secretary himself. Mallory "possessed in regard to naval affairs a kind of impulsive progressivism, which, although it sometimes led him astray, enabled him in other instances to . . . develop with boldness sound new principles."[16] He also had good people. In the early months of 1861 more than three hundred officers—about one fifth of the total—left the U.S. Navy and cast their lot with the South. Although Mallory could not begin to find useful billets for this number of officers, he had a large pool from which to fill a few key positions.[17] The Federal navy, in contrast, suffered from a seniority system—long deplored by Semmes, among others—that had produced an officer corps often lacking in imagination and initiative.

In strategic terms, Mallory faced three tasks. One was to keep open the important waterways of the South; this objective would depend heavily on Confederate fortunes on the ground and, for this reason alone, was doomed to failure. A second was to break the Federal blockade, so as to permit the South to import strategic goods and, depending on the policy adopted by the Davis government, to export the cotton that was the South's great economic asset. The South would prove unable to break the blockade, but Mallory's rapid introduction of a handful of ironclad vessels would cause considerable heartburn in Washington.

The secretary's final objective was to take the war to the enemy, through commerce raiders, in such a way as to force the Federals to sue for peace. Here, there were some decisions to be made. Were privateers the most appropriate response? In both of America's wars against Britain, the U.S. Navy had been heavily outnumbered. To compensate for numerical inferiority, the United States had issued letters of marque for privateers—privately owned vessels whose masters were permitted to retain part of the proceeds from any enemy vessels they might seize.

For all their aura of romance, privateers had never proved their worth. Professional naval officers, Semmes among them, disdained privateers as ineffective, undisciplined, and more interested in building their personal fortunes than in fighting the enemy. But in the absence of a Confederate navy, the government at Montgomery was prepared to endorse privateering. On April 17, 1861, President Davis called on Southern skippers to apply for letters of marque and reprisal. A flurry of applications followed, and Northern merchants petitioned the government in Washington for protection against rebel predators.

Semmes supported this initiative, but he could also see its limitations. The legal status of privateers was cloudy, because under the 1856 Declaration of Paris it was no longer permissible for belligerents to issue letters of marque.[18] But for the Confederacy, the immediate problems were practical rather than legal. If there were virtually no ships for the navy, where were privateers to come from? Moreover, if the South's ports were blockaded, what was a privateer to do with his prize? Ultimately, in the words of one author, "Confederate privateers never amounted to much more than paper sharks."[19]

One final option remained to the Confederates: cruisers able to sustain themselves at sea, and there to prey on the enemy's commerce. As belligerent vessels they had a legal status. Their commanders would be dedicated Confederate officers. And although no suitable vessels were available in the South, they could perhaps be purchased and equipped abroad. Semmes had no desire to profit from the war—he would leave this to the Yankees—and for this reason he had no interest in commanding a privateer except perhaps as a last resort. With his highly developed sense of honor, he asked only for a command in the Confederate navy.

Meanwhile, Semmes had won his first battle: convincing Secretary Mallory that he was qualified to command a cruiser in wartime. To offset his age, the Alabamian had impressive credentials. He had served gallantly in the Mexican War and had commanded ships at sea. He believed in commerce raiding as a strategy for the Confederate navy. He had a solid grounding in international law, on which he could draw in any dealings with foreign officials. Above all, Semmes had zeal: He was a true believer in the Confederate cause.

An April morning found Semmes in Mallory's office, listening to the secretary deplore the absence of seagoing vessels for the navy. Mallory passed him a collection of reports on available ships, reports that catalogued their numerous deficiencies. One of these caught Semmes's eye. It described a steamer of about five hundred tons that had been built for the passenger trade. She was equipped with a low-pressure engine and was said to be capable of making nine or ten knots. But she had no accommodations for a wartime crew and carried fuel for only five days' steaming. The shortage of bunker space seemed a critical flaw, and the officers who had examined her had condemned the *Havana* as having no military value.

Semmes handed the reports back to Mallory, pointing to the one on the *Havana*. "Give me that ship," he told the secretary. "I think I can make her answer the purpose." On April 18, Mallory signed off on an order that designated Semmes commander of the newly named C.S.S. *Sumter*.[20]

CHAPTER 6

"Doing a Pretty Fair Business"

When the *Sumter* left the *Brooklyn* hull-down in the Gulf of Mexico, the Confederacy had its first cruiser on the high seas. The *Sumter* was alone, opposed by the eighteen-hundred-odd guns of the existing U.S. Navy, a force that even then was in the process of quadrupling in size. But all on board were euphoric over their daring escape from the Mississippi. They had done it! The raider's first night in the Gulf was marked by the appearance of the Great Comet, which crossed the northern sky with spectacular brilliance. The crew of the *Sumter* saw the comet as a good omen, as they did the extra round of grog with which they celebrated their escape.

Semmes could now decide on his course. Given the large number of Federal warships in the Gulf, he had no wish to linger there. He chose instead to steam for Cuba—then a Spanish colony, one with considerable trade with the United States—where he might find enemy merchantmen and coal, but where he would not expect to encounter Federal warships.

As time went on, the *Sumter*'s deficiencies as a commerce raider would become apparent. But her immediate prospects were good, with or without a comet. International law, as it existed in 1861, made enemy property at sea subject to capture and confiscation. This tenet made any maritime power vulnerable, for not even the most powerful country could protect its entire merchant fleet from an enemy with seagoing warships. In two wars against Britain the United States had made commerce raiding an important part of its strategy. It had been hopelessly outclassed at sea in both the Revolution and the War of 1812. But John Paul Jones, commanding the *Ranger*, had raided English harbors during the Revolution and captured numerous merchantmen. In the War of 1812, David Porter, in the *Essex*, had made the difficult voyage around Cape Horn to ravage British shipping in the Pacific.

Technology, meanwhile, was a boon to commerce raiding. With a fresh breeze from their best quarter, many sailing vessels of the 1860s were faster than a primitive steamer like the *Sumter*. But the mere fact that the Confederate raider could make nine or ten knots under steam, without regard to the wind, made her a deadly predator at a time when virtually all merchantmen were sailing ships. In a relatively confined body of water such as the Caribbean, where much of the commerce followed traditional sea-lanes, an armed steamer like the *Sumter* was truly a fox in the chicken coop.

But this technological advantage was theory in July 1861. As Semmes pointed his ship toward Cuba, he had much to consider. Britain had issued a statement of neutrality in the American conflict; this declaration had the effect of recognizing the Confederacy as a belligerent but not as a de jure government. Other European governments had not yet acted but were expected to follow Britain's lead. London's action was important to Semmes, for under international law a belligerent vessel was permitted to purchase supplies other than munitions without restriction and to make such repairs as might be necessary to stay at sea. He planned to exploit to the utmost the privileges implicit in belligerent status.

On the morning of July 3 the *Sumter* passed south of the western tip of Cuba, heading east. Semmes planned to make a sweep along the southern coast of Cuba, take on coal, continue on to Barbados, coal again, and then make for the coast of Brazil. That afternoon the lookout for the first time cried "Sail ho!" from the masthead and moments later announced a second sail. Both strangers were heading westward, so the distance quickly closed. In accordance with established naval tradition, Semmes attempted to deceive his prey by flying false colors, in this instance British. He stopped the first vessel, which proved to be Spanish and was promptly released. The second, however, was recognizably American. Now showing the Stars and Bars, Semmes brought her around with a warning shot and took *Sumter*'s first prize. She proved to be the six-hundred-ton bark *Golden Rocket,* of Brewster, Maine. The boarding party soon returned with the skipper and his papers.

In Semmes's recollection, nothing could have exceeded the astonishment of her master, William Bailey, who, however, was "not disposed to go either into hysterics or . . . heroics." The *Golden Rocket* was in ballast, outward bound to Cuba, and clearly a lawful prize. From the equipment on board Semmes appropriated the chronometer—the first of many that would fall into his hands over the next three years. The Confederate commander assured Bailey that he and his crew would be well treated, calling his own duty a painful one but one that could not be avoided. He told Bailey, "You will only have to submit, as so many thousands have done before you, to the fortunes of war."[1]

Semmes was about to burn his first Federal ship. The *Sumter* sent her boats to bring off *Golden Rocket*'s crew, together with such provisions—cordage, sails, and paints—as the raider required. Night fell. A party from the *Sumter* set to chopping up pine bunks aboard the prize, laying a pile of chips and straw in several parts of the vessel. These flammables were in turn sprinkled with butter and lard from the ship's stores and then ignited. At about 10:00 P.M., flames leaped up from the aptly named *Golden Rocket.*

Semmes watched the fire devour his first victim. He had earlier ordered the American flag flown by the *Golden Rocket* brought to him, and it had awakened a barrage of conflicting emotions. He had served that flag and had defended it; now he was waging war against it. As he later recalled the night:

> The wind, by this time, had become very light, and the night was pitch-dark. . . . Not a sound could be heard on board the *Sumter,* although her deck was crowded with men. . . . The prize ship had been laid to, with her main topsail to the mast, and all her light sails, though clewed up, were flying loose about the yards. The forked tongues of the devouring element, leaping into the rigging, newly tarred, ran rapidly up

the shrouds. . . . A top-gallant sail, all on fire, would now fly off from the yard, and sailing leisurely in the direction of the light breeze. . . settle. . . into the sea. . . . The mizzen-mast now went by the board, then the fore-mast, and in a few minutes afterward, the great main-mast tottered, reeled, and fell over the ship's side into the sea, making a noise like that of the sturdy oak of the forests when it falls by the stroke of the axeman.[2]

The destruction of the *Sumter*'s first prize appears to have been an emotional moment for everyone on the raider. For the first and only time during the war, the *Sumter*'s officers collected a purse for a captive's heartbroken skipper. Semmes invited Bailey to mess with the *Sumter*'s officers, and his crew had the run of the raider's deck. Semmes would always take pride in his treatment of those whom he captured. "We were making war upon the enemy's commerce," he later wrote, "not upon his unarmed seamen."[3]

The following day was the Fourth of July, and this fact again awakened mixed emotions in Semmes. Normally he would have been invited to join his officers in the wardroom, and the crew would have been issued extra grog. Semmes ordered that there be no observance. That afternoon the lookout spotted two sail, and a blank cartridge from the *Sumter* brought each vessel to a halt. One was the brig *Cuba,* the other the *Machias,* both from Maine. Each was carrying sugar, which the manifests showed to be British-owned.

Had this been the War of 1812, the captured enemy vessels would have been sent with a prize crew to the nearest American port, where the cargo would have been remitted to its neutral owners, the ships sold, and the proceeds divided between the U.S. government and the crew of the *Sumter*. This was 1861, however, and the Federal blockade made it difficult for any Confederate ship to send its prize to a Southern port. Given this situation, Semmes probed the limits of international law. Britain and France had prohibited belligerents from bringing prizes to their ports, but Spain had not. Semmes put prize crews aboard the *Cuba* and the *Machias* and told them to follow him to the Cuban port of Cienfuegos.

On the evening of July 5, off the Cienfuegos lighthouse, he stopped two more sugar traders, the *Ben Dunning* and the *Albert Adams.* In each case the ships were American but the cargoes Spanish. He put prize crews on both, which, when added to the *Machias,* made up a four-ship convoy. Then, as Semmes prepared to move into

Cienfuegos with his three prizes, his lookout reported a steam tug, with three American vessels in tow, coming down the narrow strait from Cienfuegos Bay.

Semmes intended to add all three American ships to his already considerable bag, but he could not molest them within the three-mile limit, or "marine league." The *Sumter* therefore ran up Spanish colors, and Semmes ordered his prize crews to do the same. To justify his loitering in the area, Semmes signaled that he required a pilot. The unsuspecting American vessels separated from the tug and set a course seaward, leaving the tug free to attend to the *Sumter*. A Spanish pilot clambered aboard the raider and asked Semmes where he wished to go. To the Spaniard's astonishment, Semmes replied in fluent Spanish that he planned to capture yonder American ships just as soon as they passed into international waters. "We are *Confederados*," Semmes paraphrased his remarks to the pilot, "and we have *la guerra* with the *Americanos del Norte*." When the helpful pilot confirmed that his late charges were at least five miles from shore, the *Sumter* ran up Confederate colors and set out in pursuit.[4]

In acting as he did, Semmes violated a tenet of international law that forbade a belligerent from launching a strike from neutral waters. The *Sumter* should have allowed her quarry a twenty-four-hour head start. But Semmes was selective in his interpretation of international law, and by the evening of July 6 the *Sumter* was surrounded by no fewer than six U.S. merchantmen.

Semmes had burned his first prize, *Golden Rocket,* in part as a means of announcing his arrival. Now, as he led his string of prizes into Cienfuegos harbor like a mother duck, he turned his attention to legal aspects of his captures. Given the Federal blockade of Southern ports, he hoped that he might be able to adjudicate his prizes outside the Confederacy. Some adroit diplomacy would be required, however, for the initial Spanish reaction to the arrival of Semmes's convoy was less than friendly. Not recognizing the Stars and Bars, guards at the fort had sent a volley of small-arms fire through the *Sumter*'s rigging as an order to halt.

Semmes sent an officer to the *comandante,* who was apologetic about the shooting. Semmes, suitably appeased, invited the Spaniard to the *Sumter,* where they shared a bottle of wine as Semmes provided a highly colored description of the war in North America. The *comandante* regretted his misunderstanding and assured Semmes that he would be properly received once he had arrived in Cienfuegos.

Semmes sent an officer, Robert Chapman, to the city, with the dual mission of arranging coaling for the *Sumter* and delivering a letter to the Spanish governor. The letter noted the prizes recently taken by the *Sumter* and laid out a program that Semmes hoped to "sell" to Spanish authorities:

> I have sought a port of Cuba with the expectation that Spain will extend to the cruisers of the Confederate States the same friendly reception that, in similar circumstances, she would extend to cruisers of the enemy. In other words, that [Spain] will permit me to leave the captured vessels within her jurisdiction until they can be adjudicated by a court of admiralty of the Confederate States.

Here, Semmes was venturing into uncharted legal waters. It was doubtful whether any neutral would allow Confederate cruisers to "park" their prizes for an indefinite period, but Semmes made the best case he could:

> A rule which would exclude our prizes from [Spanish] ports . . . although it should be applied, in terms, equally to the enemy, would not, I respectfully suggest, be an equitable or just rule. . . . One of the most important [belligerent rights] in a war against a commercial people is that which I have just exercised, of capturing his property on the high seas. But how are the Confederate States to enjoy . . . the benefit of this right, if their cruisers are not permitted to enter neutral ports with their prizes, and retain them there in safe custody, until they can be condemned and disposed of? They cannot send them into their own ports.[5]

The governor of Cienfuegos, Don José de la Pozuela, had no intention of responding to Semmes's letter, which he promptly telegraphed to his superiors in Havana. But he did extend the hospitality of the port to the *Sumter,* and this involved more than the sale of coal. Lieutenant Chapman, reputedly the handsomest of the *Sumter*'s officers, appears also to have been the one, after Kell, on whom Semmes most relied. While bargaining for coal, Chapman was fêted by local citizens at the best club in Cienfuegos. One evening the party lasted all night, and Semmes had his first evidence that the upper classes in much of the Caribbean were supporters of the Confederate cause.

Meanwhile, Semmes was puzzled as to what had become of one of his earlier captures, the brig *Cuba*. He left a message for the prizemaster he had put aboard her, Midshipman A. G. Hudgins, telling him to parole the crew of his prize, turn the ship over to the local governor for safekeeping, and make his way back to the Confederacy as best he could. Semmes himself could not afford to dally in Cienfuegos. No sooner had the *Sumter* arrived than the U.S. consul had telegraphed Havana, imploring his colleague to rush any available Federal warship to Cienfuegos. Semmes knew that the United States maintained a naval station at Key West and that the navy's continuing search for Confederate privateers would eventually bring a warship to Havana.

During the night of July 7 the *Sumter* headed back to sea. She had taken on a hundred tons of fuel and five thousand gallons of water to replace the supplies that had been jettisoned off New Orleans. Semmes left a local agent in charge of his six prizes, but having less than total confidence in how their legal status would be resolved, he kept the crews aboard the *Sumter* as prisoners. Even if U.S. representatives were to regain the ships, there would be no crews to man them.

Semmes had no way of knowing that he had lost the *Cuba* forever, under unusual circumstances. During the night of July 4–5, the skipper and two officers of the *Cuba,* having free run of their ship, had seized the keys to the arms locker and regained control of the vessel. Putting the Confederate prize crew in irons, Captain Strout and his men set sail for New York.*

---

*Years later the Yankee skipper gave his version of what had happened: "We were unarmed and were allowed to keep on deck," Captain Strout wrote in the *Magazine of History* in 1908. "I got a chance to talk to Jim Babbage and Jim Carroll, my first and second mates, and we determined to recapture the vessel. On July 8 [*sic*] I found the prizemaster asleep on the round-house. Immediately we got possession of all the arms. The prize crew got on to the racket and ran for their weapons. Finding them gone two drew their sheath knives and one got an axe and rushed at where we were. The mainsail was down and lay between us. One of them tried to jump over it and I hit him over the head with a cleaver. . . . He fell, scrambled back, and did not attempt to return. My mates and the cook were now armed with revolvers and one of my seamen had a cutlass. 'If you stir,' I shouted to the prize crew, 'I will blow your heads off.' They didn't stir. When I ordered them to surrender they yielded. . . .

"I had on board only four pairs of irons. I put one on the prizemaster and the others on three of the most dangerous of the others. The rest we tied with ropes. . . .

The little *Sumter* had made her presence felt in a big way during her first week at sea, capturing eight enemy vessels. Federal warships, already en route to Cienfuegos, would encounter the first of many frustrations when they discovered that the *Sumter* had flown the coup. Yet Semmes's attempt to find a neutral sanctuary for his prizes was destined to fail. Unknown either to him or to Spanish authorities, Queen Isabella had, on June 17, issued a proclamation of neutrality with respect to the American war based on the positions taken by Britain and France. None of these neutrality proclamations addressed the rights of belligerent warships, but the United States sought to blur the distinction between privateers, which had been outlawed by the Declaration of Paris, and commissioned warships like the *Sumter,* which had long-established rights to make repairs and take on supplies in neutral ports.[6] Spain, with her exposed Caribbean colonies, could not afford to antagonize the United States. To Semmes's fury, authorities in Cuba eventually returned the six vessels captured by the *Sumter* to their owners on the basis of a polite fiction: that they had been captured within Spanish territorial waters.[7]

Meanwhile, the *Sumter* steamed eastward along Cuba's southern coast. Semmes's goal continued to be the coast of Brazil—the intersection point for several important sea-lanes—but he was already experiencing difficulty with his vessel's short steaming range. For six

---

Nothing of importance happened until the 14th day of July, when the prizemaster, whose irons had been removed at his urgent request, managed to get a pistol and perched himself in the maintop. Then he took out a cigar and lighted it and called out that he had something to say to me. 'Do you intend to carry me to New York?' he asked. I told him that I did. He blew out some smoke, laughed, and said, 'Well, you'll never do it alive.' 'All right,' said I, 'then I'll carry you dead.' At that he yelled, 'It's your time to dodge,' and fired at me. The bullet struck the deck at my feet and I did dodge. Johnny Reb told the truth that time. He fired again and I did some more lively hopping. Then I ran below and got my pistol. . . .

"I got on deck at last and proceeded to even things up. He was swinging around in the maintop and I was dancing around on deck. I suppose it was the funniest looking duel that ever was. He used up all his cartridges without hitting me, and I shot at him three times without coming anywhere near him. Then I lodged a ball in the mast just above his head and the next shot I got him in the arm. It was the right arm, and it was broken above the elbow. He dropped his weapon to the deck. All this time he had been holding his cigar in his left hand. He was the nerviest man I ever saw. He threw the cigar away and came down. I dressed his wound and locked him up. I kept guard over him until we reached New York on July 21." See George Dalzell, *The Flight from the Flag* (Chapel Hill, N.C.: University of North Carolina Press, 1940), 39–40.

days the *Sumter* bucked head winds that reduced her speed to five knots, damaged one mast, and sent her seasick captain to his cabin. On July 10 he wrote in his journal,

> At 1:30 this morning I went upon the companion ladder, to give some directions to the officer of the deck . . . and while so doing I felt a sudden sickness of the stomach and reeling of the brain. I laid my head on my arm, thinking the sensation would pass off, but in a moment more I lost consciousness and tumbled from the top to the bottom of the ladder upon the cabin floor. . . . Confined to my hammock during the day.[8]

Down to only two days' worth of coal, Semmes altered course to the south. He could not afford to expend all his fuel, lest he encounter a Federal warship that he could not outrun under sail. Given the contrary winds from the east, he decided to head south and refuel at the Dutch colony of Curaçao. For the first time the *Sumter* cruised under canvas unaided by steam. The lookout spotted one sail on the horizon, but Semmes, concerned about his fuel, did not pursue her. He had seen no enemy warships since New Orleans, but if he were obliged to stop for coal every week, as he was now doing, his movements would become predictable and unacceptably risky.

For the moment, however, his most irritating enemies were American consuls. Although the Lincoln administration would, in practice, accord the Confederacy belligerent rights, Washington's official position was that the Richmond government had no legal standing and that neither the *Sumter* nor the Confederacy's privateers were anything more than pirates. American consuls in ports of the Spanish Main were instructed to advise their host governments that the Southern "insurgents" had none of the rights traditionally accorded to belligerents.

The charge that he was a pirate would dog Semmes throughout the war and after. Nothing infuriated him more, and he reserved a special loathing for the Federal diplomats who sought to poison the minds of local officials at his ports of call. At Curaçao he wrote at length to the local governor, specifying the belligerent rights due the *Sumter*, and once again sent his letter by way of the urbane Lieutenant Chapman. Word came back that a council of state was deliberating the matter. Semmes's patience, never a strong point, was wearing thin.

> After the lapse of an hour or two . . . I told my first lieutenant that, as our men had not been practiced at the guns for some

time, I thought it would be as well to let them burst a few of our eight-inch shells at a target. Accordingly . . . a great stir was made about the deck as the guns were cast loose, and pretty soon, whiz! went a shell across the windows of the council-chamber, which overlooked the sea. . . . By the time we had fired three or four shells, all of which burst with beautiful precision, Chapman's boat was seen returning and . . . we ran out and secured the guns.[9]

Whether or not Semmes's gunboat diplomacy carried the day, local authorities decided to allow the *Sumter* to refuel and to make repairs. The raider spent a week in Curaçao, where she obtained a new fore-topmast to replace one sprung in the gales off Cuba and a new coat of black paint. The crew received its first liberty since going to sea, and Semmes found time for a stroll around the town, which he found picturesque but rundown. In a practice that he would employ repeatedly, Semmes let slip in conversation that the *Sumter*'s next cruising ground would be off Cuba. Cuba was, of course, the one area to which he had no intention of returning.

The *Sumter* left Curaçao on July 24, the ship fully coaled and her skipper's health restored. The following morning the lookout spotted sail, and the *Sumter* gave chase. The vessel in question proved to be a New England schooner, the *Abby Bradford,* headed for Venezuela. Semmes had not yet given up on his hope of parking prizes in neutral harbors, and he turned with his prize to the Venezuelan port of Puerto Cabello. There he was disappointed yet again. The U.S. consul protested, and local authorities delayed any decision. Semmes may have anticipated such temporizing, for rather than waiting for a decision that might well be negative he decided to attempt a new and dangerous tack. He put a prize crew aboard the *Bradford* and instructed the prizemaster, a young midshipman named Ruhl, to run the blockade into New Orleans. He entrusted Ruhl with a letter to Secretary Mallory in which he summarized the *Sumter*'s cruise to date. Semmes did not deem it prudent to discuss his future movements but concluded, "We are all well, and 'doing a pretty fair business,' in mercantile parlance, having made nine captures in twenty-six days."[10]

It was just as well that Semmes was security-conscious for his letter to Mallory fell into enemy hands—the only occasion on which one of his dispatches was intercepted. Prizemaster Ruhl was careless in his approach to the Mississippi passes, and the *Abby Bradford* was captured by David D. Porter's *Powhatan*. The prize was returned to her owners, but the Federals learned little from Semmes's report that they did not know already. And the incident had one interesting result: Believing the *Sumter* ripe for capture, Porter asked permission to pursue her. Permission was granted, and he set off in a game of cat and mouse that pitted two major figures of the naval war against one another.[11]

Semmes, of course, had not yet heard that the *Bradford* had been recaptured or that the six vessels at Cienfuegos were being returned to their owners. Nor would he know for many months the fate of the *Cuba*. Running east along the Venezuelan coast, the *Sumter* intercepted an American bark, the *Joseph Maxwell,* on July 27. Because she carried cargo belonging to a Venezuelan trading firm, Semmes thought that Venezuelan authorities might be more cooperative than they had been with respect to the *Abby Bradford*. He returned to Puerto Cabello, to ask of Venezuela what he had asked of Spain: permission to leave his prize in a Venezuelan port pending a resolution of its status. But the U.S. consul had been busy since Semmes's departure the day before, and the local governor demanded that Semmes deliver up the *Joseph Maxwell* until Venezuelan courts should determine its status. This was hardly what Semmes had in mind, and the *Sumter* left Puerto Cabello for the last time. Semmes put a prizemaster aboard the *Joseph Maxwell* and ordered him to join the six vessels that, he believed, were still detained at Cienfuegos.

From the outset, Federal pursuit of the *Sumter* had been disorganized. Secretary of the Navy Gideon Welles personally controlled the disposition of Federal vessels, with little participation by senior navy officers. Welles was a former newspaper editor from Connecticut whose appointment was designed to give New England a place in the war cabinet; his flowing white beard had led Lincoln to call him Father Neptune. Welles's character was above reproach, but he was abysmally ignorant of naval matters.

Following the *Sumter*'s escape from New Orleans, Welles had scolded Captain Charles Poor of the *Brooklyn* for failing to intercept the raider. The tightening of the Federal blockade was Welles's first priority, and Poor had set a bad example. But with the *Sumter* now at sea, what should the Federals do? Welles was not prepared to significantly weaken the blockade to pursue one cruiser, and here his logic was sound. His failure lay in his inept deployment of those vessels that he did send.

During the late summer of 1861, three Federal warships, the *Powhatan,* the *Iroquois,* and the *Keystone State,* had the capture of the *Sumter* as their primary mission. Other Federal warships knew of the Confederate raider and were told to destroy or capture her if she were encountered. But the Federals had no meaningful strategy for bagging their prey. In ordering one vessel, the *Shepherd Knapp,* to the West Indies, Welles informed her captain that his task was "to capture or destroy the vessels of the rebels and protect legitimate commerce of your own flag." But Welles had no suggestion as to how this was to be accomplished beyond instructing Captain Eytinge, "You will exercise your crew at the great guns, and occasionally with shot and shell."[12]

Semmes was very conscious of his ship's limitations—her light armament, modest speed, and limited fuel capacity. But balanced against these liabilities were certain assets. Not only was a raider allowed to deceive her quarry by the use of foreign flags, but the *Sumter* was able to further disguise her appearance by lowering her funnel. The fact that she was a screw steamer rather than a paddle wheeler was an additional advantage, for there was nothing to indicate from a distance that she was a steamship at all. And, as noted earlier, a steamship of any kind enjoyed a tremendous advantage over a quarry dependent on unpredictable winds.

As for eluding her pursuers, the *Sumter* had one tremendous asset: the vast expanse of the seas. Whereas all American merchant vessels were prey to the *Sumter,* she herself was a nautical counterpart to the needle in a haystack. Concerned as he was with his own problems, Semmes had only a vague idea of the havoc he was creating among the enemy. He would have relished the report of one U.S. consul to Secretary of State Seward, which concluded, "Your Excellency cannot possibly imagine the effect which the presence of the *Sumter* on this coast has had on American trade. It is quite possible that it will be entirely suspended."[13]

CHAPTER 7

"Semmes Was Too Clever"

During its first month at sea the *Sumter* had captured ten enemy ships, only one of which had been destroyed. Far from being a pyromaniac, Semmes had searched diligently for a means of dealing with prizes in a way that would turn a profit for his government and for those aboard the raider. Soon, however, he would learn than none of the countries represented in the Caribbean were prepared to play the roles he assigned them. As a result, Semmes henceforth would burn most of his prizes.

From Puerto Cabello the *Sumter* set a course east toward the British colony of Trinidad. The ship was buffeted by head winds, and progress was slow. One afternoon she passed over the coral reefs off Tortuga, and for an hour Semmes forgot the war and became the earnest naturalist of his earlier travels in Mexico. Slowing engines on his ship, he marveled at the clearness of the water, the rainbow-hued tropical fish, the multicolored plants, and above all, the great clusters of coral, which he compared to miniature cathedrals. The hour passed quickly. Semmes then ordered the officer of the deck to resume speed, and the *Sumter* once again was the predator of the seas.[1]

Sails were few, however, and the *Sumter* had a largely uneventful cruise to Trinidad. Outside Port of Spain a British merchantman dipped her colors to the raider—a courtesy that Semmes never failed to note, and one that he probably viewed as a good omen. In any case, his August 4 arrival at Port of Spain marked the first visit by the *Sumter* to a British port. The attitude of British authorities there would constitute an important precedent for the remainder of her cruise and for other Confederate warships as well.

Semmes sent an officer to call on the governor, who returned word that the *Sumter* could expect the same hospitality that would be extended to Federal vessels; the Confederates were free to purchase anything except contraband of war. This was all that Semmes could ask, but how Britain chose to define contraband was important as well. In particular, was coal considered contraband? British colonial authorities concluded that it was not, a welcome decision for the Confederacy because commerce raiding could be carried on only by steamships, and Confederate steamers were dependent on coal obtained in neutral ports.[2]

Meanwhile, there was some unfinished business. Semmes still had on board the very apprehensive eight-man crew of the *Joseph Maxwell*. The Federal navy had recently captured a Confederate privateer, the *Savannah,* and had threatened her crew with hanging in accordance with a proclamation by President Lincoln that the crews of Confederate vessels would be treated as pirates. Semmes had warned the crew of the *Maxwell* that they were hostages and that their fate depended on the treatment ultimately accorded the crew of *Savannah*. Fortunately, newspapers in Port of Spain reported that the crew of the Confederate privateer had been accorded prisoner-of-war status.

The crews of the *Savannah* and the *Joseph Maxwell* were pawns in a game whose principal players were in Washington and London. Although the United States had not been a party to the Declaration of Paris, the Lincoln administration now embraced its principles, and as a corollary sought to portray all vessels flying the Confederate flag as either privateers or—better still—simply pirates. As such, they would be entitled to none of the privileges normally accorded belligerents. The British were far too sophisticated to accept this reasoning, but the main argument against it was humanitarian. Were Confederate soldiers to be treated in accordance with the laws of war, but Confederate sailors routinely hanged? A justice of the U.S. Supreme Court, Robert Grier, wrote in 1861 that he would have no part in wartime "piracy" cases: "I have other business to attend to, and do not mean to be delayed here from day to day in trying charges against a few unfortunate men . . . out of half a million that are in arms against the government. Why should this difference be made between men captured on land and on the sea?"[3]

Semmes, of course, had no way of knowing that the Yankees were retreating from their threat to hang Confederate sailors. Before releasing the crew of the *Joseph Maxwell,* he called the ship's mates to his cabin. He had been fully prepared to hang them, Semmes said, but he was glad that this had not proved necessary. They and their shipmates were free to leave.[4] Would Semmes in fact have hanged sailors whose only "crime" was to have served on a U.S. ship? He acknowledged in his memoirs that to have carried out this threat would have exceeded his authority, but he carefully avoided saying what he would have done. Semmes later stopped short of executing deserters from his own ships, however, and one suspects that he would have found extenuating circumstances on behalf of the crew of the *Joseph Maxwell.*

Port of Spain had proved to be a very satisfactory stop. Semmes and his officers basked in a warm if unofficial reception, the first of many in the far-flung ports of the British Empire. There were no official salutes, but the raider's decks were crowded with visitors, and Semmes had ample opportunity to regale officers of the Royal Navy with his version of the war in America.

A day or two after the *Sumter*'s arrival Semmes was visited by the master of a Baltimore brig then in port. He was ready for sea, the master told Semmes, but he wanted to know Semmes's intentions. Semmes told the master that his ship would not be molested, adding that his instructions were to give special consideration to Maryland vessels, in the hope that the state that Semmes had once called home would eventually side with the Confederacy.[5]

While at Trinidad, Semmes exchanged calls with the skipper of a British steam frigate, H.M.S. *Cadmus.* When Captain Hillyar expressed puzzlement about the causes of the war in North America, Semmes gave his standard explanation, with emphasis on the North's economic exploitation of the South. He held forth on the iniquities of the tariff, as a result of which, he maintained, the South had been reduced to the status of a dependency. But what of slavery? Hillyar asked. That issue, Semmes replied, was a red herring:

> With the exception of a few honest zealots, the canting, hypo-critical Yankee cares as little for our slaves as he does for our

draught animals. . . . When a burglar designs to enter a dwelling for the purpose of robbery, he provides himself with the necessary implements. The slavery question was one of the implements employed, to help on the robbery of the South.[6]

One wonders about Captain Hillyar's reaction to this diatribe. In his official report Hillyar focused on naval matters, noting that he was not impressed with the *Sumter* as a ship. He thought her too lightly constructed for a man-of-war, and he doubted whether her guns were mounted high enough to be fired in high seas. But if Hillyar was not impressed with the *Sumter*, he was quite taken with her commander. Of Semmes he wrote, "There is no doubt he will do an enormous amount of damage before he is taken, for he seems a bold, determined man and well up to his work."[7]

Coaling was slow, and the raider was further delayed when First Officer Kell discovered corrosion in the boilers. To keep the crew entertained Semmes encouraged them to stock up on fruit from the bumboats that surrounded the raider at her anchorage. When the *Sumter* finally departed on August 5, her boats and stern nettings were filled with oranges, bananas, and other tropical fruit, and she looked more like an excursion boat than a warship. Kell even allowed the sailors to bring aboard a variety of tropical wildlife. The *Sumter* got under way to the squawk of parrots and the incongruous sight of monkeys swinging through the rigging.

Semmes's immediate goal continued to be the sea-lanes off the bulge of Brazil, and from Trinidad he set a course to the southeast. The weather was fine; only Yankee ships were lacking. Semmes, who referred to his crewmen collectively as "Jack," would write nostalgically of this leg of the *Sumter*'s cruise:

> With the fore-castle and quarter-deck awnings spread, we do not feel the heat, though the sun is nearly perpendicular at noon. Jack is "overhauling" his clothes'-bag, and busy with his needle and thread, stopping now and then to have a "lark" with his monkey, or to listen to the prattle of his parrot. The boys of the ship are taking lessons in knotting and splicing, and listening to the "yarn" of some old salt, as he indoctrinates them in these mysteries.[8]

The *Sumter* was averaging about eight knots, and Semmes had initially hoped to make a direct run to São Luís on the north coast of

Brazil. Once again, however, the raider's fuel consumption forced a change in plans. On August 11, with just thirty hours' coal left, he let the steam go down and set a course for French Guiana, some three hundred miles away.

The *Sumter* arrived at Cayenne on August 15, and there Semmes met his first unfriendly reception. When he sent an officer to the governor to inquire about coaling, that official replied that the Confederates would have to spend five days in quarantine before disembarking and that in any case no coal was available. His attitude was considerably more hostile than that of the French government, probably because he had received no instructions. Rather than debate the authorities, Semmes weighed anchor and retraced his course to neighboring Suriname. Coal was available, but here too there were problems. The U.S. consul contacted the local coal merchants and attempted to purchase their entire inventories, appealing to them "not to sell a pound to that rascally steamer sailing under the name *Sumter*." The merchants were not intimidated, however, and several visited the *Sumter* in person to make arrangements for bunkering.[9] Perhaps they were impressed by Confederate prospects. Word of the Confederate victory at Manassas reached Suriname while the *Sumter* was there, prompting Semmes to order an extra round of grog for his crew.[10]

Meanwhile, it was clear that the *Sumter* required more than coal. Although she had undergone repairs just two weeks earlier at Trinidad, the raider was now in need of a refit. In addition, Kell was convinced that if two water tanks were removed the raider could accommodate more coal and increase her cruising range. The upshot was that the *Sumter* stayed twelve days in Suriname, and although the port of Paramaribo did not afford facilities for a full overhaul, Kell succeeded in enlarging her bunkers.

As first officer, or "Luff," in the argot of the sea, thirty-eight-year-old John McIntosh Kell was proving to be all that Semmes could hope for. While Semmes dealt with tactics, diplomacy, and prize adjudication, Kell managed the day-to-day operation of the ship and her unruly crew. At six feet two, the Georgian was tall for his time, with a broad forehead, blue eyes, and brown hair. His most striking feature was a magnificent full beard that reminded at least one acquaintance of a Scottish chieftain—hardly surprising, for Kell's roots were in Scotland. The captain of a warship at sea was often remote from the crew, and the first officer did much to set the tone on a ship. Dr. Francis Galt, the young Virginian who served as surgeon on both the

Sumter and the *Alabama,* wrote after the war that Kell had an especially keen sense of justice and made a point of dealing fairly with his
crew.[11] He appears to have combined a firm hand in disciplinary matters with a personal warmth often lacking in Semmes.

Alas, not even Kell could maintain discipline once a ship dropped
anchor. Months before, when the *Sumter* was still fitting out in New
Orleans, Semmes's cousin Thomas had thoughtfully presented him
with a slave named Ned to serve as cabin steward aboard the raider.[12]
According to Semmes, Ned—the only black on the ship—was "happy
as the days were long [and] a great favorite with the crew." In
Paramaribo, however, he and another steward deserted. Semmes had
a ready explanation. "I have not the least doubt that they were
seduced away by the U.S. Consul, a man of no character . . . and
some Yankee skippers that were in port."[13] After all, why would anyone want to leave the *Sumter*?

The raider sailed from Suriname on the last day of August and
arrived at São Luís, Brazil, on September 6. Her cruise had begun
dramatically with the escape from New Orleans and the string of
prizes off Cienfuegos. Now some of the gloss was gone. Semmes had
spotted only four sail since leaving Trinidad, and all had been either
neutral or too distant to chase. Keeping the *Sumter* at sea was a challenge, even with enlarged bunkers. The $10,000 in gold with which
she had left New Orleans was being eaten up by fuel bills, for there
had been little or no cash on the raider's prizes. Semmes knew nothing of the activities of his pursuers, but his frequent stops for coal
were leaving a dangerous trail.

Semmes had only Kell with whom to discuss his worries, and the
Sumter's high-strung commander was showing signs of stress. Off São
Luís he could see no sign of a pilot boat. Rather than anchor and wait
for a pilot, he chose to make his own way, relying on charts. The
Sumter had passed the most dangerous shoals when she struck a
sandbar. The impact was enough to cause those on deck to lose their
balance, and the thought flashed across Semmes's mind that he might
have difficulty explaining the loss of the Confederacy's only cruiser
on a Brazilian sandbar. But the tide was running out, and with
engines at full astern the *Sumter* worked her way free. Aided by a
local fisherman, Semmes piloted his vessel to anchorage.[14]

Semmes was ill. Because the voyage from Suriname had been a
smooth one, this malaise was presumably unrelated to his earlier seasickness. His disposition did not improve, however, when the welcome at São Luís proved cool. Although the *Sumter* had arrived on

Brazil's independence day, he and his officers were excluded from the festivities because Brazil did not recognize the Confederacy. Had the *Sumter*'s officers been invited, the independence celebrations would have assumed a symbolic importance, perhaps as a portent for the Confederacy. Shut out as he was, Semmes dismissed them with contempt. "We were a race of Anglo-Saxons," he would later write, "proud of our lineage, and proud of our strength, frowned upon by a set of half-breeds."[15]

While the *Sumter* docked for repairs, Semmes checked into a local hotel for rest. He chose well, for the owner of the Hotel Porto, Senhor Porto himself, was delighted to have the cruiser captain under his roof and volunteered to play political adviser. Senhor Porto was a devotee of fast horses, and in the course of a daily carriage ride with his guest, the Brazilian helped Semmes cope with the local officialdom. Semmes's initial request for an appointment with the provincial president had been refused. Now, with Porto's patronage, all doors were open to him. He called on the president and displayed his commission. Semmes's description of the interview is interesting as a reflection of Semmes the diplomat:

> I then read to his Excellency an extract or two from the letter of instructions which had been sent to me by the Secretary of the Navy, directing me to pay all proper respect to the territory and property of neutrals. I next read the proclamations of England and France, acknowledging us to be in possession of belligerent rights, and said to his Excellency that, although I had not seen the proclamation of Brazil, I presumed she had followed the lead of the European powers—to which he assented.[16]

But what of coal? the president asked. Semmes was able to cite here the example of the British at Trinidad. Contrary to the allegation by the U.S. consul, Semmes purred, the British had determined that coal was not contraband. It was a bravura performance, in no way diminished by the contempt in which Semmes held the countries of Latin America and their nettlesome bureaucrats. He got his coal, and the *Sumter* was repaired, painted, and provisioned. Indeed, São Luís proved a lucky stop. Almost out of cash, Semmes had made the acquaintance of an expatriate Texan named Wetson who was working in Brazil as an engineer. Hearing of Semmes's plight, Wetson lent him $2,000, which allowed Semmes to meet the *Sumter*'s bills and still take a small amount to sea.[17]

While in São Luís, Semmes rethought his cruise. It was late in the season for the *Sumter* to be operating on trade routes off Brazil. The southeast trade winds combined with the strong current would make operations off Cape St. Roque fuel-intensive and for that reason perhaps unproductive. Changing plans, Semmes decided to head north to the equatorial calm belt. There his engines would give him a critical edge over any merchant vessel he might encounter.

On the morning of September 25, ten days after leaving São Luís, Semmes heard the cry of "Sail ho!" for the first time in several weeks. Flying the Stars and Stripes, the *Sumter* overhauled a Maine-built brigantine, the *Joseph Park*. The prize was in ballast, having been unable to obtain a cargo in the Brazilian port of Pernambuco because of fear of the *Sumter*. Semmes found on board the *Joseph Park* a letter to her master warning him to avoid the usual sea-lanes on his return to Hampton Roads. No wonder pickings were lean: The Yankees were learning to vary their routes!

Semmes resumed his course northward. The Alabamian was always a very private person, but this period appears to have been one of special reflection. He wrote in his journal:

> *Friday, September 27th.* This is my fifty-second birthday, and so the years roll on, one by one, and I am getting to be an old man! Thank God that I am still able to render service to my country in her glorious struggle for the right of self-government. . . . We have thus far beaten the Vandal hordes that have invaded and desecrated our soil; and we shall continue to beat them to the end. . . . My poor distressed family! How fondly my thoughts revert to them today. . . . May our Heavenly Father console, cherish and protect them.[18]

Meanwhile, Semmes decided that, rather than burn the *Joseph Park,* he would employ her as a scout. The lookouts on a ship such as the *Sumter* could rarely scan more than twenty-five or thirty miles, but a second vessel could extend the range of search significantly. Semmes put Lieutenant William Evans in charge of the *Joseph Park,* and for three days she and the *Sumter* patrolled as a team, but to no avail. Semmes then burned the *Joseph Park,* for he was hardening to the necessity of destroying his prizes. First Spain, then Holland, Venezuela, and Britain had denied him the option of sending prizes to their ports. In the end he would burn—first from the *Sumter,* then from the *Alabama*—all but twenty-one of the eighty-two vessels that fell into his hands.

Moving slowly northward, the *Sumter* encountered few sail, and those invariably were neutrals. On one occasion the *Sumter,* flying U.S. colors, stopped what turned out to be a British vessel, the *Plover.* Her captain asked Semmes's boarding officer—apparently William Evans—if he was searching for the *Sumter.* Evans was not sure whether the master was joking or not, but because the raider *was* flying U.S. colors Evans kept a straight face, confirming that they were in fact looking for the Confederate raider. Well, the Englishman remarked, "it will take a smarter-looking craft than yours" to catch Semmes.[19]

On the morning of October 27, as the *Sumter* prepared for Sunday muster, the lookout spotted a sail. After a six-hour chase, a blank cartridge from the raider halted a two-hundred-ton schooner, *Daniel Trowbridge,* outward bound from New York to Guiana. This particular prize was a godsend to Semmes, for her holds bulged with provisions, including many luxury goods. For three days, boats from the raider ferried sheep, pigs, preserved meats, lobster, fancy crackers, cheese, and flour from the *Trowbridge* to the *Sumter.*[20] When a boarding party finally torched the *Daniel Trowbridge,* the Confederates felt so kindly toward her that they raised three cheers for their floating commissary. Semmes, typically, was less effusive. He clapped the *Trowbridge*'s master in irons for alleged "insolence" toward one of his officers.[21]

In her last three months at sea the *Sumter* had captured only two prizes, *Joseph Park* and *Daniel Trowbridge.* But Semmes was satisfied, for he correctly attributed the shortage of game to his having thoroughly disrupted American trade in the Caribbean. Certainly he was giving the U.S. Navy fits. On September 9, 1861, a twenty-one-year-old midshipman, Alfred T. Mahan, on board a Federal warship, took pen in hand and somewhat daringly addressed a letter to Assistant Secretary of the Navy Gustavus Fox. The ravages of the *Sumter,* Mahan wrote, had reached a level embarrassing to the U.S. Navy. Yet the rule that allowed a belligerent vessel a twenty-four-hour start over a pursuer in a neutral harbor made it almost impossible to catch a rebel steamer. What was to be done? Mahan suggested the use of decoys—sailing vessels equipped with a hidden pivot gun. If such a vessel encountered the *Sumter,* it might inflict enough damage to disable her.[22]

In World War I, the Royal Navy was to have some success with Q-ships, decoy vessels with hidden guns, which lured German submarines to the surface and then destroyed them. But this was 1861, and no one took up the imaginative proposal from the future author of *The Influence of Sea Power Upon History*. Mahan's scheme would have greatly increased the risk Semmes took in approaching the most innocent-appearing U.S. merchantman.

Not that the *Sumter* was suffering from lack of attention. In New York, insurance rates were rising and the press was filled with stories of alleged Confederate atrocities. The president of the Pacific Mail Steamship Company was so fearful that Semmes might waylay one of his steamers bearing gold from California that Gideon Welles authorized a limited convoy for such vessels in the waters off Panama. Meanwhile, David D. Porter, commanding the *Powhatan*, had his own plan for snaring the *Sumter*, based on his acquaintance with Semmes in the Old Navy. He wrote to Welles:

> Let the Department fit out some fast steamers with rifle guns and send one to the bay of Samaná at the east end of Haiti [Hispaniola]. He will be found there or I'll lose my head. . . . There is also a place in the same island, Ocoa Bay, well known to Semmes (I was there with him), where a thousand vessels might lie concealed and no one know of it.[23]

Porter was mistaken, of course; neither the *Sumter* nor any of her prizes was in Haitian waters. The letter may have been intended to prod the Navy Department into awarding the writer a more active command. If so, Porter succeeded in his objective. On August 14 the *Powhatan* was detached from the blockade squadron and sent after the *Sumter*.

The connection between Semmes and Porter is intriguing. In his readings in naval history, Semmes had been impressed with the career of Porter's father, also named David, who in the War of 1812 had taken the frigate *Essex* around Cape Horn to plunder British commerce in the Pacific. Physically small but combative by temperament, the senior Porter was attracted to unaccompanied cruising. He also reveled in command authority; he cheerfully compared the captain of a warship to a petty despot, writing, "He stands alone, without the friendship or sympathy of one on board."[24] Did Raphael Semmes model himself to some degree after David Porter? If so, it is ironic that his most persistent pursuer in the year of the *Sumter* was to be the commodore's son.

Once on Semmes's trail—along with the *San Jacinto*, *Iroquois*, *Niagara*, and *Keystone State*—Porter developed a keener appreciation

of the problems inherent in finding a single ship under a skillful commander. He followed Semmes's cold trail to Cienfuegos and thence
to the Spanish Main. Four days after Semmes had left São Luís,
Porter dropped anchor there, and for a time it appeared that the
hound might tree the fox. Despite Semmes's attempts to leave a false
trail, Porter concluded correctly that he had decided to forgo Cape
St. Roque in favor of an area he could reach without expending too
much coal. The *Powhatan* weighed anchor and headed north. On
October 8, her lookout spotted a distant light across the dark sea,
and Porter set out in pursuit. The light disappeared. Years later,
Porter concluded that the distant light must have been the *Sumter*,
perhaps seventy-five miles away. Semmes concurred, but placed the
probable distance between the ships at forty miles.[25]

Then as now, the seas were vast.

On November 9, the *Sumter* dropped anchor at Fort-de-France on
the west coast of Martinique. Because the island was a French possession and France was a potential friend of the Confederacy, Semmes—
in fresh linen and dress uniform, complete with sword—called
personally on the governor. Governor Maussion de Cande was
friendly, but suggested that although the *Sumter* was free to purchase
coal in Martinique, it would be better if he knew nothing about it. In
this connection, he noted that the commercial harbor of St. Pierre
would be less conspicuous than Fort-de-France.[26] Meanwhile, the
Sumter's crew had been granted its first liberty since leaving New
Orleans. Although only one watch at a time was allowed ashore, the
result was a rash of brawls and desertions; Kell and his officers spent
countless hours retrieving crewmen from the bars and brothels of the
town.

One bit of news cheered Semmes. While at Fort-de-France he first
heard of the *Trent* affair, in which the U.S.S. *San Jacinto,* commanded by Charles Wilkes, had forcibly removed two Confederate emissaries from a British mail packet, the *Trent*. Semmes had known
Wilkes before the war and had credited him with more intelligence
than to commit an act that was certain to infuriate Britain. He
hoped for a breach between Britain and the United States, but
Washington eventually backed down and returned the Confederate
envoys. To Semmes was left the honor "to have been pursued by
six frigates [*sic*] and one of them caught Mssrs. Mason and Slidell
instead of catching me."[27]

On November 13, the *Sumter*'s crew having returned from their
brawling "liberty," Semmes moved up the coast to St. Pierre for coal-

ing. Satisfied that all was well with his ship, he went off for an evening stroll on the island, accompanied by his clerk, Breedlove Smith.

> The air was soft and filled with perfume, and we were much interested in inspecting the low-roofed and red-tiled country houses, and their half-naked inmates . . . [who] presented themselves, from time to time, as we strolled on. We were . . . objects of much curiosity, and the curiosity was evinced in the same way, respectfully. Whenever we stopped for water . . . the coolest "monkeys"—a sort of porous jug or jar—and calabashes, were handed us, often accompanied by fruits and an invitation to be seated.[28]

The *Sumter* was taking on coal in St. Pierre the following afternoon when danger loomed. A U.S. Navy steam sloop, the thousand-ton *Iroquois,* rounded the tip of the island and took up station outside the harbor. Her skipper, Captain James Palmer, had been at St. Thomas when he heard that the *Sumter* was at Martinique. Palmer had weighed anchor with commendable promptness and had reached St. Pierre in thirty-six hours.

Palmer, whose eight guns far outweighed *Sumter*'s five, and whose ship was far more rugged than the raider, hoped to pounce on the *Sumter* as the smaller vessel left port. But the rules of war complicated his task. If *Iroquois* were to anchor in the harbor, Semmes would be allowed a twenty-four-hour head start once he had finished coaling. If Palmer stayed in international waters, he would have to patrol a harbor mouth fifteen miles across. It was a daunting task, and it helps to explain the willingness with which Semmes had moved his ship to St. Pierre.

The two adversaries studied each another through their glasses. Semmes continued his coaling during the day, while Palmer contemplated a provocation. That night he entered the harbor and headed his ship directly for the *Sumter*. Semmes called his crew to quarters and cleared for action, but the *Iroquois* sheared off at the last minute. To Semmes's surprise—for such harassment was a violation of French waters—Palmer repeated this maneuver several times before returning to his station offshore. Palmer was unable to provoke Semmes into firing the first shot, but the men of the *Sumter* slept at their guns until the morning light.

Semmes registered an immediate protest at Palmer's attempts at intimidation, and Maussion de Cande sided with the Confederates.

He sent a warship to warn Palmer either to anchor in the port or to take up a position outside the three-mile limit. Semmes, meanwhile, acted in a manner calculated to bait his enemy: He ignored the *Iroquois* and continued to take on fuel and supplies. For Semmes, a single Federal warship was little more than a nuisance; to evade her from a harbor as wide as St. Pierre was hardly a challenge compared with the *Sumter*'s escape from the Mississippi delta more than four months before. Time, however, was not on Semmes's side. If another Federal warship were to put in an appearance the odds would worsen considerably.

Palmer, meanwhile, had been in contact with the U.S. consul at St. Pierre, hoping to devise a method by which the latter could signal the *Iroquois* of any movement by the *Sumter*. The consul was no help, but Palmer enlisted the master of an American lumber schooner to signal the *Sumter*'s course if she were to head to sea. Even so, the Federal commander was pessimistic. He wrote to Welles on November 17, "I feel more and more convinced that the *Sumter* will yet escape me, in spite of all our vigilance and zeal. . . . To blockade such a bay as this . . . obliged as we are by the neutrality laws to blockade at 3 miles' distance, it would require at least two more fast steamers."[29]

The war of nerves continued. Semmes discovered Palmer's system of warning lights and protested to the authorities, but to no avail. He waited for a dark night, hoping that one would come before another Federal vessel joined the *Iroquois*. On November 23 the sky was still clear, but Semmes decided that he could wait no longer. At noon he summoned Kell and ordered that every man be at his station by sundown.

The *Sumter* raised steam but attempted to put out as little smoke as possible. A few minutes before 8:00 P.M. the raider hoisted anchor and slipped her moorings. Semmes peered anxiously into the night, confirming that the *Iroquois* was positioned in the northern half of the bay. Pointing south, the black-hulled *Sumter* was almost invisible against the volcanic soil of the bluff. Semmes directed one of his officers to keep a close watch on the Yankee schooner in the harbor, and he soon got the word he expected. The officer ran to Semmes at his station on the horse block, near the helmsman. "I see them, sir! I see them! Look, sir, there are two red lights, one above the other, at the . . . mast head." The schooner doubtless was signaling that the *Sumter* was under way, headed south.[30]

Semmes waited until he could see that the *Iroquois,* too, was under way. He then changed course, doubling back across the bay to the northern shore. There was an anxious moment when the chief engineer, Miles Freeman, informed Semmes that he would have to stop engines in order to cool the bearings. But the *Iroquois* was slow to discover that she had been tricked, and a welcome squall helped hide the *Sumter* as she steamed out of the bay at full speed. Even so, it was an anxious night. Semmes relieved one of his lookouts, who for most of the evening reported false sightings of the *Iroquois*. Semmes himself stayed on deck until 4:30 A.M. before turning in.

His departure from Martinique could not have been better timed. On November 24, the day after *Sumter*'s escape, a second Federal steamer, the *Dacotah*, arrived at St. Pierre to help deal with the raider. When Secretary of the Navy Welles received Palmer's report detailing the *Sumter*'s escape, he relieved Palmer of his command. Four months later, however, Welles reinstated him, implicitly acknowledging that the captain of the *Iroquois* had not been negligent.

Admiral Porter had his own interpretation; he wrote in his postwar memoir that "Semmes was too clever for Palmer."[31] But Semmes's escape had been facilitated by international law, which favored ships attempting to evade blockaders. Palmer wrote to Welles after the *Sumter*'s escape,

> I shall be glad to understand from the Government whether they wish me to respect international law in the case of the *Sumter,* which gives her so great immunity and makes every port her asylum. I was informed at Martinique that France would regard it as an act of war if I attacked her anywhere within the marine league of the island.[32]

CHAPTER 8

Farewell to the *Sumter*

Semmes kept his vessel on a northward course throughout the night and the following day. He had much on his mind. It seemed folly to remain in the Caribbean with a ship that was no match for any of the Federal vessels she might encounter. In any case, with American merchantmen avoiding the usual sea-lanes, game was likely to prove scarce. Yet what was the alternative?

About November 25 Semmes made up his mind: He would take his ship across the Atlantic. It was a daring decision. The lightly built *Sumter* had not been designed for work that would keep her at sea months at a time. Even now her boilers were corroded, she leaked at the seams, and she was taking additional water through a crack in her propeller sleeve. Semmes doubtless hoped to exchange the *Sumter* for a more seaworthy vessel, but if that proved impossible—and he was unlikely to find a prize with the steam propulsion essential for a cruiser—he might be able to drydock the *Sumter* in a neutral port. There was a final argument in favor of taking the raider across the Atlantic. The *Sumter* was an instrument of indirect as well as direct damage to the Federal economy. Her mere appearance in European waters would affect insurance rates and might lead Gideon Welles to take additional vessels from blockade duty to search for her.

On November 25, almost immediately after turning into the Atlantic, the *Sumter* overtook a Yankee square-rigger, the *Montmorenci,* which, at 1,183 tons, would be the largest ship taken by the *Sumter*. Her master and part-owner, Joseph T. Brown, hoping that Semmes might spare his ship, offered Semmes a gift of wine and cigars. With his contempt for the obsequious, Semmes might have burned Brown's ship out of sheer contrariness, but his legal training would not permit it. Her cargo being neutral, Semmes released the *Montmorenci* under a ransom bond of $20,000, the first of twelve prizes that he would release on bond during the course of the war.[1] Captain Brown was not mollified, however. Like the masters of other ships captured by Semmes, he had unkind words for the Confederate commander once it was safe to speak them.

The next day, November 26, the *Sumter* encountered a small American schooner, the *Arcade,* carrying barrel staves to Guadeloupe. "The staves being well seasoned," wrote Semmes, "she made a beautiful bonfire, and lighted us over the seas some hours after dark."[2]

Although Semmes was now burning most of his prizes, he was sensitive to the public relations impact of the *Sumter*'s destructive cruise. While charges that he was a pirate were ridiculous—he had a commission from the president of the Confederacy—the picture of unarmed merchant ships being burned on the high seas was not flattering to him or his government. To counter charges that the *Sumter* was a pirate or a privateer, Semmes permitted no random plundering of prizes and was flexible in questions involving personal possessions. When he learned that a spyglass removed from the *Arcade* had been awarded to her master for saving lives in a marine disaster, he returned it to its owner.[3]

The *Sumter* spotted her next prize on December 3, some four hundred miles southeast of Bermuda. The raider was under sail, for Semmes was conserving his coal against the possibility that he might encounter a Federal warship. To raise steam would require two hours, so Semmes resorted to guile. Covering his hinged funnel with a sail, he hoisted French colors and plodded along on course. Not expecting an enemy so far out to sea and perhaps deceived by the *Sumter*'s appearance, the stranger showed the Stars and Stripes and made no effort at evasion. A gun brought her to, and the *Sumter* had her fifteenth prize. The ironically named *Vigilant* was in ballast, bound for the West Indies. Semmes transferred her complement to the *Sumter* and burned her at dusk.

The raider moved out of the Gulf Stream into the cold, gray Atlantic. Semmes had estimated that it might take as long as fifty days to cross the ocean under sail. He had begun this leg with water enough for sixty-one days, but the presence of twenty-one prisoners from his last three prizes reduced this margin. In addition, the *Sumter* was encountering heavy weather. A cold rain beat down, obliging the Confederates to house their prisoners belowdecks. "What with the active rolling and tumbling of the ship," Semmes complained, "we have but little comfort."[4] The raider groaned in her timbers, and the clank of the bilge pumps was constant.

On the morning of December 8 the lookout reported a ship five miles away. Fearing that she might be a Federal cruiser Semmes fired his boilers, raised the funnel, and hoisted U.S. colors. The stranger proved to be a whaler, the *Eben Dodge,* twelve days out of New Bedford en route to the Pacific whaling grounds. Despite rough seas, the *Sumter* took from her prize a welcome supply of boots, pea jackets, and other warm clothing; the Confederates also appropriated two new whaleboats. Then the *Eben Dodge*—the first of many whalers to fall victim to Semmes—was put to the torch. Wrote Semmes: "The flames burned red and lurid in the murky atmosphere, like some Jack-o'-lantern; now appearing . . . now disappearing, as the doomed ship rose upon the top, or descended into the abyss, of the waves."[5]

Semmes now had forty-three prisoners on his vessel, counting twenty-two from the *Eben Dodge,* so that prisoners numbered almost half as many as crew. Heretofore, prisoners from the *Montmorenci, Arcade,* and *Vigilant* had virtually free run of the ship. Now, to guard against any uprising, Semmes directed that half the prisoners, officers excepted, be handcuffed in shifts. The captives seemed to understand the reason for this precaution, but Semmes would be pilloried in the Northern press.

The *Sumter* struggled eastward, once again under sail alone. On December 11 the barometer plunged, prompting Semmes to remark on "as ugly looking a morning as one could well conceive; thick, dark, gloomy weather, with the wind blowing fresh from the east, and threatening a gale."[6] In fact, although it was late in the season, the *Sumter* was caught in a hurricane. She was buffeted by winds from various directions until, after midnight, came a pause of some two hours. During the calm the quartermaster informed Semmes that a portion of the starboard bow had given way and that the gun deck was awash. By the time the winds picked up again the ever-reliable Kell was attending to the damage. Years later Semmes still remembered this storm as one of the worst of his long career:

> The sea was mountainous, and would now and then strike the *Sumter* with such force as to make her tremble in every fiber of her frame. I had remained on deck during most of the first watch, looking anxiously on, to see what sort of weather we were going to make. The ship behaved nobly, but I had no confidence in her strength.[7]

The morning light was welcome, but it brought no relief from the elements. The wind howled, the *Sumter* lost her jibboom, and Semmes wondered whether his ship's small bilge pumps would be able to deal with the water on board. The masters and mates of the captured ships offered to assist in any way they could, prompting Semmes to call them "gallant men." But they were Yankees, and Semmes declined their services. At last, on December 13, the storm abated. But after a period of relative calm, Christmas Eve brought more heavy weather in what was the most severe Atlantic winter in recent memory.

Christmas! For Semmes, the holiday touched everything that he cherished—family, church, and home. "How great the contrast between these things and our present condition," he chronicled in his journal. "A leaky ship, filled with prisoners of war, striving to make a port through the almost constantly recurring gales of the North Atlantic!"[8] Semmes concluded that the weather and contrary winds would make it difficult to reach the Azores, so he set a course for Gibraltar, one that offered the option of stopping at Madeira in an emergency. He took inventory of his drinking water once again. Although he appeared to have enough for thirty-eight days at the standard ration of one gallon daily per man, he reduced this amount by one quart.

On December 28 the *Sumter* reached the great sea-lanes off West Africa. At long last the skies were blue, and winter storms were a thing of the past. Semmes stopped several ships, but all proved to be neutral, as did others hailed in the final days of 1861. But he had cause for satisfaction in having crossed the Atlantic in only thirty days in the most adverse weather imaginable. And he picked up one bit of welcome intelligence from an English bark: A second Confederate cruiser, the *Nashville,* was in action and had burned a Yankee clipper in the English Channel. Semmes knew nothing of the *Nashville* or of any other Confederate raiders, but it was heartening to know that the little *Sumter* was no longer alone in flying the Stars and Bars on the high seas.

By the time Semmes wrote his Civil War memoirs, the exploits of his two wartime commands had become part of Confederate mythology. For Semmes himself, time would have cast a kindly glow over almost all who had served on the *Sumter* or the *Alabama*. Although he would write frankly of his disciplinary problems, he treated them as shortcomings endemic to the nineteenth-century seaman, the generic sailor he called "Jack."

Semmes took good care of his crew. He had a surgeon on board— there would be two on the *Alabama*—and he no longer punished with the lash. But he was a strict disciplinarian, and a man not given to explanations. Communication on his ships was a one-way process. In the recollection of one officer,

> Captain Semmes was an austere and formal man, and with the exception of Dr. Galt, the surgeon, and Mr. Kell, his first lieutenant, he rarely held any intercourse with his officers except officially. He waxed the ends of his moustache (which the sailors called his "st'unsail booms") and he would pace the quarter-deck alone, twisting and retwisting those long ends.[9]

The disciplinary problems Semmes confronted were quite different from those faced by Confederate army officers. While his land-bound counterparts at home attempted to turn farmers into soldiers, Semmes had been able to recruit experienced seamen—the majority British— for the *Sumter*. And whereas any land battle afforded frightened recruits an opportunity to cut and run, sailors had no such option. Semmes never worried about the behavior of his men under fire.

At the same time, the *Sumter*'s crew of mercenaries had none of the devotion to the Southern cause that would make the Confederate soldier renowned for his steadfastness and resilience. The most drastic punishment Semmes administered aboard the *Sumter* grew out of a slur against the Confederacy by a member of his crew, George Whipple, a New Englander who had shipped on the *Sumter* in New Orleans to avoid being drafted into the Confederate army. Returning, drunk, from shore leave (possibly in Martinique), he had shouted curses at Semmes and the Confederate flag. Normally, drunkenness on liberty might cause a crewman to lose his grog ration for a couple of weeks. In the case of Whipple, however, Semmes ordered him put in irons and a straitjacket; later, he was tied up by his thumbs.[10]

Alcoholism was so prevalent among his crew that Semmes had a standing rule that no liquor was allowed on ship. This was no hardship for Semmes, who drank nothing stronger than sherry, and his officers served wine in the wardroom. The crew was provided with grog twice a day, as in the Royal Navy, but this was no substitute for an alcoholic orgy. Therefore, whenever a prize was taken, the *Sumter*'s boarding officer attempted to destroy any liquor supply before it could be smuggled aboard the raider. Semmes had no illusions about reforming "Jack," but he insisted on maintaining fighting efficiency between liberty ports.

Semmes knew that he could never relax discipline aboard ship. At about the time the hurricane was abating in mid-December, fire broke out belowdecks on the *Sumter* when a prisoner's pipe ignited his mattress. The blaze was quickly extinguished, but Semmes held it to be the responsibility of two sentries who had been guarding the prisoners; he suspended their grog for a week. Touching on the incident in his memoirs, Semmes commented, "I made it a rule on board the *Sumter* that punishment should follow the offense, with *promptitude* and *certainty* rather than severity."[11]

Nevertheless, the *Sumter* was not a happy ship in the final weeks of 1861. Most of the crew had been enticed on board the raider by the promise of prize money, but Semmes's practice of burning his victims, beginning with the *Joseph Park*, made it unlikely that there would be any prize money. The *Sumter*'s hands were not versed in international law—most, in fact, were illiterate—but they could sense that their ship was somehow "different." If the *Sumter* was a true man-of-war, why did she not send her captures to a British port? Could it be that her crewmen were nothing more than pirates, as the Yankee newspapers claimed? Morale that December was not improved by the presence of the forty-three prisoners, in weather conditions that required the crew to share their cramped quarters below.

One practice of Semmes's caused considerable comment on his ship. Although his rule was that nothing but ship's funds, provisions, and clothing were to be taken from the *Sumter*'s prizes, Semmes himself made interesting exceptions to this rule. He took from each prize its flag and its chronometer. In quiet times Semmes himself attended to winding the chronometers, for he had become interested in them as a young officer in Norfolk; they were part of the orderly, scientific universe with which he associated himself. Much later, they would become the basis for the only prize money his officers would ever receive.

The first days of the new year saw the *Sumter* moving north up the bulge of Africa, part of a stream of vessels entering or exiting the Mediterranean. One day the raider boarded sixteen vessels, not one of them American. Semmes had planned to linger for a few days off the Spanish port of Cádiz, north of Gibraltar, before putting in for repairs and had husbanded three days' coal for this phase of the cruise. Unfortunately, a final gale in the *Sumter*'s stormy crossing so battered his ship that her pumps were once again under strain. The leak in her propeller sleeve was worsening, and Semmes felt that he had no choice but to head directly for Cádiz.

Sumter entered port on the morning of January 4 and hoisted the signal for a pilot. The day was gray, but Semmes was pleased to return to a city that he had long regarded as one of Europe's most charming. "The city of Cadiz is a perfect picture as you approach it," he wrote, "with domes and towers and minarets and Moorish-looking houses of a beautiful white stone. The harbor was crowded with shipping . . . and a number of villages lay around the margin of the bay . . . picturesquely half hidden in the slopes of the surrounding mountains."[12]

Picturesque Cádiz, however, was not the best port for Semmes to have chosen. The more powerful European powers, Britain and France, could afford to grant belligerent rights to the Confederacy, because neither country feared the United States. Indeed, the Lincoln administration's policy was to avoid any foreign crisis until the war at home was won. Spain, in contrast, could not take the United States for granted. Her colonies in the Western Hemisphere, which included Cuba and Puerto Rico, were highly vulnerable, and however formidable the Confederate army was on land, the U.S. Navy was supreme in the Caribbean. The upshot was that Semmes received a cool reception in Cádiz. Until explicit permission was received from Madrid, he was not even permitted to offload his prisoners. Six days after dropping anchor, he was still awaiting authorization to dock his ship.

On January 12 the *Sumter* was at last authorized to make repairs at the Carraca naval yard, some eight miles east of the city. The first examination of the raider's hull was reassuring. Although a section of the false keel was gone, as were strips of her copper bottom, the hull was sound. After three days in drydock the raider emerged with a new propeller housing and new copper where required. But nothing was done for her boilers, and the yard managers, in Semmes's view, seemed very anxious to see him gone. There were other problems. Five of his crew deserted on January 13, and eight more after the *Sumter* returned to Cádiz. Semmes ordered that no boat leave the *Sumter* without an officer, and he warned that anyone else attempting to desert would be shot.[13]

Quite apart from these problems, Semmes was low on funds and was obliged to wire Confederate authorities in London for money with which to pay for his repairs. Before any money arrived, however, nervous Spanish functionaries had ordered the *Sumter* to leave. Semmes protested this edict and was granted a twenty-four-hour stay, but he chose not to press the matter: He had heard in Cádiz that six Federal ships, each more powerful than his own, were closing in. With coal enough to make it to Gibraltar, he put out to sea on January 17. As the *Sumter* departed, a boat was seen pulling in great haste toward the raider; one of the occupants was waving a great envelope. Semmes did not stop to receive it. Smarting from his treatment by Spanish authorities, he probably realized that Gibraltar should have been his goal in the first place. For once, his legalistic perspective had served him badly. Confident of his rights as a belligerent, he had not allowed for the reaction of a weak neutral, one fearful of antagonizing the United States. Henceforth, Semmes would rarely enter any but a British or French port.

The *Sumter* passed the Pillars of Hercules in the small hours of January 18 and was off Gibraltar at dawn. The early light disclosed several vessels to the east, and Semmes became convinced—viewing their "symmetry and beauty of outline," the "taper and grace" of their spars, and the whiteness of their cotton sails—that two of them were American. The *Sumter* used the last of her fuel in getting up steam. Perhaps Semmes suspected that his ship's days were numbered, because he attempted no deception. Showing Confederate colors, he brought the first vessel, the bark *Neapolitan*, to a halt. She was bound from Sicily to Boston with fifty tons of sulfur, and Semmes brushed aside her master's insistence that his cargo was British-owned. Sulfur was an essential ingredient in gunpowder; *Neapolitan*'s cargo was almost certainly destined for some Civil War battlefield. It was contraband, and Semmes spared his latest prize only long enough to board the second American vessel, *Investigator,* which proved to be carrying neutral cargo and was released on bond. The *Neapolitan* made a dramatic spectacle, however, "burned in the sight of Europe and Africa, with the turbaned Moor looking upon the conflagration on one hand, and the garrison of Gibraltar and the Spaniard on the other."[14] She was the first ship burned by the *Sumter* whose cargo was explicitly military, and Semmes took special pleasure in putting her to the torch.

Gibraltar! Semmes had not visited the fortress since his days as a midshipman; how much had changed since then! Dusk was falling as the *Sumter* edged slowly into the historic harbor. Flames from the burning *Neapolitan* cast a glow over the strait, and hundreds of spectators along the Spanish coast and "the Rock" watched as Semmes nudged his little ship toward the man-of-war anchorage. He could hardly have choreographed a more dramatic arrival.

The raider and her officers met with a warm reception from the British. Quite apart from their traditional sympathy for underdogs—which the British believed the Confederates to be—many Britons were still miffed at the Federal seizure of Confederate emissaries from the *Trent,* even though the Lincoln administration had released the Southerners with an apology. No quarantine was imposed on the *Sumter,* and it seemed that every British officer in Gibraltar came to call on her commander. One visitor found it hard to believe that the ship he was inspecting was the raider about which he had read so much:

> I could scarcely believe that so poor a vessel could have escaped so many dangers. She is a screw-steamer with three masts, a funnel strangely out of proportion to her size, and a tall, black hull, so high out of water that she gives you the idea of being insufficiently ballasted. . . . She is crank and leaky. Her engines are partially above the lower deck, and . . . are surrounded by a cylindrical casing of 6-inch wood covered with half-inch bars—very poor protection against an 8-inch shot.[15]

Semmes made a round of official calls at the base and received all the courtesies he could have desired. Sentries snapped to attention when he walked through the narrow lanes of the town. "All the nations of the earth seemed to have assembled upon the Rock," he later recalled. "As each nationality preserved its costume and its language, the quay, market-place, streets and shops presented a picture witnessed in few if any other towns of the globe."[16] Semmes marveled at Gibraltar's renowned colony of apes. He dined at Royal Navy messes, received guest privileges at clubs and reading rooms, and had the use of a British orderly. The *Sumter* herself was the scene of many festivities, and Semmes remarked on the ability of his officers to party through the night without apparent ill effects.

Time was running out on the raider, however, and part of the problem was money. Semmes's total cash on hand consisted of $137, including $86 taken from the *Neapolitan*. He wrote to the Confederate office in London that he was crippled by lack of funds at a time when, with a sound vessel, he could make his presence felt in the Mediterranean.[17] He also worried about the effects on British policy of the resolution of the *Trent* affair. He wrote Lieutenant James North in London that the British "were so badly frightened in their late quarrel with the Yankees, and have been so delighted to get out of it without a war, that I am afraid we shall never bring them up to the mark again. . . . Thank God we are independent of them all, and can whip the Yankees without their assistance."[18]

While in Gibraltar, Semmes became friendly with a colonel of the Coldstream Guards, Arthur Freemantle. On January 30, Freemantle took Semmes on a tour of the fortress, including the great tunnels that contributed much to its reputation for invincibility. Later, they rode on horseback to the peak of the Rock. While the two men studied the distant sail, a British signalman remarked that he had had a fine view of the action two weeks earlier when Semmes had burned the *Neapolitan*. "Are there many Yankee ships passing the Rock now?" Semmes asked. The signalman replied that there were very few.[19]

On the morning of February 8, the *Warrior*, pride of the Royal Navy, eased into the harbor. Launched in 1860, the new man-of-war, constructed of iron throughout and heavily armored as well, shared with France's *Gloire* the distinction of being the most formidable naval vessel of the day. Semmes, on visiting *Warrior*, was much impressed. He concluded that the era of wooden ships was coming to a close, writing in his journal that with a vessel like the *Warrior* he could destroy the entire fleet that was blockading the ports of the South.[20]

As skipper of the *Sumter*, Semmes had proved himself not only a skillful captain but also a diplomat capable of making the best possible case for the Confederacy in various ports of call. Now, in Gibraltar, he read the year-end report of the Federal secretary of the navy, which bristled with references to the "piratical" *Sumter*. The report hinted darkly at retaliation against powers to whom the raider's illegal "character" was well known. Semmes concluded that some response was called for, and he chose as his medium a letter to *The Times* of London:

> Mr. Welles . . . in imitation of the dirty and mendacious press of the Yankee States, calls me a privateer. He knows better than this. He knows that a privateer is a vessel that bears a letter of marque, and that I am cruising under no such letter. He knows that I have been regularly commissioned as a ship of war of the Confederate States. If he and his deluded associates insist upon calling the citizens of the Confederate states "rebels," under the idea that those states still form a part of the old Yankee concern, then he might characterize me as a rebel man-of-war. But if I am this, so were all the ships of the American colonies commissioned by the Virginian, George Washington.

Semmes then sought to rub salt in the wounds of his enemies:

> I feel honored to have been pursued by six frigates, and one of them caught Messrs. Mason and Slidell [on the *Trent*] instead of catching me. . . . But I am fleeing from these ships, says Mr. Welles. Soft, Mr. Welles. He would have me, I suppose, fall into the Yankee trap he has set for me, and rush to the encounter of his six frigates, each of which is twice the size of my weight of metal. He dares not send a ship of equal force to meet me, and if he did dare to . . . I venture to say that the officer would not dare to find me.[21]

Semmes's letter shows him to have been not merely a seagoing diplomat, but a propagandist of no mean skill. Nevertheless, he could not help wondering whether his ship would ever cruise again. He had hoped to install new boilers at Gibraltar, but his hosts, so obliging in most matters, had refused to permit the installation of machinery that would increase the raider's effectiveness. Meanwhile, the U.S. consul, Horatio Sprague, succeeded in denying Semmes access to privately owned coal in Gibraltar, warning that anyone who supplied the *Sumter* would be blackballed by U.S. ships. On top of these problems, the *Sumter* continued to be ravaged by desertion. Nineteen crewmen—including the infamous Whipple—vanished during the first half of February, prompting Semmes to comment, "The devil seems to get into my crew."[22]

On January 25 Semmes received a telegram from London, directing him not to make repairs and not to leave port; a letter would follow. On February 2 the promised letter arrived, advising Semmes that Commissioner William L. Yancey intended that he assume command of a new cruiser then under construction in Liverpool.[23] Although arrangements were far from settled, this is the first indication that people in high places wanted him to command the newest and most advanced of Confederate cruisers, the future *Alabama*.

Meanwhile, Semmes had at last received some money, a draft for $16,000. This was $4,000 less than he had requested, but better than nothing. Ever resourceful, he ordered his paymaster, Henry Myers, to Cádiz, to contract for coal there and to have it shipped by charter boat to Gibraltar. Myers was accompanied by Tom Tunsall, a former U.S. consul in Cádiz who had sided with the South. On February 18 the two Confederates boarded a French packet boat that plied the Mediterranean. Once again, Federal diplomats proved Semmes's nemesis. When the two Confederates left their ship at Tangier for a stroll on shore, the U.S. consul learned of their presence and used his influence with local Moroccan officials to have them arrested and locked up in his residence. The Confederates attempted to bribe their guards, and when this proved unsuccessful one of the two succeeded in prying open his irons and escaping as far as the garden before being recaptured. The consul then called on the U.S. Navy, which sent the cruiser *Ino* to take the two prisoners on board.[24]

Semmes did the best he could for his two agents, penning démarches to Moroccan authorities and attempting, unsuccessfully, to enlist the good offices of the British. Nothing worked. The captain of the *Ino*, Lieutenant Josiah Creesy, turned his two prisoners over to the skipper of a merchant vessel bound for Boston. There Myers and Tunsall, whose capture on neutral ground was clearly illegal, were nevertheless imprisoned in Fort Warren.[25]

Meanwhile, the *Sumter*'s position was becoming desperate. Not only was she still without coal and without prospect of repairs to her boilers, but the U.S. Navy was putting in an appearance. On February 12 the *Tuscarora* briefly entered the harbor before taking up station at the nearby Spanish port of Algeciras. Three weeks later the *Kearsarge*, a spanking-new steam sloop commanded by Charles W. Pickering, entered Gibraltar and for a time moored near the *Sumter*.

The stillness of the night was broken first by a chorus of "Dixie" from the *Sumter,* followed by a presumably more vigorous rendition of "The Star-Spangled Banner" from the fully manned *Kearsarge.* Rather than remain at Gibraltar and give the *Sumter* a twenty-four-hour lead should she depart, the *Kearsarge* moved into international waters, where she was soon joined by the *Ino.*

All this represented a bit of overkill, for the *Sumter* was not going anywhere. Although Semmes knew that he could obtain coal eventually, the presence of three Federal warships guaranteed that there would be no repetition of his daring escape from Martinique. On March 6 he wrote to James Mason, the Confederacy's envoy in London, recommending that the *Sumter* be laid up. Mason replied that Semmes should do nothing; for a disabled vessel, the *Sumter* was doing well in occupying the attention of so many enemy warships. Semmes again asked to be relieved, and this time he included a request from his officers that their ship be laid up. On April 7 Mason came through with the necessary authorization, and Semmes paid off those of the *Sumter*'s crew who remained.[26] There were not many. Of the ninety-two crewmen who had shipped aboard at New Orleans, only forty-six had resisted the temptations of port.

Like many a mariner before him, Semmes had become very attached to his ship. It had served both him and his cause well.

> She had run me safely through two vigilant blockades, had weathered many storms, and rolled me to sleep in many calms. Her cabin was my bedroom and my study, both in one, her quarter-deck was my promenade, and her masts, spars and sails my play-things. . . . She had fine qualities as a sea-boat, being as buoyant, active, and dry as a duck . . . and these are the qualities which a seaman most admires.[27]

On April 11 Semmes turned his ship over to Midshipman Richard Armstrong, commanding a skeleton crew of twelve. Semmes implies in his memoirs that he had no plans at this time beyond conferring with Confederate authorities in London and then making his way to Richmond. But he knew that a new cruiser was under construction somewhere in Britain.

Semmes's record with the *Sumter* had been remarkable: In a cruise of six months she had captured no fewer than eighteen vessels. Although seven of these had been released by Spanish authorities, and only seven destroyed, the raider's cruise had made a sufficient impression on Washington that, in December 1861, she was being pursued by a number of Federal vessels that otherwise would have been tightening the Union blockade of the South. Semmes estimated the total cost of operating the *Sumter* at $28,000, the value of one of her lesser prizes. John Kell said it best, writing after the war: "I have always felt that the little *Sumter* has never had full justice done her. . . . No ship of her size, her frailness, and her armament ever played such havoc on a powerful foe."[28]

The *Sumter,* along with a few Confederate privateers, had an indirect effect on the Federal merchant marine as well. In 1861 the premium for war risk insurance on American ships ranged between 1 and 3 percent of the insured value, but by the end of the year it was 4 percent.[29] Some shipowners saw the handwriting on the wall. During 1860 forty-one ships had been transferred from U.S. to British registry. During 1861 this figure rose more than 300 percent, to 126.[30]

Over time, the British wearied of having the *Sumter* on their doorstep. Prodded by London, Confederate authorities agreed to the raider's sale, and on December 9, 1862, she was sold at auction for $19,500 to a British trading company. The "sale" in fact proved a means of getting the *Sumter* safely away from Gibraltar, for her purchaser was acting on behalf of Confederate representatives.

Renamed, appropriately, *Gibraltar,* the erstwhile raider went to Liverpool, where she was outfitted as a blockade runner. In July 1863 she successfully ran the blockade into Wilmington, North Carolina, but she lacked the requisite speed for a blockade runner and appears to have made only one voyage. In June 1866 she was sold once again, this time at Liverpool. Shortly thereafter she foundered in a storm in the North Sea. A tired ship had encountered one gale too many.

CHAPTER 9

The Mysterious 290

On April 14, 1861, Semmes, Kell, and several other of the *Sumter*'s officers took passage on a British mail steamer for Southampton. Semmes doubtless hoped that his record with the *Sumter* would gain him command of the new cruiser under construction somewhere in Britain.

James Bulloch was the principal Confederate agent in charge of purchasing and equipping ships for the Confederacy. A Georgia native, Bulloch had joined the U.S. Navy as a midshipman in 1839, thirteen years after Semmes. Like Semmes, he had found the peacetime navy a lackluster existence. He resigned after fourteen years and took a position with a New York shipping line. Prematurely bald and with sideburns that made him appear older than his thirty-eight years, Bulloch was intelligent, level-headed, and a firm believer in the Southern cause.

In the spring of 1861 Bulloch had been skipper of the *Bienville,* a steamer plying between New York and several Southern ports. He was in New Orleans when the Civil War erupted, and he immediately offered his services to the Confederate government. But he refused to turn over his ship to Confederate authorities, insisting that he was honor-bound to return the *Bienville* to her owners in New York.

Once he had fulfilled this obligation, Bulloch made his way back to the Confederacy.*

In May, Secretary of the Navy Mallory informed Bulloch that he was being sent to Europe as a purchasing agent for the department. Mallory authorized the purchase of six steam-powered vessels for the navy, and the Confederate Congress appropriated $1 million for this purpose.[1]

Bulloch arrived in England in early June and went about his work in the greatest secrecy. He first visited the major British ports in search of ships that might be converted to military use. When his inquiries proved fruitless, he considered the possibility of constructing vessels from scratch. Here, the legal problems were formidable. Bulloch engaged a prominent solicitor to advise him regarding Britain's Foreign Enlistment Act, one provision of which prohibited the outfitting of warships for belligerent powers. The solicitor concluded that the law permitted construction of a warship in Britain so long as the vessel did not take on its military equipment in British waters. Having surmounted this major obstacle, Bulloch contracted with the William C. Miller Company of Liverpool for the *Oreto,* the vessel destined to become the first Confederate cruiser contracted for abroad.[2]

The procedures that Bulloch employed in this first, critical purchase he would follow later in the case of the *Alabama.* First, he went to great pains to disguise the *Oreto*'s Confederate connection, planting rumors that his ship was destined for an Italian buyer. Then he arranged for a ship whose master he trusted—the *Bahama,* which would bring Semmes from Nassau to Britain—to convey the *Oreto*'s ordnance to a rendezvous in the Bahamas. By arming the cruiser in international waters, he would avoid contravening the Foreign Enlistment Act. U.S. consular officers were not fooled by Bulloch's operation, but British officialdom was slow to react. On March 24, 1862, *Oreto* headed for sea, disguising her departure for the Bahamas

---

*Semmes may have been thinking of the *Bienville* incident when he wrote after the war, "It may be [asked] whether . . . Southern naval officers, in command, would not have been justified in bringing their ships with them, which would have been easy for them to do. But, on the other hand, they had been personally entrusted with their commands by the Federal Government, and it would have been treason to a military principle, if not to those great principles which guide revolutions, to deliver those commands to a different government. Perhaps they decided correctly—at all events, a military or naval man cannot go very far astray who abides by the point of honor." Semmes, *Memoirs of Service Afloat,* 92.

with the trappings of a trial run.[3] After many tribulations she would gain fame as the C.S.S. *Florida*.

Bulloch had scarcely concluded his negotiations for the *Oreto/Florida* when he met with representatives of another Liverpool yard, John Laird Sons, about a second cruiser. On August 1 (while the *Sumter*, across the Atlantic, was coaling at Trinidad) Bulloch signed a contract for the ship that would become the most successful and most famous of all Confederate vessels, the *Alabama*.

Bulloch had ideas for her design, and he made sure that they were followed. Although many vessels were then being constructed with iron hulls, Bulloch decreed that the new cruiser was to be of oak, for in isolated parts of the world it was easier to repair a wooden ship than an iron one. He specified reinforced decks to accommodate ordnance and munitions. To ensure that the new cruiser would perform well under canvas, he required that her twin-blade screw be retractable. To increase her endurance, he specified that she have a condenser to distill drinking water from the sea. Bulloch assumed that he himself would command the new ship—he had made sea duty a condition of his accepting the mission to England—and he insisted that only the finest materials go into his brainchild.

The number "290" appeared above the slip in which Bulloch's vessel was under construction. The number indicated only that she was the 290th order to be filled by the Laird yards, but the vessel's relative anonymity fed the alehouse rumor mill. Why did this ship not have a name, as other vessels under construction did? Among those who believed that something was amiss with the *290* was Thomas Dudley, the able U.S. consul in Liverpool. Dudley studied newspaper notices and quizzed seamen in the taverns. He hired spies, whom he called detectives, and attempted to gather enough evidence that the *290* was destined for the Confederacy to pursuade Crown authorities to act.[4]

Bulloch's first purchase, the *Florida,* had already reached Nassau and was preparing to take on her guns when Semmes and the other officers from the *Sumter* arrived in London. There, Semmes and Kell shared a parlor and two bedrooms in a rooming house on Euston Square. The captain of the *Sumter* was already something of a celebrity, and James Mason undertook to show him the sights in Britain. Some in Confederate service found Mason pompous and of limited value as an envoy. Not Semmes, who would write: "In his company I saw much of the society of the English capital, and soon became satisfied that Mr. Davis could not have entrusted the affairs of the Confederacy to better hands."[5]

Semmes also met Bulloch, with whom he discussed matters relating to the *290*. Bulloch still hoped to command this ship, but given Semmes's seniority and his record with the *Sumter,* the younger man offered to place himself under Semmes's instructions. Semmes, in a generous moment, declined to override the instructions from Mallory that designated Bulloch to command the new cruiser. He wrote in his memoirs: "It being evident that there was nothing available for me, I determined to lose no time in returning to the Confederacy."[6]

In fact, however, Semmes rather enjoyed his fame in London, and he took his time booking passage home. For much of May he was the guest of the Reverend Francis Tremlett, whose parsonage near Hampstead was becoming a rendezvous for Confederate naval officers in London. In late May, however, Semmes, accompanied by Kell and Galt, left London for Nassau aboard a British vessel, the *Melita*. They arrived there on June 13, to find the port bustling with commerce growing out of blockade running. The harbor was thronged with ships, the warehouses filled with munitions and luxury goods.

Semmes checked into the Royal Victoria Hotel, which housed a large contingent of Confederate naval officers. One of them was John Maffitt, who had been designated to command the *Oreto/Florida*. The British had begun an investigation into her status, and Maffitt was obliged to keep his distance from his command pending completion of the admiralty inquiry. For Semmes, however, there was good news. An officer newly arrived from Richmond told him that he had been promoted to the rank of captain for his accomplishments with the *Sumter*. Still more important, an order from Mallory directed him to return to London immediately and assume command of the *290*.

Semmes could hardly believe his good fortune. His reply to Mallory, dated June 15, 1862, shows a busy mind at work:

> In obedience to your order, assigning me to the command of [the *Alabama*], I will return by the first conveyance to England. . . . I will take with me Lieutenant Kell, Surgeon Galt, and First Lieutenant of Marines Howell. . . .
>
> It will, doubtless, be a matter of some delicacy and tact to get the *Alabama* safely out of British waters, without suspicion, as Mr. Adams, the Northern envoy, and his numerous satellites in the shape of consuls and paid agents, are exceedingly vigilant in their espionage.

We cannot, of course, think of arming her in a British port; this must be done at some concerted rendezvous, to which her battery and a large portion of her crew must be sent, in a neutral merchant vessel. The *Alabama* will be a fine ship, quite equal to encounter any of the enemy's steam sloops of the class of the *Iroquois, Tuscarora* and *Dacotah,* and I shall feel much more independent in her, upon the high seas, than I did in the little *Sumter.*[7]

Several weeks passed before Semmes was able to book passage back to Britain. He chafed at the delay, but the layover was a pleasant one. From his hotel window he watched the comings and goings of blockade runners supplying the embattled Confederacy. They brought news of the war, some of it good, some disturbing. The fall of Forts Henry and Donelson on the Tennessee and Cumberland rivers was ominous, as was the bloody Confederate defeat at Shiloh. But in the crucial eastern theater, General George B. McClellan's campaign against Richmond had been repulsed.

Condemned to delay, Semmes and his officers enjoyed the hotel fare at the Victoria and the companionship of the wives of officers on the blockade runners. There were evenings of whist and billiards. For two weeks, Raphael Semmes and John Maffitt, the two officers destined to be the most famous raiders of the war, were under the same roof. In recalling this interlude Semmes sounds almost envious of his dashing young colleague. "Maffitt," he wrote, "was the life of our household. He knew everybody, and everybody knew him. . . . Being a jaunty, handsome fellow, he was a great favorite with the ladies."[8]

On July 13, Semmes and his fellow officers at last set out for England on the *Bahama*. Arriving at Liverpool on August 8, Semmes immediately went to see Bulloch, who informed him that his ship had already put to sea. The tale he told was one of intrigue triumphant.

Aware that the escape of the *Florida* had alerted both the Yankees and the British to Confederate activities in Britain, Bulloch had taken pains to ensure that nothing interfered with the delivery of the new cruiser. He and others identified with the Confederacy stayed far away from the *290*. He hired detectives to keep an eye on Dudley and other U.S. representatives. Most important, he recruited a spy at 10 Downing Street, the prime minister's office, to provide warning of any move to impound his ship.

Bulloch had traveled to Richmond in February, and at that time there was no suggestion that anyone other than he would command the new cruiser. He was back in England when the *290,* now bearing the cover name *Enrica,* was launched on May 15. While workmen at the Laird yard installed her engines and boilers, Bulloch arranged for her departure. He chose officers from among those Confederates then in England, loaded supplies, and saw to the first coaling. He made no move to recruit a crew, lest he tip his hand to British authorities, but he did charter a 350-ton bark, the *Agrippina,* to transport the cruiser's guns and munitions to an agreed rendezvous. Then, in mid-July, Bulloch received the order he may have dreaded: He was to turn over his command to Semmes, who was even then en route back to England from Nassau.[9]

Bulloch swallowed his disappointment and readied the *Enrica* for sea. He engaged an Englishman, Matthew J. Butcher, as the cruiser's interim master, to recruit a crew, ostensibly for a voyage to the West Indies. For all Bulloch's precautions, U.S. representatives were hot on his trail. On July 21, 23, and 25, minister Charles Francis Adams confronted the Palmerston government with new affidavits regarding the *Enrica*'s military character. On Saturday, July 26, Bulloch received word, probably from his Downing Street spy, that it would not be safe for his ship to be in Liverpool another forty-eight hours.[10]

The Confederate agent went immediately to the Laird yards and told the partners that he required a day-long trial of his ship. He ordered Captain Butcher to get a crew on board and be ready to weigh anchor with the morning tide on Monday. This second trial was, to the casual observer, a festive occasion. The ship was dressed in flags, and guests of both sexes were invited for what appeared to be an outing. Only Butcher was told that the ship would not be returning that afternoon. Accompanied by a tender, the *Enrica* moved slowly down the Mersey River. There were music and dancing on board, as well as a sumptuous luncheon. After several runs on the river the guests were told that, because *Enrica* would be staying out for the night, they would be returned on the tender. The guests transferred to the tug *Hercules,* and the *Enrica* continued downstream.[11]

Bulloch had directed Butcher to take the *Enrica* to Moelfra Bay on the coast of Wales and to wait for him there. He himself returned to Liverpool to gather a few final items of equipment for the *Enrica* and to check on her crew. An assistant had been recruiting sailors, ostensibly for a voyage to Havana, and the early hours of July 30 found some thirty-five to forty seamen milling about the dock, "and nearly as many women, of that class who generally affect a tender solicitude for Jack when he is out-ward bound, and likely to be provided with an advance-note."[12]

Bulloch tried to lure the men on board without the doxies, but the latter would have none of it. As a result, it was a crowded tug that arrived at the *Enrica*'s anchorage that afternoon. Once aboard the ship, all were fêted with food and grog. Butcher told them that the *Enrica* would not be returning to Liverpool, but he offered generous terms to those men willing to contract for a voyage to Havana, perhaps with intermediate stops. His offer of a month's pay in advance was the clincher. All but three of the sailors signed up, turning over the advances to their female companions, who cheerfully returned to town on the tugboat. Bulloch could not afford to dally, for he had heard that the Federal sloop *Tuscarora* was in the vicinity. With neither guns nor a trained crew, *Enrica* would be easy prey.

Bulloch returned to Liverpool, confident that Butcher would take the ship safely to the agreed rendezvous at Terceira, in the Azores. It became clear on his return that the *Enrica*'s hasty departure had been well advised. On Friday, July 25, the Palmerston government had in fact decided to detain the ship. In accordance with standard procedure, the necessary papers were sent to the queen's advocate, Sir John Harding, for his approval. But Harding's wife failed to tell the authorities that her husband had suffered a nervous breakdown and was in no condition to review the *Enrica* dossier. The papers were eventually returned to Downing Street, but not before the ship had sailed. By the time the detention order had reached customs officials in Liverpool, the *Enrica* was twenty-four hours into the Atlantic.[13]

This was the story that Semmes heard from Bulloch on his arrival in Liverpool on August 8. He could expect to command a fine ship, but he would have to meet her in the Azores. In addition to the officers who had returned with him from Nassau, he recruited Lieutenant Arthur Sinclair, a veteran of the *Sumter,* and recalled Midshipman Richard F. Armstrong from Gibraltar, where he had been in charge of the laid-up raider. Semmes visited the Confederacy's British bankers, the firm of Fraser, Trenholm & Company, to make last-minute financial arrangements. Then, after five days in Liverpool, Semmes, Bulloch, and the junior officers boarded the *Bahama,* the same ship that had brought Semmes from Nassau and that Bulloch, with his usual foresight, had chartered to take them to the Azores. Bulloch's intense interest in the ship he had created led him to accompany Semmes to Terceira for her christening.

After a week's voyage from Liverpool, the *Bahama* reached the Azores on August 20. As the morning mist lifted, Semmes could make out Porto Praya, with its white houses dotting the mountainside. Soon he could see the spars of the *Enrica,* and, to his considerable relief, no sign of any enemy warship, for the task of arming the *Enrica* would require several days. While the *Bahama* dropped anchor, Semmes examined the cruiser that would be his home for the next two years. His first impression was one that never left him: "She was, indeed, a beautiful thing to look upon."[14]

Like the *Sumter*, the *Enrica* was a bark, which is to say that her foremast and mainmast were square-rigged, while the aft (mizzen) mast was fore-and-aft rigged. In addition, she had steam propulsion, with a retractable funnel. There, however, the resemblance between the vessels ended. The new cruiser, at 1,040 tons, had more than twice the displacement of the little *Sumter*. Semmes's new command was 220 feet in length, 32 feet in beam, and drew 15 feet of water fully loaded. Her two engines were rated at 300 horsepower each, but on a trial run they had generated considerably more. As Bulloch had specified, the twin-bladed screw could be retracted into a well—the operation took about fifteen minutes—when steam was not required. The cruiser carried a year's supply of spare parts and a double suit of sails. Her bunkers held 350 tons of coal, enough for about eighteen days' steaming. The condensing apparatus in which Bulloch had taken such pride was capable of providing a gallon of water a day for each of the *Alabama*'s complement of about 120. Her cost had been £47,500, or approximately $237,000 in the dollars of that time.[15]

As for armament, the cruiser's most potent weapons were a 110-pounder Blakely rifle in the forward pivot and a smoothbore sixty-eight-pounder astern that could fire either solid shot or shell. In addition, the cruiser mounted broadside six of the standard thirty-two-pounders of the day.

The *Alabama* was a transitional craft in every sense of the word. Comparatively few warships would be designed, as she was, to accommodate both sail and steam propulsion; although sailing vessels would be employed in commerce well into the twentieth century, the requirement that naval vessels be both reliable and maneuverable would mandate the transition from sail to steam. In terms of armament the *Alabama*'s thirty-two-pounders were a throwback to Nelson's day, but her two pivot guns were ancestors of the turrets on twentieth-century dreadnoughts.

Semmes fell in love with the ship that was to be "not only my home, but my bride":

> Her model was of the most perfect symmetry, and she sat upon the water with the lightness and grace of a swan. She was barkentine rigged, with long lower masts, which enabled

her to carry large fore-and-aft sails. . . . Her sticks were of the best yellow pine, that would bend in a gale like a willow wand, without breaking, and her rigging was of the best of Swedish iron wire. The [construction] of the vessel was light compared with vessels of her class in the Federal Navy, but this was scarcely a disadvantage, as she was designed as a scourge of the enemy's commerce, rather than for battle.[16]

Only a trained observer could have seen any beauty in the ship that day. Her overworked crew was busily transferring stores from the *Agrippina* and would soon be moving guns, munitions, and other gear from the *Bahama*. Her decks were cluttered with gun carriages, cordage, barrels of beef and pork, and various other supplies. The *Enrica* had made the voyage to Terceira with a crew of about sixty, and now, begrimed with coal dust, they attempted amid much profanity to bring about some degree of order. The weather proved uncooperative. A fresh wind sprang up from the east that afternoon, raising enough of a sea that Semmes ordered all three ships to proceed to the lee side of the island. There work resumed.

The transfer of supplies to the cruiser took three days. Semmes took on board the flags and seventeen chronometers that he had taken from prizes while commanding the *Sumter*. On the morning of August 22 the last gun was mounted, the powder and shell were stowed, and the *Agrippina* was sent on her way. The remainder of the day was occupied in coaling from the *Bahama*, but at 10:00 P.M. the hammocks were piped down and the "main-brace was spliced"—grog was served the weary crew.[17]

On the morning of August 24, the *Enrica* and the *Bahama* steamed slowly out of Terceira to just beyond the three-mile limit. Semmes faced a formidable challenge in recruiting additional hands, but, ever the sea lawyer, he would do his recruiting in international waters. By now, no one on either vessel had any illusion as to *Enrica*'s role. Similarly, every sailor knew that Semmes could hardly go to sea with a ship as undermanned as the cruiser now was. Those "Liverpool rats" who were considering signing articles aboard the man-of-war were prepared to drive a hard bargain.

The cruiser had been scrubbed clean, and seamen from the *Bahama* and *Agrippina* were invited aboard, for Semmes had prepared a ceremony for that sunlit Sunday morning. The officers were in full uniform—Confederate gray rather than the traditional blue, which occasioned some snickering among the sailors. The boatswain's whistle summoned all hands to the quarterdeck, where an officer ordered heads bared. Semmes, erect and resplendent in his dress gray with gold braid, mounted a gun carriage. He read first his commission as a captain in the Confederate navy, then the order from Secretary Mallory directing him to take command of the newly christened C.S.S. *Alabama*. As he finished, he signaled to a gunner who fired a salute. At the same time, the British ensign ran down the halyards and the Confederate flag—the Stars and Bars—floated in the breeze. A hastily assembled band played "Dixie," amid loud huzzahs from the assembled sailors, most of whom had never set foot in the American South.[18]

It was a scene worthy of Hollywood, but it only set the stage for what was to follow. Semmes again spoke from the gun carriage, first telling the sailors that they were released from their contracts and free to return to Liverpool if they chose to do so. He followed this with his version of the war in America—how the Southern states had legally dissolved their ties to the Union, only to be faced with invasion by a cruel and powerful foe. He moved on to his plans for the *Alabama*. There would be hardships: cruises in many climates, boarding of ships in foul weather, and always the risk of a clash with the U.S. Navy. And although the *Alabama* was a commerce destroyer, she was not a privateer: Strict discipline would be maintained at all times.

On a more positive note, Semmes promised that there would be good food on his ship and grog twice a day. He would pay double the Royal Navy wage scale, in gold. Finally, if all went well there would be prize money—perhaps a great deal of prize money![19] A skillful salesman, Semmes appealed both to his listeners' self-interest and to their sense of adventure:

> Now, my lads, there is the ship; she is as fine a vessel as ever floated. There is a chance which seldom offers itself to a British seaman—that is, to make a little money. I am not going to put you alongside a frigate at first, but after I have got you drilled a little, I will give you a nice little fight. There are only six ships that I am afraid of in the U.S. Navy. We are going to burn, sink and destroy the commerce of the United States. Your prize-money will be divided proportionately, according to each man's rank, something similar to the English Navy. . . . There is Mr. Kell on the deck, and all who are desirous of going with me, let them go aft, and give Mr. Kell their names.[20]

Semmes stood down from the gun carriage, and a squeal from the boatswain's pipe dissolved the assembly. The men scattered about the ship in small groups, comparing notes on Semmes's speech and the *Alabama*'s prospects. Gradually, small knots of men began forming about Kell, captain's clerk Breedlove Smith, and paymaster Clarence Yonge. Some executed half-pay tickets, providing for half of their wages to go to wives and sweethearts. All who volunteered signed articles of war, subjecting themselves to disciplinary rules comparable to those of the Royal Navy. Semmes wrote:

> The *democratic* part of the proceedings closed as soon as the articles were signed. The "public meeting" just described was the first and last ever held on board the *Alabama*. . . . When I wanted a man to do anything after this, I did not talk to him about "nationalities" or "liberties" or "double wages," but I gave him a rather sharp order, and if the order was not obeyed in "double-quick," the delinquent found himself in limbo. Democracies may do very well for the land, but monarchies, and pretty absolute monarchies at that, are the only successful governments for the sea.[21]

Whatever his recruiting technique, Semmes now had a crew. Eighty seamen from the *Agrippina* and the *Bahama* signed aboard the raider, leaving her somewhat understrength but adequately manned.

Late that night, James Bulloch said his farewells and returned to the *Bahama* for the anticlimactic voyage back to Liverpool. Semmes in turn set a course to the northeast and directed chief engineer Miles Freeman to let his fires go down. The wind freshened appreciably. Semmes left the quarterdeck for the ladder leading down to his cabin—the cabin that would be his home for nearly two years. For the first of many times he passed the great double steering wheel just forward of the mizzenmast. In it was carved the motto "Aide-toi et Dieu t'aidera"—the French-language version of "Help yourself and God will help you." Semmes had had no part in choosing the motto, but it coincided with his sentiments exactly.

"I now turned into an unquiet cot," Semmes wrote, "perfectly exhausted after the labors of the day, and slept as comfortably as the rolling of the ship, and a strong smell of bilge-water would permit."[22]

CHAPTER 10

The Pirate Semmes

The *Alabama*'s first day without her consorts was cloudy, with a fresh wind and rough seas. Areas belowdecks were a shambles, for the heavy weather made the stowing of gear difficult and even dangerous. Not until the *Alabama*'s third day at sea was the last shot box stowed below, the iron rings for the pivot guns laid on the deck, and Semmes's books unpacked in his cabin. The captain was seasick—always an embarrassment—and feeling the stress; he wrote of trying to get some sleep "so as to quiet my worn nerves."[1]

After the storm abated, he kept his ship under easy sail for several days, away from the main sea-lanes. The *Alabama* proved to be a fine sailer under canvas. She had been constructed largely of green timber, however, and considerable caulking was required to make her tight.

Once his ship had achieved some degree of order and the crew had been exercised at the guns, Semmes set a course for his first hunting ground. Bulloch's choice of the Azores as the *Alabama*'s rendezvous had placed the raider in the heart of a major whaling ground at the peak of the season. Cruising near the thirty-ninth parallel on September 5, Semmes chased a brig that managed to outsail the *Alabama* but led the raider to her first prey. The 454-ton *Ocmulgee* was the easiest of captures, for she lay alongside her latest kill, sails furled, listing from the weight of a great sperm whale. The *Alabama* had been flying the U.S. flag, and Semmes would long remember the look of astonishment on the face of master Abraham Osborn as the *Alabama* hoisted Confederate colors before making the capture. Semmes sent his second lieutenant, Richard Armstrong, to the whaler to fetch the master and his papers. Once he regained his composure, Osborn told Semmes that when he saw the *Alabama* flying U.S. colors he assumed that the Federal government had sent a ship to look after the American whaling fleet.[2]

It was dark by the time the *Alabama* had taken aboard *Ocmulgee*'s thirty-seven-man crew and relieved the prize of beef, pork, and other stores. Semmes decided not to burn his prize that night, lest the blaze frighten away the other whalers he assumed to be in the vicinity. Her timbers permeated with whale oil, *Ocmulgee* made a splendid blaze the following morning.

Sunday, September 7, saw the first of many "musters"—inspections—aboard the *Alabama*. Semmes was pleased at the appearance of his crew. A week before they had looked like a group of waterfront vagrants; now, in white shirts and blue duck trousers, they were beginning to look like the crew of a warship. A muster centered on the reading of the articles of war, which were a fearful recitation of the crimes that might be committed aboard ship and the punishments that must surely follow. Semmes recalled cheerfully, "The penalty of death frequently occurred in them, and they placed the power of executing this penalty in the hands of the captain and a court-martial."[3]

That same day, Semmes paroled the officers and crew of the *Ocmulgee* and allowed them to stock their boats with provisions from the whaler. The *Alabama* was within a few miles of Flores, the westernmost island of the Azores, and the sea was calm. Semmes watched benignly as his late prisoners rowed their heavily laden boats to their temporary refuge.

The prisoners had scarcely shoved off when the *Alabama*'s lookout spotted sail. The stranger—a schooner—was wary of the *Alabama*, for she raced under full sail for the safety of the three-mile marine league off Flores. Semmes, flying British colors, succeeded in cutting off his prey and fired a blank cannon as a signal to halt. The schooner sped on, and this time Semmes put a solid shot between her masts, causing her to heave to. She turned out to be American: the *Starlight* of Boston, with a crew of seven.

Semmes had heard in London of the misadventures of Henry Myers, the *Sumter*'s popular paymaster, who had been abducted in

Morocco and kept in irons before being imprisoned in Fort Warren. In retaliation, Semmes now had the men of the *Starlight* placed in irons. In his words,

> I pursued this practice, painful as it was, for the next seven or eight captures, putting the masters and mates of the ships, as well as the crews, in irons. The masters would frequently remonstrate with me, claiming that it was an indignity put upon them; and so it was, but I replied to them that their country had put a similar indignity upon an officer and a gentleman who had worn the uniform of the navies of both our countries.[4]

The next day, September 8, Semmes landed the crew of *Starlight* on the island of Flores. Their period in irons had been brief.

That afternoon the *Alabama* was pursuing a ship that turned out to be Portuguese when she came upon a Boston whaler, the *Ocean Rover*, carrying eleven hundred barrels of oil. Semmes again delayed burning his prize, instead allowing *Ocean Rover*'s crew to make for the island in a night procession of whaleboats. Both *Starlight* and *Ocean Rover* were close by the next morning when the lookout spotted sail. Again there was a chase, and again the *Alabama*, without using her engines, overtook her prey. Lieutenant Armstrong boarded the prize, which turned out to be the 398-ton whaler *Alert*, sixteen days out of New London. Laden with supplies, *Alert* was an especially valuable prize.*

While the *Alabama*'s boarding party relieved this latest victim of pork, bread, and a welcome supply of Virginia tobacco, Semmes fired *Starlight* and *Ocean Rover*. A few hours later, *Alert* added a third plume of smoke to the fall afternoon. Unopposed and in perfect weather, Semmes was decimating an important sector of the New England economy, its whaling fleet. The availability of the Azores as a place to deposit his prisoners made it unnecessary for him to encumber the *Alabama*. The presence of a single Federal warship in the Azores would have sharply restricted Semmes's freedom of action, but, alas for the whalers, there was no such warship.

---

*She also had a history. *Alert* was the ship on which Richard Henry Dana Jr. had served on a voyage from San Diego to Boston in 1836. She became one of two ships on which Dana based his famous narrative, *Two Years Before the Mast*. See Charles G. Summersell, ed., *The Journal of George Townley Fullam* (University of Alabama Press, 1973), 20.

Semmes had barely fired *Alert* when the cry of "Sail ho!" sent the raider in pursuit of its fifth prize, the whaling schooner *Weathergauge*. Two days later, the *Alabama* seized and burned one of her smallest prizes, the 119-ton brig *Altamaha*. That evening, Semmes was half asleep in his cabin when he was roused by a report that the *Alabama* had just passed a large ship sailing on the opposite course.

> I sprang out of bed at once, and throwing on a few clothes, was on deck almost as soon as the quartermaster. I immediately wore ship [reversed course], and gave chase. . . . By this time the [ship] was from two-and-a-half to three miles distant, but was quite visible to the naked eye in the bright moonlight.[5]

The *Alabama* exhibited her fine sailing qualities in catching her prey, the 349-ton whaler *Benjamin Tucker*, eight months out of New Bedford. Semmes fired her that morning, September 14, after enlisting one of her crew—the first of many recruits from the *Alabama*'s victims.[6]

By now Semmes's boarding officers were becoming quite adept at firing ships, several of them having served their apprenticeship aboard the *Sumter*. Arthur Sinclair, who wrote a memoir after the war, described the approved technique:

> First, you cut up with your broadaxe the cabin and forecastle bunks, generally of white pine lumber. You will find, doubtless, the mattresses stuffed with straw, and in the cabin pantry part at least of a keg of butter and lard. Make a foundation of the splinters and straw, pour on top the lard and butter. One pile in cabin, the other in forecastle. Get your men in the boats, all but the incendiaries, and at the given word—"Fire!" shove off, and take it as truth that before you have reached your own [vessel], the blaze is licking at the topsails of the doomed ship.[7]

The next day was uneventful, but on September 16 the raider captured the whaling schooner *Courser*, out of Provincetown, Massachusetts. Semmes was impressed with the ship's master, Silas Young, whom he described as "a gallant young fellow, and a fine specimen of a seaman." Semmes was tempted to spare his ship, but did not.[8]

By then the *Alabama* was carrying about seventy prisoners from four prizes, and once again Semmes took advantage of his proximity to Flores. He paroled all the crews, allowing them to load their effects into whaleboats from the four vessels. Because it might be some time before they could get passage home, Semmes even allowed the sailors to stock the boats with supplies. Evening saw a convoy of eight heavily laden boats pulling for Flores in a manner that reminded some of a regatta.[9]

Semmes had once previously exercised his crew at the *Alabama*'s guns; now, after sending *Courser*'s crew off to Flores, he used the schooner for target practice, firing three rounds from each of the *Alabama*'s guns. The results were unimpressive, but Semmes put the best face on the drill, writing in his journal that the results were acceptable for green hands. In any case, it was necessary to conserve ammunition, for powder and shell were contraband and would be difficult to replace.[10]

On Wednesday, September 17, the *Alabama* took her ninth prize, the 346-ton bark *Virginia,* after a three-and-a-half-hour chase. Her master, Shadrach R. Tilton, believed his vessel to be fast, but conceded that she had stood no chance against the *Alabama*. Semmes burned her late in the afternoon, and the glow was visible after nightfall. A portion of the following day was wasted in chasing what proved to be a French brig, but in the afternoon the raider stopped an American whaling bark, *Elisha Dunbar*. The wind had been increasing all day, and Semmes was pleased to see that his ship, in overtaking the *Elisha Dunbar* under sail, performed well in heavy seas. But by the time the prize had heaved to, the waves were so high that Semmes was concerned for the safety of his boarding party. He instructed them to bring nothing from the prize except her crew, her chronometer, and her flag, and he watched anxiously until the transfer was complete.

The master of *Elisha Dunbar,* David R. Gifford, later testified about what had happened under the *Alabama*'s guns. After an armed boarding party had informed him that his ship was a prize, he was ordered on board the *Alabama* with his papers, and his crew ordered to follow with a bag of clothing each. Semmes told Gifford that his ship was to be burned, but when Gifford protested that he had no effects except the clothes he was wearing, he was allowed to return to his ship for a small trunk. "It was blowing very hard at the time," Gifford recalled. "We were all put in irons, and received the same treatment that Captain Tilton's officers and crew did, who had been taken before."[11]

Sinclair, for one, thought that Gifford had given up far too easily; in his judgment, the seas were too heavy for the *Alabama* to have employed her battery had her intended victim sailed on. *Elisha Dunbar* was loaded with whale oil, and the conflagration when she was fired was one that Semmes remembered years later:

> This burning ship was a beautiful spectacle, the scene being wild and picturesque beyond description. . . . The thunder began to roll and crash, and the lightning to leap from cloud to cloud in a thousand eccentric lines. The sea was in a tumult of rage; the winds howled, and floods of rain descended. Amid this turmoil of the elements, the *Dunbar,* all in flames and with disordered gear and unfurled canvas, lay rolling and tossing upon the sea. Now an ignited sail would fly away from a yard, and scud off before the gale; and now the yard itself, released from the control of its braces, would swing about wildly, as in the madness of despair, and then drop into the sea.[12]

Elisha Dunbar, the *Alabama*'s tenth victim, represented an interesting milestone. She brought the aggregate value of ships destroyed by the raider, as estimated by her officers, to $232,000, almost exactly what the Confederacy had paid for her.[13] Henceforth, every prize taken by the *Alabama* would be "profit."

For nearly a week after burning the *Elisha Dunbar,* the *Alabama* battled gale winds that carried her northwest of the Azores. Semmes knew that the end of the Atlantic whaling season was approaching; he knew also that he could not loiter indefinitely in the Azores without encountering a Federal warship. Toward the end of September he set his course west toward Newfoundland. He was thinking of taking the war to the enemy's front yard; time would tell whether his scheme was practical.

On October 3, about two hundred miles from Newfoundland, the *Alabama* spotted two ships coming toward her—the first sail in nearly two weeks. Their lines and sails identified both as American, and Semmes set an interception course. The first, the 839-ton *Brilliant,* was laden with flour and grain; the $164,000 evaluation of this prize by the Confederates made her the most valuable of the *Alabama*'s captures to date. The *Brilliant*'s master and part-owner, George

Hagar, implored the Confederates to spare his ship, but Semmes turned a deaf ear.

Brilliant's companion, the *Emily Farnum*, became the first American vessel stopped by the *Alabama* whose master was able to produce documentation acceptable to Semmes that he carried neutral cargo; she was released on bond. Because they were no longer near the Azores, Semmes required *Emily Farnum*'s master to accept his prisoners from the *Virginia*, the *Elisha Dunbar*, and the *Brilliant*.[14] Any ship that escaped the torch could be expected to perform some service.

Semmes stipulated, in releasing *Emily Farnum*, that she continue on to her destination, Liverpool, lest word of his presence off Newfoundland reach Federal authorities. According to Semmes, *Farnum*'s skipper, N. P. Simes, pledged that he would do so, only to change course for Boston as soon as the *Alabama* was out of sight. Although Semmes as a cruiser captain took advantage of every ruse sanctioned by international law, he was a man of his word, and his deepest contempt was reserved for men who were not. Semmes wrote sarcastically of Simes's deception, "This being nothing more than a clever 'Yankee trick,' of course there was no harm done the master's honor."[15]

Communications were slow—to Semmes's considerable benefit— but the captain of the *Alabama* was beginning to get extremely bad press in the North. On his return to the United States, Captain Tilton of the *Virginia* testified to the rigor with which he had been treated:

> I went on the quarter-deck [of the *Alabama*] with my son when they ordered me into the lee waist, with my crew, and all of us were put in irons, with the exception of the two boys, and the cook and steward. I asked if I was to be put in irons? The reply of Captain Semmes was that his purser had been put in irons, and his head shaved by us, and that he meant to retaliate. We were put in the lee waist, with an old sail over us, and a few planks to lie upon. . . . The steamer's guns being kept run out, the side ports could not be shut, and when the sea was a little rough or the vessel rolled the water was continually coming in on both sides.[16]

Semmes later conceded that Tilton's account was substantially accurate.

Brilliant was the first New York–based vessel destroyed by the *Alabama,* and the outcry on Wall Street following the arrival of captains Simes and Hagar did much to establish the image of Semmes the pirate. On October 21 the New York State chamber of commerce convened a special meeting to consider actions to be taken in response to the *Alabama*'s depredations and roundly denounced Semmes's treatment of prisoners. "The conduct of the captain of the pirate to the crew of the captured vessels was most inhuman," the chamber concluded. "The unfortunate men were clustered together on the deck, manacled, without room to lie down at night . . . while the rest were compelled to stand; and in heavy weather they were continually washed by the sea—exposure and trials which only the stoutest and strongest men could endure."[17]

For years, going back even before hostilities, Semmes had despised New England merchants as a class. Now it was the North's turn to demonize him. One of the whaling captains whose ship Semmes had burned was quoted in the New York *Herald* to the effect that although Semmes may once have appeared to be a gentleman, he had entirely changed:

> He sports a huge mustache, the ends of which are waxed . . . and it is evident that it occupies much of his attention. His steward waxes it carefully every day, and so prominent is it that sailors of the *Alabama* call him "Old Beeswax." His whole appearance is that of a corsair, and the transformation appears to be complete from Commander Raphael Semmes, United States Navy, to a combination of Lafitte and Kidd.[18]

It was no coincidence that the vilification of Semmes began with the return of the crews of the *Virginia* and the *Elisha Dunbar.* The men of these two vessels probably had the most difficult time of any prisoners taken by Semmes during the war. They were captured too far from the Azores to be released in their own boats, and they were on the *Alabama* during some very rough weather. The *Virginia* and *Elisha Dunbar* were the last ships whose officers were routinely ironed in retaliation for the treatment the Federals had accorded Henry Myers.

Nothing infuriated Semmes more than to be called a pirate. He viewed any such charge not merely as an ad hominem attack, but as an aspersion on his honor and the legitimacy of his government. It was just as well for Semmes that the Northern reporters did not bother to research his own writings. They would have found in his

Mexican War memoir a scathing indictment of commerce raiders that operated with mercenary crews. For a privateer to be legal under the law of nations, Semmes had written, "it was necessary that at least a majority of the officers and crew of each cruiser should be *citizens*." Any vessel that failed to meet this prerequisite, in his view, "would have become, from that moment, a *pirate*."[19]

Semmes's sensitivity to the charge of piracy is understandable: The *Alabama* was operating with an almost exclusively British crew.

Semmes was pleased with the officers he had with him on the *Alabama*, several of whom, of course, had previously served on the *Sumter*. John Kell was the man upon whom he relied, for although the captain liked the spirit of his other officers, virtually all were in their twenties. The two who ranked immediately behind Kell, Richard Armstrong and Joe Wilson, had entered the U.S. Naval Academy in 1857; Semmes was old enough to have been their father. Aboard the *Alabama,* the traditional isolation of a captain in time of war was underscored by the age difference between Semmes and his officers.

As for the crew, Semmes viewed all sailors in much the same light: lazy, morally corrupt, incapable of any lasting loyalty, and totally unable to handle alcohol. Under the right leadership, however, something could be made of this unpromising material. He considered the *Alabama*'s first months at sea, removed from the temptations of port, as his one chance to whip his wharf rats into some kind of fighting unit, for Semmes had no intention of limiting his war against the North entirely to merchantmen. In his recruiting speech, he had promised his sailors a fight, and he fully intended to oblige.

Semmes, like many other skippers, treated sailors as wards of the state, incapable of making decisions for themselves. The smallest items of clothing, down to boots and underwear, were controlled by the ship's paymaster, who doled them out as need could be demonstrated and docked each sailor's pay appropriately. There were limits to any captain's effective reach, however. A wise skipper did not look closely into life in the forecastle, nor did his officers. At times there was no law between decks except that which was enforced by the crew themselves. The bullies hazed the "quiet" men until a boatswain or some tough seaman intervened. Drunkenness at sea was uncommon, but despite all precautions there was some smuggling of liquor from the *Alabama*'s prizes.

The raider's crew included four "boys"—riverfront toughs who had made their way onto the *Bahama* and subsequently signed aboard the *Alabama*. They were "powder monkeys," responsible for odd jobs but ranking below even ordinary seamen. One day, when the *Alabama*'s pet cat disappeared, suspicion immediately fell upon the ship's boys, particularly a troublemaker named Robert Egan. Convinced that he was responsible for the missing cat, the crew had Egan "spread-eagled" in the mizzen rigging. At this moment the lookout spotted a sail, and the raider cleared for action. When the tampion was removed from the muzzle of the aft pivot gun, what should emerge but the cat! Egan confessed, saying that he had always wanted to see a cat fired out of a cannon.[20]

Although Semmes deplored his sailors' habits, he had no illusions about reforming them. He maintained a satisfactory state of discipline by a policy of speedy punishment. At the same time, he knew what was important to maintain morale. He could sense about how long he could expect his crew to function effectively without a liberty port, and when necessary he managed to find a port of call, even in wartime, for a few days of debauchery.

Each day one quarter of the crew was "exercised," usually at the guns but at times with small arms, because the capture of an enemy ship by boarding was still deemed feasible in the early days of steam. Semmes acknowledged that a primary objective of the exercise was to keep his crew busy. "I found the old adage that 'Idleness is the parent of vice' as true upon the sea as upon the land," he wrote. "My crew were never so happy as when they had plenty to do and but little to think about."[21]

On the *Sumter*, Semmes had posted a list of regulations to be observed. The *Alabama* doubtless followed a similar regimen:

1. The deck will never be left without a lieutenant, except that in port a Midshipman may be assigned to keep the First Lieutenant's watch.

2. The quarterdeck will at all times be regarded as a place of parade, and no sitting or lounging will be permitted thereon. . . .

3. Officers will wear their uniforms at all times, when on board ship & when on shore on duty.

4. No officer will remain out of the ship after 10 P.M. without the special permission of the Commander.

5. Each division of Guns will be exercised at least three times a

week, and there will be an exercise at general quarters twice a week. . . .

6. The Crew will be mustered at quarters for inspection every morning at 9 o'clock (except Sundays) and every evening at sunset.

7. On Sundays there will be a general muster for inspection at 11 A.M. when the officers will appear in undress, with epaulettes.

8. The Chief Engineer is to keep the Commander informed at all times (through the First Lieutenant) of the conditions of his engines, boilers &c: and he is to see that his assistants &c. are punctual & zealous, in the performance of their duties, and report such as fail therein to the First Lieutenant.

9. There will be an Engineer at all times on watch in the Engine Room when the ship is under steam; and the Engineers on watch will report every two hours to the officer of the Deck how the engines are working &c.

10. The Marine officer will drill his guard once every day, when the weather is suitable, and the duty of the Ship does not interfere therewith.

11. The firemen will be exercised at least once a week, when the pumps, hose &c. are to be adjusted, and used as in the case of actual fire.[22]

Sunday, after muster, the ship was given a thorough cleaning, below as well as topside. Still, there was plenty of free time for the seamen of the *Alabama,* and in good weather they could be found engaged in domestic activities such as mending clothes. There was entertainment, too, for the *Alabama,* like every other vessel of any size, had a ship's fiddler to help pass the time of an evening. Above all there was talk, much of it about prize money. Semmes's sailors, none of whom had served on the *Sumter,* were puzzled as to how there could be prize money from ships that were not sold but burned. At the same time, they observed the care with which the *Alabama*'s officers noted the value of each ship and its cargo before they were destroyed. Surely, after the war, a grateful Confederate government would find some way to reward the crew of its most effective raider!

Whatever their questions, they learned little from their commander. Semmes cultivated an aura of remoteness. He kept his plans secret from all his officers except Kell, despite the fact that the chance of a leak to the enemy was minimal. Although many captains joined their officers for some meals, Semmes generally dined alone. After his evening meal he would often stroll to the quarterdeck for a single cigar. Occasionally he would be joined there by Kell, Dr. Galt, or one of the other officers, and there would be some general conversation about the war or friends at home. Lest there be any impairing of discipline, Semmes took care "to tighten the reins, gently . . . the following morning."[23]

Semmes normally retired about 9:00 P.M. to his triangular cabin in the stern of the raider. There he had a small Catholic shrine, and he probably said prayers before going to sleep. His thoughts were often of home and family. He had doubtless received one or two letters from Anne since leaving New Orleans with the *Sumter,* for he would have directed her to write him at any port that he might visit. But with two sons—soon to be three—in Confederate service, Semmes must have passed some uneasy nights.

Who could have expected such a long, destructive war?

CHAPTER 11

Off the Grand Banks

Federal authorities had known since late August that they faced a grave threat on the high seas in the form of the *Alabama*. Neutralization of the raider was a formidable challenge, but one that the U.S. Navy might have met had its ships been deployed with some imagination. To intercept Federal merchantmen, Confederate cruisers were obliged to operate in well-known and well-defined sea-lanes. While Secretary of the Navy Welles could not be expected to read Semmes's mind, he could have posted ships in the areas most likely to attract the enemy. Instead, there was no effective pursuit. In October 1862, while the *Alabama* approached the New England coast, Welles was ordering the U.S.S. *Tuscarora* to the Azores. On October 6, while Semmes was burning grain ships off New England, Captain Pickering of the *Kearsarge* reported that he, too, was at the Azores and that the *Alabama* had in fact destroyed ten U.S. whaling vessels in waters around the islands.[1] Federal captains were skilled at filing reports, but often lacked initiative.

On October 18 Welles grumbled in his diary, "The ravages by the roving steamer *290,* alias *Alabama,* are enormous. England should be held accountable for these outrages." And so England would be, but meanwhile Welles had to deal with the merchants and insurance companies of his native New England. Responding to demands that vessels be sent in search of the *Alabama*, Welles sent several gunboats to the raider's last known position, off Nova Scotia.[2]

On October 7, some three hundred miles northeast of Newfoundland, the *Alabama* spotted a suspicious sail at dawn and subsequently halted an American bark, the *Wave Crest*, laden with grain for Britain. After condemning her, Semmes made the *Wave Crest* a target for his gunners—their second such exercise on the *Alabama*. That evening, at 9:00, the lookout spotted a sail in the moonlight. After what Semmes described as a "beautiful, picturesque chase" of several hours the raider had her prey. Semmes's victim was the New York–based brigantine *Dunkirk*, carrying grain to Lisbon.

By a quirk of fate, the crew of the *Dunkirk* included George Forrest, a troublemaker from the *Sumter* who had jumped ship at Cádiz. Semmes ordered him placed in double irons, and on October 9 convened a court-martial, headed by John Kell, to try him. Proceedings were just under way when, shortly after noon, the *Alabama*'s lookout spotted sail. The court adjourned while the raider chased and captured a 1,300-ton packet ship, *Tonawanda*.

The trial resumed at 4:00, and within half an hour had delivered a verdict of guilty. The penalty for desertion was death, but—perhaps on Semmes's suggestion—Forrest was sentenced not to swing from the yardarm but to serve without pay or prize money for the remainder of the *Alabama*'s cruise. This was a remarkably light sentence, and Semmes would have cause to regret it, but the *Alabama* was still understrength and seamen were in short supply.[3]

Meanwhile, what to do with the *Tonawanda*? The ship's cargo of grain was not documented as neutral, but the ship carried seventy-five passengers, including thirty women and children. Semmes would have liked to burn *Tonawanda*, but he was already carrying prisoners from the *Wave Crest* and the *Dunkirk* and could burn his latest prize only if he could find a vessel for his prisoners. He took an $80,000 bond from *Tonawanda*'s master, but put a prizemaster aboard with orders to stay close to the *Alabama*. Two days later, on one of the North Atlantic's few fine days, the *Alabama* captured and burned yet another grain ship, the *Manchester*, bound from New York to Liverpool. On October 13, Semmes placed all his prisoners aboard the *Tonawanda* and sent her on her way.[4]

The most persistent strain in Semmes's writings is his hostility toward "Puritans," by which, in practice, he often meant all New Englanders.

The roots of Semmes's hostility are not entirely clear. Although he deeply resented what he perceived as the North's prewar exploitation of the South, he did not hold all Northerners responsible.

Semmes's hostility toward Yankees was based in history and religion. He associated Catholicism with liberty and virtue, Puritanism with narrow intolerance. For Semmes the Civil War was a holy war, and he often took special pleasure in burning New England–based ships. When the *Alabama*'s boarding officer brought a number of Protestant religious tracts from the *Dunkirk,* Semmes examined them closely. They had been shipped for distribution in Catholic Portugal even though, as one tract noted, dissemination of such material in Portugal was illegal. Semmes viewed the tracts as one more example of Yankee/Protestant duplicity.[5]

Like his Confederate army counterparts, however, Semmes found it difficult to sever every emotional tie to the flag that he had served for so many years. At the close of the *Trent* affair, when Washington had averted a crisis by apologizing to Britain, Semmes confessed to a feeling of mortification "that an American nation had been so greatly humbled before [a European power]; for although the Federal States were my enemies, as between them and foreign nations I could not but feel something like family attachment."[6]

The *Alabama* enlisted two hands from *Tonawanda*. The first was an ordinary seaman; the second was none other than a slave, David White, who had been on his way to Europe with his master. Slavery was still legal in those states that remained in the Union, and White's case was not unique. The situation appealed to Semmes's sense of the ironic. Inasmuch as the North was treating enemy-owned slaves as contraband of war, Semmes did the same. He appropriated White from his owner, pronounced him free, and put him on the rolls as a wardroom "boy." According to Semmes, White, though frightened at first, became delighted with his "emancipation" and attached himself to Dr. Galt.[7]

Semmes himself had little need for White's services. On the *Alabama* as on the *Sumter,* he had at his disposal a personal servant as well as a clerk. On his voyage from Nassau to Liverpool on the *Bahama,* he had noticed one of the stewards on board, "a pale, rather delicate, and soft-mannered" young man named Bartelli. Semmes found him respectful and obedient, qualities he admired, but upon making some inquiries was told that Bartelli had a serious drinking problem. As the voyage went on, Semmes observed with disapproval the harshness with which the British captain treated Bartelli and asked if he might speak to the fellow about serving aboard the *Alabama*.

Semmes liked a reclamation project. He offered Bartelli a position as steward, with the stipulation that he never touch alcohol aboard ship. Bartelli accepted, and in time became "a capital servant," who looked after Semmes "like a woman."[8] Equally important, he had no trouble with alcohol while on the *Alabama*.

Among the most sought-after items on any prize taken by the *Alabama* were Northern newspapers, which even for Confederates constituted news from "home." The standard practice aboard the *Alabama* was for captured newspapers to be reviewed by Semmes's secretary, Breedlove Smith, whose cubicle was immediately outside the captain's cabin. Items of interest were passed promptly to Semmes; the papers eventually circulated among the officers and then among the crew.

For Semmes, newspapers were an intelligence bonanza. For instance, the October 5 issue of the *New York Herald*—scrounged from the *Manchester*—contained the entire order of battle for Federal gunboats. Semmes studied it closely. Although the grand total of gunboats was 192, Semmes knew their characteristics and concluded that no more than 13 were superior to the *Alabama*.[9] Like Robert E. Lee, Semmes made good use of enemy journals; he wrote after the war, "Perhaps this was the only war in which the newspapers ever explained, beforehand, all the movements of armies and fleets to the enemy."[10]

On October 15, in heavy weather, the *Alabama* encountered an American bark, the 365-ton *Lamplighter*. The seas were so high that the party from the *Alabama* had difficulty boarding the prize, and Lieutenant Sinclair, for one, thought that her master could have made a successful run for it had he been more daring. *Lamplighter*'s principal cargo was tobacco, of which the boarding party managed to plunder a supply for the *Alabama* before putting their prize to the torch.[11]

The following day the raider found herself in a storm—in fact, a hurricane—that Semmes described as one of the most severe he had ever experienced. Master's Mate George Fullam provided a terse summary in his journal:

> 9:30—Blowing a perfect hurricane, the sea rising to a fearful height, and the ship labouring heavily. Shortly after, a squall of extraordinary violence struck us, we being under close

reefed maintopsail, reefed maintrysail and foretopmast stay-sail. The heavy strain on the main braces caused the weather bumkin to snap in two, the yard flew forward bending upwards until it was almost double, when with a sudden crash it broke in two, splitting the topsail with a noise equal to the loudest thunder. A sea striking immediately after smashed in the whale boat; it was soon cut away.[12]

Two men were assigned to the wheel, and even so it once spun out of control. Men who had to stay on deck either clung to the bulwarks or were lashed to their posts. The air was so filled with spray that some of the *Alabama*'s officers were reminded of a blizzard. Even at the height of the storm, however, Semmes was a scientist as well as a sailor. When the wind suddenly abated after two hours he was certain that the storm was cyclonic; he timed the vortex with his watch, coolly informing Kell that in a few minutes the winds would resume from the opposite direction. After half an hour the wind and rain returned in all their fury, but Semmes knew that the worst would soon be over. Four and a half hours after the storm struck, the *Alabama* was "rolling and tumbling about in the confused sea which the gale had left behind it, with scarcely wind enough to fill her sails."[13]

For three days the raider held her position under gray skies in rough seas. The crew worked almost around the clock making repairs, but Semmes noted in his log that he had to find a prize from which to obtain new yards and new boats. On October 23, the *Alabama* captured a 945-ton grain ship, the *Lafayette*. The prize had documents alleging that her cargo was British-owned, but Semmes, in his admiralty proceedings, declared them spurious. Semmes was so thoroughly versed in maritime law, and so suspicious of the documentation he was now encountering, that only airtight evidence of neutral ownership, duly sworn and notarized, could pass muster. The *Lafayette* was put to the torch.

By this time the *Alabama* was about 250 miles from New York City, and Semmes faced a key decision. Some days earlier he had confided a daring plan to Kell: He planned to take the *Alabama* into New York harbor and fire the ships he found there. Would not the element of surprise neutralize whatever Federal vessels might be in the area? In Kell's recollection, Semmes was fully committed to such a raid until the hurricane of October 16, which had left the raider in what Kell called "a very disabled condition."[14] A month later, writing to James Bulloch in London, Semmes offered a different explanation. "I was obliged to forego [sic] my 'raid' off New York harbor, as I found when I had approached . . . within 250 miles, I had but four days' coal on board."[15] For whichever reason, there would be no dramatic incursion into New York harbor.

Semmes's orders from Secretary Mallory with respect to the *Alabama* did not survive the war. Judging from the wide discretion that Mallory had given him with command of the *Sumter,* however, it seems safe to infer that Semmes enjoyed considerable latitude in carrying out his commerce-destroying mission with the *Alabama.* Whether such discretion extended to a high-risk raid into the enemy's greatest port is debatable, but Semmes probably would have been justified in undertaking an operation that, if successful, would have required the Federals to strengthen defenses in all their port cities.

By this stage of the *Alabama*'s cruise her officers had become quite adept at identifying the nationality of the ships they encountered. This was a pertinent skill, because it was clearly to the raider's advantage to avoid fruitless chases. Semmes had with him a master's mate, James Evans, who had sailed on the privateer *Savannah* at the beginning of the war. Semmes himself was no slouch at identifying a ship from her lines and sails, but he soon turned this responsibility over to Evans. "When he pronounced a ship a Yankee," wrote Semmes, "I was always sure of her."[16]

On October 26 the *Alabama* captured a small grain schooner, the *Crenshaw,* three days out of New York. Her documents indicated that the cargo was British-owned but named no individual as owner, and in Semmes's reading of the law any manifest that failed to identify the purchaser was defective. He burned this latest victim. The officers of the *Alabama* were angered to read, in papers taken from the *Crenshaw,* of the charges of brutal treatment that had been lodged by Captain Hagar of the *Brilliant.* Nevertheless, there was no more routine manacling of prisoners. Indeed, the weather having turned cold, prisoners from the *Lafayette* and *Crenshaw* were moved below-decks.[17]

After yet another storm, the *Alabama* spotted a sail on October 28. The vessel in question was American, the 284-ton bark *Lauretta,* and her documents alleging neutral ownership of her cargo did not meet Semmes's exacting requirements. Sworn and notarized affidavits contended that the cargo belonged to citizens of Portugal, Italy, and Britain, but Semmes judged them to be fabricated, and he burned

Lauretta. Her master subsequently gave a New York journal his account of an admiralty court in which the only opinion that mattered was that of Captain Raphael Semmes, C.S.N.:

> The papers of the bark were, at the command of Semmes, taken by Captain Wells on board the *Alabama.* . . . Semmes took first the packet which bore the Portuguese seal, and with an air which showed that he did not regard it as of the slightest consequence, ripped it open and threw it on the floor, with the remark that "he did not care a d—n for the Portuguese." The Italian bill of lading was treated in a similar manner, except that he considered it unworthy even of a remark.
>
> Taking up the British bill of lading and looking at the seal, Semmes called upon Captain Wells, with an oath, to explain. It was evidently the only one of the three he thought it worth his while to respect.
>
> "Who is this Burden?" he inquired sneeringly. "Have you ever seen him?"
>
> "I am not acquainted with him; but I have seen him once, when he came on board my vessel," replied Captain Wells.
>
> "Is he an Englishman—does he look like an Englishman?"
>
> "Yes," rejoined the captain.
>
> "I'll tell you what," exclaimed the pirate. "This is a d———d pretty business—it's a d———d Yankee hash, and I'll settle it."[18]

Notwithstanding that this fierce dialogue came from a Yankee journal, "quoting" a master whose ship had been burned by the *Alabama,* parts of it ring true. Semmes had little respect for the lesser powers of the world, and he had grown suspicious of documents alleging British ownership. Sinclair would later write that Semmes rarely displayed temper, except when suspicious manifests sent him to searching his library for reasons to discount them. "Then," Sinclair remarked, "there's many a 'd———n your eyes.'"[19]

The next day the raider stopped a brigantine, *Baron de Castine,* bound for Cuba with a cargo of lumber. Semmes concluded that she was of little value, and instead of burning her used her as a refuge for the forty-odd prisoners he had on board. "I charged the master of this ship," Semmes wrote in his memoirs, "to give my special thanks to Mr. Low, of the New York Chamber of Commerce, for the complimentary resolutions he had passed in regard to the *Alabama.* The more the enemy abused me, the more I felt complimented."[20]

By the end of October the *Alabama*'s cruise off the Grand Banks was over. Semmes had dealt a blow to the grain trade between New York and Britain, much as he had previously ravaged the New England whaling fleet. But whereas operations in the Azores seemed remote to those not directly affected, it was a different matter to have a raider operating with impunity a day's sail from New York City. The consternation in U.S. financial centers caused by the *Alabama* in the final months of 1862—the rise in maritime insurance rates, the rush to switch vessels to British registry, and the attempts to fabricate ownership documents on cargo—would have pleased Semmes immensely had he known of it.[21]

Although the *Alabama* was having a major effect on ocean commerce, her effect on Northern morale was limited by a factor beyond Semmes's control. On September 17, 1862, Federal forces had repulsed Lee's Army of Northern Virginia at Antietam, at a cost of nearly twelve thousand Union casualties. For most Americans, North and South, the material cost of the war, on land or at sea, was by now far overshadowed by its human cost.

Although Semmes of the *Alabama* had not caused the death of a single person, the final months of 1862 brought new charges of brutality and "piracy" against him. To some extent, these were a predictable outgrowth of his practice of burning most of his prizes. They were abetted, too, by the return of prisoners from the whalers captured around the Azores, whose accounts of having been placed in irons aboard the *Alabama* lost nothing in the telling. But Semmes himself did nothing to discourage his detractors. There was something Mephistophelian about the slight, intense figure with the slim, tapered fingers and the flashing gray eyes. Semmes's mustache appears to have grown heavier and more sinister as the *Alabama*'s cruise went on. His tendency to smack his lips occasionally in conversation evoked the image of a seagoing Dracula, drinking the blood of the U.S. merchant marine. His taunting of the New York chamber of commerce had a piratical, in-your-face ring to it. Most skippers owned a share of the ships they commanded, and this share was not always insured. To a captain who had just been told that his ship was to be burned, Semmes—sitting behind the desk in his cabin, twisting the tips of his mustache—was the devil incarnate.

There were commercial considerations, too, in the propaganda charges against Semmes. Many of the marine insurance policies of the day included coverage against piracy—a holdover from the era of true buccaneers when Raphael Semmes was a midshipman. Now, skippers and shipping companies alike sought to collect on their policies, to no avail. The owner of the first ship Semmes had burned, the *Golden Rocket,* had sued for compensation under a piracy clause but had lost in both state and federal courts. Subsequent victims, however, doubtless hoped for more favorable results.[22]

Finally, there was the question of the *Alabama*'s strange origins. An article in *Harper's Weekly* summed up the U.S. case against Britain:

> Here is a vessel built in a British dock-yard, by a member of the British Parliament—Mr. Laird; armed with British guns, manned with British sailors; fitted out under the auspices of British officials, in defiance alike of the remonstrances of our Minister and of the Foreign Enlistment Act. . . . If this craft be not a British pirate, what would constitute one?[23]

Meanwhile, Semmes was in search of a new hunting ground. The principal impetus appears to have been the same one that obliged him to abort the raid into New York harbor: He was low on coal and could never tell when he might run into a Federal warship. Fortunately for Semmes, the thoughtful James Bulloch had chartered a tender, the *Agrippina,* to supply the raider with coal. The *Agrippina* was scheduled to arrive at Martinique shortly, and Semmes set a course for the Caribbean.

After the war, in his history of the Civil War navies, Admiral David D. Porter would write of Semmes, "Was there ever such a lucky man as the Captain of the *Alabama*? If he wanted a cargo of provisions it fell into his hands. If he required to visit a dock-yard to fit out his ship, a vessel came along filled with cordage, canvas and anchors."[24] There was some basis for Porter's lament. As the *Alabama* sailed south during muster on Sunday, November 2, the lookout spotted a sail. A few months earlier, such a development would have led Semmes to suspend his Sunday routine and call his crew to quarters. Now, the reading of the Articles of War continued while the raider pursued a 376-ton whaler, *Levi Starbuck*. A blank shell brought her to.

Because the *Levi Starbuck* was just beginning her voyage, she was a floating warehouse. The October hurricane had depleted the *Alabama*'s supply of spare spars, sails, and cordage, but replacements from the captured whaler made up for these. Moreover, *Levi Starbuck* provided such antiscorbutic vegetables as cabbages and turnips, a welcome relief from the *Alabama*'s diet of salt pork, dried beef, and beans.

The raider continued on her course south, running against the Gulf Stream toward the West Indies. During the night of November 7 the lookout spotted sail, and the *Alabama* set out in pursuit. She was being given a good run by the stranger when a larger ship, characterized by James Evans as clearly American, came up from the south. Semmes captured the larger vessel, the *Thomas B. Wales,* returning from Calcutta to Boston with a cargo of jute, linseed, and saltpeter. Saltpeter was, of course, an ingredient for gunpowder and, as such, contraband; Semmes was about to burn his first contraband cargo since the *Neapolitan* off Gibraltar.

As luck would have it, the Confederates found that the main yard of the *Thomas B. Wales* almost exactly matched that of the *Alabama,* which had been carried away during the hurricane, and so the *Alabama*'s boarding party removed it before burning the prize.[25] The raider enlisted no fewer than nine hands from the *Wales*'s crew, the most recruits ever signed from a single prize. They raised the *Alabama*'s complement to 110—ten fewer than called for, but as close to fully manned as the raider had been to date.

The *Thomas B. Wales* was carrying as passengers a former U.S. consul in India, George H. Fairchild, his English wife, and their three young children. Semmes was at his most chivalrous where women were concerned, but in this instance he even took to Mr. Fairchild, who "although a New Englander, was, apparently, an unbigoted gentleman." Semmes turned over two cabins to the master and the Fairchild party and appears to have found them good company; he wrote nostalgically in his log of his pleasure at hearing "the merry voices of children."[26] He would later have occasion to congratulate himself on the kind treatment accorded the Fairchilds.

To avoid any chance encounter with a Federal warship, Semmes kept the *Alabama* well out at sea as he sailed for the Caribbean. Winds were light and progress slow, but on November 18 the Confederate raider passed St. Pierre, almost exactly a year after the *Sumter*'s dramatic escape from the *Iroquois* there. This time Semmes headed for Fort-de-France, where the governor—still Maussion de Cande—again gave the Confederates a friendly reception. He expedited the landing of the prisoners from the *Levi Starbuck* and the *Thomas B. Wales* and authorized Semmes to use any repair facilities he required.

The *Alabama*'s arrival was no surprise, because her tender, the *Agrippina,* had arrived eight days before. Her skipper, Captain

McQueen, was becoming a problem. Instead of waiting for the *Alabama* offshore, or inventing a story to justify an extended stay at Fort-de-France, Captain McQueen had spoken openly of his role as tender to the *Alabama* and had even mentioned the raider's approximate arrival date. Semmes needed coal, but he could not take the chance that McQueen's loquaciousness would bring a couple of Federal warships into view. He ordered McQueen to a new rendezvous, the barren islet of Blanquilla off the Venezuelan coast.[27]

Meanwhile, Semmes played host to groups of curious Frenchmen who came to examine the "pirate" vessel. His crewmen, less formally, did a brisk business with a fleet of bumboats that crowded about the raider, peddling fruit, pipes, and various sweets. Semmes was in his cabin that evening, enjoying some fruit that Bartelli had obtained, when he heard a loud commotion on deck. Kell also heard it and was going forward to investigate when he barely escaped a belaying pin aimed for his head. Several crewmen began to abuse Kell, and when the first officer ordered others to seize the culprits, they refused.[28]

At this moment Semmes appeared on deck. There he found a "surly and sulky crowd of half-drunken sailors gathered near the foremast, using mutinous language and defying the authorities of the ship." The gray eyes flashed, and Semmes ordered Kell to beat to quarters. At the rattle of the drum, most of the crew made an effort to reach their battle stations. The officers, meanwhile, armed themselves with pistols. Kell described what followed:

> We then passed among them as they stood at their guns, the eagle eye of Captain Semmes pointing out the most disorderly and riotous to be ironed. There were about twenty of the culprits. He then ordered them to be taken to the gangway, and called out for the quartermasters to provide themselves with draw-buckets, and beginning with the most drunken culprit to douse them thoroughly with water. The buckets came down in quick succession.[29]

At first the mutineers were defiant, but the water kept coming. Soon they began to gasp for breath and to shiver with cold. Some begged for mercy, promising model behavior. The water treatment went on for some two hours before Semmes ordered Kell to beat the retreat.

So ended the only mutiny on board the *Alabama*. Because it stemmed from drink smuggled aboard the raider, it was less serious than a premeditated attempt to defy authority. Nevertheless, it was a reminder to Semmes that discipline aboard his ship was a fragile commodity. Just two days before he had written in his journal that he had never seen "a better disposed or more orderly crew."[30]

The mutineers, for the most part, appeared to bear no grudge against their captain. Most probably recognized that commanding a crew such as that of the *Alabama* was no bed of roses. In his memoir, Semmes would quote good-humoredly a joke that made the rounds of his ship. "Old Beeswax," the saying went, "sure knows how to water a fellow's grog!"[31]

Semmes's worry that the Federals might make a connection between the *Alabama* and the *Agrippina* proved fully justified. On November 19, the day after the *Alabama*'s "mutiny," a large warship arrived at Fort-de-France. Semmes ordered his ship readied for battle and soon learned that his adversary was the 1,450-ton, fourteen-gun *San Jacinto,* the ship that had precipitated an international incident the previous November when its commander, Charles Wilkes, had removed Confederate emissaries from the British packet *Trent.* The *San Jacinto* now had a new commander, William Ronckendorff.

Many Federal vessels had pursued the *Alabama*; the *San Jacinto* was the first to find her. If Semmes's memoirs are to be credited, he never considered challenging the *San Jacinto,* which, in his words, "threw more than two pounds of metal to my one," and had a crew twice the size of the *Alabama*'s.[32] George Fullam, however, suggests that Semmes was initially tempted to fight; he wrote in his journal: "At first it had been our captain's intention to go out and give the enemy battle, but after deliberation he determined to wait until darkness set in."[33]

Aboard the Federal vessel, meanwhile, there were dreams of glory. The *San Jacinto* entered the harbor from the west and could make out the *Alabama* at anchor some three miles away. According to Lieutenant Ralph Chandler, the *San Jacinto*'s executive officer, he urged his skipper to attack the *Alabama* in French waters:

> A cry of delight ran through the ship and the crew rushed to their stations and cast loose the guns without an order or the sound of the drum. I rushed to the poop deck where the captain was and said, Capt. Ronckendorff, here is your opportunity. . . . The [*San Jacinto*] is as strong as oak and iron can make her, and we can run that ship down before she can get

her anchor. I was surprised when the Capt. remarked, "I am not the man to take such a responsibility."[34]*

Meanwhile, Semmes planned his escape. His own ship had an edge over the enemy's in speed, and Semmes was confident that he could elude *San Jacinto*—assuming, of course, that she was not reinforced. He could not afford to dally, lest a second enemy ship appear, and the gray light of a short November day suggested the advisability of an immediate breakout.

The French officials were notably friendly. Governor Maussion de Cande, who had been so helpful to Semmes at the time of the *Sumter*'s visit, reminded Ronckendorff that if he were to anchor in the harbor he would be obliged to give the *Alabama* a twenty-four-hour lead when she left. Not surprisingly, the Federal commander chose to wait outside the marine league. To avoid any repetition of the harassment that the *Sumter* had suffered at the hands of the *Iroquois,* French authorities stationed a gunboat near the *Alabama*'s anchorage. Her commander obligingly provided Semmes with charts showing the best channels out of Fort-de-France.[35]

Semmes decided to take advantage of what promised to be a dark, rainy night. Before weighing anchor he darkened ship and ran out all guns. The thirty-two-pounders were loaded with solid shot, the two pivot guns with shell. The raider weighed anchor at about 7:15 and forty-five minutes later was headed for the harbor's southern exit. Gradually, her speed was increased to fourteen knots. With all the assistance that the Confederates received from French authorities and the weather, the raider was in little danger. Semmes wrote laconically in his log, "Having gotten on board some supplies . . . and having received a pilot at 7:30 p.m., we got underway and ran out of the harbor, without seeing anything of the old wagon that was blockading us."[36]

---

*Late in the war, in October 1864, a different Federal commander, in a Brazilian rather than a French port, would behave very differently. Captain Napoleon Collins of the U.S.S. *Wachusett,* upon spotting the Confederate cruiser *Florida* in the harbor of Bahia, attacked the Confederate vessel at her anchorage and made off with her. The Lincoln administration expressed its regrets to Brazil, even as the damaged *Florida* sank in mysterious circumstances off Newport News. By this time, the government in Washington was quite willing to incur some diplomatic embarrassment in return for the destruction of one of the enemy's most effective cruisers.

For several days Ronckendorff searched various coves and inlets for the *Alabama,* misled by the master of an American vessel who insisted that the *Alabama* was still in the vicinity. Finally, Ronckendorff could only report to Welles that the raider had escaped, "notwithstanding all our vigilance." In reply, Welles sent a stinging reprimand.

Once again, Semmes's seamanship and knowledge of international law had stood him in good stead.

CHAPTER 12

"Give It to the Rascals!"

Semmes caught up with the *Agrippina* on November 21 and accompanied her to Blanquilla. Having chosen this particular site for its isolation, he was not pleased to find a Yankee whaling schooner, *Clara L. Sparks,* at anchor there, processing the oil from a recent kill. Semmes nevertheless moved into the harbor, flying the Stars and Stripes. The master of the whaler, seeing U.S. colors, rowed to the *Alabama* in one of his boats and was welcomed on board. After receiving a guided tour of the raider, he declared it the very ship to give the pirate Semmes his comeuppance.

The situation appealed to Semmes's caustic vein of humor. He sent for the master and told him what ship he was on and to whom he was speaking. According to Semmes,

> An awful vision seemed to confront him. His little schooner, and his oil, and the various little 'ventures' which he had on board, with which to trade with the natives along the coast . . . were all gone up the spout! . . . But I played the magnanimous. I told the skipper not to be alarmed; that he was perfectly safe on board the *Alabama* and that out of respect for Venezuela, within whose maritime league we were, I should not even burn his ship.[1]

What Semmes did require was for the master to stay aboard the *Alabama* until the raider had finished coaling, lest he inform some U.S. warship of his whereabouts.

Privacy assured, Semmes made coaling the occasion for a thorough airing of the *Alabama* and for some diversion for her crew. The officers organized hunting parties on the island; the crew swam and were allowed on shore in shifts. Semmes tried out the *Alabama*'s gig under sail and studied the local flora and fauna. He puttered along the island for miles, putting into first one cove and then another, occasionally fishing, occasionally hunting for shells, always alone.[2]

Back on his ship, Semmes had a disciplinary matter to attend to. He ordered a second court-martial for the incorrigible George Forrest, who, on top of his previous sins, had been one of the ringleaders of the Martinique "mutiny." The court sentenced Forrest to be discharged from the ship. He was landed on Blanquilla with his bag and hammock, but his mates made up a purse of $80 for him to take into exile.[3]*

After five days Semmes prepared for departure. When the master of the *Sparks* began thanking him for his release, Semmes cut him short. No thanks were in order, Semmes told the man who had called him a pirate. "If you had been three miles from shore I would have burned you as quick as any vessel! Now go and tell the truth. Do not lie as the rest of you have done."[4]

On November 26 the *Alabama* set sail for the Windward Passage, between Cuba and Haiti. Four days out she stopped a schooner that proved to be Spanish but, having visited Boston, had a supply of American newspapers, some as recent as November 13. From them Semmes learned that a Federal expedition under General Nathaniel P. Banks was about to depart by ship for Galveston with the objective of invading Texas. There had been earlier rumors of such an expedition, and it was these rumors as well as his rendezvous with the *Agrippina* that had brought Semmes to the Caribbean. The fact was that

---

*More than a year later, the U.S. delegation in London distributed a sixteen-page pamphlet titled "Narrative of the Cruise of the *Alabama* by One of Her Crew." The purported author of the pamphlet, George Forrest, alleged that he was "frequently punished by having his hands and legs fastened to the rigging, the punishment being known as the 'Spread Eagle.'. . . He would be kept in this position for four hours." In fact, only Forrest appears to have been punished in this manner, and on only one occasion. Philip Van Doren Stern, *When the Guns Roared* (New York: Doubleday, 1965), 279.

Semmes was spoiling for a fight; having abandoned his cherished plan to raid New York harbor, he considered how the *Alabama* might disrupt Federal operations off Galveston.

For the moment there was nothing for the *Alabama* to do about the Banks expedition, which would not be in the Gulf until mid-December. The raider cruised east along the island of Hispaniola (today divided between Haiti and the Dominican Republic) as Semmes contemplated the possibility of intercepting one of the "gold steamers" from California. The practice in those days before the Panama Canal was for goods from California to travel by ship to Panama, cross the isthmus by rail, and then be loaded aboard another steamer for the final run to New York. In the absence of a U.S. Navy escort, the gold steamers were a tempting target for Confederate cruisers.

On November 30 the *Alabama* captured her first prize in three weeks, the 136-ton bark *Parker Cook* of Boston. What this prize lacked in size she made up in quality, for she was loaded with provisions that were in short supply on the *Alabama,* including bread, cheese, and dried fruit. For half a day the raider lay alongside her prize, transferring her larder. Then Semmes applied the torch. The Confederates appraised her at a modest $10,000, but her destruction brought the estimated value of ships destroyed by the *Alabama* to $1,194,300, more than four times the raider's original cost.[5] Six days later Semmes stopped another small American vessel, the schooner *Union.* Because her cargo was neutral, Semmes took a bond for just $1,500 and made the master take his prisoners from the *Parker Cook.*

Such small fry no longer interested the *Alabama*'s crew, who decided that their captain had his eye out for one of the gold ships. In Sinclair's recollection, the raider had never had so many volunteer lookouts. "Everybody is sure of being rich before night—not on paper, in promises to pay of the Confederate Congress which may only be redeemed at best in shin plasters, but in hard, shining, substantial gold!"[6] Because the newpapers that Semmes studied so carefully included ship sailings, the *Alabama* was not searching for a needle in a haystack. Moreover, the sea-lanes traveled by the treasure ships were well known to Semmes; in patrolling the straits between Cuba and Hispaniola he had positioned his ship on their preferred route. The excited sailors on the *Alabama* estimated that each sailor's share from a gold ship would be around $8,000.

On the morning of December 7, Semmes was finishing breakfast when he heard the lookout's cry, "Sail ho!"

The "Where-away?" of the officer of the deck, shouted through his trumpet, followed, and in a moment more came the rejoinder, "Broad on the port bow, sir!" "What does she look like?" again inquired the officer of the deck. "She is a large steamer, brig-rigged, sir," was the reply.[7]

The *Alabama* had indeed encountered one of the treasure ships, the steam packet *Ariel*. Unfortunately, she was heading west rather than east and would have no gold. Nevertheless, she was one of the largest and most valuable ships to be encountered by the *Alabama,* and her capture would be one of the more unusual episodes in the war at sea. The stranger passed while the *Alabama* was still raising steam, and Semmes could make out gaily dressed women on her deck, as well as groups of men in uniform. The raider, flying U.S. colors, drew friendly waves from the passengers. Semmes studied the stranger through his glass and concluded that the *Ariel* was not a warship but that she *was* quite fast—a very modern paddle wheeler.

The *Alabama* raised steam and lowered her propeller in preparation for the chase. Once in gunshot range, she ran up the Stars and Bars in the place of the U.S. flag and fired a blank warning shot. The result delighted the buccaneer in Semmes. In his account, "The ladies screamed—one of those delightful, dramatic screams, half fear, half acting, which can only ascend from female voices."[8] The Yankee master, however, was not prepared to lay to. He ignored the first warning shot, and Semmes could tell from the increased volume of smoke that he was making a run for it. Not until the *Alabama* fired two "live" warnings, one of which glanced off her mast, did the *Ariel's* great paddle wheels cease to turn.

Dr. George Read, a California rancher, was a passenger on the *Ariel* that Sunday afternoon. He had been seasick from the time of his ship's departure and was eating "a plain cooked potato" when he heard the *Alabama's* first cannon. Climbing to the hurricane deck, Read could clearly see the two projectiles fired by the raider when the *Ariel* failed to halt. The packet's deck was crowded when the warning shots were fired, but it emptied quickly.[9]

In his memoirs, Semmes waxed romantic over what followed. Having been told that there was much anxiety among the packet's passengers,

> I sent for my handsomest young lieutenant [Armstrong] . . . and when he had come to me, I told him to go below, and array himself in his newest and handsomest uniform, [and to]

buckle on the best sword there was in the wardroom. . . . I gave him my own boat, a beautiful gig . . . and directed him to go on board the *Ariel* and coax the ladies out of their hysterics.

According to Semmes, Armstrong made his way to the prize and assured the passengers that they were in the hands of Southern gentlemen, not ruffians and pirates.

Presently a young lady, stepping up to him, took hold of one of the bright buttons that were glittering on the breast of his coat, and asked him if he would not permit her to cut it off, as a memento of her adventure with the *Alabama*. He assented. A pair of scissors was produced, and away went the button! This emboldened another lady to make the same request, and away went another button; and so the process went on, until when I got my handsome lieutenant back, he was like a plucked peacock.[10]

After telling the passengers that their private property would not be molested, Armstrong demanded the ship's papers and the key to her safe. He took the contents of the safe, mostly currency, and brought the *Ariel*'s master, Albert J. Jones, to the *Alabama* for Semmes's standard admiralty proceedings.

For all his gallantry, Semmes now faced a problem. He was eager to burn the *Ariel*, for she was owned by "Commodore" Cornelius Vanderbilt, who had donated one of his other vessels to the U.S. Navy. But instead of a steamer filled with gold, he had on his hands a packet with some five hundred passengers, including a rather embarrassed company of U.S. Marines. Semmes paroled the 140 marines and played for time. To discourage any attempt to overcome his small prize crew, he kept Captain Jones and his chief engineer on board the *Alabama*. Then he went in search of another prize to which he might transfer his prisoners.

For several days the *Alabama* patrolled the Windward Passage in search of a suitable vessel. On December 9, while pursuing a ship that turned out to be German, the cruiser's engines failed because of a broken valve casting. Her innovative chief engineer, Miles Freeman, estimated that repairs would take anywhere between one and three days; Semmes cautioned his officers to keep the *Alabama*'s condition secret lest the *Ariel* attempt to escape. He also called off his search for a new prize and accepted a $261,000 bond from Captain Jones. The well-heeled passengers on the *Ariel* would not have to transfer to some cattle boat, leaving their worldly goods behind to be burned. According to Kell, as the raider pulled away, "the ladies called for 'three cheers for Captain Semmes and the *Alabama*,' which were heartily given, with a waving of handkerchiefs and adieus."[11]

There was no cheering in Washington. Gideon Welles noted gloomily in his diary, "We had yesterday [December 28] a telegram that the British pirate *Alabama* captured the *Ariel*, one of the [Panama] steamers, on her passage from New York. . . . Abuse of the Navy Department will follow."[12]

Charles Wilkes was another of Welles's problems. The onetime explorer had been publicly praised by Welles for his initiative in seizing Mason and Slidell from the *Trent*. When the Lincoln administration repudiated Wilkes's action, Welles had to find a suitable position for a man whom he had lauded and whom the Northern public regarded as a hero. In an action unusual in wartime, Wilkes had refused the first command offered him, that of the James River Flotilla. Unwilling to risk a confrontation, Welles then posted Wilkes to the West Indies Squadron to watch for rebel cruisers and blockade runners.

Wilkes had pursued the *Sumter* in the final months of 1861, and he now felt that he had some insight into Semmes's thought processes. Believing that the Alabamian would stop at Grand Cayman Island, Wilkes proceeded there in his flagship, the *Wachusett*, in mid-December. Finding no sign of the *Alabama* there, he decided to try his luck at Cienfuegos, Semmes's first port of call in the *Sumter*. Once again the Federals were relying on guesswork.

Meanwhile, the Confederates appeared to be gaining the upper hand in the land war. Setbacks along the Mississippi were overshadowed by victories in the east, and the year had closed with the Battle of Fredericksburg, one of Robert E. Lee's easiest victories. Alongside such battles, General Banks's proposed expedition into Texas did not loom especially large. Nevertheless, Semmes saw it as an opportunity. He determined to do what mischief he could to the Federal fleet he expected to find off the Texas coast.

Timing was everything, and Semmes devoted the interval between his capture of the *Ariel* and the anticipated arrival of Banks's force at Galveston to maintenance. His first priority was the raider's engines. Semmes found a secluded bay on the north shore of Jamaica where he could make repairs. In his description, "Nothing but the puffing of the bellows, the clinking of the hammer on the anvil, and the rasping of files was to be heard for 48 hours."[13]

Repairs were completed on December 12, and Semmes took his ship westward along Jamaica's north coast. A three-day storm blew the raider almost to Central America, and once again the *Alabama* found herself in the path of the gold steamers. But Semmes now had other designs, and he proceeded to Yucatán for a previously scheduled rendezvous with the *Agrippina*. The raider passed the latter half of December among the tiny Arcas Islands, off Campeche. Semmes assured his crew—still disappointed at missing a treasure ship—that he planned some excitement for them. He also careened his ship for the first time to clean her bottom and received the last of the *Agrippina*'s coal. He then sent the tender back to Liverpool for a new load of fuel, to be delivered at their next rendezvous, off the coast of Brazil.

In his journal, Semmes marked the new year with a maxim: "Success, as a general rule, attends him who is vigilant and active, and who is careful to obey all the laws of nature." Semmes was nothing if not vigilant and active, and with his crew spoiling for a fight, Semmes was about to oblige them. For the first but not the last time, he was going to deviate from the orders that directed him to avoid battle with enemy warships. The *Alabama* weighed anchor on January 5 to search for the Banks expedition. Contrary to Semmes's information, however, Banks's destination was New Orleans, a city already under Federal control; he had arrived there with thirty thousand men on December 15. However, the area around Galveston was far from quiet. The port city had been captured by a Federal naval expedition in October 1862 and subsequently had been garrisoned by the Federals. A Confederate force under General John B. Magruder resolved to recapture the city, however, and had done so on New Year's Day, 1863.

Unaware of these late developments, the *Alabama* sailed north toward Galveston, expecting to find Banks's transports. On the afternoon of January 11 came the cry from the masthead, "Sail ho," followed by "Land ho." But the lookout, under questioning, reported no merchant fleet such as would have carried Banks's army, only five warships. In due course one of the five was seen to fire into the city. Semmes remarked to the officer of the deck that there had been "a change of programme here. The enemy would not be firing into his own people, [so] we must have recaptured Galveston."[14]

Semmes's reading was correct, but it left him in a ticklish spot. He had promised his crew some action, but he was in no position to take on five Federal warships. As in many situations during the war, the enemy came to his rescue. The *Alabama*'s lookout called out from the masthead that one of the Federal steamers was headed for the raider.

Commanding the Federal squadron off Galveston was Commodore Henry H. Bell. Upon seeing the *Alabama* in the distance, Bell had signaled one of his ships, the *Hatteras,* to check her out. The *Hatteras,* a 1,126-ton side-wheeler, was one of the "instant" warships that had allowed the U.S. Navy to expand to more than four hundred vessels by December 1862. She had been a passenger vessel on the Delaware River before the war and in 1861 and 1862 had enjoyed some success in capturing Confederate blockade runners. Now, however, maintenance problems had cut her top speed to seven or eight knots. Still more ominous, her armament—four thirty-two-pounders, two thirty-pounders, and a twenty-pounder howitzer—was far inferior to that of the *Alabama.*

At about 3:30 P.M., Commander Homer Blake of the *Hatteras* acknowledged Bell's signal and headed into the Gulf. The *Hatteras* was the forty-year-old Blake's first command, and he had been her skipper for only two months. After more than an hour's steaming, Blake's executive officer, Henry Porter, caught a glimpse of the strange sail and told Blake that it looked to him like the *Alabama.* The prospect of engaging a heavily armed cruiser was not inviting, yet it presented an opportunity of sorts. The *Hatteras* could not be expected to defeat the *Alabama,* but she might damage her sufficiently to allow her to be taken by other vessels of Bell's squadron.

Semmes turned his ship about, lowered the propeller, and headed slowly out to sea. He was in complete control of the situation, for if the ship pursuing him proved too powerful for the *Alabama* to engage, he could still outrun her. Blake, on his part, was not fooled by the stranger's seeming nonchalance; he signaled to Bell that the suspicious vessel was a steamer and cleared his own ship for action. By 7:00 P.M., when darkness had fallen and the *Hatteras* was within a mile or two of the *Alabama,* Blake observed that his quarry "had ceased to steam and was lying broadside on, awaiting us."[15]

The *Hatteras* now hailed the stranger, asking her identity. Semmes identified his ship as "Her Majesty's steamer *Petrel.*" He then asked the *Hatteras* to identify herself, which Blake did. The Federal commander replied that he would send a boat on board, and soon the creak of tackle could be heard across the water. The *Hatteras*'s boat had scarcely begun to pull in the direction of the raider when Semmes turned to Kell and asked if he was ready for action. When Kell replied in the affirmative, Semmes told him to identify their vessel as the *Alabama* and then to open fire. Kell called out through his trumpet, "This is the Confederate States steamer *Alabama*!"[16]

With that, he gave the order to fire. The two ships lay only about a hundred yards apart, and the Federal response was immediate. The *Alabama* was fighting her starboard guns, the *Hatteras* her port broadside. As the two vessels exchanged fire, the distance between them narrowed so that at one point it was not more than forty yards, and both combatants supplemented their heavy weapons with rifle fire. George Fullam wrote,

> [It] was a grand though fearful sight to see the guns belching forth, in the darkness of the night, sheets of living flame, the deadly missiles striking the enemy with a force that we could feel. Then, when the shells struck her side, and especially the percussion ones, her whole side was lit up and showing rents of five or six feet in length.[17]

Semmes's command post was the horse block, a raised platform on the quarterdeck that offered some perspective on the action. Because most of the *Hatteras*'s fire was toward the *Alabama*'s stern, the horse block was highly exposed, and George Fullam was impressed with his captain's poise. "As [shots] came whizzing over him, he with usual coolness would exclaim 'Give it to the rascals'; 'Aim low men'; 'Don't be all night sinking that fellow.' When for all . . . we knew, she might have been an ironclad or a ram."[18]

Semmes's gunners needed little encouragement. "That's from the scum of England!" shouted one, who had presumably been reading the enemy press on the subject of the *Alabama*. "This one's from a London wharf-rat!" shouted another.[19] The fire from the raider's forward pivot was accurate and deadly.

After perhaps seven minutes, a shell from the 110-pounder Blakely entered the *Hatteras* at the waterline, exploding in the sick bay. A thirty-two-pounder struck the walking beam, knocking the engine out of line and causing it to vibrate badly. Still another disabled the engine, releasing so much steam that the pumps became inoperable and the engineers were forced to evacuate the engine room. The fire in the sick bay went out of control and threatened the magazines.[20]

In Galveston, the Federals could see the flash of the guns, followed by the sound of heavy weapons. Commodore Bell belatedly suspected that the *Hatteras* was in over her depth and went to her rescue in his flagship, the *Brooklyn*. He was too late. Blake made a halfhearted attempt to turn toward the *Alabama* and board her. With her superior speed, however, the raider pulled ahead of the *Hatteras* and prepared to cross her bow. Blake had had enough. With his ship settling and fire threatening his powder, he ordered the magazines flooded and a lee gun fired in token of surrender. When there was no response from the *Alabama*, he fired two more distress signals. Turning to his captain, Porter asked, "Is it possible that that fellow is going to leave us in this way?" Blake replied that he didn't know.[21]

Then a voice from the *Alabama* offered assistance, and boats from both vessels began ferrying prisoners to the raider. Blake, on the *Alabama*'s deck, handed Semmes his sword "with deep regret." Whereupon Semmes, in a gesture that went beyond normal protocol, invited the Federal officer to use his own cabin.

By Semmes's reckoning the entire action had lasted only thirteen minutes; others clocked it slightly longer. Sinclair thought that the *Alabama* had fired perhaps six broadsides. Casualties on both sides were remarkably light; the *Alabama* had only one man wounded while the *Hatteras*, despite the punishment she had taken, had only two killed and five wounded. Semmes attributed the low casualty total to the fact that most of the *Alabama*'s shots took effect at the waterline.[22] Ten minutes after the last survivor was rescued the *Hatteras* went down by the bow. At daybreak the *Brooklyn* spied her mast, pennant still flying, protruding from the shallow Gulf waters. Later that day Federal authorities learned some details of the disaster. Acting Master L. H. Partridge had been in charge of the boat from the *Hatteras* that had been sent to investigate the *Alabama*. When firing began, Partridge had at first attempted to follow the combatants, then had thought better of it. Eventually he concluded that *Hatteras* must have been captured and made for the coast. He confirmed that the mysterious steamer had been the *Alabama*.[23]

Admiral Porter wrote after the war that Semmes's expedition to Galveston had been boldly conceived. "No one can deny," he wrote, "that Semmes displayed great daring in thus bearding the lion in his den, and entering waters he knew to be full of his enemy's gunboats."[24] The affair of the *Hatteras* could hardly have gone better for Semmes. He had wanted some action for his crew, and the enemy had obligingly supplied a large but inferior vessel. The *Alabama* had been struck seven times but had suffered no significant damage. In his log and his formal report, Semmes sought to make the *Hatteras* a more formidable opponent than the facts justified, crediting her with a total of eight guns. He conceded "a great disparity in weight of metal in our favor," but insisted that by fighting at close range he had made his opponent's smaller guns almost as dangerous as heavier ones.[25]

Whatever the disparity between the ships, and it was considerable, the engagement between the *Alabama* and the *Hatteras* was something of a milestone. For the first time, a steam warship had been sunk by another steam warship. In defiance of landsmen's expectations, a duel between a wooden ship and an iron vessel of the same approximate size had brought a quick victory to the wooden ship. Raphael Semmes had defeated a Federal warship in single combat, a feat that no other Confederate vessel would match.

Semmes headed back into the Gulf, his ship crowded with no fewer than 118 Yankee prisoners.

CHAPTER 13

The Trail of Fire

One of the secrets of Semmes's success as a commander was that he never relaxed his vigilance and was quick to punish anyone who did. Even as he took on board the last of the crew of the *Hatteras,* he scoured the night sky for any sign of other Federal warships. Once the last enemy sailor had been rescued and the *Hatteras* was gone, the raider steamed south at full speed. The U.S.S. *Brooklyn*—the same ship that had failed to prevent the *Sumter*'s escape from New Orleans in 1861—was now one of two Federal vessels that searched unsuccessfully for the elusive *Alabama*.

On January 13 the raider's lookout spotted a sail dead ahead, and Semmes, in U.S.-patrolled waters, hoisted the Stars and Stripes. The stranger, flying British colors, looked familiar to Semmes, who soon realized that she was none other than his own tender, the *Agrippina*. Because the *Alabama* had hoisted U.S. colors, officers on the raider feared that their tender, on seeing an "enemy," might jettison her mailbags—bags filled with letters for their families. But Captain McQueen probably recognized the raider; in any case, he continued on his course. The *Alabama*'s officers, for their part, were careful to conceal the *Agrippina* connection from the prisoners on board.[1]

146

Semmes set a course southeast for Jamaica, where he planned to unload his Yankee guests. The presence of 118 prisoners strained accommodations on the raider, and the discomfort was exacerbated by frequent squalls. For the most part, however, the Federal prisoners accepted their fate with good humor. Kell was on deck on the day after the encounter with the *Hatteras* when he was approached by Captain Blake, whom he had known before the war. Blake saluted, inquired as to Kell's health, and remarked to the effect that fortune favors the brave. Kell thanked him, adding gravely, "We take advantage of all of fortune's favors."[2]

Sinclair, for his part, found the prisoners "a rather jolly sort." He had known Blake's first officer, Henry Porter, before the war, and Porter was so pleased to find a friend on the *Alabama* that he stood Sinclair's watches with him. Porter was much impressed with the cruiser's speed and was interested that grog was still served the crew. Congress had eliminated the grog ration for the U.S. Navy the previous July.[3]

The *Alabama*, fighting adverse currents and winds, was nine days in reaching Jamaica, then a British colony. On January 20, however, the raider dropped anchor at Port Royal, where Semmes was able to release his prisoners in care of the U.S. consul. It was good to be on firm land in a friendly port; although Britain was officially neutral in America's war, large segments of British society, especially in the colonies, supported the South. Businessmen with interests in shipping or cotton were inclined to favor the Confederacy for reasons of trade, while other upper-class Britons recognized that their erstwhile colony would become a formidable commercial rival if it remained united. Even among the working classes, many saw the South as a victim of aggression.

Semmes was grateful for the friendly reception, for he was feeling the the strain of his lonesome command:

> On the high seas, with the enemy all the time in full chase of me, constant vigilance was required to guard against surprise; and my battle with the elements was almost as constant as that with the enemy. When I reached the friendly shelter, therefore, of a neutral port . . . my over-taxed nervous system relaxed in a moment, and I enjoyed the luxury of a little gentlemanly idleness.[4]

For Semmes, "gentlemanly idleness" took the form of a four-day holiday as guest of a Reverend Fyfe, who may have learned of Semmes from Francis Tremlett in London. Semmes turned his ship over to Kell and set off in Fyfe's carriage for a delightful ride of ten miles along macadamized roads to his host's home in the mountains. After three days of total rest, word came from Kell that the *Alabama* was ready for sea. Semmes had earlier agreed to speak before a gathering of the British community, however, and at noon on January 24 he was introduced, to great applause, at the Commercial Exchange in Kingston. According to the *Tribune and Daily Advertiser,*

> [Captain Semmes] expressed his delight at the sympathy which he had detected in the community for the cause he represents. In England he had met the same cordial reception which he received here—nine-tenths of the people of that country being sympathizers with the South. He lauded the South as an advocate of free trade and promised her ports would be thrown open to the world.
>
> During his whole speech, not one word did he utter in allusion to his own daring exploits—a proof that associated with true valor is a modesty as honorable as it is in striking contrast with the bombastic displays which belong to the North.[5]

The relative calm that Semmes found at the *Alabama*'s anchorage was deceptive, for the raider's arrival had occasioned great excitement at Port Royal. Not only was she a *British* ship—constructed in Britain and sailed by Britons—but she had just sunk an enemy warship and had prisoners to prove it. These had scarcely been landed when the raider was inundated by a host of local officials and citizens. In Sinclair's recollection, at no time during his two years on the *Alabama* was there as much confusion on board as in Kingston.[6] As much to clear the decks as anything, Kell sent the crew off on liberty by watches.

When it was time for a new group to go ashore, there was, of course, no sign of the first liberty men. From bar to brothel, the officers of the *Alabama* sought to coax their drunken crewmen back to the ship. Sinclair quoted one madam as saying, "Tell 'Old Beeswax,' your old piratical skipper, to go to sea, burn some more Yankee ships, and come back. We'll give up the boys then, and you shall have your turn."[7] By paying off the brothel keepers the *Alabama*'s officers were able to buy some cooperation in getting their sailors back. But they had to call on the local police for assistance as well.

Somehow, Kell had managed to coal the ship and to repair the superficial damage that had been inflicted by the *Hatteras*'s thirty-two-pounders. But seven of the *Alabama*'s crew had deserted and were nowhere to be found. Many would not be missed, but the matter of the ship's paymaster, Clarence Yonge, was serious. Yonge had been sent ashore with £400 to pay some bills, but Kell heard reports from the waterfront that the paymaster was spending ship's funds on drink and had contacted the U.S. consul. Kell ordered Yonge brought back under arrest; one of Semmes's first actions on returning to the *Alabama* was to dismiss the paymaster and put him ashore.[8]

By January 25, 1863, the raider had completed her repairs and was ready for sea. Semmes took her out that night. The morning light found the *Alabama* in the passage between Jamaica and Hispaniola, under sail to the north. That same day the raider took her first prize since the *Ariel*, some seven weeks before. This latest victim was the brig *Golden Rule*, of New York, heading for Panama. Capture of the *Golden Rule* was especially satisfying in that she carried masts, spars, and rigging for a Federal warship, the *Bainbridge*, then at Panama. There being no possibility of neutral ownership, Semmes's decision to burn his prize was an easy one. The next day, off Santo Domingo, he captured another brig, the *Chastelain*. The Boston-based *Chastelain* was in ballast, but the *Alabama*'s prize crew removed her chronometer and $700 in gold before putting her to the torch.[9]

Meanwhile, Semmes was disposing briskly of the disciplinary cases stemming from the stopover in Jamaica. Before the raider's grim-visaged commander paraded a motley collection of sailors, many still exhibiting signs of their recent orgy, including tattered clothing, broken noses, and bloodshot eyes. Some were in irons. The most prominent miscreants were Tom Bowse and Bill Bower, who, after being returned to the *Alabama*, had jumped ship, seized a dory manned by two Jamaicans, and attempted to row back to town. Kell had promptly sent the ship's cutter, manned by five sailors, after them. As the cutter closed the gap, Bowse and Bower forced first one of the Jamaicans, then the other, into the water. The cutter lost ground each time it stopped to pick up one of the swimmers, but eventually Bowse and Bower were apprehended and brought back to the *Alabama*. Now, cold sober, the two sailors faced Raphael Semmes. Their stern captain suggested that they were guilty not only of desertion but of attempted murder:

"Murder!" replied Bowse, with a start of horror, "we never thought of such a thing, sir; . . . it was only a bit of a joke, you see sir, played upon the officer of the cutter. We knew he'd stop to pick [the Jamaicans] up, and so give us the weathergauge of him."

"That may do very well for the murder," I now rejoined, "but what about the desertion?" "Nary-a-bit of it, your honor," again replied Bowse; "we only meant to have a bit of a frolic, and come back all in good time, before the ship sailed." "Just so," added Bower; "the fact is, your honor, we were hardly responsible for what we did that night; for we had a small drop aboard, and then the moon was so bright, and Moll Riggs she had sent us such a kind message!"

The moonlight and Moll clinched the argument, and turning to the master-at-arms, with an ill-suppressed smile, I directed him to turn the prisoners loose.[10]

For the most part, the officers and men of the *Alabama* respected their captain and occasionally feared him; they had little disposition to analyze his command techniques. It is a commentary on the brutality of some of Semmes's peers that one of the *Alabama*'s crewmen characterized his captain as "always kind and polite . . . I think he is a fine and good man."[11] Another wrote his sweetheart in Liverpool, "Captain Semmes (or the admiral, as we call him both fore and aft) is of the opinion that the war will be settled in the beginning of the year," presumably on terms favorable to the South. "In that case," he added, with an eye toward his share of the crew's prize money, "we shall be provided for for life."[12]

One officer who observed his skipper closely was Arthur Sinclair. Sinclair wrote after the war that Semmes knew exactly how to keep himself "near to the hearts and in the confidence of his men," without in any way compromising his position as their commander. Semmes did not appear to pay much attention to developments off the quarterdeck, Sinclair noted, but he overlooked very little.[13]

On January 28 the *Alabama* put into Santo Domingo, showing the Confederate flag in that Spanish colony for the first time. Semmes paroled his prisoners from the *Golden Rule* and the *Chastelain* and put out to sea the following day. There were rumors that enemy warships were patrolling the Mona Passage, between Haiti and Puerto Rico. No Yankees were encountered, but Semmes was not inclined to dally in the enemy's backyard, and he set a course for the Atlantic.

On February 3 the *Alabama* stopped a small schooner, the *Palmetto,* ten days out of New York with a general cargo of foodstuffs. She did not give up readily and for several hours led the cruiser on a chase in which Semmes again tested the speed of his ship under sail alone. In the absence of any claim of neutral ownership for *Palmetto*'s cargo, Semmes burned her.[14]

The *Alabama* was not yet in the major sea-lanes and for several days spotted only occasional sail. Semmes instructed his boarding officers to identify the raider as the U.S.S. *Dacotah,* a Federal gunboat of approximately the *Alabama*'s size, in order to avoid confirming that the *Alabama* had left the Gulf. Not until February 21 did the raider stop another American ship, and then she stopped two on the same day. Master's Mate Evans identified one of the two sail as clearly American, and the *Alabama* overhauled a 1,121-ton New Bedford clipper, the *Golden Eagle,* laden with guano for Ireland. Semmes left the clipper under prizemaster George Fullam and set off in pursuit of the other ship.

She proved to be the bark *Olive Jane,* en route from Bordeaux to New York with a cargo of delicacies including canned meats, olives, and French wines and brandies. Semmes was always interested in varying his ship's menu, but the disciplinary problems in Jamaica made him extremely wary of *Olive Jane*'s liquid cargo. He put Sinclair in charge of the boarding party, with strict instructions that not a single bottle from the prize was to make its way to the *Alabama.* The raider then returned to the *Golden Eagle,* which was found to be a lawful prize and was fired the same day.

Semmes rarely discussed the emotions of the merchant captains with whom he dealt and to whom he delivered life-or-death sentences regarding their ships. He liked them to be stoic and to accept as the fortune of war whatever verdict he decreed; certainly he wasted little time on sympathy. "Well, Captain!" Semmes told one skipper who had led the *Alabama* on a long chase. "So you wanted to be unsociable! . . . Well, never mind, I've come to you. By the way, Captain, you had probably forgotten my 'little teakettle' below, where I get my hot water. No use in running, skipper. Steam will fetch you when canvas fails."[15]

The oceans were wide and the sea-lanes broad. A slight variation in course could be the difference between having a prosperous voyage and becoming the *Alabama*'s latest victim. One of Semmes's officers remarked to a Yankee master whose ship had just been burned, "Just think, Captain, if you had altered your course only a quarter of a point at daybreak we should never have seen you." The unhappy skipper replied, "That shows how little you know about it. I did alter my course a quarter of a point at daybreak, and that's how I [came to] this fix."[16]

Sinclair would study the faces of the mariners who emerged from Semmes's cabin; their "downcast eyes and lugubrious countenance" usually reflected the fate of their vessels. Soon, along the *Alabama*'s rail "may be seen the officers and crews of the burning prizes, conversing in subdued whispers." Aboard the raider there was usually sympathy for those who had just lost their seagoing home. Officers and crew alike admired the cool bearing of the American sailor in the face of adversity.[17]

February had proved to be an indifferent month, with only three prizes to show for the first three weeks. With the capture of *Olive Jane* and *Golden Eagle*, however, the *Alabama* had entered the principal sea-lane between New England and the Pacific. Despite an abundance of sail, for several days the raider boarded only neutral ships. Then, on February 27, she stopped the *Washington*, of New York, with a cargo of Peruvian guano consigned to Antwerp. Semmes accepted a $50,000 bond for the *Washington*, after her skipper agreed to take the prisoners from the *Alabama*'s last two prizes. Two days later the raider captured yet another guano ship, the *Bethiah Thayer*. Because the fertilizer she carried was documented as property of the Peruvian government, Semmes again settled for a bond from her captain.[18]

On March 2 the *Alabama* stopped another vessel, the 1,047-ton *John A. Parks*, of Hallowell, Maine, carrying a cargo of white pine lumber. Her papers appeared in order, with notarized certificates naming specific British residents of Montevideo as purchasers of the cargo. Alas, among the papers was a letter from a New York export-import house noting that the cargo had been certified as neutral solely as a hedge against seizure. Semmes invited skipper John Cooper of the *Parks* to join him for a cup of coffee, telling him, at the same time, that he would be burning his ship. Later, Semmes wrote facetiously that Cooper declined the coffee, "but I am quite certain that the ship was burned."[19]

From the "tollgate" that Semmes established at the thirtieth parallel, the *Alabama* worked gradually south. On March 15 she stopped a Boston ship, *Punjaub*, after a chase in the fog that began at midnight and ended a little before dawn. The *Punjaub* was carrying a cargo of jute and linseed, properly certified as British, from Calcutta to London. Semmes released her on bond, after requiring that her skipper take on the crew of the *John A. Parks*.[20]

The raider was approaching the equator when, on March 23, she added two more victims to her already impressive list of prizes. The *Morning Star* of Boston, carrying British goods from Calcutta to London, Semmes released on bond. The whaling schooner *Kingfisher*, from Fairhaven, Massachusetts, was less fortunate. In Semmes's account,

> We set fire to her just at nightfall, and the conflagration presented a weird-like spectacle . . . amid the rumbling of thunder, the shifting but ever-black scenery of the nimbi, or rain clouds, and the pouring and dashing of torrents of rain. Sometimes the flames would cower beneath a drenching shower, as though they had been subdued, but in a moment afterward they would shoot up, mast-head high, as brightly and ravenously as before.[21]

The six-month cruise of the *Sumter* had demonstrated that the Federal merchant marine was vulnerable to commerce raiders, but the tiny Confederate navy was never in a position to mount a coordinated offensive on the high seas. Once the *Sumter* was cornered at Gibraltar, there was a hiatus of seven months before the *Alabama* struck the New England whalers off the Azores. The Confederates had high hopes for the *Florida,* commanded by Semmes's friend John Maffitt; but, ravaged by yellow fever, she had been forced to take refuge in Mobile during the fall of 1862. As of New Year's Day, 1863, the *Florida* had not made a single capture.

Confederate fortunes took a turn for the better with the new year. On January 15, Maffitt escaped from Mobile and began a cruise that would net him twenty-four prizes before bad health obliged him to give up his command. (Semmes heard of the *Florida*'s escape from newspapers seized from the *John A. Parks*.) For a time, the *Florida* under Maffitt would be as feared as the *Alabama* under Semmes. In January 1863, each captured three prizes. The following month the *Alabama* made three captures, the *Florida* one. Then, in March, the *Alabama* captured seven ships—her largest monthly total since the bonanza of grain ships off New England in October 1862—while the *Florida* burned four others. The two raiders, operating independently, were a formidable pair, and they were soon to be joined by another cruiser, the *Georgia*.

The U.S. shipping industry was on its way to being ruined by the *Alabama* and her consorts. During 1863, 348 U.S. ships, totaling 252,579 tons, would be sold to British interests—four times the tonnage transferred the previous year.[22] In the North, meetings were held and resolutions passed, denouncing Semmes and Maffitt and imploring the Navy Department to do something about the rebel cruisers. Horace Greeley, editor of the *New York Tribune,* was especially caustic, on one occasion listing eighteen vessels that were allegedly searching for the *Alabama* and adding, "It seems strange that the energy and resources of the country cannot result in ridding the ocean of a pestering pirate."[23] London's *Punch* ran a limerick:

> There was an old fogy named Welles,
> Quite worthy of cap and bells,
> For he thot that a pirate,
> Who steamed at a great rate,
> Would wait to be riddled with shells.[24]

If the war could be won by embarrassing the government in Washington the Confederate cruisers were every bit as successful as Jeb Stuart's cavalrymen and John Mosby's raiders. But were commerce destroyers having any effect on the outcome? The answer was by no means clear. The misfortunes of the Northern shipping industry did not carry great weight with the Lincoln administration. And while the depredations of Confederate cruisers forced Secretary Welles to shift some ships from blockade duty, there is no evidence that this move significantly weakened the blockade.

The Northern merchant fleet was vanishing, some in crackling flame, others in a maze of legal documents. But was anyone paying attention?

On March 25, just above the equator, the *Alabama* took two more prizes. Both were from Boston and both carried salt, from Liverpool to Montevideo and Calcutta, respectively. The captain of the *Charles Hill* claimed that his cargo was British-owned, but he could offer no proof. Semmes probably would have burned his ship in any case, but its fate was sealed when Semmes found a letter from her owners urging the skipper to have his documents endorsed as English property, and his cargo certified by the British consul.

The case of the *Nora* was less straightforward. The bill of lading specified that the cargo was the property of a British subject, one W. N. de Mattos, but the information was not given under oath. It is a measure of the aggressiveness with which Semmes conducted his admiralty hearings that he condemned the *Nora* on such a technicality. He transferred thirty tons of coal from her and from the *Charles Hill* before burning both ships on March 26.

"If there was ever a contrast to Raphael Semmes," one author has written, "it was John Ancrum Winslow." Like Semmes, Winslow had stayed in the navy in the drab prewar years, despite bouts of poor health. Unlike Semmes, Winslow, though born in North Carolina, remained loyal to the Union. In the early years of the Civil War he served with Commodore Andrew Foote's gunboat flotilla on the Mississippi, but he did so without distinction. He ran the gunboat *Benton* aground and was himself injured in the mishap when struck by a flying chain. His professional prospects were not enhanced when he was quoted by a Baltimore paper as saying, following the Confederate victory in the Second Battle of Manassas, that it was too bad that the rebels had not bagged "Old Abe."[25]

Inexorably, however, Winslow's name rose on the seniority list, and in July 1862 he was promoted to captain. An officer of this rank would often command a flotilla, but little in Winslow's record suggested that he was qualified for such responsibility. Ultimately, he received orders to travel to the Azores and there to await his command, the steam sloop *Kearsarge,* then undergoing repairs at Cádiz. Winslow arrived in the Azores on Christmas Eve, 1862, lonely, dispirited, and suffering from a painful eye affliction. Not until April 1863 did he take command of the *Kearsarge* and begin cruising European waters in search of Confederate cruisers.

Semmes's most persistent pursuer at this stage of the war was no officer of the U.S. Navy but Secretary of State William H. Seward. In his instructions to U.S. envoys, Seward had long insisted that Confederate cruisers were pirates and as such not entitled to take on supplies of any kind in neutral ports. This was an extreme position— one that the Confederates were fairly successful in countering—but Semmes's bitter complaints about the activities of U.S. consuls suggest that the implied threat of U.S. retaliation against nations that assisted Confederate cruisers was a continuing source of concern.

Seward now seized on the case of the *Nora* for yet another protest to the British government. Writing to Foreign Secretary Lord John Russell, he characterized the construction and equipping of the *Alabama* in Britain as a criminal act. Recalling that the British government had been fully warned of the planned role for the Lairds' *290,* Seward insisted yet again that London take responsibility "for the damages which the peaceful, law-abiding citizens of the United States sustain by the depredations of the *Alabama*." In making the *Nora* the basis for this particular protest, Seward may have deliberately chosen an instance in which the cargo destroyed in a U.S. ship was British-owned. The protest concerning the *Nora* would become a key part of the U.S. position in the postwar negotiation of the *Alabama* claims.[26]

Seven desertions in Jamaica had left the *Alabama* undermanned. The prisoners from the *Nora* and the *Charles Hill* represented a promising source of recruits, however, and the raider's most active recruiters were her own crewmen, who had a personal interest in keeping the ship up to strength. With the officers remaining carefully in the background, members of the *Alabama*'s crew mingled with the prisoners over an evening pipe to determine which ones might be prepared to sign aboard the raider. For those most likely to fit in there was a sales pitch: double pay in gold; grog twice a day; tobacco; and the prospect, however uncertain, of prize money amounting to thousands of dollars after the war. In Sinclair's recollection,

> The bid has been made. Our worthies of the lee-scuppers are lost in revery. They are thinking of the character attached to this lone rover (pirate), what might be their fate if captured, and of other consequences of casting off home protection by the act of enlistment. There is an ominous silence on the group for a while. . . . All at once a concerted move is made for the mainmast, the captain and first "luff" sent for, and shortly . . . we have secured half a dozen splendid specimens of old Neptune's bantlings.[27]

Ultimately, ten men from the *Charles Hill* and the *Nora* signed on with the *Alabama*.

CHAPTER 14

Ruling the Waves

When Semmes took his ship out of the Gulf of Mexico into the Atlantic, he had three objectives. First, he wanted to leave an area that was heavily patrolled by the enemy. Second, he wanted to cruise in a major sea-lane, where ships would come to him without excessive expenditure of fuel on his part. Finally, he wanted to operate near enough to the Brazilian mainland to conveniently meet the *Agrippina* for refueling at their prearranged rendezvous.

So the *Alabama* worked her way south in the early days of spring, crossing the equator for the first time on March 29. Visibility was poor for several days, but on April 4, between intermittent squalls, the lookout spotted a tall ship steering on the same southerly course as the raider. After an all-day chase the *Alabama* boarded the 853-ton *Louisa Hatch,* carrying a cargo of top-quality Welsh coal from Cardiff to Ceylon.[1] Fortune was smiling on the *Alabama* yet again, for her bunkers were almost empty. Although the scheduled meeting with *Agrippina* was for the purpose of fueling, the Confederates had no assurance that their tender had sailed safely to Liverpool and back with a fresh supply of coal.

Semmes had chosen as their rendezvous the island of Fernando de Noronha, a volcanic outcropping some two hundred miles off north-

ern Brazil, in the middle of the sea-lane between North America and
Cape Horn. Fernando de Noronha was valued by sailors as an aid to
navigation but was visited by few ships, for the harbor was poor and
the island itself was a Brazilian penal colony. Fernando promised the
privacy that the *Alabama* required while coaling.

Semmes put George Fullam aboard the *Louisa Hatch* with a prize
crew and told him to follow the *Alabama* to Fernando de Noronha.
The thick weather made for difficult navigation; Semmes, who was his
own navigator, complained that whenever he wished to "shoot" his
position, a squall would come up and obscure the sun. "Such was the
case today," he wrote on April 7, the second day in a row he had no
observation for latitude. He was moved to philosophize: "But I
endeavor to profit by these trials, as they teach me a lesson of humility. What is man, that the sun should shine for him? And then, in our
stupidity, we fail to see things in their true light; all the occurrences of
nature, being in obedience to wise laws, must, of course, be the best."[2]

On April 10 Semmes made out the thousand-foot peak of
Fernando de Noronha, a granite shaft that Semmes compared to the
steeple of a cathedral. The raider and her prize moved to the anchorage, but there was no sign of the *Agrippina*. Nor would the tender
ever appear. The story that later reached Semmes was that Captain
McQueen had restocked his ship as planned, but, becoming alarmed
lest he fall into Federal hands, had sold the *Alabama*'s coal in one
port or another and disappeared.[3]

Clearly, Semmes had done well not to burn the *Louisa Hatch*. But
he had a problem, in that Brazil had followed the lead of the
European powers in refusing to permit Confederate cruisers to offload
prizes in her territorial waters. Once again, however, fortune favored
the Confederates. On the day after the *Alabama* dropped anchor, two
representatives of the governor visited the ship. Their demeanor was
friendly, and they raised no objection when Semmes suggested that he
might start loading coal from his prize in their harbor.

The next day, Semmes and Dr. Galt—newly promoted to paymaster in place of the renegade Yonge—made an official call on
Governor Sebastião José Basilio Pyrrho. Semmes found the governor
"a thin, spare man . . . of sprightly manners and conversation." They
arrived just as the governor and his entourage were sitting down to a
late breakfast of roast meats, breadfruit, and various tropical delights,
and the two callers were pressed to join the party. Semmes was very
much taken with the blond teenage daughter of one German-speak-
ing guest.

The occasion took on a comic-opera quality when the governor explained to Semmes and Galt that his guests were in fact convicted felons in his charge. The German with whom Semmes had been speaking, he explained, was no common criminal but a gentleman "who, in a moment of weakness, had signed another gentleman's name to a check for a considerable amount."[4] Wine and cigars appeared, after which the governor led his guests on a horseback tour of his little dominion. "We passed within a stone's throw of the Peak," Semmes wrote, "and were more struck than ever with the grandeur of its proportions and the symmetry of its form."[5]

Back at the harbor, however, the transfer of coal from the *Hatch* to the *Alabama* was proceeding slowly under the oppressive equatorial sun. No job on the cruiser was more disagreeable than that of coaling. By the time it was done, a layer of coal dust covered the decks and bulwarks; it even seeped into cabins, storage areas, and crew's quarters below. The coaling at Fernando de Noronha took five days, but Semmes used the time to stock up on other provisions as well. Despite the high prices for fresh vegetables, Semmes believed that his crew had been too long on a salt diet, and he filled his ship's larder with antiscorbutics.

On April 15, just as coaling was completed, two whaling ships appeared offshore. The skipper of each came to the harbor in his whaleboat, apparently to barter for supplies, and each made for the *Louisa Hatch*. Neither the *Alabama* nor her prize was showing any colors, but Fullam, from the deck of the *Hatch,* chatted easily with the two skippers in their boats. The two captains identified their ships as the *Lafayette* and the *Kate Cory*. When one of them asked about the bark nearby—the *Alabama*—Fullam told them not to worry; she was a Brazilian packet that had just delivered convicts to the island. Suddenly, both captains broke off the conversation, crying out "Stern all!" and "Double-quick!" They had simultaneously spotted a Confederate flag spread out to dry on one of the *Hatch*'s booms.[6]

The two skippers' carelessness was about to cost them their ships. Semmes had gotten up steam as soon as he spotted the whalers, and now he began maneuvering the *Alabama* out of the harbor. He judged the two Yankees to be four or five miles offshore, and thus beyond the protection afforded by the marine league. The two ships were easy prey. Semmes burned the *Lafayette*—the second ship of that name to be captured by the *Alabama*—but for a time spared the *Cory,* with a view toward using her for his prisoners. Then a

Brazilian schooner appeared and Semmes was able to persuade her skipper to take over his prisoners in return for some provisions. This arrangement left Semmes free to burn both the *Cory* and the *Louisa Hatch,* which by then had been thoroughly plundered. Four recruits from the *Louisa Hatch* brought the *Alabama*'s complement up to full strength for the first time.[7]

The raider left Fernando de Noronha on April 19, after the governor had presented Semmes with a fine turkey, and his wife had sent him a bouquet of roses. For all the bonhomie, Governor Basilio was concerned about the extent to which Semmes was taking advantage of his hospitality, and not without reason. By the time the *Florida* stopped at the island two weeks after the *Alabama*'s layover, Basilio had been replaced and the reception accorded the *Florida* was decidedly hostile.[8]

Although Semmes was uneasy about the missing *Agrippina* and concerned about leaks in the *Alabama*'s steam tubes, he was optimistic about the cruise. He was looking forward to working the sealanes off Brazil, which he had been unable to do in the *Sumter*. He noted in his journal that the ship's progress out of the equatorial heat and into the southeast tradewinds "had an electric effect upon my people."[9]

In the small hours of April 24, the *Alabama* reversed course to pursue a whaling bark, the *Nye,* carrying five hundred barrels of whale oil. After capturing and burning her, Semmes noted that she was his sixteenth whaler; he had exceeded the number Commodore David Porter had taken on his famous cruise in the *Essex* during the War of 1812.[10] Two days later, on April 26, the raider stopped another American ship, the 699-ton *Dorcas Prince,* carrying coal from New York to Shanghai. Semmes had no room for her coal, and the newspapers she carried were more than a month old. He took her twenty-man complement on board the raider and put her to the torch.[11]

When three unproductive days followed, Semmes concluded that he was too far out to sea and set a course for the waters off Bahia, present-day Salvador. There, on May 3, he captured two American ships, the 483-ton *Union Jack,* bound from New York to Shanghai, and a 973-ton Boston clipper, the *Sea Lark,* bound for San Francisco. By Confederate estimates, *Sea Lark* was the most valuable vessel destroyed by the *Alabama*; because of her varied cargo, Kell estimated her value at $550,000.[12] There was no attempt to disguise ownership, and the *Alabama*'s boarding party spent the better part of a day in looting the clipper before burning her.

The *Union Jack,* too, was carrying U.S. cargo, but she posed problems to Semmes. First, she carried a number of passengers, including three women and two children. One of the women was a "stewardess" to the skipper, Charles P. Weaver—a category of passenger of whom Semmes was quite disdainful. In the case of Captain Weaver's companion, his attitude was fully reciprocated; she was so reluctant to board the *Alabama* that the Confederates had to tie her into a boatswain's chair to get her aboard the raider. Once on the *Alabama,* the feisty Irishwoman, whose name is lost to history, marched up to Semmes and denounced him as a pirate. This was one charge for which Semmes would never stand still; when the woman refused to stop her tirade, he ordered that she be doused with water—perhaps the only time he treated a prisoner so roughly.[13] The episode must have been distasteful to the Alabamian, for he failed to mention it in either his journal or his postwar memoir. Soon, his normal chivalry was again in evidence. When one of the women from the *Union Jack* complained to Sinclair that her opera glasses had been among nautical instruments appropriated from the ship, Sinclair spoke to Semmes and the glasses were returned.[14]

The burning of the *Sea Lark* and the *Union Jack* coincided with one of the high-water marks of Confederate arms: Lee's great victory at Chancellorsville on May 3, 1863. It would be weeks before Semmes knew either of the victory or of the subsequent death of General Stonewall Jackson, but Semmes's own labors for the Confederate cause were impressive. In eight months at sea, the *Alabama* had sunk one Union warship and burned thirty-seven merchantmen, the latter with an estimated total value of some $2.5 million—ten times the purchase price of the *Alabama.*

Now, with eighty-four prisoners on his ship, Semmes set a course for Bahia. There he discharged his prisoners, but was annoyed to encounter a representative of the provincial president who charged the *Alabama* with violations of Brazil's neutrality while at Fernando de Noronha. The specific charges were that Semmes had used the island as a base from which to pursue enemy ships and that he had burned the two American whalers within Brazil's territorial waters. Curiously, there was no mention of the Confederates' leisurely plundering of the *Louisa Hatch,* which was a violation of international law that even Semmes would have had trouble refuting. Addressing the points raised by the Brazilians, Semmes replied that his objective in stopping at Fernando de Noronha had been to supply his ship, not to use the island as a base, and that the appearance of two U.S. vessels off the island had been fortuitous. He then insisted that he had taken special care to burn the *Louisa Hatch* and the *Kate Cory* outside the marine league.[15]

Semmes's reply had a ring of authority, and the *Alabama* was promised the normal courtesies due a belligerent warship. A British merchant hosted a great ball for her officers, at which, Sinclair recalled, they "danced and flirted" until the small hours of the morning. The crew once again took shore leave in shifts and once again disgraced themselves. When Semmes called on the provincial president, the latter remarked that the *Alabama*'s crew had been behaving very badly. Semmes sadly agreed, adding that his excellency would oblige him by arresting and jailing the rioters.[16]

The following morning Semmes learned that an unidentified warship had entered the harbor during the night. He ordered that the *Alabama* hoist Confederate colors and was delighted when the stranger did the same. The new arrival was the *Georgia*, commanded by William L. Maury, the newest addition to the Confederate commerce raiders. For the first and only time, the Confederacy had three cruisers at sea.

Bahia was the scene of a warm reunion. Semmes had known William Maury before the war—he was a cousin of the renowned Matthew Maury—and one of the *Georgia*'s officers, Robert Chapman, had served under Semmes on the *Sumter*. As usual, the local British colony did all it could to make the Confederates welcome. The owners of a railroad hosted an excursion into the countryside, featuring the best of food and drink. Semmes's only problem was the nervousness of the local authorities, unhappy at finding not one but two Confederate cruisers on their doorstep. Prodded by the U.S. consul, the provincial president for a time refused coal to the *Georgia* and sent a letter to Semmes urging that the *Alabama* move on. Semmes replied that his ship was not yet ready and sent off another division of his crew on liberty. At about this time, a telegram from Pernambuco announced the arrival at that Brazilian port of a third Confederate cruiser, the *Florida*. In Sinclair's words, "We can straighten up now and . . . boast of the 'Confederate squadron of the South American station.'"[17]

Semmes, the senior of the two Confederate captains in Bahia, told Maury that he planned to leave on May 21 and that because they were both headed south, Maury should allow the *Alabama* a day's head start to increase their range of search. Before the *Alabama* departed she took 528 pounds of powder from the *Georgia*, doubtless on Semmes's initiative.[18] Because the *Alabama* had been involved in only the brief engagement with the *Hatteras* up to that time, and firing practice had been rare, the *Alabama*'s powder supply should not have been badly depleted. Semmes's requisition suggests that he may have been anticipating problems with his powder—problems that would prove critical a year later.

The *Alabama* headed south under sail. Once again Semmes was homesick, as each hour took the raider farther from his embattled homeland. "I am now two long years and more absent from my family," he wrote in his journal, "and there are no signs of an abatement of the war." He wondered whether anything short of an invasion would bring the North to terms, "unless, indeed, it be the destruction of their commerce, and for this I fear we are as yet too weak."[19]

Semmes probably had received personal mail at Jamaica and possibly again at Bahia; the practice of most naval officers was to encourage relatives to write to them at a number of plausible ports of call. Semmes had known before sailing on the *Sumter* that his wife and daughters planned to live with Anne's family in Cincinnati. He may or may not have heard of her subsequent problems. As reports of the *Sumter*'s operations had filtered back to the North, Anne's position had become increasingly uncomfortable. Newsboys sold fake "extras" under her window, proclaiming the capture of the "pirate" Semmes.[20] Her correspondence came under surveillance by Federal authorities.[21] If any of her husband's letters were intercepted, however, the authorities would have learned little, for Semmes was a very discreet correspondent.

General John A. Dix, a prominent New York politician, was commander of a military district in the North. On March 4, 1862, he wrote to George Pendleton, an Ohio congresssman, about Anne Semmes, describing her situation as "a very unpleasant one," and noting that she wanted to go south. Dix thought not only that she should be allowed to depart but that she should be forced to go, to share the privations that secession had brought to the country.[22] But the mills ground slowly. Federal authorities at first urged Anne Semmes to move to the Confederacy, then refused permission.

A year later, General Horatio G. Wright, commander of the Department of the Ohio, abruptly ordered Anne to go south. She and her daughters were escorted to Baltimore and moved from there by boat to City Point, Virginia, on the James River. They crossed into the Confederacy under a flag of truce in April 1863 and proceeded to

Richmond. When Belle Boyd, the fabled "rebel spy," was released from a Northern prison and allowed to go south, she wrote from Richmond in the fall of 1863 that Mrs. Semmes had treated her "with as much attention as though I had been her own daughter."[23]

Anne Semmes had been opposed to secession and, at least initially, to her husband's siding with the Confederacy. But she was a loyal wife, and the harassment to which she was exposed in Cincinnati appears to have strengthened her commitment to the Southern cause. The circumstances of her travel south added insult to injury: She was required to pay for her transportation from Cincinnati to City Point, and some medicines in her effects were confiscated as contraband. Anne Semmes, the tepid secessionist, arrived in Richmond a dedicated Confederate.

All three of the Semmes boys were in Confederate service. Young Raphael had been only twelve when the war began, but out of deference to his father, the age requirement for midshipmen was waived and he was sent to the training ship *Patrick Henry*.[24] Spencer, the oldest, was a staff officer with the Army of the Tennessee. Oliver, twenty-four, had been commanding an artillery battery in General Richard Taylor's army when he was captured in a skirmish in southwest Louisiana. He and about fifty other prisoners were being transferred by boat from Fortress Monroe to a Northern prison when a group led by Oliver overcame the guards and conned the boat to a landing in southeast Virginia. The escaped Confederates made their way to Richmond after a three-week trek through the Dismal Swamp.[25]

On the night of May 26 the *Alabama* spied a rakish-looking vessel that led the raider on an extended chase. Semmes refused to use his engines, but—his pride thoroughly engaged—he supervised the pursuit. Midnight brought a change of watch, but the quarry was as far away as before; the change of watch at 4:00 A.M. saw no lessening of the gap. Semmes was on deck all night, but at first light he turned command over to Kell and went below. A couple of hours later he heard a gun and then received a report. The ship they had chased all night was Dutch!

For the most part, however, hunting was good. Four days out of Bahia the *Alabama* captured a New York–based ship, the *S. Gildersleeve*, carrying coal to Calcutta. Although her cargo was said to be British-owned, Semmes found the documentation defective and condemned her. As Semmes was dealing with the *Gildersleeve*, his lookout reported another ship close by. The latter turned out to be the small bark *Justina,* American but with a neutral cargo. Semmes took a bond for just $7,000, but obliged her master to take his prisoners from the *Gildersleeve.*[26]

Not since encountering the string of grain ships off New England had the *Alabama* had such an easy time. Her officers marveled at the absence of any enemy vessel off the "bulge" of Brazil, but none appeared, and the *Florida* and *Georgia* also were making easy captures along the sea-lanes between North America and Cape Horn. The *Alabama*'s foray into the Gulf of Mexico had led Welles to send some additional ships to the Gulf, but he did little to interfere with Confederate cruisers off Brazil.

What little he did came to naught. Charles Wilkes, commanding the West Indian squadron, was responsible for maintenance of the blockade and the pursuit of Confederate cruisers. But he spent much of his time bickering with British colonial authorities, and he was as impetuous in 1863 as when he had boarded the *Trent* two years before. Through some channel, Secretary Welles had heard in March that the *Alabama* would shortly be stopping at Fernando de Noronha. (Given Semmes's secrecy with regard to his movements, Welles's source may have been the garrulous Captain McQueen of the *Agrippina,* the one person whom Semmes was obliged to take into his confidence.) In any case, Welles dispatched a powerful side-wheeler, the *Vanderbilt,* to patrol the waters off Brazil, only to have Wilkes commandeer her as his flagship.

This left only one U.S. warship—the U.S.S. *Mohican*—pursuing three Confederate raiders in the South Atlantic. The Federal warship was active, missing the *Florida* by a week at Pernambuco and arriving at Bahia three days after the *Alabama* had departed. But one ship was not enough. When, in May, the marine insurance companies of New York City complained bitterly to Welles of the *Alabama*'s captures in the South Atlantic, the navy secretary had all the reason he needed to relieve Wilkes for diverting the *Vanderbilt.* "I, of course, shall be abused for the escape of the *Alabama,*" lamented Welles, "by those who know nothing of the misconduct of Wilkes."[27]

Whatever Welles's problems, Semmes was astonished that the U.S. Navy made no serious effort to impede his operations off Brazil. Although Semmes sought to mislead his pursuers, his ability to do so was limited. His captures were reported, and from them it should have been possible to anticipate his probable courses of action. The seas were wide, but they were not infinite. Semmes wrote after the war,

If Mr. Welles had stationed a heavier and faster ship than the *Alabama*—and he had a number of heavier and faster ships— at the crossing of the 30th parallel; another at or near the equator . . . and a third off Bahia, he must have driven me off or greatly crippled me in my movements. A few more ships in the other chief highways, and his commerce would have been pretty well protected.[28]

In the absence of such dispositions, Semmes was able to stay a jump ahead of any pursuers. After discharging prisoners from one of his prizes, he would calculate how long it would take for their reports to reach Washington and for a ship to be dispatched to the place where the *Alabama* was last reported. By then, of course, the raider would be long gone.

In the small hours of May 29 the *Alabama*'s lookout reported a distant sail in the moonlight. After a four-hour chase the raider fired a warning shot that was ignored; a second shot, however, brought her to. The *Alabama*'s forty-ninth victim was the 1,074-ton *Jabez Snow,* of Rockport, Maine, carrying coal and cordage to Montevideo. Semmes disavowed her master's claim to be carrying neutral cargo because the affidavits in question had not been executed under oath. He was pleased to find several letters on board that alluded to weakness in the maritime economy; he was less pleased to find that the *Jabez Snow*'s master had on board a woman described as a "chambermaid." Semmes wrote prudishly in his journal, "These shameless Yankee skippers make a common practice of converting their ships into brothels, and taking their mistresses to sea with them."[29]

Three days later the *Alabama* was, in Semmes's term, "standing leisurely across the great highway" when the lookout spotted sail. After a long chase the raider halted the bark *Amazonian,* of Boston, bound for Montevideo. The documents alleged that the prize's varied cargo was French-owned, but Semmes was not persuaded and ordered the *Amazonian* burned. The following day he stopped an English brigantine and persuaded her skipper, in return for a captured chronometer, to take over the *Alabama*'s forty-one prisoners.[30]

On June 5 the raider captured a 1,237-ton clipper, *Talisman,* bound for Shanghai. Her principal cargo was coal, but she also had on board four twelve-pounder cannon, and Semmes relieved her of two of them before burning the ship. The following day he stopped a ship whose lines showed her to be American, only to find that she had a British crew and in fact had been sold to British owners.

Semmes grumbled in his journal that although a prize court might conclude that the transfer had been only nominal, he could not burn her based solely on this presumption. In time, he would become less deferential.

The *Alabama,* in heavy weather, worked her way south to a point off Rio de Janeiro. It was winter in the Southern Hemisphere, and the crew of the raider wore heavy clothes. On June 16, the cruiser stopped two more American-built vessels that turned out to be British. On June 20, however, she captured a 348-ton American bark, the *Conrad.* Sinclair thought her the most handsome clipper he had ever seen—"new, well-found, and fast."[31] *Conrad's* papers indicated that her cargo—mostly wool from Argentina—was British, but Semmes concluded that the fact that she was en route to New York was prima facie evidence that the cargo was American. Semmes's logic is questionable, for goods consigned by a British merchant might well be British-owned, even if shipped to New York. His decision was a measure of his increasing aggressiveness as a sea lawyer, but then he was eager to get hold of the *Conrad.*

An accepted means of augmenting a cruiser fleet in the nineteenth century was to arm a captured vessel and commission her as a satellite cruiser. The *Alabama's* appropriation of two cannon from the *Talisman,* followed by her capture of the speedy *Conrad,* were an invitation for Semmes to try his hand at this tactic. He wrote in his journal on June 21,

> Today I commissioned the prize bark *Conrad* as a Confederate States cruiser and tender to this ship, under the name of the *Tuscaloosa.* . . . We supplied her with the 2 brass 12-pounder rifled guns captured from the *Talisman,* 20 rifles, 6 revolvers, ammunition, etc. . . . At 5 p.m. Lieutenant Commanding Low hoisted his flag, firing a gun simultaneously, and cheered. We hoisted our colors and cheered in reply, and shortly afterwards the two vessels separated. May the *Tuscaloosa* prove a scourge to Yankee commerce![32]

To command the *Tuscaloosa,* Semmes chose English-born John Low, who had been living in Savannah in 1861 when he was recruited by James Bulloch for the Confederate navy. Low had followed Bulloch to Britain, made a trip through the blockade on the blockade runner *Fingal,* and ultimately was assigned to the *Alabama.* There he shared with George Fullam the responsibilities of principal boarding officer. Semmes regarded Low as an excellent seaman, and he was a natural choice to command the *Tuscaloosa*. Semmes provided him with three officers and eleven sailors and directed him to cruise between Brazil and South Africa and to meet the *Alabama* at Cape Town in September. For all the effort Semmes put into manning and equipping his consort, the *Tuscaloosa* was to prove a disappointment as a raider and a source of continuing concern to Semmes.

One of the few advantages the Confederacy enjoyed in the Civil War was the fact that it was fighting a defensive war. It aspired to no Northern territory and fought only for the right to secede. Whatever plan the Davis administration might claim to be following, its actual strategy was to inflict such losses on the North as to force the North to quit. An active peace movement in the North, one with close ties to the Democratic party, was a constant source of encouragement to Richmond.

The early months of 1863 brought mixed military results for the Confederacy—reverses along the Mississippi to balance Lee's string of victories in the East. But the peace movement was growing in the North, and the possibility of foreign intervention on behalf of the Confederacy could not yet be dismissed. Thus, June 1863 represented the last time in which a Confederate victory was a reasonable prospect. As Lee marched his army into Pennsylvania, the tiny Confederate navy did its bit to add to war weariness in the North. Of the approximately 220 ships captured by Confederate cruisers during the war, seventy-two—more than 30 percent—were taken in the crucial first half of 1863. The *Alabama* alone captured twenty-six of the seventy-two.[33]

Ultimately, this naval effort was wasted. Semmes would write in his memoirs that at the outset of the war the North could not comprehend the threat posed by Confederate commerce raiders, and when the threat materialized the North was "too deeply engaged in the contest to heed it." In a strategic sense Semmes was correct, for the North never allowed the targeting of its merchant marine, and the resulting sale of U.S. ships to neutral owners, to influence its war aims. But the Confederate cruisers nevertheless had an impact beyond their numbers. In January 1863, for instance, Secretary Welles wrote to Admiral Samuel F. Du Pont that the blockade had been seriously weakened by the detachment of Federal cruisers to pursue the *Alabama* and the *Florida*.[34]

Moreover, Washington could not ignore the panic in shipping circles caused by the Confederate raiders. Lacking confidence in the navy's ability to deal with the *Alabama* and the *Florida,* New York's chamber of commerce and Boston's board of trade urged the government to license privateers to go after them. This recommendation, in turn, triggered a round of fighting within Lincoln's cabinet. Secretary of State Seward favored the commissioning of privateers, not because he saw them as any threat to Confederate cruisers but because they represented an implied threat to Britain, should that nation permit the sale of any more warships to the Confederacy. The ever-suspicious Welles, in contrast, was certain that Seward and his friends only wanted to seize prizes that otherwise would fall to the U.S. Navy.

In March 1863, to Welles's dismay, Congress passed a bill that authorized the president to commission privateers. Seward warned the British minister that the construction of any more vessels like the *Alabama* would be an unfriendly act and that unless Britain took appropriate preventive steps he feared for the peace. Ultimately, Lincoln declined to commission any privateers, but London was put on notice that any conflict with the United States would be costly to the British merchant marine.[35]

CHAPTER 15

"Daar Kom die *Alabama*"

The *Conrad*—captured on June 20, 1863—was the *Alabama*'s twelfth prize in her cruise off Brazil and the raider's fifty-second overall, excluding the *Hatteras*. Semmes had made his ship the talk of the seagoing world, but he was about to fall on lean times. Of the *Alabama*'s eventual total of sixty-four prizes, fifty-two were taken in her first ten months at sea—that is, between September 1862 and June 1863. During the following twelve months, the raider would burn or otherwise dispose of only twelve enemy ships, an average of one a month.

There were several reasons for this decline, the most obvious being the "flight from the flag"—the sale of U.S. ships to neutral owners. A related reason was the understandable preference on the part of American exporters for neutral vessels that were exempt from seizure. A third factor was that Yankee skippers were getting smarter; they had belatedly learned to avoid the traditional routes that Semmes patrolled so effectively. A final factor related to enemy pursuit. Although Semmes ridiculed Welles's practice of sending ships to wherever the *Alabama* had last been seen, this tactic did have the effect of keeping the raider on the move and limiting her ability to double back.

There were early signs, too, that the *Alabama* was no longer the fleet vessel she once had been. On June 15 Semmes complained that his ship had become "very dull under canvas," having averaged just eight knots that day. Nor was Semmes himself at his best. Two weeks later he complained in his journal of the *Alabama*'s "rolling and tumbling about, to my great discomfort." Youth, he philosophized, "loves to be rocked by a gale, but when we have passed the middle stage of life we love quiet and repose."[1]

The *Alabama* was then at what Semmes described as "the forks of the great Brazilian highway"—the point where the sea-lane divides into branches for Cape Horn and the Cape of Good Hope. Semmes chose the latter, planning to work the waters off South Africa for traffic to and from the Indian Ocean. After parting from the *Tuscaloosa* on June 21, the *Alabama* sailed on an easterly course. Unfortunately, an inventory of food stocks taken after three days' sailing revealed that the raider had bread enough for only thirty days, forcing Semmes to reduce the daily bread ration to half a pound per man.[2] Worst yet, a second inspection three days later revealed that most of the remaining bread had been damaged by weevils. Semmes put his ship about and headed for Rio de Janeiro, more than eight hundred miles away. He could not sustain his crew on salt pork alone.

When Admiral Porter complained, after the war, of Semmes's extraordinary good fortune, he may have had in mind the capture of the *Anna F. Schmidt*. Four days after changing course for Rio, and after a frustrating run of eleven vessels that proved to be neutral, the *Alabama* stopped the *Anna F. Schmidt*, a Maine-based vessel whose California-bound cargo included a large quantity of bread in airtight casks. Semmes fired her—valued at $350,000, she was second only to the *Sea Lark* in value—but not before confiscating the precious bread. He then set a new course for the Cape of Good Hope.[3]

Shortly after midnight on July 6 the lookout spotted a sail that proved to be the *Express,* of Boston, carrying guano from Callao, Peru, to Antwerp. Captain William Frost reported to his owners that the weather was thick, and that three shots had been fired in his direction before he realized that they were not distress signals. Semmes, writing after the war, recalled that the master had his wife on board, and Semmes thought it sad that she and her maid, having braved Cape Horn, should be carried off to possible new dangers off the Cape of Good Hope.[4] According to Frost, Semmes nevertheless fired the *Express* with everything on board, including his and his wife's clothing.[5]

The month that followed was the most barren of the *Alabama*'s cruise to date. The raider was outside the major sea-lanes, and such ships as were encountered proved to be neutral. Semmes found this situation frustrating, and his journal entry for Sunday, July 26, is an incongruous juxtaposition of the spiritual with the material. After detailing how he had boarded three neutrals that day, Semmes wrote, "I have thus spent a busy Sabbath day, without having time even to read a chapter in the Bible, and all for nothing—one Dutchman and two Englishmen."[6]

The *Alabama* arrived off the Cape of Good Hope on July 28. Not knowing whether the enemy had posted a ship near the Cape, Semmes avoided Cape Town and went instead to Saldanha Bay, sixty miles up the coast. His choice was a good one. The *Alabama*'s officers were pleasantly surprised to find no other ships in an excellent natural harbor. Kell set to work overhauling the raider, paying special attention to her machinery and caulking. The rough South Atlantic seas had opened some of the *Alabama*'s seams, and the fact that the vessel had been constructed of incompletely seasoned wood was proving to be one of her few weaknesses.

Semmes, who had never before set foot on the continent of Africa, went ashore for a stroll on August 1 and met a group of Boer farmers coming to look at his ship. They presented him with a wild peacock, which Semmes likened to an American turkey without the latter's bright plumage.[7] The crew was given liberty, and the relative isolation of Saldanha Bay from the fleshpots of other ports promised relief from the disciplinary problems that had plagued the *Alabama*'s officers in previous ports of call. Alas, not even the opportunities for hunting and fishing in a veritable nature preserve could keep Semmes's sailors from the flowing bowl. After a drunken crewman had threatened one of his officers, Semmes wrote in his journal,

> I have a precious set of rascals on board—faithless in the matter of abiding by their contracts, liars, thieves, and drunkards. There are some few good men who are exceptions to this rule, but I am ashamed to say of the sailor class . . . that I believe my crew to be a fair representation of it.[8]

Semmes was a firm believer in the beneficial effects of naval discipline on even the least promising human material, but the *Alabama*'s crew was shaking his faith.

Meanwhile, his ship was overwhelmed with visitors. The *Alabama* had become world famous. British expatriates had long regarded the cruiser as their own, in part because of her British crew. In Saldanha Bay, Boer farmers were no less interested in the raider, and Semmes's officers passed the time showing visitors around her. The local residents, in turn, brought fruit, game, and fowl and attempted to be hospitable even though most spoke little English. "All day long they came, the men carefully examining the guns, the women shyly examining the officers."[9]

The weather was unusually mild for winter, which it was, in the Southern Hemisphere, and the *Alabama*'s officers took turns going ashore on hunting expeditions. Returning from one such trip, one of the ship's engineers, Simeon W. Cummings, handled his rifle carelessly while climbing into a boat. The rifle discharged, killing Cummings instantly. When Sinclair reported the incident to Semmes, he thought his captain "much affected . . . a tear creeping slowly down his weather-beaten cheek."[10] Although Sinclair may have been carried away in his description, most of the men of the *Alabama* were shaken by the death of a young man so far from home. In contrast to their counterparts in the Confederate army, those on board the raider were unfamiliar with violent death. Cummings was buried with full military honors, the *Alabama*'s boats proceeding to shore with muffled oars and flags at half-staff. The stone erected to mark Cummings's grave became the only Confederate monument in Africa.[11]

Semmes had hoped to meet both the *Tuscaloosa* and the wandering *Agrippina* at Saldanha Bay, but once his repairs were complete he decided to wait no longer. To his considerable relief, however, he met the *Tuscaloosa* on his first day out. Low had had an unproductive cruise, his one prize having been released on bond. Semmes now ordered him to proceed to Simon's Bay, on the east side of the Cape, to refit and await orders.[12]

The *Alabama* was just off Cape Town on the afternoon of August 5 when she spotted an approaching sail that appeared to be American. Calling for steam, Semmes moved to cut her off before she reached territorial waters. The *Alabama* showed British colors and, because the winds were light, was able to overtake her prey at a distance that Fullam estimated by cross bearing to be five miles offshore. Not since the *Alabama* had burned the two whalers off Fernando de Noronha had one of Semmes's captures been visible from shore, but word that the raider was on her way to Cape Town had reached the capital, and many white South Africans were following the civil war in America with intense interest. A reporter for the *Cape Argus* described the capture of *Sea Bride*:

> The Yankee came around from the southeast, and about five miles from the Bay, the steamer came down upon her. The Yankee was evidently taken by surprise. . . .
>
> Like a cat, watching and playing with a victimized mouse, Captain Semmes permitted his prize to draw off a few yards, and then he upped steam again and pounced upon her. She first sailed around the Yankee from stem to stern, and stern to stem again. The way that fine, saucy, rakish craft was handled was worth riding a hundred miles to see. She went around the bark like a toy, making a complete circle, and leaving an even margin of water between herself and her prize.[13]

The *Sea Bride*, a 447-ton bark from Boston, was carrying a general cargo to the east coast of Africa. She would prove to be one of the *Alabama*'s more controversial prizes. Having plans for her but knowing that he could not take her into a British port, Semmes instructed prize officer George Fullam to stand offshore for the time being. From the heights overlooking Table Bay, thousands of South Africans of all races watched the fabled Confederate raider work her way slowly into the anchorage.

Part of Semmes's value to the Confederacy lay in his versatility: He was cruiser captain, diplomat, and propagandist in one. He made a point of showing off his vessel and his officers at any friendly port, and the welcome at Cape Town may even have exceeded that in Jamaica. Gifts, including flowers and fruit, arrived daily. By some mysterious process, the *Alabama* was on its way to becoming a legend in South Africa—a colony thousands of miles removed from the American South, whose people had little understanding of America or of the war that had brought the *Alabama* to its shores. The fact that both South Africa and the Confederacy were dedicated to keeping blacks in slavery or subservience appears to have had little role in the process. A song, "Daar Kom Alabama, Alabama Kom oor die See," which may have originated in the Cape Malay community, lasted into the twentieth century:

> Here comes the *Alabama,* the *Alabama*
> comes o'er the sea,
> Here comes the *Alabama,* the *Alabama*
> comes o'er the sea,

Girl, girl, the reed-bed girl, the reed bed is
made up for me,
On which I can sleep.
Girl, girl, the reed-bed girl, the reed bed is
made up for me,
On which I can sleep.[14]

Aboard the raider, Semmes's faithful steward, Bartelli, posted himself outside the captain's cabin and refused admittance to all unless
they presented a card and were properly announced. Even so,
Semmes wore himself out signing autographs. More photographs of
the *Alabama* and her officers were taken at Cape Town than anywhere else, including a famous photograph of Semmes posed alongside one of his pivot guns. John Kell showed off the raider's Blakely,
telling visitors how its shells had exploded "with magnificent effect"
in the engagement with the *Hatteras*. Semmes wrote later that the
deck of his ship was at times so crowded that the officers could hardly move, but he noted approvingly that the visitors represented "a
generous outpouring of the better classes."[15]

Among the adulation, one reporter provided a thoughtful description of the notorious Semmes:

He has nothing of the pirate about him—little even of the
ordinary sea captain. He is rather below middle stature with a
spare body frame. His face is care-worn and sun burnt, the
features striking—a broad brow with iron-grey locks straggling over it, grey eyes, now mild and dreamy, then flashing
with fire as he warms in conversation, a prominent nose, thin
compressed lips and well-developed chin. . . . He was dressed
in an old grey, stained uniform . . . with battered shoulder
straps and faded gold trimmings.[16]

For all the welcome, Semmes soon found himself in a controversy
over the capture of *Sea Bride*. The U.S. consul made the standard
charges that the *Alabama* had escaped illegally from Britain and was
not a true ship of war. On top of this, he charged that *Sea Bride* had
been captured within the marine league. Fortunately for Semmes,
witnesses from Cape Town backed up his assertion that his prize was
more than three miles offshore, and local authorities rejected the U.S.
protest.

The question of what to do with *Sea Bride* vexed Semmes. Because
she had now been certified as a legal prize, he wondered whether he

could not dispose of her in some way more profitable than burning. His hopes were realized when a local merchant, Thomas Elmstone, offered to purchase the *Sea Bride* provided that the deal could be closed at some location away from Cape officialdom. Semmes agreed to turn the ship over at Angra Pequena (now Lüderitz) on the coast of present-day South-West Africa (Namibia), a part of the continent not then claimed by any major power.

Meanwhile, Semmes needed coal, and to obtain it he planned to go to Simon's Bay, where he had directed the *Tuscaloosa*. Simon's Bay was protected from the winds off the Atlantic, and a gale on August 7 made the prospect of a more sheltered anchorage especially appealing. So it was that on August 9 the *Alabama* rounded the Cape of Good Hope. Approaching her anchorage, she stopped an American bark, the *Martha Wenzell,* bound from Akyab, Burma, to Falmouth with a cargo of rice. After boarding his victim, Semmes realized that he was within neutral waters—there defined as a line drawn from opposite headlands of the bay. When Semmes told him that his ship would be released the *Wenzell*'s master was profuse in his thanks. Semmes replied curtly that he regretted not being able to burn her.[17]

The Confederate captain was not always so abrupt, however. A few days later, Edward Cooper, master of an American bark anchored close to the *Alabama,* decided to query Semmes as to his intentions toward his ship. Cooper's vessel, the *Urania,* was in a somewhat unusual situation in that she was under charter to an Englishman. In Cooper's recollection,

> I announced myself in the privateer's [*sic*] gangway as master of the Federal bark (then the only Northern vessel in port) and desired an interview on business with Captain Semmes. The officer in charge of the deck received me with smiling politeness . . . another officer brought a message from Semmes that he would be at liberty to receive me presently, and ordered that I might be shown the vessel in the meantime.

When Semmes received Cooper, he heard him out and remarked that if the *Urania*'s papers confirmed what Cooper had told him, the most that he had to fear was being bonded.

> When on point of retiring I smilingly asked Semmes if there was truth to the report current on shore that for hoisting the "old flag" so near to his vessel he had . . . theatened to hang

the saucy Yankee captain when he caught him. Semmes almost laughed, and assured me, while bowing me out, that . . . [there was] not the slightest truth in the report, and seemed rather to think the better of me for doing what I had done, as the only Federal vessel in port. "You have no right to any other flag, sir," were his last words to me.[18]

The *Tuscaloosa*, which was waiting at Simon's Bay, represented yet another headache for Semmes. Although the Confederates maintained that she was as much a Confederate warship as the *Alabama*, British authorities were less certain. She had been commissioned without being formally condemned, and her hold was filled with wool—hardly the cargo of a man-of-war. For the moment, however, local officials had accepted her as a warship and were allowing her to take on provisions.

At Simon's Town, Semmes instructed Lieutenant Low to pick up the *Sea Bride* at Saldanha Bay and take her to Angra Pequena. The *Alabama* would meet him there and complete the sale of *Sea Bride* and perhaps of the *Tuscaloosa*'s cargo as well. Semmes spent several days in coaling and in dealing with the usual disciplinary problems. The *Alabama* suffered a record number of desertions at the Cape, in part because of the lush colony's inherent appeal and in part because of efforts by the energetic U.S. consul, Walter Graham, to induce defections.

Although Semmes was a severe disciplinarian, he also believed in redemption. Boatswain's Mate Brent Johnson was a veteran sailor, an artist in scrimshaw, and one of the senior petty officers on the ship. In Cape Town, however, he was court-martialed for threatening an officer with his knife while under the influence. The charge was a serious one, and the verdict of the court was draconian: The prisoner was stripped of his rank, denied all pay and prize money due him, and sentenced to three months' solitary confinement before being discharged. Semmes affirmed the sentence, but he expressed regret at having to do so. A month later he remitted the sentence and put Johnson back on the rolls as a seaman. Three months later he was returned to his rank as petty officer.[19]

On August 15 the *Alabama* left Simon's Town for a brief cruise off the Cape before joining her consorts at Angra Pequena. It was an unproductive excursion—only neutrals were boarded—and the raider now faced a formidable opponent in South African waters, the 3,360-ton, fifteen-gun U.S.S. *Vanderbilt*. The *Vanderbilt*'s veteran skipper,

Captain Charles Baldwin, had anticipated that the *Alabama* would be operating off South Africa and was cruising off the Cape for much of the raider's stay. His ship was both faster and more powerful than the *Alabama,* but consumed coal so prodigiously that she was constantly in need of bunkering.

Working her way up the west coast, the *Alabama* met only neutrals. Seas were heavy, the raider was having difficulty with its water condenser, and tempers were short. Writing in his journal, Semmes again complained of motion sickness and of his protracted life at sea:

> I am supremely disgusted with the sea and all its belongings. The fact is, I am past the age when men ought to be subjected to the hardships and discomforts of the sea. . . . The very roar of the wind through the rigging, with its accompaniments of rolling and tumbling, hard, overcast skies, etc., gives me the blues.[20]

On August 28 the *Alabama* reached Angra Pequena, where the *Tuscaloosa* and the *Sea Bride* were waiting. Semmes had arranged the sale of *Sea Bride* to Elmstone for $16,940, and the *Tuscaloosa*'s cargo of wool to a British syndicate for a sum to be credited to a Confederate account in Britain. The *Sea Bride* was the only prize that Semmes sold during the war. He later reflected that he might have sold some of his earlier prizes in a similar manner, but that his mission was to destroy the enemy's commerce, not to turn a profit.[21]

Semmes had resolved to take the *Alabama* to Asian waters, and with this in mind he directed Low to cruise off Brazil for three months and then to meet the *Alabama* at Cape Town. His theory was that, because the Federals knew that both the *Alabama* and the *Georgia* were in South African waters, it should be safe for the lightly armed *Tuscaloosa* to return to the busy trade routes off Brazil. By this time the *Alabama*'s condenser had broken down completely, and Semmes was reduced to sending the pitcher from his cabin to the *Tuscaloosa* for refilling. Fortunately, Elmstone, the *Sea Bride*'s purchaser, was able to provide the *Alabama* with a twenty-day supply of water from his own schooner.

The *Alabama* had now been in South African waters for a month, with nothing to show for it except the proceeds from the *Sea Bride*. The raider worked her way back to Simon's Town, where Semmes learned that he had barely missed the *Vanderbilt*. On the night of September 11, the *Alabama* had passed a large warship—almost certainly the *Vanderbilt*—so close that officers on the deck could hear the splash of her paddle wheels.[22] The poor visibility and the *Alabama*'s low silhouette had allowed the raider to go undetected.

At Simon's Town the news was all bad. Semmes learned there of the Confederate disasters at Gettysburg and Vicksburg the previous July. "Our poor people seem to be terribly pressed by the Northern hordes of Goths and Vandals," he wrote in his journal, "but we shall fight it out to the end."[23] He lingered at Simon's Town for nine days, waiting for coal to arrive from Cape Town, and once again the *Alabama*'s officers dined in splendor on shore. The local Royal Navy commander, Admiral Sir Baldwin Walker, invited Semmes and Kell to dinner at his quarters and there passed on a warning. Captain Baldwin of the *Vanderbilt,* who had dined with him a few nights before, had said that if he caught up with the *Alabama* he would attempt to ram her. Semmes played with the tips of his mustache but did not appear unduly concerned. He conceded that the Federal vessel was faster than his own, but he considered the *Alabama* too maneuverable to be rammed.[24]

While the *Alabama*'s officers sampled the good life, her sailors deserted in record numbers. By the time Semmes was ready to sail on September 23, twenty men—roughly a sixth of the enlisted complement—were gone. Some would be unlamented; among the missing was the useless Robert Egan, tormenter of the ship's cat. But the deserters included some able seamen whom the *Alabama* would not be able to replace, including Michael Mahoney, the ship's fiddler. For the first time Semmes appears to have misjudged his crew, whose motives were never other than mercenary. Since the *Alabama* had begun her cruise, the prize money due each member of her crew had reached several thousand dollars under a complex formula in which half the value of a prize accrued to a cruiser's officers and men. In the forecastle, the principal topic of conversation was money—prize money—and what might be done with it back in England. Never mind that, in past wars, prize money had been paid only for ships that had been captured, sold, and paid for—not for vessels burned at sea.

However unrealistic these expectations, they had been whetted by the sale of *Sea Bride.* At last they would have something of prize money other than calculations on scraps of paper! In the face of these expectations, Semmes applied all the proceeds from the *Sea Bride* sale to the *Alabama*'s operating funds; there was nothing for his crew.[25] Small wonder that morale on the raider lagged after Cape Town.

On the positive side, the ship gained two promising warrant officers. Baron Maximilian von Meulnier was an officer of the Prussian navy. He and a colleague, Julius Schroeder, were on leave and traveling around the world when their ship was wrecked near Table Bay. The two applied for billets on board the *Alabama* and impressed Semmes with their education and their apparent willingness to fight if the need arose. Semmes gave them both appointments as warrant officers and never had cause to regret his action.[26]

Even with the recruiting of the two Germans, the *Alabama* was short a dozen hands. What was to be done? In any important port, unemployed sailors gravitated to "crimps"—dockside employment operators who provided lodging and liquor on credit. Because the system worked to the advantage of the shipping industry, skippers of ships taking on new hands were careful to pay off the crimps with money from the wages of the seamen they shipped. Semmes had little use for crimps as a class, but when one approached him in Simon's Town, he listened. A belligerent was not supposed to recruit in neutral ports, but had Semmes not lost a score of seamen in a neutral port?

Semmes recruited the crimp's eleven men, whom he characterized as "whiskey-filled vagabonds." Punctilious as always, he accepted them as "passengers" until they could be legally enlisted outside the three-mile limit. It was a poor bargain, but it was the best to be had. On hearing that the *Vanderbilt* had appeared at Cape Town, Semmes went to sea on the night of September 24, hurrying into the Indian Ocean before a fierce easterly gale.

CHAPTER 16

In Asian Waters

For three days the *Alabama* ran east with the gale. Semmes's intention was to follow the fortieth parallel, where the currents would be in his favor. The seas were heavy but the cruiser made good time. Semmes passed his fifty-fourth birthday on September 27, once again away from his family. As usual on such occasions he was moved to introspection, writing in his journal,

> My life has been one of great vicissitude, but not of calamity or great suffering, and I have reason to be thankful to a kind Providence for the many favors I have received. I have enjoyed life to a reasonable extent, and trust I shall have fortitude to meet with Christian calmness any fate that may be in store for me. . . . My dear family I consign with confidence to His care, and our beloved country I feel certain He will protect and preserve, and in due time raise up to peace, independence and prosperity.[1]

In two weeks the *Alabama* covered 2,400 miles under sail, a very satisfactory average of 171 miles per day. There was little traffic, Yankee or neutral, but Semmes told himself that he should not expect much game until he neared the South China Sea. There he could expect to intercept ships carrying rice from Burma and Western goods

to China, often by way of Singapore. In any case, he would demonstrate that Yankee ships could operate safely in none of the Seven Seas!

On October 12 the raider passed the islands of St. Peter and St.
Paul, a navigational halfway mark on the route from Cape Town to
the Sunda Strait. Semmes thought these remote granite outposts the
perfect station for a meteorologist. They were frequently used as navigational aids by India-bound ships, and Semmes thought of lingering
in the vicinity, but heavy weather prompted him to continue toward
his immediate objective, the Sunda Strait.

Off present-day Indonesia, Semmes spoke to the master of an
English bark who told him that a Federal cruiser, the *Wyoming,* was
patrolling the strait. Semmes was not impressed. Two days later, on
October 28, the raider stopped a Dutch vessel, whose master told
Semmes that he had seen the *Wyoming* off the town of Anger in the
strait. In these last days of October the *Alabama* began encountering
merchant ships in some profusion, but all proved neutral. Semmes
was confined to his cabin for several days by an illness that he blamed
on the tropical heat. Nevertheless, he made a critical decision: His
orders notwithstanding, he would seek out the *Wyoming* and fight
her. He wrote in his journal, "The *Wyoming* being a good match for
this ship, I have resolved to give her battle. . . . We will do our best,
and trust the rest to Providence. . . . I shall violate no [sovereign]
right if I assault my enemy within a marine league of one of these
islands."[2]

Semmes's eagerness to take on the *Wyoming* reflected both his
combativeness and his frustration over the disappearance of U.S.
merchant shipping. In preparing for battle Semmes decided to
employ his starboard guns, and he shifted two thirty-two-pounders
from the port to the starboard side to strengthen his broadside from
that quarter. The Federal vessel was commanded by an able officer,
David S. McDougal, but his ship—unknown to Semmes—was in even
worse shape than the *Alabama.* Only months before, *Wyoming* had
participated in an undeclared war against Japanese warlords over
transit rights through the Inland Sea. A joint bombardment of
Japanese forts by British, French, and U.S. warships eventually
secured the right of free passage, but only after the *Wyoming* had suffered eleven hits and an equal number of casualties. McDougal, who
had expected to return to the United States, instead found himself on
station in the Sunda Strait.[3]

Semmes had not captured a ship for three months—the last was
the *Sea Bride*—and he was even more restless than usual. Passing off

his own ship as the U.S.S. *Mohican,* en route to relieve the *Wyoming,* he spoke to neutral merchantmen and milked them for information. Finally, off Java Head, the raider spotted a ship whose lines marked her as American. She proved to be the *Amanda,* bound from Manila with a cargo of sugar and hemp. Although the cargo was documented as British, her papers were not executed under oath and Semmes condemned her. Burned at night, the *Amanda* lighted up the sea for many miles.[4]

The next day the *Alabama* passed through the Sunda Strait into the South China Sea. Semmes made the passage under both sail and steam, with extra lookouts, for he fully expected to encounter the *Wyoming* and engage her. But fortune did not favor Semmes with a man-of-war. On November 9 McDougal had set off for Christmas Island, some two hundred and fifty miles south of Java, to check out a report that the island was being used as a base by Confederate cruisers. Thus, instead of encountering *Wyoming,* the *Alabama* emerged from the Sunda Strait to spot an American clipper ship, *Winged Racer.* The result was the *Alabama*'s fifty-seventh capture. In Semmes's words, "The *Winged Racer* was a perfect beauty—one of those New York ships of superb model, with taut, graceful masts and square yards. . . . There was no claim of neutral property, and condemnation followed the capture as a matter of course."[5]

Semmes was in no hurry to fire this latest prize, for he had made so few captures in the latter half of 1863 that he was low on supplies. Now, as he studied *Winged Racer*'s manifest, he found numerous items, including sugar, coffee, and tobacco, that were in short supply on the raider. The Confederates plundered their prize from 3:00 P.M. until well into the night, while Malay bumboats surrounded both vessels, hawking their own wares of fruit and poultry. The Malays had no idea what Semmes had in store for the ship that was supplying him so generously; when flames suddenly leaped up from the doomed clipper, the local boatmen cast off their lines and pulled away in alarm.

By the light of the burning *Racer* the *Alabama* made her way into the Java Sea, heading north. The raider was under sail on the morning of November 11 when the cry of "Sail ho!" came from the masthead. The stranger's first mate, in a report to the Navy Department, described what happened next:

> On the morning of the 11th November, about 70 miles northeast of Batavia, at 10 a.m. saw a steamer abeam, bearing

right down on us. About twenty minutes after she hoisted American ensign. We ran our colors up and kept on our course. In about twenty minutes more she fired a blank shot, we still keeping on our course. About 11:45, being then about 3 miles off, she hauled down the ensign, ran up the Confederate flag, and gave us a shot. We crammed on every sail we could carry, 14-knot breeze blowing, and dropped her until she got about a point on our quarter.[6]

The 1,098-ton *Contest* was yet another famous New York clipper, and her master, Frederick J. Lucas, had no intention of giving up without a fight. The crews of pursued and pursuer alike became engrossed in a high-stakes race that Sinclair would call "the Derby of the Gaspar Strait." For a time the *Alabama* seemed to be falling behind. Semmes ordered more steam, only to be told by engineer Matthew O'Brien that the engine could stand no more. Semmes then ordered some of the crew aft and moved several guns in an effort to trim ship, but even then the raider barely held her own. Semmes fretted at his ship's dull sailing, but eventually the prize was his:

> As the sun gained power, and drove away the mists of the morning, the breeze began to decline! Now came the triumph of steam. . . . It was not until all hope was evidently lost that the proud clipper-ship, which had been beaten rather by the failure of the wind than by the speed of the *Alabama,* shortened sail and hove to.[7]

Semmes congratulated Captain Lucas on his seamanship and privately regretted that he had neither the men nor the guns to convert the *Contest* into another satellite raider. A number of the *Alabama*'s officers examined the prize closely, having experienced her speed firsthand. Still, her fate was sealed, and at 9:00 P.M. the Confederates put her to the torch. In Sinclair's recollection, Captain Lucas "is leaning against the rail, looking on in silence. His brow is unruffled, and face calm. We will not inquire into his thoughts. He has merited our respect by his pluck, and we know how he must feel to lose such a ship. But he admits no personal grudges."[8]

Semmes resumed his northerly course toward the South China Sea, posting only the standard lookouts, for he no longer expected to encounter the *Wyoming.* Indeed, when the Federal vessel returned to the Sunda Strait and learned of the *Alabama*'s depredations, Captain

McDougal took his ship to Singapore in the mistaken belief that he would find the raider there.

The *Alabama* was once again in an important sea-lane, but all was not well aboard ship. Her officers, halfway around the world from their beleaguered homes, were loyal but homesick. The crew still bristled from having seen nothing of the money from *Sea Bride.* Semmes wrote in his journal on November 13 that he had had yet another row with his "rascals" that day. After he had distributed some cigars from the *Winged Racer* to officers and crew, "the latter threw theirs overboard in a contemptuous manner, whereupon I arrested the ringleaders for punishment, etc."[9]

The first mate of the *Contest,* James Babcock, spent ten days as a prisoner on the *Alabama* and was not impressed:

> Discipline very slack, steamer dirty, rigging slovenly. Semmes sometimes punishes, but is afraid to push too hard. . . . Crew insolent to petty officers; was told by at least two-thirds of them that they will desert on first opportunity. . . .
>
> *Alabama* is very weak; in any heavy sea her upper works leak badly. . . . While on board saw drill only once, and that at pivot guns, very badly done; men ill disposed and were forced to it; lots of cursing.[10]

One of Semmes's skills as a commander was a sense for just how far his sailors could be pushed. Although he continued to board ships in the South China Sea, his goal was the coast of present-day Vietnam, which promised seclusion both to repair his ship and to provide some recreation for his crew. Still, there was little rest for Semmes in these treacherous waters. Sinclair thought that his captain was beginning to show the strain of his third year at war without a home port.[11]

On December 2 the *Alabama* reached Pulo Condore, a group of mountainous islets off the coast of Vietnam. Because they were said to be uninhabited, Semmes toyed with the idea of claiming them for his government as a naval base. But on the day after his arrival he spied a small gunboat flying French colors and from its commander discovered that France had occupied the islands and had stationed a small garrison there.[12] The young governor seemed pleased to have visitors and quickly granted Semmes permission to repair and refit. While Kell put his carpenters to work, off-duty watches were granted alcohol-free shore leave for hunting and fishing. Semmes wrote in his journal, "The crew dined [on bullock] today, their first meal of fresh meat since Simon's Town nearly three months ago; and yet we have no one on the sick list. Causes: good water, temperance, strict government, and, as a consequence, a reasonable degree of contentment."[13]

Pulo Condore represented the northernmost point of the *Alabama*'s Asian cruise. Semmes would have liked to extend it into the northern Pacific—he wanted American shipping to feel threatened everywhere—but the condition of his ship and crew argued otherwise. Both Semmes and Kell remembered their ship's indifferent performance in the chase with the *Contest*. Now, in the bay of Pulo Condore, Kell and the ship's carpenter constructed a primitive caisson that permitted crewmen to clean the ship's bottom from a waterproof compartment below the waterline.

With his refit complete on December 14, Semmes weighed anchor for Singapore. As he approached the British colony he encountered a warship that he thought might be the *Wyoming*, but she proved to be British. The raider entered Singapore harbor on December 21, and the sight warmed Semmes's heart. He counted twenty-two American vessels lying idle in the roads, immobilized by reports and rumors of the *Alabama*! The scene was a reminder of the indirect effect of a raider on an enemy's shipping; the threat of destruction alone kept many vessels tied up.

Although Semmes took comfort from the immobilized Yankee merchantmen, the welcome accorded the *Alabama* in Singapore fell short of that accorded her in other ports of the British Empire. With Confederate fortunes on the wane and the local economy pinched by the slack sea trade, the raider was not received with the hospitality that had marked her calls at Jamaica and Cape Town. The English-language press charged Semmes with avoiding battle with the *Wyoming* or with any vessel of his own size. The editor of the *Straits Times* wrote that, however much the international community might admire the South's quest for independence, it was under no obligation to countenance the Confederacy's "corsair fleet."[14]

While the *Alabama* took on coal Semmes walked the streets of a city he had not previously visited. He admired the Singapore Chinese, whom he found peaceful yet hardworking. "The Chinaman," in Semmes's view, was "born to industry." He considered the Chinese, in many respects, "the most wonderful people of the earth."[15]

One evening a group of the *Alabama*'s officers were playing billiards at a local hotel when they were approached by several American merchant skippers, who invited the Confederates to join them at the bar. For a while all went well, with much bonhomie and swapping of sea stories. Then one of the skippers, whose ship was presumably among those laid up in the harbor, proposed a toast that, in Sinclair's words, "bore on its face an affront"—perhaps a tribute to Union arms. The provocative toast prompted an all-out brawl in which the Confederates claimed victory. Whichever side won the fight, the Southerners did not linger, but raced back to their ship in cabs, one jump ahead of the local police.[16]

The *Alabama* put to sea on Christmas Eve, headed toward home at last. Ten crewmen had deserted in Singapore, but Kell had been able to find replacements for four. The *Alabama* had scarcely entered the Strait of Malacca when the lookout spotted a sail. The stranger responded to the raider's gun, and Semmes sent a boarding party under George Fullam over to her. The ship's papers, all in order, showed her to be the British *Martaban,* eight hundred tons, with a cargo of rice from Burma to Singapore. Fullam returned and reported to Semmes that although the prize's papers were in order, he believed them to be counterfeit.

For the only time in the war Semmes called for his gig and personally boarded a prize. As he examined the *Martaban,* everything about her seemed American, from the graceful hull and square sails to the food—codfish and potatoes—being prepared in the galley. Her name had been freshly painted on the stern; her master, Samuel Pike, seemed the prototypical Yankee. Semmes told Pike that he was going to burn his ship, a statement that brought a fiery rejoinder from the American skipper. The British government, he warned, would not stand for such action. Semmes told the skipper to simmer down; his British registration was clearly bogus.

In his postwar memoirs Semmes admitted to no doubts concerning the propriety of burning the *Martaban.* At the time, however, as flames from the burning ship lit the Malacca Strait, he was less certain. For more than two years at sea he had played a sure hand. Not once, with either the *Sumter* or the *Alabama,* had he embarrassed his government by destroying a neutral ship. Now he had just fired a vessel whose papers showed her to be of British registry, and although the chance of British intervention in the American war was now remote, Britain was one power that the Confederates did not wish to antagonize.

That afternoon he called Captain Pike to his cabin. Placing him under oath, Semmes asked whether the sale of his ship had been legitimate. Pike replied reluctantly, "I do not state this." Had the transfer been made to avoid capture? Pike agreed that it had been.

The following morning Semmes, still worried, again questioned Pike and received much the same answers. Semmes was now satisfied and on Christmas Day allowed the Yankee skipper and his crewmen to row in their boats to the Portuguese port of Malacca.

The destruction of the *Martaban,* formerly the *Texan Star,* had repercussions throughout the shipping community. The "flight from the flag" had seen hundreds of ships change from U.S. to foreign registry to avoid the threat of Confederate cruisers. Were all such vessels now subject to Semmes's whim? His destruction of the *Martaban* was defensible in terms of international law, but was threatening to British shipping interests. The alarm, first manifested in Singapore, made its way to London and brought action by the British government. In June 1864, the vice admiral of the Atlantic Fleet, citing the case of the *Martaban,* would direct officers under his command to capture and send to Britain any vessel believed to have burned a ship with British papers.[17]

The *Alabama*'s captain was showing the stress of nearly three years at sea, but he continued to sow panic among his country's enemies. When a Russian fleet visited San Francisco in the fall of 1863, the city was full of rumors that the *Alabama* had crossed the Pacific and was about to attack San Francisco. The Russian admiral assured Californians that his ships would protect them.[18]

The crew of the raider had just finished their noon meal on December 26 when the lookout spotted two ships at anchor in the strait. The ever-reliable Evans pronounced them American, and Semmes ran up the Confederate flag—probably his first use of the new Confederate colors, consisting of a blue cross in a red square, in the corner of a white field. The *Highlander,* of Boston, and the *Sonora,* of Newburyport, were both in ballast, so there was no possibility of their being protected by neutral cargo. The captain of the *Highlander,* Jabez Stone, clambered up the raider's side and, offering Semmes his hand, remarked ruefully that he was pleased to meet him at last. "I have dreamed of you, captain, night after night; you have been a perpetual nightmare to me for more than two years. Every sail that peeped up over the horizon I conjured into the *Alabama*." Stone asked to be allowed to travel in his ship's boats to Singapore, and Semmes agreed.[19]

Stone's stoicism was a sharp contrast to the attitude of Captain Lawrence Brown of the *Sonora.* Brown considered the capture of his ship analogous to "an eagle swooping down on a humming bird." He was not impressed with either the *Alabama* or her famous captain.

He thought the ship dirty, with some ten or fifteen tons of coal on her deck, and her officers shabbily dressed. He refused Semmes's hand and, in the standard interview in the captain's cabin, took pleasure in telling the Alabamian that his latest victim carried nothing but sand. As Brown later told it,

> My boat was searched, and a quadrant belonging to the mate and other articles were passed up on the deck of this bold cruiser. I asked [Semmes] if we could go now, as it was not safe towing alongside his craft. He said, "You have no water in your boat." I said, "Only that which leaked in." He said, "You hang on to me and I'll tow you toward your ship and you can get some." She was then one mass of flames. I looked at him and said, "I never sent a man where I would not go myself, and that is no place for me." He then said, "You can clear out. You are the most impertinent man I have dealt with."[20]

New Year's Day found the *Alabama* exiting the Strait of Malacca for the Indian Ocean, on a course for home. George Fullam wrote in his journal, "We Alabamians have exceeding cause to be grateful for our almost miraculous preservation during the past year."[21] Semmes, for his part, wrote sadly, "Another year of war and toil and privation has passed over me, leaving its traces behind."[22] For two weeks the raider traversed the Bay of Bengal, the poor morale that had marked her months in Asian waters partly dissipated by thoughts of home— not that anyone on board the *Alabama* had a clue as to where their captain would take them. Still, there was no longer the danger of a run-in with the *Wyoming*. Sinclair would recall this leg of the cruise as one marked by choral serenades in the evening, for which Semmes would bring his camp stool and cigar to the bridge.

> Oh, don't you hear the old man say,
> Goodbye, fare thee well; goodbye fare thee well.
> We're homeward bound this very day,
> Hurrah my boys, we're homeward bound!

There were sea chanties and plantation songs, but the singalong traditionally concluded with "Dixie" and "Bonnie Blue Flag."[23]

The raider was pitching in moderate seas one day when a seaman, Henry Godson, who had only recently come off the sick list, fell overboard from the forecastle. Lieutenant Joe Wilson, the officer of the deck, ordered the ship stopped, a lifeboat manned, and a buoy thrown to the swimmer, but it was by no means certain that the feeble Godson could remain afloat long enough to be rescued. Coxswain Michael Mars, who had fought a shark for sport when the *Alabama* was in the Caribbean, disregarded a warning from Kell and dove into the sea to help his shipmate. Mars, a strong swimmer, reached Godson in time and was the hero of the hour. At the next muster, Semmes, who had disciplined Mars on several occasions, took the opportunity to praise his bravery.[24]

The *Alabama* encountered few ships in the Indian Ocean but on January 14, off what is now Sri Lanka, she captured and burned the 1,097-ton *Emma Jane,* of Bath, Maine, in ballast to Burma. After landing his prisoners on India's Malabar coast, Semmes set a course for Africa. The *Alabama* crossed the equator for the third time on January 30 and ten days later dropped anchor off the volcanic Comoro Islands between the northern tip of Madagascar and Mozambique. Semmes was flattered that even here the inhabitants had heard of his ship. He had planned this as a rest stop, but was amused that his sailors—unable to buy whiskey from the Muslim residents—returned from shore leave early. "My vagabonds on shore looked rueful and woe-begone," Semmes wrote. "Nature had no beauties for them, and there was no liquor to be had."[25]

Semmes cruised off the Cape of Good Hope for the first days of March, but after nine days of fruitless searching he anchored at Cape Town. There he found the same warm welcome he had experienced the previous August, but he had to deal with a vexing problem regarding his satellite cruiser, the *Tuscaloosa.* That luckless vessel had now been seized by British authorities.

When the *Tuscaloosa* had entered Simon's Bay six months before, local officials had accepted her as a duly commissioned Confederate warship. When she returned in January 1864, however, British authorities informed John Low that his ship would not be permitted to leave and might be returned to her previous owners. When his protests proved unavailing, Low paid off his crew and set off for Britain. Once again, Federal diplomacy was proving more damaging to the Confederates than Gideon Welles's navy.

Semmes considered Admiral Sir Baldwin Walker a friend, but he was furious at the seizure of the *Tuscaloosa.* While taking on supplies in Cape Town he composed an extended protest to Baldwin in which he contended that no government other than his own could look into the antecedents of a Confederate warship.[26] Walker forwarded the protest to London, and Semmes would win an empty victory when, months later, Whitehall ordered the *Tuscaloosa* released to the Confederates. By then, however, there were no Confederates at the Cape to reclaim her. At the end of the war, the ill-starred cruiser became the property of the United States.[27]

In contrast to its earlier, extended stay in South African waters, the *Alabama* spent only three days at Cape Town, the minimum time necessary to take on supplies. The war news was terrible: Sherman had devastated Georgia, and Grant was tightening his grip around Richmond. Sinclair thought it time for the South to make peace. Semmes said nothing.

The raider weighed anchor on March 25, steaming slowly out of Table Bay to the accompaniment of cheers and waving handkerchiefs from boats in the harbor. A fast American packet ship, the *Quang Tung,* had just arrived, and Semmes would have liked to capture her as he had *Sea Bride*. But the packet was clearly in territorial waters, and the *Alabama* steamed slowly past her, the U.S. and Confederate flags at one point almost touching, the crews of the two vessels staring at one another in silence.[28]

Once at sea Semmes banked his fires and set course for St. Helena. As his ship dipped into the long Atlantic swell, Semmes brooded over the newspapers he had picked up in Cape Town. The Yankee government and the British press assumed that the South was beaten. Well, he would show them! "No power on earth can subjugate the Southern States, although some of them, as Maryland and Kentucky, have been guilty of . . . making war with the Yankees against their sisters."[29] He grumbled about Britain's apparent switch of sympathy toward the Yankee "victors." Given the state of his ship, however, Semmes felt he had no choice but to make his way to a British or French port where the *Alabama* might be thoroughly overhauled and repaired.[30] The prospect was not pleasant, for the enemy would not be idle while the dreaded *Alabama* was restored to fighting trim. Meanwhile, he told Kell, "should we fall in with one of [the enemy's cruisers], not too heavy for us, we will give him battle before we go into dock."[31]

The raider sailed northwest, under topsails only, to the sea-lanes off Brazil that had proved so fruitful the previous year. Semmes was restless, for he had not taken a prize since the *Emma Jane* on January 14. On April 22, however, the lookout spotted an apparent Yankee and the raider gave chase. After a long pursuit, the *Alabama*'s warning gun brought its victim to. She was the 976-ton *Rockingham,* of

Portsmouth, with a load of guano from Peru. It had been months since the *Alabama* had engaged in gunnery practice, and Semmes now made the *Rockingham* a target. Sinclair recalled that the ship's cabin was badly shattered and that some damage was done to the hull.[32] George Fullam thought the gunnery "excellent," and Semmes wrote in his journal that the firing had been "with good effect."[33] Others, including Kell, were more critical. The master of the *Rockingham* later testified that out of twenty-four rounds fired in ideal conditions, four took effect in his ship's hull and another three in the rigging.[34] The prisoners from the *Rockingham* attributed this to poor shooting, but Kell concluded that one in three shells had failed to explode.[35]

Five days later, still off the bulge of Brazil, the *Alabama* made out a large ship heading directly toward her. Neither ship changed course and neither showed any colors, but Semmes suspected correctly that the stranger was a Yankee. The *Alabama* made her sixty-fourth capture without changing course. The 717-ton *Tycoon* was carrying a large cargo of general merchandise, and the Confederates helped themselves to fresh apparel before burning her.

On May 2 the *Alabama* crossed the equator for the fourth and last time. She encountered heavy rains, but spirits were high, for all hands now realized that they were headed for Europe, if not for England. For six weeks the raider plowed slowly north. On May 12 Semmes wrote in his journal that, "suspecting our fuses to be bad, we got up some shells today and tried several. They all proved to be bad, and so we have commenced to re-fuse all the shells in the ship." Nevertheless, when the raider fired a shell in the direction of a suspicious vessel a few days later, it failed to explode.[36]

Shells were not the only problem. Semmes wrote in his journal on May 21 of a British ship that had overhauled and passed the *Alabama*. "Our bottom is in such a state that everything passes us. We are like a crippled hunter limping home from a long chase."[37] In an oft-quoted passage in his memoirs he would expand on the hunting metaphor:

> [The *Alabama*] was like the wearied fox-hound, limping back after a long chase, foot-sore and longing for quiet and repose. Her commander, like herself, was well-nigh worn down. Vigils by night and by day . . . and the constant excitement of the chase and capture had laid, in the three years of war he had been afloat, a load of a dozen years upon his shoulders.

The shadows of a sorrowful future, too, began to rest upon his spirit. The last batch of newspapers captured were full of disasters. Might it not be that, after all our trials and sacrifices, the cause for which we were struggling would be lost? . . . The thought was hard to bear.[38]

The *Alabama* passed close by the Azores, recalling the raider's first, profitable operations there against the American whaling fleet nearly two years before. Now there were no enemy ships to be found.

During her twenty-two months at sea, the *Alabama* had never visited a Confederate port. Yet she had traveled some 75,000 miles and had overhauled 294 vessels, 64 of which were U.S.-owned merchantmen in international waters. Of these 64, the *Alabama* had commissioned 1—the *Conrad*—into Confederate service, and sold another, *Sea Bride*. Of the remaining 62, 52 had been burned and another 10 bonded. The Confederates placed the value of ships captured at slightly more than $5 million; after the war, in the arbitration of the "*Alabama* claims," her victims would be appraised at some $6.75 million. Along the way Semmes had sunk the one enemy warship to engage him—the only defeat of a Federal warship in single combat during the war. Semmes's record would not be approached by any other sea raider until the era of the submarine.

At the same time, the *Alabama* was about to demonstrate the weakness of all naval vessels: eventually, they must find a port for maintenance and refitting. For a dominant naval power, such port calls entail little more than an interruption in operations. For a weak naval power like the Confederacy, every anchorage is fraught with peril. The threat of being blockaded, either in a home port or in that of a neutral, is ever present. In the absence of a home port, the *Alabama* was now obliged to find neutral repair facilities, at a time when Confederate fortunes were waning and the U.S. Navy was at full strength.

As his ship approached the English Channel, Semmes made a final, fateful decision as to where he would land. His choice was Cherbourg, France, rather than any British port, and his reasons were primarily political. He knew, from the affair of the *Tuscaloosa* as well as from the newspapers, that official sentiment in Britain had turned against the Confederacy. He could not be certain of his reception in France, but he was probably correct in believing that it would be more friendly than in Britain.

On June 10, in a gray morning drizzle, the *Alabama* halted off the Lizard to pick up a Channel pilot. Semmes, who was suffering from a cold and fever, felt a surge of relief at turning over the helm to a pilot and at having brought the *Alabama*'s remarkable cruise to a successful end. He did not realize that his ship's saga was not yet over.

Semmes's boyhood home in the Georgetown section of what is now Washington, D.C. *Author's photo*

Captain Raphael Semmes, C. S. Navy. *Library of Congress*

The *Sumter* escaping the *Brooklyn*, as described in Semmes's memoirs.
Semmes, Memoirs of Service Afloat

Semmes leans nonchalantly against his aft pivot gun in a photo taken at
Cape Town. *Library of Congress*

Winslow Homer depicts the consternation on a Federal ship as the *Alabama* is sighted. *Harper's Weekly*

Artist's representation of the *Alabama*. *National Archives*

A scarce song sheet honorin[g] Semmes and his crew, publishe[d] in Richmond in 1864. *Georg[e] Dunn & Co.*

A different opinion: Thomas Nast's portrayal of "Semmes the pirate." *U.S. Army Military History Institute*

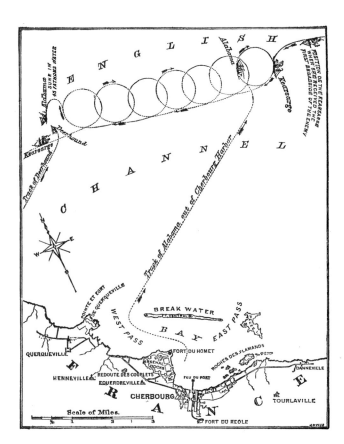

Alabama's last battle, as
rted in 1885.
atury Magazine

One of the *Kearsarge*'s destructive pivot guns in action against the
Alabama. *Library of Congress*

The *Alabama* is abando[...]
Library of Congress

From the right, Semmes, John Kell, and a Dr. Weblin, in a photograph taken in Southampton after the battle with the *Kearsarge*. Semmes is concealing his bandaged hand. *Gary Hendershott Collection*

Mobile, Ala.
May 6th 1870

My dear little God-son.

I have received your nice little letter, together with your likeness. You have grown to be quite a little man since I saw you, and your health seems to be much improved. You are, no doubt, beginning to learn to spell, and, by and by, you will be a "big boy", and go to school; but this will be after you come back from the Indian Spring, where you are going with your papa, who, I am sorry to hear, is not very well. Tell mama she must take good care of papa, and make him well again, so that when you get to be that big boy I speak of, he may tell you all about the "picture book" I sent you, and explain to you how the Alabama did the Yankees. In the mean time, you must be a good little boy, and do all that papa and mama tell you, so that you may grow up to be a man, by & by, like your papa.

Your off. God-father R. Semmes

A letter from Semmes to his young godson, Raphael Semmes Kell. He writes that his father might explain "how the *Alabama* did the Yankees." *Michael Masters Collection*

The Semmes house in Mobile, circa 1930. It is now part of the First Baptist Church. *Library of Congress*

CHAPTER 17

Showdown off Cherbourg

"Look not too long in the face of the fire."

—Herman Melville

At about noon on June 11 the *Alabama* dropped anchor off Cherbourg. Semmes asked and received permission from the commander of the port to land his prisoners from the *Rockingham* and the *Tycoon*. The next day was Sunday, but Semmes nevertheless called on the port commander to request approval to use the French government facilities for docking and repairing his ship.

The admiral received Semmes courteously but hinted that Confederate cruisers were perhaps showing too much partiality for French government facilities—a reflection of the fact that the war had turned against the Confederacy and that France, like Britain, was now eager to distance itself from the losing side. Only the emperor could give the *Alabama* access to French navy docks, the admiral said, and Napoleon III was on holiday in Biarritz. The admiral would forward Semmes's request, but the implication was that there would be no decision for several days.[1]

Semmes, still unwell, returned to his ship to await developments. Flag Officer Samuel Barron, in Paris, was the senior

Confederate navy officer in Europe, and Semmes began reporting to him. He wrote on June 13 that he had money enough to pay off his crew—he proposed to give them "an extended run on shore"— but would require additional funds for repairs to his ship. Semmes did not expect to take the *Alabama* to sea again. "As for myself," he wrote, "my health has suffered so much from a constant and harassing service of three years, almost continuously at sea, that I shall have to ask for relief."[2] Semmes thus became the third commander of a Confederate cruiser to request leave for reasons of health, Maffitt of the *Florida* and Maury of the *Georgia* having preceded him.

On the same day, June 13, Semmes received word that changed all these plans: The U.S.S. *Kearsarge* was en route to Cherbourg and would be arriving imminently. Clearly, Semmes's tour as commander of the *Alabama* was not over. He suspended all plans for leave and exercised his crew at the guns. On the morning of June 14 Semmes and Kell watched through their glasses as the black-hulled *Kearsarge* steamed into Cherbourg harbor, well away from the *Alabama*. Her captain, John Winslow, sent a boat ashore asking French authorities to turn over to him the *Alabama*'s recent prisoners. When this request was denied, the *Kearsarge* steamed out and took up station outside the breakwater.

The 1,031-ton *Kearsarge* was a few months older than the *Alabama,* having been commissioned in January 1862. Both Semmes and Kell had seen her before; she had been one of the three Federal cruisers blockading the *Sumter* off Gibraltar in March 1862. Now, neither Confederate officer noted a slight change in her lines. On the suggestion of his first officer, James S. Thornton, Winslow had followed an example set by Admiral David Farragut in draping chains along the hull amidships to protect his engines. To make the addition less unsightly, the chains were covered with boards, forming a box about fifty feet long.[3]

The *Kearsarge* had spent two years in European waters, the past year under Winslow, seeking but never finding the *Alabama*. Like Semmes, the fifty-two-year-old Winslow was not in the best of health. A disease that navy doctors diagnosed as malaria had nearly blinded his right eye. Unlike Semmes, the irascible Winslow was in disfavor with his superiors, a result of his undistinguished service on the Mississippi and his public criticism of President Lincoln. For Winslow to be commanding only a third-class steamer like the *Kearsarge* was clear evidence that he had been given the lowliest posting consistent with his rank.

The *Kearsarge* had been at Flushing, the Netherlands, on June 12 when Winslow received a telegram from William Dayton, the U.S. minister in Paris, informing him of the *Alabama*'s unexpected appearance at Cherbourg. Was his dogged pursuit of Confederate raiders at last to be rewarded? Winslow immediately prepared his ship for sea, using a bugle to recall his crew from shore. Prudently, he took time to telegraph the nearest U.S. warship, the *St. Louis,* at Tangier, directing her commander to proceed to Cherbourg with all possible haste.[4]

Meanwhile, Semmes had already made a crucial decision: He would fight the *Kearsarge.* His decision was the product of both logic and his own combative temperament.

The *Kearsarge* was the third Federal vessel to have "caught" the *Alabama,* the first two having been the *San Jacinto* and the luckless *Hatteras.* Semmes could attempt to escape the *Kearsarge,* as he had earlier eluded the *San Jacinto* in western waters. There were two channels for ships leaving Cherbourg, and although they were only two miles apart it would be difficult for a single ship to cover them both, particularly at night. Any escape would have to be attempted quickly, however, for the Yankees had doubtless put out a call for reinforcements. But what if the *Alabama* should break out? Her officers were weary, the crew homesick, and the ship herself desperately in need of drydocking. It would be difficult to keep the *Alabama* at sea in her present state, and in any case, to what purpose? Her very success as a commerce raider had made prizes scarce.

A second possibility was for Semmes to lay up the *Alabama* as he had the *Sumter* when that vessel was blockaded at Gibraltar. The *Kearsarge* would doubtless be reinforced within days, and no one could expect the *Alabama* to take on two or three enemy warships. After a period of convalescence Semmes would be offered another ship if one were available, but he would have to recruit and train a new crew for any new command. Meanwhile, the thought of the *Alabama* laid up—rotting away at some French wharf—was anathema to her captain. For the moment there was only one enemy vessel outside the breakwater, and that was the *Kearsarge.* Semmes carried in his mind a list of Federal gunboats too powerful to be challenged, and the *Kearsarge* was not on it.

Semmes's decision reflected a number of other factors in addition to his reluctance to bid farewell to the ship that had made him famous.

One, almost certainly, was the reduced utility of any Confederate cruiser in 1864. Because commerce raiding was no longer profitable, he could justify putting his ship at risk in a way that he could not have done a year or two earlier. Another factor in Semmes's thinking was the indifferent level of professionalism he had observed in the U.S. Navy throughout the war. He remembered Winslow from the Mexican War as a competent officer, but so too, presumably, were Palmer of the *Iroquois* and Blake of the *Hatteras*. The first ship he had eluded; the second he had sunk in thirteen minutes.

The critical factor, however, was Semmes's own aggressive personality. As early as February 1862, in his letter to *The Times* of London, Semmes—then commanding the little *Sumter*—had publicly hinted that he was prepared to take on any enemy ship of his own size. Subsequently, with the *Alabama,* he was even less inclined to limit his activity to the enemy's merchant marine. He had cruised in South African waters almost within sight of the powerful *Vanderbilt,* convinced that if he encountered the Yankee side-wheeler his ship could handle her. Two months later, spoiling for a fight, he had hoped to encounter the *Wyoming* in the Sunda Strait. Now, with the war apparently lost, Semmes could at least strike a blow for the honor of the Confederate navy. He would defeat an enemy warship more powerful than his own, and he would do so in the great theater that was Europe!

Another psychological factor was at work as well, for Semmes was in search of personal vindication. Throughout his three years on the *Sumter* and then the *Alabama,* he had been called a pirate or a privateer. Another man might have shrugged off such canards, but Semmes was hypersensitive to any charge that touched on his honor. Facing an enemy warship that outgunned him, what better way to defy those who called him pirate than to fight and sink the *Kearsarge*? What pirate would deliberately seek combat with a warship more powerful than his own? In the words of one historian, Semmes fought "because he had to and because he wished to."[5]

On the afternoon of June 14, with the *Kearsarge* waiting offshore, Semmes summoned Kell to his cabin. As his first officer took a chair Semmes said abruptly, "Kell, I am going out to fight the *Kearsarge*. What do you think of it?"[6] This statement tells much of Semmes and his style of command. The critical decision had been made; Kell was now free to comment on it. Semmes had rarely consulted his first officer on matters of strategy during their three years together, and he was not now looking for a debate. He went on:

As you know, the arrival of the *Alabama* at this port has been telegraphed to all parts of Europe. Within a few days, Cherbourg will be effectively blockaded by Yankee cruisers. It is uncertain whether or not we shall be permitted to repair the *Alabama* here, and in the meantime the delay is to our advantage. I think we may whip the *Kearsarge,* the two vessels being of wood and carrying about the same number of men and guns. Besides, Mr. Kell, although the Confederate States government has ordered me to avoid engagements with the enemy's cruisers, I am tired of running from that flaunting rag![7]

Kell was not convinced that his captain's decision was wise, and he reminded Semmes of some of the disparities between the two antagonists. The *Kearsarge* mounted two eleven-inch pivot guns, which, while lacking the range of the *Alabama*'s pivots, packed considerably more punch at ranges under a thousand yards. And whereas the *Alabama* had been built for speed, her opponent had the sturdy construction of a man-of-war. Kell reminded Semmes that their powder was defective, as evidenced in the target practice against the *Rockingham,* and that only one fuse in three had detonated properly. Semmes brushed the warning aside, remarking, "I will take the chances of one in three."[8]

Kell set to work to prepare for battle. The raider took on a hundred tons of coal, in part to keep her hull low in the water and in part to protect her engines. The yards were slung in chains, the deck holystoned, and the brasswork polished. Guns, magazines, and shell rooms were carefully examined. To Kell's dismay, several barrels of powder were found to be defective because of exposure to dampness and had to be thrown overboard. He could only hope that the remaining powder, packed in cannisters, would prove sound.

Word that they would be fighting the *Kearsarge* spread like lightning through the *Alabama.* No one seemed surprised at Semmes's decision to fight, and few wanted to miss the battle. The motley collection of wharf rats whom Semmes had browbeaten across the seven seas were eager to risk their lives for a country most had never seen. They worked to a song:

> We're homeward bound, we're homeward
>   bound,
> And soon shall stand on English ground.
> But ere that English land we see,
> We first must fight the *Kearsargee.*[9]

Semmes wrote in his journal,

> My crew seem to be in the right spirit, a quiet spirit of deter-
> mination pervading both officers and men. The combat will
> no doubt be contested and obstinate, but the two ships are so
> equally matched that I do not feel at liberty to decline it. God
> defend the right, and have mercy on the souls of those who
> fall, as many of us must.[10]

On June 15 Semmes penned a letter to M. Bonfils, the Confederate
agent in Cherbourg. Bonfils was to to inform his U.S. counterpart
that Captain Semmes hoped the *Kearsarge* was not at Cherbourg solely to pick up the prisoners discharged by the *Alabama*. Semmes issued
a formal challenge: "I desire you to say to the United States consul
that my intention is to fight the *Kearsarge* as soon as I can make the
necessary arrangements. . . . I beg she will not depart before I am
ready to go out."[11] Ever prudent, he then entrusted to Bonfils's care
the raider's operating funds—some 4,700 gold sovereigns—and the
sixty-odd chronometers that the *Alabama* had collected during her
epic cruise. The flags that Semmes had taken from his prizes stayed
on board.

For three days the *Alabama*'s crew coaled and drilled for battle.
The emphasis on boarding drill, complete with pistols and cutlasses,
convinced many on the raider that Semmes—secretive as always—
planned to lay his ship alongside the *Kearsarge* and board her. On
June 15 a representative of the port admiral asked Semmes whether
his request for coal did not imply a withdrawal of his earlier applica-
tion for permission to make repairs. Semmes agreed that it did.
Although French authorities would not allow either belligerent warship to recruit new crewmen, two of the *Alabama*'s petty officers,
von Meulnier and Schroeder, who returned from Paris to be in on the
fight, were allowed to rejoin their ship.

By the afternoon of June 18, Confederate preparations were complete. Semmes advised the port admiral of his intention to engage the
Kearsarge the following day, Sunday. Was there a touch of the super-
stitious in Semmes's makeup? The crew thought Sunday his lucky
day; the commissioning of the *Alabama,* the capture of the *Ariel,* and
the defeat of the *Hatteras* had all taken place on Sundays.

Even on the day before the battle there was no shortage of visitors.
Several friendly Frenchmen, including the loyal Bonfils, warned
Semmes against fighting a "superior force." Bonfils was so upset that

he wired the Confederate minister in Paris, John Slidell, urging him to forbid Semmes from fighting. Slidell declined to interfere, stating that he had full confidence in Semmes's judgment.[12]

In Cherbourg there was talk of Winslow's having employed chains to protect his ship's hull. Among those who had heard such rumors was Semmes's own secretary, Breedlove Smith.[13] But Cherbourg was full of rumors—the *Alabama,* for instance, was alleged to have recruited sailors from a British man-of-war—and if Semmes heard anything about chains he was undeterred. A last-minute visitor to the raider was Commander George T. Sinclair, a Confederate naval agent in Europe, who had come from Paris to view the battle. He thought the *Alabama*'s officers "jaded and worn out," but wrote of Semmes: "He seemed to have weighed the matter well in his own mind, and determination was marked in every line of his faded and worn countenance."[14]

Saturday night, many of the *Alabama*'s officers attended a banquet in Cherbourg hosted by local Confederate partisans. Responding to toasts, the officers vowed that they would either sink the *Kearsarge* or "make another corsair" out of her—a hint that the result they most desired would be to capture the *Kearsage* and in so doing exchange the *Alabama* for a stauncher and more seaworthy vessel.[15] While his officers exchanged toasts, Semmes slipped into one of the *Alabama*'s boats and was rowed to the town. There, by special arrangement, he celebrated Mass in a small Catholic church. He was back on his ship by 10:00 P.M.[16]

Semmes's challenge had been relayed to John Winslow on Wednesday, June 15. Semmes's sarcasm in asking that he not depart was wasted on Winslow; having pursued rebel raiders for more than a year, the stolid Yankee had no intention of leaving station for any reason. From his position just off Cherbourg, Winslow ordered that his ship's guns be unlimbered, lookouts be alert to any movement in the harbor, and ammunition be readied for immediate action. He ordered special precautions against a surprise attack at night.[17]

In contrast to Semmes, who asked no one's advice on how to fight the *Kearsarge,* Winslow called in his officers to discuss tactics. He speculated that the battle would be fought on parallel lines and that Semmes would seek sanctuary in French territorial waters should the fighting go against him. Visitors from Cherbourg told of comings and goings on the *Alabama*: the loading of coal, the removal of specie, and the sharpening of swords and cutlasses. The initiative lay with

Semmes, for he alone would determine the day and time of the engagement.

On the morning of Sunday, June 19, at about 10:00, the *Kearsarge*'s crew had been inspected and dismissed to attend religious services. The morning was warm, with only a hint of haze. Winslow was about to read from the Scriptures when the lookout cried, "She's coming out, and she's heading straight for us!" Winslow laid his Bible aside and picked up his spyglass. The drums beat to quarters.

Whatever happened on June 19 would take place before a great audience. Cherbourg was overflowing with visitors who had come to see the battle, and some fifteen thousand people crowded along the bluffs that afforded the best view of the Channel. There was plenty of betting. The two ships were screw steamers of about the same tonnage, each powered by two engines. The *Alabama*, with a crew of 149, boasted as its forward pivot the 110-pounder Blakely that was considered one of the most advanced weapons of the day. The *Kearsarge*, with a complement of 163, mounted seven guns—one fewer than her antagonist—but the word among navy professionals was that her two eleven-inch Dahlgrens were formidable weapons indeed. One boat in the harbor carried painter Edouard Manet, complete with pencils and sketchbook; he would convert his initial sketches into a famous painting of the battle. Among others who happened to be in Cherbourg that weekend was John Lancaster, a wealthy English businessman who was on holiday with his family in his sleek yacht, the *Deerhound*. His children had elected to watch the battle rather than go to church, and the *Deerhound* left the harbor early in the morning to find a good viewing point in the Channel.[18]

On the *Alabama*, chief engineer Miles Freeman started his fires about 6:00 A.M. Shortly thereafter, the port admiral informed Semmes that the French ironclad *Couronne* would escort the *Alabama* to sea, to ensure that there was no violation of French waters. Semmes inspected his crew at muster, commenting on their smart appearance in white shirts and blue trousers. Among the officers he spoke to was Arthur Sinclair. "How do you think it will turn out today, Mr. Sinclair?" he asked. The young officer, startled at the question, could only stammer that he was sure that the crew "will do their full duty, and follow you to the death." "Yes, that's true," Semmes replied, and resumed his pacing.[19] Commander George T. Sinclair, Arthur's cousin, was one of the last visitors to the ship. He urged Semmes to keep away from the enemy's eleven-inch guns, drawing from the Alabamian a rare hint as to his battle plan. In an apparent reference to his Blakely, Semmes replied, "I shall feel him first and it will all depend on that." When Sinclair asked that he be allowed to join the *Alabama* for the battle, Semmes demurred. He was honor bound not to increase his complement.[20]

The *Alabama* got under way a few minutes before 10:00 A.M. She steamed past the *Couronne*, which fell in behind her. She approached the breakwater, moving, in Semmes's memorable description, "with the lightness and grace of a swan." As the raider passed a French liner, the *Napoleon*, her crew cheered the *Alabama* and a band played "Dixie."

As soon as the *Alabama* passed the breakwater, her officers could see the *Kearsarge* some five miles away. Semmes pointed directly toward her. Then, calling the crew aft, he mounted a gun carriage and gave a brief but rousing exhortation:

> Officers and Seamen of the *Alabama*!—You have, at length, another opportunity of meeting the enemy—the first that has been presented to you since you sank the *Hatteras*! In the meantime, you have been all over the world, and it is not too much to say, that you have destroyed and driven for protection under neutral flags, one half of the enemy's commerce, which, at the beginning of the war, covered every sea. This is an achievement of which you may well be proud; and a grateful country will not be unmindful of it. The name of your ship has become a household word wherever civilization extends. Shall that name be tarnished by defeat?

Semmes's words drew from more than a hundred voices a cry of "Never!" He went on:

> Remember that you are in the English Channel, the theatre of so much of the naval glory of our race, and that the eyes of all Europe are at this moment upon you. The flag that floats over you is that of a young Republic, who bids defiance to her enemies, whenever and wherever found. Show the world that you know how to uphold it! Go to your quarters.[21]

As the *Alabama* steamed toward her opponent, sailors opened the magazines and shell rooms, filled tubs of water with which to combat fires, and sanded the decks to prevent their becoming slippery with blood. Semmes planned to fight his starboard guns, and to strengthen his broadside he shifted one of his port thirty-two-pounders to star-board. This caused the ship to list slightly, but it also reduced the amount of hull exposed to enemy fire.[22]

Winslow spotted his opponent at about 10:20. He turned his ship away, in part to avoid any infringement of French territorial waters but primarily to deny Semmes a sanctuary inside the marine league should things go badly for the Confederates. About seven miles from shore the *Kearsarge* reversed course and headed directly for the *Alabama*. Winslow's plan, according to his official report, was to run his antagonist down and thus at least cripple her. When the two ships were about eighteen hundred yards apart, however, Semmes turned to port. Were the gunners ready? he asked Kell. When Kell said they were, Semmes gave the order to open fire.

The *Alabama*'s pivot guns opened the battle at about 10:57 A.M. For several minutes only the raider was in effective range, but her shots were high and had no effect except in the *Kearsarge*'s rigging. When the range was down to about nine hundred yards, Winslow reconsidered his plan to close on the *Alabama* lest he receive "raking fire"—a full broadside from the enemy's starboard guns. The *Kearsarge* turned to port and returned fire with her own starboard battery, attempting at the same time to reach a position from which to rake the *Alabama*. It quickly became apparent that the *Kearsarge* was the faster of the two vessels, and that Semmes was unlikely to get into a position from which to rake his opponent. With the range narrowed to less than seven hundred yards, the brief period when the *Alabama*'s guns outranged those of her antagonist had passed.

Naval gunnery in 1864 had progressed somewhat since Nelson's day, with the development of rifled cannon; nevertheless, 10 percent accuracy under battle conditions was still considered acceptable shooting. In the clash between the *Alabama* and the *Kearsarge*, at least fifteen minutes passed before either ship inflicted any significant damage. Then a shell from the *Alabama* passed through the *Kearsarge*'s starboard bulwarks and exploded on the quarterdeck, wounding three members of a gun crew. A few minutes later the Federal vessel was struck again. A 110-pound projectile from the *Alabama*'s forward pivot glanced off the *Kearsarge*'s counter and lodged in her stern post. The stern post—a great, curved timber that anchored the planks of the upper hull—was a vulnerable point on any vessel, and the impact, according to the *Kearsarge*'s surgeon, shook the ship from stem to stern.[23] Had the shell exploded it might have crippled the Federal warship. But it did not.

Almost immediately, the battle began to turn. A shot from the *Kearsarge* destroyed the *Alabama*'s steering apparatus; for the remainder of the engagement the Confederate cruiser could only be steered with tackles. Shells from the *Kearsarge*'s Dahlgrens began to smash into the raider. "The firing now became very hot," Semmes wrote in his report:

> The enemy's shot soon began to tell upon our hull, knocking down, killing and disabling a number of men in different parts of the ship. Perceiving that our shell, although apparently exploding against the enemy's sides, were doing but little damage, I returned to solid shot firing, and from this time onward alternated with shot and shell.[24]

At about this time Semmes reportedly said of his enemy, "Confound them, they've been fighting twenty minutes and they're cool as posts!"[25]

Lieutenant Joseph Wilson—"Fighting Joe" to his messmates—commanded twenty-two men at the *Alabama*'s aft pivot. He was about to fire a round when a shell from the *Kearsarge* exploded alongside the gun, killing or wounding all but a few of his division. Coxswain Michael Mars, one of the uninjured, took in the devastation and shoveled the human fragments into the sea. While Mars cleared and resanded the deck, Kell ordered the crew of a thirty-two-pounder to man the pivot. At one point in the action a shot from the *Kearsarge* cut down the *Alabama*'s colors. They were quickly run back up the mizzenmast.

Winslow commanded his ship from a chest on the *Kearsarge*'s starboard quarter; Semmes commanded, as he had against the *Hatteras,* from the horse block. Sinclair recalled Semmes "leaning on the hammock-rail, at times watching earnestly the enemy, and then casting his eye about our ship. . . . Nothing seemed to escape his active mind or eye."[26] Midway in the action a shell fragment inflicted a painful wound to Semmes's right hand. He called on a petty officer to bandage it but did not leave the quarterdeck.

By now the sailors on both ships had stripped to the waist to work the heavy guns. They were drenched with sweat and black from smoke and powder. From time to time there were pauses in the firing when one of the combatants was obscured by smoke. The two ships were fighting clockwise on a circular track, much of the time at a range of about five hundred yards. They made seven complete circles in the course of the action, reminding one Northern sailor of two flies crawling around on the rim of a saucer.[27] Only steamships could have fought as they did, maintaining a circular course in light winds; the day of ramming and boarding an enemy was past.

William Alsdorf was a loader at one of the *Kearsarge*'s Dahlgrens, and his narrative catches some of the excitement on the Federal cruiser:

> Our 1st Lt. Thornton went along to each Gun telling the Gunners to take good aim. "Don't fire, boys, unless you have good aim, for one hit is worth 50 thrown away." Every man was doing his duty. There was no flinching. . . . Both of our ships were completely enveloped in smoke, but as we were fighting in a Circle we soon ran out of it and then the Shells flew thick & fast.[28]

Semmes was so preoccupied with keeping the *Kearsarge* from crossing his stern that he made no attempt to supervise his gunners, leaving that task to Kell. Unfortunately for the Confederates, the *Alabama* had few experienced gunners. Commander Sinclair, watching from the shore, noted that although the *Alabama* was firing at least three shots for every two of her opponent, she usually fired high. A sailor on the *Alabama* later admitted that the raider's guns were badly handled. "The men all fought well," he said, "but the gunners did not know how to point and elevate the guns." Nor was gun laying the only problem. John Bickford, a loader on the *Kearsarge*, insisted that the failure of many Confederate shells to explode was not the fault of the ammunition. According to Bickford, many unexploded shells still bore the lead caps that the loaders should have removed to expose the fuse.[29] Commander Sinclair noted something else: The smoke from the *Alabama*'s guns was much heavier than that of her opponent, at times resembling heavy steam. The raider's powder had deteriorated far more than Semmes had realized.[30]

After some forty-five minutes of battle, an eleven-inch shell passed through the *Alabama*'s starboard side and exploded inside, collapsing a coal bunker and raising a cloud of coal dust that brought cheers from the *Kearsarge*. Other rounds struck between the mainmast and mizzenmast, near the waterline. Once again the *Alabama*'s colors were shot away, and once again they were replaced. With steam pressure falling and his ship down by the stern, Semmes attempted one last throw of the dice. He ordered Kell to hoist jibs and trysails, to shift guns to the port side in order to raise some shot holes above water, and to point for the French coast. As Winslow had predicted, Semmes was heading toward French territorial waters.

But time was running out. One of his engineers informed Semmes that the water was almost up to the furnace fires. Semmes heard this report over the crash of guns and the shouts of his gunners, then said, "Return to your duty!" Those belowdecks considered this a death sentence, but they remained at their posts.

Semmes now ordered Kell to inspect below, and the first officer was appalled at what he saw. Surgeon David Llewellyn was at his operating table, but the casualty he had been treating had just been swept away by a shell. Water was entering the hull through holes the size of a wheelbarrow, and over the creak of timbers Kell could hear the popping of air bubbles from drowned compartments. He returned to the quarterdeck and told Semmes that the ship could not float for more than ten minutes. By this time Winslow had maneuvered his ship between the *Alabama* and the French coast and was nearly in position to rake his foe. A few minutes after noon Semmes made the most painful decision of his naval career, telling Kell to cease firing, shorten sail, and haul down the colors, remarking that it would never do "for us to go down with the decks covered with our gallant wounded."[31]

The *Alabama*'s final, chaotic moments do not lend themselves to orderly narrative. Although the raider was now attempting to surrender, previous pauses in her firing had been followed by renewed fighting, and the Federals were wary. If Semmes's report is to be credited, the *Kearsarge* fired repeatedly on the *Alabama* after the latter had flown a white flag. The Federals, for their part, charged that the *Alabama* fired several rounds after her nominal surrender and that their ship had merely returned fire.

A few minutes after noon, with a white flag now visible on the *Alabama*'s spanker boom, the *Kearsarge* ceased firing. The once-graceful raider was a woeful sight. There were great gaps in her bulwarks, and several spars were supported aloft only by their wire rigging. The funnel was riddled with holes. The deck had been torn up by the *Kearsarge*'s fire and was littered with the *Alabama*'s own shell boxes. The raider, still under sail, forged slowly ahead, leaving a trail of wreckage and a few bobbing heads astern.[32]

Kell put Fullam and Wilson in charge of the *Alabama*'s two sea-worthy boats, filled them with wounded, and sent them to the *Kearsarge* with a request for assistance. Aboard the Federal cruiser, Fullam looked up and down the deck of the *Kearsarge* and asked about Federal casualties. When told that only three men had been wounded, he was incredulous. "My God!" he exclaimed. "It's a slaughterhouse over there."[33]

On the *Alabama,* Semmes ordered that every man attempt to save himself. Kell urged crewmen over the side, telling them to find a plank or spar. As the ship settled by the stern, a knot of men gathered amidships around their captain. In Semmes's recollection, "One tendered me this little . . . kindness, and another, that."[34] There was no panic. Semmes wanted to save his journals, and Bartelli sloshed through waist-deep water in the captain's cabin to retrieve them. Michael Mars, a strong swimmer, offered to take the books. The faithful Bartelli helped Semmes take off his boots and don a life preserver.

With the *Alabama*'s bow now high in the air, Semmes and Kell were among the last to leave the ship.* The sea was filled with bobbing heads, but Winslow—to Semmes's everlasting scorn—was slow in sending boats to their assistance. John Lancaster, who had viewed the battle from the *Deerhound,* ordered his captain, Evan P. Jones, to save such survivors as he could. Kell, clinging to a wooden grate, estimated that he had been in the water for twenty minutes when he was spotted by one of the *Deerhound*'s boats. "I was pulled into a boat," he recalled, "in which was Captain Semmes, stretched out in the stern-sheets, as pallid as death."[35] A boat from the *Kearsarge* approached within hailing distance and asked if anyone had seen Semmes. Kell, wearing a seaman's cap, replied quickly that his captain had drowned.[36]

Once on the *Deerhound,* Semmes was introduced to Lancaster as the captain of the *Alabama.* The Englishman told him that he believed all survivors had been picked up; where did Semmes want to go? Raphael Semmes was wounded, half-drowned, and shattered by the loss of his ship. But he still had his wits about him. "I am now under English colors," he whispered, "and the sooner you put me with my officers and men on English soil, the better."[37]

---

*According to legend, Semmes and Kell each threw his sword into the sea rather than surrender it to the victors. It is unlikely, however, that either had time for such heroics. A press clipping in the Kell papers that repeated the sword-throwing episode bears a note in Mrs. Kell's hand, "My husband said this did not happen." (Personal communication from Norman Delaney to the author, August 2, 1993.)

While Semmes caught his breath, his ship was in her death throes. The mainmast, which had been damaged by gunfire, crashed into the sea as the *Alabama*'s bow rose higher in the air. Dr. Browne, the surgeon aboard the *Kearsarge,* was struck by the way the raider assumed a near-perpendicular position as her ordnance and engines collapsed into the stern. He thought it remarkable that her final plunge— shown in the victor's log as taking place at 12:24 P.M.—brought no cheering from the crew of the *Kearsarge,* only silence.[38]

From the *Deerhound,* Semmes turned for a last look at the ship he had loved:

> A noble Roman once stabbed his daughter, rather than she should be polluted by the foul embrace of a tyrant. It was with a similar feeling that Kell and I saw the *Alabama* go down. We had buried her as we had christened her, and she was safe from the polluting touch of the hated Yankee![39]

CHAPTER 18

Defeated but Not Conquered

While the *Deerhound* made for Southampton, there was confusion as well as elation on board the *Kearsarge*. A prisoner from the *Alabama* mistook Winslow for a steward and asked him, naturally, for a drink. Winslow obligingly gave him whiskey and then pointed toward the American flag, remarking, "That is the flag you should have been under."[1]

What the battle lacked in competitiveness it would shortly make up for in controversy. When the *Deerhound* first appeared, Winslow had urged Captain Jones to render all possible assistance to the *Alabama*'s survivors. It had never occurred to him that the yacht, after picking up Semmes, Kell, and thirty-seven others, would then head straight for England. Thornton, Winslow's executive officer, later testified that he was waiting for an order to fire at the *Deerhound* and was very upset when no order came.[2]

Aboard the yacht, Captain Jones had briefly consulted with John Kell as to whether he should surrender the survivors to the *Kearsarge*. Kell, though hardly a disinterested party, suggested that the Confederates were now under British protection and that the *Deerhound* should proceed to Southampton. Several of the survivors sought to express their appreciation to the yacht's owner, John Lancaster. The textile tycoon replied that no special thanks were required; he would have done the same for the Federals if the battle had turned out differently.[3]

Winslow himself bore some responsibility for Semmes's imminent arrival in England, for he had been slow in sending help to those struggling in the water. It was as if, in his concern over the wily Semmes, he expected the sinking *Alabama* to somehow rise from the waters and spring at his ship. Two of Winslow's boats had been destroyed in the action, however, and this fact may have delayed his rescue efforts. Aboard the *Kearsarge* the victors were magnanimous. Winslow mustered all hands briefly, congratulating them on their victory and concluding that "God must be on our side." He told his sailors to provide the prisoners with dry clothing and to report any expense to him. The grog tub was unlimbered, and rebel prisoners joined Federal sailors in "splicing the main brace."

Casualties aboard the *Alabama* had been heavy. Although only nine men were killed in the action, twenty were wounded and twelve more drowned after the ship foundered. Among the drowned were Semmes's diffident valet, Bartelli, who appears to have told no one that he could not swim; the ship's assistant surgeon, David Llewellyn, another nonswimmer, whose makeshift life preserver failed in the water; and David White, the onetime slave from Delaware whom Semmes had graciously "emancipated."

In contrast, there were no immediate fatalities aboard the *Kearsarge*, although one of her three wounded crewmen later died. The Federal ship had been fortunate; two rounds from the *Alabama* had passed through gun ports but had inflicted no casualties. Winslow, in his official report, wrote that the *Alabama*'s gunnery had at first been rapid and wild, but that it improved toward the close of the action.[4] He estimated that the *Alabama* had fired some 370 shot and shell—more than twice his own number—and that 13 or 14 had struck the *Kearsarge*'s hull and some 16 or 17 others had damaged her rigging.[5] The most visible damage to the *Kearsarge* was a great hole in her funnel where one of the Confederate shells had exploded. Winslow reported that the *Kearsarge* had fired 173 rounds; he did not speculate on how many of these took effect, but the devastation inflicted on his opponent spoke for itself.

Captain Jones of the *Deerhound* thought Semmes "a most miserable object to look at" when he was first helped aboard the yacht. He thought that the Alabamian, with his flamboyant mustache, owed his freedom to Kell's quick thinking in the lifeboat. As the *Deerhound* made its way to Southampton, Jones noted the attitude of the *Alabama*'s crewmen toward their officers. He thought that Semmes appeared to be "greatly reverenced" by his crew, but that Kell had their "deepest regard."[6]*

The *Deerhound* reached Southampton on the evening of the battle. Semmes and Kell checked into Kelway's Hotel there and quickly discovered that they were celebrities. The British, with their traditional respect for the underdog, concluded that Semmes had bravely challenged a superior opponent and given him a good run for his money. On the day after their arrival in Southampton, Semmes and Kell visited a tailor's shop to purchase some clothing. The proprietor was so delighted at his distinguished company that he insisted they take tea with him, but the Confederates had to cut short the visit when the crowd seeking a glimpse of Semmes grew so large as to block the street.[7] Letters and testimonials poured into Kelway's. A sister of William E. Gladstone, chancellor of the exchequer, offered to finance a successor to the *Alabama*.[8] Schoolboys wrote, asking to serve on Semmes's next command. When it became known that Semmes's sword had gone down with his ship, a group of Royal Navy officers raised funds for a splendid replacement, with an elaborate if biased inscription:

> Presented to Captain Raphael Semmes, C.S.N., by officers of the Royal Navy and other friends in England, as a testimonial of their admiration of the gallantry with which he maintained the honour of his country's flag and the fame of the *Alabama* in the engagement off Cherbourg, with a chain-plated ship of superior power, armament and crew, June 19th, 1864.[9]

From Cherbourg, Commander Sinclair wrote Commodore Barron on the afternoon of the battle that he had just spoken to a French

---

*In making his escape on the *Deerhound*, Semmes may have eluded more than a Yankee prison. By one of those coincidences that abound in the Civil War, one of the sailors on board the *Kearsarge* was George Whipple, the deserter from the *Sumter*, who had never forgiven Semmes for the punishments he had endured on that ship. Whipple was discovered concealed on the *Kearsarge* with a rifle, waiting for Semmes to be brought aboard. When his shipmates were unable to dissuade Whipple from attempting to kill Semmes, they reported him to an officer, and his plot was nipped in the bud.

official who had watched the engagement from the sea wall. He quoted the Frenchman as saying, "The Confederates have lost their ship, but not their honor."[10] Barron in turn wrote Secretary Mallory that Semmes was far more of a hero to Frenchmen after the battle than he had been before.[11]

The question of why Semmes chose to fight the *Kearsarge,* considered in the previous chapter, is more easily answered than the question of why he subsequently made such an issue of the *Kearsarge*'s chains. For the rest of his life Semmes would maintain that he did not learn of the chains protecting the *Kearsarge* until the battle was over and he was on the *Deerhound.* In his report to Commodore Barron, he stated that "the enemy was heavier than myself in ship, battery, and crew, and I did not know until the action was over that she was also ironclad."[12] His reaction was petulant and somehow in character—the chains were a typically underhanded Yankee trick! But he would find little support for this view even from dedicated Confederates, for professional navy men recognized that Winslow had every right to protect his ship by whatever means he chose. James Bulloch wrote after the war, "It has never been considered an unworthy ruse for a commander . . . to disguise his strength and to entice a weaker opponent within his reach."[13] Another Confederate officer, Lieutenant William Parker, would write, "I can see no reason in [Semmes's] complaint. He might as well have objected to [Winslow's] slinging his yards in chains, or making any other preparations for battle."[14]

But did Semmes in fact *know* of the chains? Frederick Edge, an Englishman who interviewed survivors from the *Alabama* in Cherbourg, was told that Semmes had mentioned the chains to some of his crew but had dismissed them as being of no consequence.[15] After the war Arthur Sinclair would write that "the port admiral [informed] Semmes, a day or two before the fight, that an officer detailed to visit the *Kearsarge* . . . had reported the fact of the chain-armor . . . and strongly advised Semmes not to engage her."[16] In 1900, Dr. Galt, the *Alabama*'s surgeon and paymaster, would reveal to Kell's widow that he and "other officers" had known of the chain protection.[17] If the *Alabama*'s officers knew of the chains but were unwilling to mention them to Semmes, this fact of itself would reflect on Semmes's remote leadership.

Semmes, usually truthful in matters of fact, was probably lying when he insisted that he had no knowledge of the chains. But there may have been extenuating circumstances. Cherbourg was so full of gossip concerning the forthcoming battle that he may have dismissed rumors of chain armor as idle talk. A second possibility is that he was informed of the chains, but not until after he had issued his June 14 "challenge" to Winslow—a challenge that he felt he could not honorably withdraw. But whatever the justification, Semmes's postbattle carping showed him at his worst. In his official report to Barron, dictated from his hotel on June 21, Semmes insisted not only that he had been tricked into fighting an "ironclad" but that the *Kearsarge* had fired on the *Alabama* after she had struck her colors.[18] In contrast to Lee after Gettysburg, Semmes could not bring himself to say that the defeat was "all my fault."

But why did Semmes make such an issue of the *Kearsarge*'s chains, in the face of overwhelming opinion among naval professionals that he was talking nonsense? First, Semmes was an astute propagandist. If he could not defeat the Yankees in battle, he could at least deprive them of any glory in victory. The British and French reaction to the battle suggests that he was fairly successful in this effort. Another of Semmes's reasons was very personal. His pride was such that he could not tolerate criticism of his ship, his sailors, or his cause. The controversy over the chains, such as it was, distracted attention from the *Alabama*'s shortcomings and Semmes's own poor judgment in seeking battle.

But there is a third explanation that should not be dismissed out of hand. Semmes considered himself a representative of Southern chivalry. He lived by a code of conduct that set high standards for the man of honor. Semmes regarded his challenge to Winslow as an extension of the dueling code, and a fundamental tenet of the dueling code was that neither party should enjoy an unfair advantage. Such a view was anomalous in wartime, but it was also vintage Semmes.

Two weeks after the battle Semmes penned a personal letter to Barron in which he wrote as frankly about the engagement as he ever would. He thanked Barron for some kind words, writing that he was "oppressed with mortification for my defeat, and sorrow for my lost officers and men." He spoke of "awful disparity" between his armament and that of his opponent, but did not complain about Winslow's chains.

> I should have handled him very roughly, & perhaps have carried him down with me, but for my bad powder. Unfortunately, my magazines had been placed near the con-

densing apparatus with which we generated fresh water for the crew, & it was in consequence frequently filled with steam. We were obliged to air it very frequently to keep it at all dry. Previously to my arrival at Cherbourg, all the powder which I had in barrels was so much damaged that I was compelled to throw it overboard. I had a good supply, however, put up in cartridges & stored in copper tanks, & as this did not show any sign of deterioration, I considered that it must be good.[19]

Semmes speculated that the same deterioration had reduced the explosive power of his shells, perhaps by as much as a third, and that it had contributed to the unreliability of his fuses. "Well," he concluded, "it is the fortune of war. I am improving in general health & my wounded hand enables me to write you this note."[20]

Semmes avoided any mention of his gunners. Writing after the war, the clear-eyed Bulloch, who had read the official reports and had spoken with many who had observed the battle, gave perhaps the best contemporary assessment of it. The crew of the *Alabama* were well disciplined, he concluded, but their only battle experience had been at close quarters against the *Hatteras*. The need to conserve ordnance stores had limited their target practice, and the gunners "were wholly without the skill, precision and coolness which come only with practice and the habit of firing at a visible object and noting the effect."[21]

Semmes never discussed how he had expected to defeat the *Kearsarge*. This is a notable omission from both his correspondence and his memoirs. He had known in May that a large number of his fuses were defective. He had discovered either in Cherbourg or earlier that much of his powder had deteriorated as well. Apart from these critical problems, the *Alabama* was short of experienced gunners, and, as noted by Bulloch, those on board had been permitted little target practice. Given these circumstances, the *Alabama* was in no position to trade broadsides with her opponent.

Many of those on the raider thought that their captain's plan was to close on the *Kearsarge* and board her. But Semmes knew all too well that his ship was no longer a fast sailer; he had complained just weeks earlier that "everything passes us." How, in the age of steam, did he expect to reach a position from which to board his enemy? If Semmes thought that his pivot guns could somehow defeat the *Kearsarge* at long range he was badly mistaken. Only some combination of good luck and gross incompetence on the part of the enemy could have given him a victory.

Semmes spent a week in Southampton winding up the affairs of his lost command. Crew members were paid off in full, either in Cherbourg or Southampton; wages for those lost went to families or legal representatives. Semmes arranged for the chronometers that he had entrusted to Bonfils to be shipped to a British bank. Busywork staved off despair.

Notwithstanding that it had been a notably one-sided engagement, an aura of romance clung to the *Alabama*'s last battle. For Southern sympathizers, and there were many in Europe, the clash off Cherbourg was the Civil War in microcosm: the gallant but out-gunned South, ignoring its deficiencies in matériel, fearlessly taking on a superior force. It did not matter that the result would have no effect whatever on the land war in North America.

Reaction to the battle was predictable in the North. *Frank Leslie's Illustrated Newspaper* rejoiced in the defeat of Semmes, who was a "miserable poltroon . . . valiant only in warring on the defenseless."[22] *The New York Times* was equally partisan, rejoicing that "the pirate *Alabama* has at last gone to the bottom of the sea. After a bloody and lurid career . . . she has been annihilated on the very first occasion [*sic*] that one of our ships-of-war was enabled to get an opportunity to measure metal with her."[23]

Admiral David Farragut wrote of Winslow's victory, "I would sooner have fought that fight than any ever fought on the ocean. Only think! It was fought like a tournament, in full view of thousands of French and English, with a perfect confidence on the part of all but the Union people that we would be whipped."[24] For Semmes to have escaped was galling, however, and to no one more than to Gideon Welles. The secretary wrote to Winslow, in a letter intended for the Northern press, that Semmes's escape had been "dishonor-able" but altogether characteristic "of one who has been false to his country and flag."[25]

The people of the South were too preoccupied with immediate problems to devote much time to a setback on the other side of the Atlantic. The *Richmond Enquirer* editorialized, "We have lost the gal-lant *Alabama*, but no Federal flag floats in triumph from her mast-head. . . . It is safe to say the *Alabama* has paid for herself five hun-dred times. She could afford to die."[26] Others were less philosophical. Diarist Mary Chesnut decided that Semmes "of whom we have been so proud . . . is a fool after all—risked the *Alabama* in a sort of duel of ships. . . . Forgive who may, I cannot!"[27] B. J. Semmes, Raphael's cousin and foster brother, wrote his wife on July 13, "I suppose you have heard of the loss of the *Alabama*. Raphael is much condemned for fighting at all, and especially with his ship in bad condition."[28]

In Britain a partisan press had taken sides on the war across the Atlantic, and reactions to the clash off Cherbourg reflected contemporary editorial biases. The influential London *Times*, however, attempted to put both ship and battle in perspective:

> Fathoms deep in Norman waters lies the good ship *Alabama*, the swift sea rover, just so many tons of broken-up iron and wood . . . wearing away in the huge depository of that genuine and original marine store-dealer, Father Neptune. . . .
>
> The *Alabama* could have found no more fitting grave, for she had lived on the waters, their child and playmate. She hailed from no Southern harbor, she was warned off from many a neutral port, and went away to her wild work amid the loneliness of the watery waste. . . .
>
> Since Philip Brooke captured the *Chesapeake* there has been no more chivalric encounter between single ships than that of Sunday last off Cherbourg. . . . It was a deliberate challenge. The contest did not take either crew by surprise. . . . The *Kearsarge* had more men, carried heavier metal and was chain-plated under her outside planking. Of this latter fact, Semmes is said to have been ignorant. . . .
>
> So ends the log of the *Alabama*—a vessel of which it may be said that nothing in her whole career became her like its close! Although a legitimate and recognized form of hostilities, the capture and destruction of peaceful merchantmen is one barbarism of war which civilized society is beginning to deprecate. Yet for many reasons one can impute no moral guilt to Semmes. . . . It was his peculiar fortune to keep [to] the sea, almost alone, against a hostile navy, running the gauntlet of countless cruisers with no southern harbor under his lee, and carrying on the conflict without any of the usual forms of recruitment.[29]

To the government in Washington, the British lionizing of Semmes added insult to injury. Minister Charles Francis Adams, acting on instructions from Secretary of State Seward, denounced Lancaster's action in bringing to England the men he had rescued; in Washington's view, Semmes and his crew had surrendered their freedom when they surrendered their ship. But Adams's démarche received short shrift in Whitehall. The foreign secretary, Lord Russell, replied that in his judgment the owner of the *Deerhound* "performed only a common duty of humanity" in saving Semmes and the others. Had Lancaster and Jones acted otherwise, those rescued "would . . . in all probability have been drowned, and thus would never have been in the situation of prisoners-of-war."[30] Always the polemicist, Semmes defended himself vigorously against the charge that he was somehow obliged to turn himself over to Federal authorities once his ship had surrendered:

> I was ready and willing to complete the surrender which had been tendered, but as far as was then apparent the enemy intended to permit me to drown. . . . When my ship went down, I was a waif upon the waters. . . . I ceased at that moment to be the enemy of any brave man. A true sailor, and above all one who had been bred to arms, when he found that he could not himself save me, as his prisoner, should have been glad to have me escape from him, with life. . . . I believe this was the feeling which, at that moment, was in the heart of Captain Winslow.[31]

By the end of June, Semmes's position was in some respects more enviable than that of John Winslow. Secretary Welles's initial elation, in which he had informed Winslow that he would be put up for commodore, was short-lived. He went on to complain that Winslow's battle report was briefer than called for by regulations and that he should not have paroled those of the *Alabama*'s survivors that he rescued.[32] Meanwhile, Winslow had traveled to Paris to consult a noted oculist about his right eye, which was worse than ever. The doctor told him that he had come too late; the sight in the eye was irretrievably gone. Winslow was, nevertheless, a celebrity in France, a fact that the Federal officer found ironic. He wrote to a friend, "I have had hard service, on the Mississippi, but no honour followed; an easy victory, and every one cries hero."[33]

Semmes, in England, now had leisure in which to reflect upon his defeat. For all his protests—the *Kearsarge*'s "armor," the *Alabama*'s defective powder, the failure of his shell to explode in the enemy's sternpost—Semmes knew that he had been outsmarted and his vessel badly outfought. A British reporter thought him "to feel most acutely the complete defeat he had experienced and the death and suffering which that defeat had caused."[34] Semmes, the most private of men, would confirm this assessment in his memoirs:

> No one who is not a seaman can realize the blow which falls upon the heart of a commander, upon the sinking of his ship. It is not merely the loss of a battle—it is the overwhelming of his household, as it were, in a great catastrophe. . . . When I looked upon my gory deck, toward the close of the action, and saw so many manly forms stretched upon it . . . I felt as a father feels who has lost his children.[35]

The one question that did not arise in the wake of the battle was whether Semmes had violated his orders in challenging the *Kearsarge*. Naval men on both sides appeared to recognize that orders issued two years earlier did not prevent Semmes from exercising his discretion in circumstances very different from those that existed in 1862. And neither of the two senior Confederates in Paris, Slidell and Barron, had sought to dissuade Semmes from his decision to fight.

One of Semmes's first visitors in Southampton was a remarkable figure among Confederate sympathizers in Britain, the Reverend Francis W. Tremlett. As a young man Tremlett had attended St. John's College in Annapolis, Maryland, and had come to admire the American South. As rector of an Anglican church in a fashionable section of London, he had since the outset of the American war gone out of his way to befriend Confederate naval officers in England, including both Matthew and William Maury. He had met Semmes when the Alabamian was in Britain following the cruise of the *Sumter*. Among the small, ever-changing pool of Confederate naval officers in the London area, the cherubic Tremlett was known as "the Confederate parson."

Tremlett had earlier invited Semmes to be his guest at his parsonage, but Semmes had not been in a position to accept. Once he had taken care of the *Alabama*'s affairs, however, he and Kell both accepted the clergyman's hospitality. For Kell the interlude was comparatively brief; on July 9 he boarded a ship for his return to the Confederacy. Semmes, in contrast, was desperately in need of convalescence and had little prospect of another command. From the Tremlett home in Belsize Park, Semmes's English friends planned a trip to the Continent for their guest, and the Confederate was more than agreeable. The party eventually comprised Tremlett, his sister Louisa, a brother, and two female "friends of the family."

The travelers went first to the Low Countries, with stops at Waterloo and Spa, before taking a riverboat up the Rhine to Switzerland. At times Semmes traveled under an alias, "Raymond Smith," to ensure privacy.[36] The return trip included more than a week in Paris, however, and Confederate sympathizers there soon learned that the famous Captain Semmes was among them. A young woman from New Orleans, Marion Luckett Berry, wrote in her journal of having dined with Semmes on September 9. "He is exceedingly pleasant and agreeable," she wrote, "but very plain and homely in his appearance." Miss Berry concluded that "no stranger would judge him to be the great hero he is."*

The trip did much to restore Semmes, although he was annoyed at the number of young men from Southern states whom he encountered, all boasting of their loyalty to the Confederacy but finding sound reasons for remaining in Europe.[37] Semmes, like Kell before him, formed a warm attachment to Louisa Tremlett; he accepted from her a ring that he wore alongside his wedding band.

After a six-week holiday the Tremlett party returned to Britain in September, and on October 3 Semmes caught a liner, the *Tasmanian,* for St. Thomas. His plan was to return to the Confederacy by way of Mexico, for he could not risk capture by traveling on a blockade runner. He left the *Tasmanian* at St. Thomas, transferring to another steamer, the *Solent,* for the short run to Havana. There, Semmes was obliged to book passage on a one-time Yankee fishing schooner, redolent of codfish but under British registry, for the final run to Matamoros. She was the type of vessel whose papers Semmes would have examined closely a few months earlier. After a ten-day voyage Semmes landed at the mouth of the Rio Grande and proceeded to Matamoros by coach.

Matamoros was booming from its trade with the Confederacy—a trade that had become more important as the Federals had occupied or sealed the Confederacy's Atlantic ports. Semmes counted sixty

---

*Journal of Marion Luckett Berry, courtesy of Cameron Moseley. Semmes, in his memoir, devotes only one paragraph to his six-week European tour, and makes no mention of the stopover in Paris. Writing as he was in the devastated South, he may not have wished to call attention to his extended holiday, however well deserved.

ships offshore, while the town itself was filled with oxcarts carrying Southern cotton to the docks. Dusty Matamoros was under the control of a local warlord, General Mejia, who was profiting immensely from the trade with Texas and as a result was a friend of the Confederacy. The general welcomed Semmes as a returned hero and provided a boat to take him and his effects across to Brownsville. From there, Semmes wrote to Louisa Tremlett of his emotions on returning to the Confederacy after more than three eventful years:

> Even the uninviting sand banks of the Texas coast looked pleasant, and I felt a strange thrill as I placed my foot again upon my native land; all the more dear to me for her agony of blood & misery. . . . I fear the nation which awaits me, as I pass through this half-lawless, while chivalrous, warm-hearted state, even more than I do the four weeks journey by stage & on horseback, before me. I have just now stolen away from a levee which has lasted all the evening, composed of all the military men of the place, who have nearly wrung off my poor fingers.[38]

Semmes headed for Shreveport on November 13, with a coach and cavalry escort provided by the local Confederate commander. Remarkably, for a country in its fourth year of war, the coach was well stocked with brandy, which Semmes disdained, and Havana cigars, which he fully enjoyed. His journey across Texas became a triumphant procession. At towns like Houston, Hempstead, and Rusk, he was met by whooping Texans who often compelled him to make short speeches so that they might hear, in Semmes's ironic description, "how the pirate talked."[39]

While south Texas was relatively untouched by the war, the prospect changed as Semmes's party entered Louisiana. The Red River area had been the scene of bitter fighting, and the debris of war, including skeletons and unmarked graves, was everywhere. Semmes arrived at Shreveport, the temporary capital of Louisiana, on November 27. There he met General Edmund Kirby Smith, commander of the Trans-Mississippi Department, who told him that his son Oliver was in Alexandria, 140 miles south. Semmes had stopped in Shreveport especially to inquire about Oliver, and now he made a five-day journey to Alexandria, where father and son had a warm reunion. Following his escape from the Federal prison boat in 1863, Oliver had been attached to General Richard Taylor's forces, where he was a major of artillery. Upon Semmes's arrival he was granted a leave of absence to accompany his father as far as Mobile.

Semmes and Oliver, still with a small escort, left Alexandria on horseback on December 10, planning to link up with mail couriers to cross the Red River and the great Mississippi. The fifty-five-year-old Semmes and his son spent several days in the swamps and forests that fringed the rivers. Occasionally they had to cross a bayou, but it was the dry season, and the main obstacles were the thick undergrowth and branches that could knock a man from the saddle. Joining some Confederate couriers at the town of Evergreen, the Semmeses reached the west bank of the Mississippi on the evening of December 13. Two Federal gunboats were anchored upstream, but they did not represent a serious barrier to crossing the river. Semmes released most of his escort and loaded supplies into a skiff provided by one of the couriers. The night was still, but the crossing was without incident. In Semmes's recollection, "As we shot within the shadows of the opposite bank, our conductor, before landing, gave a shrill whistle to ascertain whether all was right. The proper response came directly, from those who were to meet us, and in a moment more we leaped on shore among friends."[40]

The Semmeses, father and son, spent the night at the house of a Confederate officer. They resumed their journey the following day, and reached Mobile on December 15. Semmes, characteristically, left no record of his reunion with his wife, Anne, after an absence of more than three years. One wonders what she thought of the ring given her husband by Louisa Tremlett. But Semmes must have been relieved to learn that all his immediate family were well. He telegraphed Secretary Mallory of his arrival, and Mallory directed him to come to Richmond when he was ready. Semmes spent the last two weeks of December with his family before leaving for Richmond on January 2, 1865. The train trip to Richmond took another two weeks because of the devastation wrought by Sherman's army. Semmes thought the people of Georgia "terribly demoralized," but he could see why. Much had changed since he had traveled "through the burning woods" to Montgomery in 1861 to offer his services to the Confederacy.

Semmes reached Richmond on January 16 and moved in with his cousin, Thomas Semmes, a member of the Confederate senate who lived in a large house on the corner of Twelfth and Clay streets. The former captain of the *Alabama* had completed a journey of some seventeen hundred miles since landing in Matamoros, a considerable feat in itself, given the state of transportation in the South. Semmes was nothing if not consistent. Having favored secession in 1861, he was now prepared to share the fate of the defeated in a war that clearly was lost.

Meanwhile, John Winslow was at last receiving his due. On December 5, 1864, President Lincoln recommended a special congressional vote of thanks to him for the "skill and gallantry" demonstrated in his sinking of the *Alabama*. Congress complied, and Winslow returned to a hero's welcome in Boston, whose shipowners had suffered so grievously at Semmes's hand. At Lincoln's request, carpenters at the Boston Navy Yard removed a section of the *Kearsarge*'s sternpost, with Semmes's shell still embedded in the oak, and boxed it for shipment to Washington.

Still, Winslow would never achieve the fame of his defeated opponent. Several years after the war, Secretary of State Seward asked him to examine a painting of the battle between the *Alabama* and the *Kearsarge* that hung in his office. Winslow considered the painting and pronounced it fairly accurate, but his tone suggested that he had reservations. Asked whether there was anything wrong, Winslow replied with some annoyance: "I wish these artists would not always be representing the *Alabama* as smaller than the *Kearsarge*. She was as large as my vessel, had as many guns, and more [*sic*] men!"[41]

CHAPTER 19

"As Hard and Determined as Flint"

The reelection of President Lincoln in November 1864, following Sherman's devastating march through Georgia, was the death knell of the Confederacy. In Richmond, only the incorrigibly optimistic could see anything except defeat in the year ahead, yet there was little talk of surrender. Such was the popular confidence in Robert E. Lee that life in the capital went on with some degree of normality even as the Yankee vise closed around the city.

The Thomas Semmeses had set a fine table throughout the war, and now they welcomed their famous cousin. Semmes himself had a round of calls to make, beginning with President Davis. He thought the president little changed in appearance since their last meeting four years before—a view at variance with that of most observers, who felt that Davis showed acutely the strain of the war years. For Semmes, Davis maintained an air of "cheerfulness and serenity" about the outcome of the war. The president told his visitor that although he deeply regretted the loss of the *Alabama*, he was sure that Semmes had acted as he thought best with respect to the

Kearsarge and had nothing for which to reproach himself.[1] Beckett Howell, Davis's brother-in-law, had been a junior officer on both the *Sumter* and the *Alabama,* and the president was doubtless relieved that he had survived the *Alabama*'s last battle.

Secretary Mallory received Semmes warmly and pressed him for details about the fight with the *Kearsarge.* He, too, must have been supportive, for their friendship survived the war. Mallory briefed Semmes on the Confederacy's latest and last cruiser, the *Shenandoah,* then en route to the Pacific. There she would fall upon the Federal whaling fleet even more destructively than the *Alabama* had in the Azores and, in the absence of word that the war was over, continue to sink Yankee whalers long after Appomattox.

Semmes, on his own initiative, visited General Lee at his headquarters near Petersburg. He told the general-in-chief of the war weariness he had observed in his journey across the South, particularly the ominous increase in desertions. Lee showed no surprise at Semmes's pessimistic narrative. Semmes thought that Lee, by his manner more than by words, appeared to recognize the inevitability of defeat.[2]

Meanwhile, the erstwhile cruiser captain was accorded the honors that the South reserved for its heroes. Both houses of the Confederate congress adopted votes of thanks, and Semmes was invited to visit the floor. On February 10, 1865, President Davis promoted him to rear admiral "for gallant and meritorious conduct in command of the steam-sloop *Alabama,*" an action that made him second in seniority only to Admiral Franklin Buchanan in the Confederate navy.[3] A few days later Semmes was appointed commander of the James River Squadron, the most prestigious naval command that the hard-pressed Confederacy could offer.

On February 18, 1865, Semmes hoisted his flag on one of the Confederacy's few remaining ironclads, the *Virginia,* on the James River a few miles south of Richmond.* Semmes's command consisted of three ironclads, each mounting four guns, plus five wooden gunboats, none of which carried more than two guns. It was a sad little flotilla. There was no prospect of employing it in offensive operations, for the lower section of the James was dominated by the U.S. Navy. However, Semmes's ironclads, supported by a series of navy-

---

*This *Virginia,* constructed at Richmond in 1863, is not to be confused with the *Virginia* (née *Merrimack*) that fought the *Monitor* in March 1862 and was subsequently destroyed to avoid her capture by Federal forces.

manned shore batteries, effectively blocked any move against Richmond by water.

Semmes found among his five-hundred-man command two officers from the *Alabama,* John Kell and Joe Wilson, but there was little else to raise his spirits. Officers and men were crowded into close, uncomfortable quarters on vessels that Semmes compared to prison ships.[4] Clothing was in short supply, and the men were often on half rations. The flotilla was manned by complements drawn largely from army units, and in assisting the navy, Lee's commanders did not send their best soldiers. Whereas Semmes's sailors on the *Sumter* and the *Alabama* had been competent seamen but not Southerners, he now commanded Southerners who were not seamen. However, he did occasionally have the company of his youngest son, Raphael, now sixteen, who continued to serve on board the training ship *Patrick Henry*.

Semmes still believed in keeping his men busy, and at Drewry's Bluff he landed them by squads and drilled them on shore. He volunteered men for picket duty with the army and occasionally sent detachments to serve in Lee's trenches. In cooperation with one of Lee's artillerymen, General Edward P. Alexander, he increased the number of mines in the James River so as to discourage any attacking fleet.[5] But there was little that Semmes could do to improve morale in his command. He was inundated with requests for furloughs—requests that he felt compelled to deny—with the result that his command was ravaged by desertion. Sometimes an entire boat's crew would disappear. If he were at sea, Semmes grumbled, it would be easy to restore discipline, but his ships "were, in fact, only so many tents," into which poured mail from regions devastated by war.[6]

Once a week Semmes, accompanied by an aide, would set off on horseback for Richmond, to confer with Mallory at the Navy Department. The secretary had little advice to offer, however, and the winter passed slowly. Semmes's health was poor; he complained of fevers, which were probably exacerbated by the cold and damp of his ironclad. In his cabin on the *Virginia,* he pored over the maps that charted the enemy's advance through the Carolinas. "The Puritan was at last in the city of the cavalier," he wrote of Sherman's capture of Columbia, South Carolina. "The coarse man of mills and manufactures had at last found entrance as a master into the halls of the South Carolina planter!"[7]

Semmes still had occasional visitors, and one of the more unusual was Thomas Conolly, a forty-two-year-old Irish member of Parliament who had run the blockade into the Confederacy in the hope of picking up a valuable cargo. The Confederate leadership attempted to put the best face on things for their well-disposed visitor, and when Conolly expressed interest in calling on the famous Admiral Semmes, the necessary arrangements were made.

Conolly was impressed with the salute he received from Semmes's gunboats and "3 huge Monitors," as he called the Confederate ironclads. He found the admiral striding the deck of the *Virginia,* "looking as hard & determined as flint with his pointed moustache & . . . weather-beaten, thin-cut face. He was surrounded by his officers and received us kindly." Semmes led his visitor across the bridge of the *Virginia* onto a barge that he was using as a temporary office. "We descended down a ladder backwards," Conolly wrote, "& found his paraphernalia of pistols, sabres, boarding pikes, compass, inkstand & writing book." The visitor was introduced to Raphael Junior, who was ill and staying with his father, and to the *Virginia*'s commanding officer, Lieutenant James Dunnington. The latter took Conolly on a tour of the ironclad that left the visitor far more impressed than the military situation warranted. According to Conolly's notes,

> Men all standing round at attention & all neatly clad in Confederate grey shirts. Then to [the] engine room at other end—through wardroom & Admiral's sleeping room, all dark but bright & clean when lighted up. Back again to Admiral's Office in the barge. . . . Semmes [declared that] he could not hope for any [foreign] intervention but was sure the Confederacy could & would fight it out to a success![8]

Semmes knew that he was speaking nonsense, but even he was surprised at the suddenness of the Confederacy's collapse when it occurred. The campaign around Richmond came to a head on March 28. Grant was attempting yet again to flank Lee's overextended lines, and Lee sent Davis the first of several warnings that Richmond would have to be abandoned. Four days later, Sheridan's cavalry smashed through Lee's lines at Five Forks, effectively turning the Confederate flank. On April 2, Lee ordered a retreat westward along both sides of the James River, in the direction of Lynchburg and Danville.

Semmes was sitting down to dinner at about 4:30 P.M. on April 2 when an aide announced the arrival of a dispatch from the Navy Department. Not anticipating anything of importance, Semmes finished his meal before reading the message. That Sunday dinner would

be his last leisurely meal for some time, because the message from
Mallory informed him that Lee was evacuating his lines and the government was leaving Richmond:

> Unless otherwise directed by Gen. Lee, upon you is devolved
> the duty of destroying your ships this night, and with all the
> forces under your command joining Gen. Lee. Confer with
> him, if practical, before destroying them. Let your people be
> rationed, as far as possible, for the march, and armed and
> equipped for duty in the field.[9]

Semmes was annoyed that Lee had not communicated his intentions directly; much time could have been saved. The Alabamian did
not know it, but Davis and his cabinet had already left Richmond by
train. Semmes immediately called his captains to the *Virginia* and told
them what lay ahead. When night fell he led his flotilla upstream
toward Richmond. He was wondering how best to sink his ships
without attracting attention when a series of explosions on the north
side of the James—caused by Lee's commanders destroying their ordnance—made such caution unnecessary. Just below the capital
Semmes evacuated his three ironclads and crowded their crewmen
onto the gunboats. Then, making good use of the experience gained
on the *Sumter* and the *Alabama,* he fired the ironclads. The *Virginia,*
loaded with munitions, exploded with a pyrotechnic display that
shook houses in Richmond.

With the morning light Semmes disembarked his command below
the capital and burned his gunboats. His was now a land command
exclusively, one that desertions had reduced to perhaps 450 men, and
Semmes had no illusions about their effectiveness as a land force. They
were carrying heavy loads that included bedding, clothing, and mess
gear, as well as food, sugar, tea, and tobacco. Worst still, they were
incapable of marching any distance without becoming footsore.[10]

Prospects for his command were not bright, but Semmes was not
about to admit defeat. Because his "troops" were incapable of any
serious marching, he headed for the railroad depot. With the enemy
at the gates, discipline—the quality that Semmes cherished above all
others—was disintegrating in the capital. The city's military commander, General Richard S. Ewell, had attempted to destroy a supply of
whiskey in a warehouse, but his guards could not prevent a mob—
largely civilian—from becoming drunk and ugly. Many of the row-
dies now headed, like Semmes, for the railroad station, in the hope of
finding a train headed south.[11]

When Semmes reached the station at the head of his motley column, he was told that the last train had left hours before. For perhaps the last time in the war the gray eyes flashed. Semmes did *not* believe that the last rolling stock had gone, and he would see for himself! Working their way through the station, which had been largely abandoned by its staff, Semmes and his officers found "a few straggling railroad cars" filled with Richmond residents still hopeful that one more train would leave the city. Semmes ordered the civilians out, telling those who complained that it was better for noncombatants than for armed soldiers to be taken by the enemy. The cars were then coupled and the James River sailors marched on board. Semmes told his engineers to see what they could do with a small steam engine that had been abandoned in the depot.[12]

By then it was nearly 8:30 A.M., and Federal troops were entering the city. In the station yard, Confederate marines knocked down a picket fence and fed the wood into the locomotive's boiler. Coupled to the heavily loaded cars, the little engine inched its way out of the depot in a cloud of smoke and sparks. It soon reached a woodpile where the engineers were able to load better-quality fuel, and Semmes now allowed civilians to fill such space as remained in the cars. The train moved out of the yards and across the James, but on encountering a slight grade on the west side of the river the straining locomotive wheezed to a halt. From his stalled train Semmes could see the columns of blue infantry, within easy rifle range, marching into the abandoned capital of the Confederacy. Fires sprang up in various parts of the city. "The prophecy of Patrick Henry was fulfilled," Semmes would write. "The very halls in which he had thundered forth his prophecy were in possession of the 'stranger' against whom he had warned his countrymen!"[13]

Semmes was considering his options when one of his engineers discovered a second locomotive abandoned nearby. The navy men coupled it to the first engine, and by midmorning the train was moving westward at about six miles per hour. From time to time it stopped to pick up stragglers—many of them, according to Semmes, generals and colonels—from the stream of refugees headed west. The train passed through Amelia Courthouse at dusk, having traveled thirty miles since leaving Richmond.

Semmes had kept some form of journal throughout the war. Now, in the pandemonium that accompanied the collapse of the Confederacy, he chronicled the debacle in a diary. "Great consternation along the roads," he wrote on April 3.[14] The train passed through Burkeville Junction at about 2:00 A.M. on April 4, ninety minutes before the town was attacked by Sheridan's cavalry.

Semmes's orders had been to join Lee's retreating army, but at this point he and his sailors were prepared to go wherever their train would take them. All day on April 4 it chuffed through southern Virginia, reaching Danville, where Davis and his cabinet had established a "temporary capital," at nightfall. Semmes's navy brigade was the last force of any size to escape from Richmond. Indeed, Semmes's achievement in extricating his little command from the James was as remarkable as any of his earlier feats at sea. But the admiral felt a bit put upon; in his memoirs he would make no charges, but would clearly imply that his command had been abandoned and forgotten in the army's precipitous retreat.

The following morning Semmes had breakfast with President Davis, who congratulated him on his escape. The president had just issued another call to arms, proclaiming a new phase of the struggle. "Relieved from the necessity of guarding particular points," he had announced, "our army will be free to move from point to point to strike the enemy."[15] Stephen Mallory did not share the president's optimism, but in one of his last acts as navy secretary he constituted Semmes's command as an army brigade. Davis in turn appointed Semmes a brigadier general, making him the only Confederate officer to hold flag rank in two services. Semmes thought that his navy rank entitled him to be a major general, but he also recognized that it was folly to debate the matter under the circumstances.[16]

When Semmes reviewed his command he found he still had about four hundred men. These he divided into two skeleton regiments, each commanded by one of his ship captains; he placed young Raphael on his own staff with the rank of lieutenant. After some rudimentary artillery drill, "General" Semmes deployed his command to defend the two bridges that spanned the Dan River. He and part of his force remained outside the town for ten days, but not all of his men could be employed in the fortifications; those not in the trenches fished in the river or gathered in groups to write letters. The first news of Lee's surrender came from paroled soldiers of the Army of Northern Virginia who streamed into Danville. Semmes was touched by the sight of these men, "some on foot, some on horseback, some nearly famished . . . and others barely able to totter along from disease."[17]

The war was lost, of course, but bitter-enders like Davis and Semmes could still point to some interesting numbers. General Joseph E. Johnston, commanding the only force of any size in the east, still had an army of some thirty thousand. In Mississippi and Alabama, General Richard Taylor commanded perhaps twenty thousand more. And across the Mississippi were a scattering of Confederate units totaling as many as forty thousand. Of course, any wishful thinking based on these numbers overlooked some other statistics. One was that Federal forces under arms now numbered more than a *million* men. Another was that Sherman's army, comprising about eighty thousand effectives, was menacing Johnston and in so doing threatened an end to all meaningful Confederate resistance east of the Mississippi.

To link up with Johnston, Davis and his cabinet traveled by rail to Greensboro, North Carolina, on the evening of April 10. Semmes and his command followed on foot five days later, but the movement turned into a disaster. The march south, much of it in heavy rain, proved an invitation to fresh desertions. "My sailors are dropping off from me at every camp," Semmes wrote in his journal on April 15, "having caught the universal contagion of desertion which has descended upon this Army."[18] The following day brought the possibility of action against the enemy, as Semmes received an order from General Beauregard to take his brigade to a break in the railroad outside Greensboro and protect supplies there.[19] This required a countermarch of more than seven miles by footsore sailors and prompted new desertions. Semmes, who was sick, wrote in his journal that evening: "A stream of vagabonds passing—some Lee's men—many [others are] deserters who are seizing horses & otherwise robbing & plundering as they go."[20]

While Semmes and his command slogged their way south, Davis was meeting with his cabinet in Greensboro. At first the president insisted on continuing the war. He proposed re-forming the Army of Northern Virginia, seemingly oblivious to the fact that the paroles granted to Lee's soldiers were conditioned on their not bearing arms against the Union. General Johnston heard Davis out but responded that to continue the war would only complete the devastation of the South and the ruin of its people. When a poll of the cabinet revealed only one vote—that of Secretary of State Judah P. Benjamin—for continuing the struggle, Davis reluctantly authorized Johnston to request surrender terms from Sherman.

Semmes and his bedraggled little band reached Greensboro on April 18. By this time his "brigade" had dwindled to perhaps 150 men.[21]* Even as Semmes set up camp, Johnston and Sherman were agreeing on terms of surrender—terms so sweeping and generous to the South that they were subsequently disavowed by the new administration of President Andrew Johnson. Semmes, however, was not interested in the terms. On arriving in Greensboro he requested authorization from Johnston's deputy, General Beauregard, to lead his command to the Trans-Mississippi Department to continue the war. Beauregard replied that any officers wishing to depart could do so, but that their units were to stay in place. Semmes's desire to continue the war, even as his command dissolved about him, was nothing short of quixotic, and he ultimately decided to stay.

Semmes first heard of the assassination of President Lincoln on April 19. His laconic diary entry—"Death of Lincoln!"—suggests surprise without regret; he would never have a kind word for the Northern leader. Years later, in his memoirs, Semmes would write that as a Christian he had a duty to ask the Lord to have mercy on Lincoln's soul. "But," he would add bitterly, "the devil will surely take care of his memory."[22]

When the Sherman-Johnston agreement of April 18 was rejected in Washington—it made no mention of slavery and would have readmitted the Confederate states on their prewar footing—the two generals met again on April 26. They quickly agreed on a five-point convention that surrendered Johnston's army but took no account of other Confederate forces and avoided political issues. As with Lee's army, officers and men were permitted to return to their homes.

But what about "pirates"? Semmes knew that he was hardly the typical Confederate army officer, and he decided to make some special arrangements. On April 30 he went to Johnston's headquarters, where he met with Johnston, Beauregard, and others, and asked that he and his officers be the first to meet with the Federal parole commissioners. The following day Semmes and his staff rode into Greensboro, where Federal commissioners had set up an office in the Britannia Hotel. After being introduced to General George L.

---

*Semmes wrote in his diary, "Command dwindled to about 90!" In his postwar memoir, he used the figure "about 250." While statistics relating to the Confederate collapse are notably unreliable, and stragglers from Semmes's command may have appeared following his journal entry, I have used a figure close to that employed by Semmes in 1865.

Hartsuff, the senior Federal commissioner, Semmes produced the muster roll for his command, and Hartsuff gave him presigned parole certificates for the number of names that appeared on it. This was not good enough for Semmes, who asked that his own form be filled out and witnessed in Hartsuff's presence. The Federal officer was puzzled but offered no objection. Semmes signed himself "Rear-Admiral in the Confederate States Navy and Brigadier-General in the Confederate States Army, commanding a brigade." When he walked out of the hotel, he carried with him a promise that he was not to be disturbed by the Federal authorities so long as he obeyed the laws of the United States. Semmes was a survivor. He had survived the wreck of the *Somers* and the sinking of the *Alabama*. He fully intended to survive the wreck of the Confederacy.

Semmes returned to his camp outside Greensboro and distributed paroles to those of his command who remained. If he had any parting words, no record of them has survived. That same day he set out on the long journey home, some nine hundred miles through the devastated South. Travel would be by road to Montgomery, Alabama, from where he hoped to take a boat to Mobile. With him were young Raphael, several other officers (including Joe Wilson), and two or three "servants," for a total of perhaps ten men. Between them they had a single wagon and several mules, but not enough for all to ride.

The parolees covered eleven miles the first afternoon, camping at Jamestown on the road to Salisbury. Semmes wrote in his diary, "Highway filled with soldiers singly & in small parties, many leading half-starved horses & all ragged and dirty."[23] The roads were bad and forage was scarce. In addition, the travelers were bedeviled by a balky wagon wheel that required repeated repairs. The weather was generally fine, however, and Semmes and his entourage could usually cover between twenty and twenty-eight miles per day. On May 6, while Joe Wilson went into a town to see about repairs to the wagon, Semmes "bathed delightfully" in a mountain stream. Two days later, however, the wagon wheel expired once and for all near the South Carolina border. Perhaps because of these logistical problems, Semmes had unkind words for the residents of Spartanburg County, South Carolina. "Population ignorant, idle, thriftless, women young & old slovenly and dirty," he wrote.[24]

The naval party carried some provisions, which they supplemented with fruit and dairy products as best they could. How they paid local farmers, if they paid at all, is not recorded. At Greenville, South Carolina, which Semmes thought "a pretty village," the town council provided them with four days' rations. When they crossed into Georgia, Semmes was surprised to find many plantations still operating with black labor. Occasionally—most often at bridges—Federal soldiers stopped the travelers, but they were allowed to proceed on showing their paroles.

On May 21 Semmes bade farewell to Joe Wilson, who left at the Alabama border to go to his home in Florida. Because John Kell had been granted sick leave before the fall of Richmond, Wilson had been the single *Alabama* veteran in Semmes's party. The following day they crossed the Chattahoochee River into Alabama, arriving at Montgomery on May 25. The admiral and his companions had traveled some six hundred miles in twenty-five days since leaving Greensboro.

Meanwhile, the war was winding down. On May 4, General Richard Taylor had surrendered his command, including Oliver Semmes, on the same terms as those accorded Lee and Johnston. Three weeks later, on May 26, the Trans-Mississippi forces of General Kirby Smith—the last Confederate force of any size—stacked their arms. President Davis and his party had been captured in Georgia on May 10; the Confederate president would be incarcerated for two years.

In Montgomery, almost as if time had stood still, Semmes was again a guest at the handsome residence of banker William Knox. By prearrangement, the traveling party dissolved there. While his officers went their own way, Semmes and young Raphael took passage on the river steamer *Peerless,* arriving in Mobile on about May 29.

Raphael Semmes was defeated in war, almost destitute financially, and effectively barred from earning a livelihood in the naval profession to which he had devoted forty of his fifty-six years. He was totally unreconstructed as to the outcome of the war and had no intention whatever of requesting a pardon from the conquerors. But he had in his pocket a document that stated that he would not be disturbed so long as he observed the conditions of his parole, and he was confident that the legal training that had proved so useful in every period of his life would enable him to earn a livelihood. Semmes now looked forward to a reunion with his wife and children.

CHAPTER 20

"A Flagrant Violation of Faith"

When the war began, Mobile, with a population of nearly thirty thousand, was one of the larger cities of the Confederacy. The city suffered comparatively little direct damage from the war, but as a result of the hostilities the cotton trade collapsed, paralyzing the local economy. In the autumn of 1863, crowds of women carrying banners reading "Bread or Blood" and "Bread and Peace" had marched down Dauphin Street armed with knives and hatchets, breaking into stores and appropriating food and clothing.[1]

Even so, the city felt the full brunt of the war only in the latter half of 1864. In August, Admiral David Farragut, after "damning the torpedoes," led his ships into Mobile Bay and defeated an outgunned Confederate flotilla. At the head of the bay, however, the city of Mobile remained in Confederate hands. Not until March 1865 did a Federal army, under General Edward R. S. Canby, march on the city from New Orleans. Mobile was strongly protected, with forts inland as well as at the entrance to the bay, but manpower was in short supply. On April 11, as Semmes and his naval brigade prepared to join

President Davis in Greensboro, General Dabney H. Maury, commanding the forces defending Mobile, evacuated the city. Federal forces occupied it the following day.

Anne Semmes appears to have spent the last two years of the war in Mobile. Once it was over and she was reunited with her husband, they had much to discuss. Two of their children had married during the war. Electra's husband was Pendleton Colston, a young Baltimore attorney; Spencer had wed a distant cousin, Pauline Semmes, whose father, General Paul Semmes, had been fatally wounded at Gettysburg. From his family Semmes learned of the declining health of his brother, Samuel, who had lived through the war in Maryland. In the summer of 1865 Raphael wrote Samuel that his wartime residence in the North was not an issue between them. "Whatever you did," Raphael assured him, "you [did] like a man of honor."[2]

Semmes was not sure that he himself wanted to live and work in the restored Union. Politics aside, he was put off by the expense of living in Mobile; Anne wrote Electra that the smallest house in the city rented for $1,500 per year and that the house they were then renting went for $1,800.[3] Nevertheless, Semmes spent the latter half of 1865 attempting to start a law practice, assisted at different times by Spencer and Oliver. He wrote his son-in-law, Colston, that although he and Spencer "have not yet *realized* anything. . . . I think we shall be able to take hold of a fair share of the practice of our one-horse city."[4] In the fall of 1865 Semmes purchased a rambling two-story frame house about four miles west of the town and named it The Anchorage. He would give the law a try.

With peace came the issues of reconstruction. The states of the erstwhile Confederacy presented a desolate picture. Their farms were in weeds and their railroads destroyed; in parts of cities like Richmond and Columbia, only brick chimneys had survived the Union armies. But if the South was subjugated, it was not prepared to admit error. Might had made right, in defiance of the Constitution. After the war as before, most Southerners regarded themselves as the injured party. If the North offered conciliatory terms for the reconstitution of the Union, they were no more than the South deserved.

Attitudes in the North were sharply divided, with few precedents to provide guidance. The assassination of Lincoln had hardened popular opinion and prompted calls for the punishment of "traitors." This sentiment had led to the arrest of a few Confederate leaders, including Jefferson Davis and Stephen Mallory, but in all but a few cases the paroles extended to Confederate soldiers and sailors were honored by the victors.

President Andrew Johnson accepted the position—earlier set forth by Lincoln—that the states of the Confederacy had never effectively left the Union. In the summer of 1865 Johnson was attempting to make Reconstruction—on his own terms—an accomplished fact before Congress reconvened in December. Because he believed he had no authority to interfere with the suffrage requirements of the individual states, he took no action regarding Negro suffrage, as the Radical Republicans demanded. The president's policies were about as conciliatory as thoughtful Southerners could expect, but Johnson gained no thanks from die-hards like Semmes, who were incensed when senior Confederate military leaders were excluded from the terms of the president's first amnesty proclamation on May 29, 1865.

In a letter to his brother, Semmes reflected on the outcome of the war and his own role:

> Having chosen my side, I gave it zealous and earnest support. I spent four years in active service, and only ceased to labor for my cause when it was no longer possible. I rendered this service without ever having treated a prisoner other than humanely, and, I may say, often kindly; and without ever having committed an act of war . . . which was not sanctioned by the laws of war. Yet my name will probably go down to posterity in untruthful histories . . . as a sort of Bluebeard or Captain Kidd. . . .
>
> I have come out of the war poor, but, God willing, I shall make a support for my family. The President treats me as an outlaw, unworthy of amnesty. I have nothing to say. If I am deemed unworthy to be a citizen, I can remain in my native land as an alien. . . .
>
> I am still in Mobile, but as yet uncertain where I shall go or what I shall do. If I save five or six thousand dollars out of the wreck of my affairs, it will be fully as much as I expect. I think of retiring into the country where, upon a small farm, I can live in obscurity and peace the few years that will remain to me.[5]

In November 1865, Semmes received letters from John Kell and his wife, Blanche, reporting the birth of a son whom they had named for him. In responding to the Kellses' letters, Semmes first wrote

Blanche how much he appreciated the honor of having a namesake. Alluding to the recent war, he added: "Although we have lost the great prize for which we struggled, neither [Kell] nor I will despair, but will endeavor to build up a future for our children, whom we will teach to respect the cause for which we have sacrificed all."[6]

At about the same time several officers from the *Alabama,* including Richard Armstrong, wrote Semmes asking whether any prize money was due them. They could not have been very hopeful, for the vessels Semmes had bonded—for sums to be paid after the war to the Confederate government—would never yield a nickel for the men of the *Alabama.* The one source of a few dollars might be the sixty-odd chronometers that Semmes had prudently sent ashore before engaging the *Kearsarge.* These had been sold in England for a sum that translated into $4,142 at the prevailing exchange rate.

Semmes wrote John Kell regarding the distribution of the proceeds from the chronometers. He had taken for himself the half that would have gone to the Confederate government, because he alone of the *Alabama*'s officers had not been paid off in London, and because he had incurred other out-of-pocket expenses at that time. Since there was no longer a Confederate government to satisfy, Semmes felt justified in keeping its share of the proceeds from the sale of items that had been preserved and sold on his own initiative. That left slightly more than $2,000 to be divided among the *Alabama*'s nine officers; Kell's share, he wrote, should be "about enough to buy Master Semmes [*sic*] a silver cup or hobby horse."[7] Semmes subsequently attempted to locate all the officers entitled to money from the chronometers; Arthur Sinclair would later record his pleasant surprise at receiving a check for his share.*

Raphael Semmes was about as unreconstructed a rebel as could be found in the South. To be sure, he had not emigrated to Mexico or South America, as some prominent Confederates had done. He remained in Mobile, however, less from choice than because he had had no tempting job offer. He put out feelers in mid-1865 for a posi-

---

*Sinclair recalled that in 1867 or 1868 he received a check from a Baltimore bank with a message from Semmes that it represented his share of the proceeds from the sale of the chronometers. Semmes asked at that time if Sinclair could provide addresses for Lieutenants Armstrong and Wilson. Sinclair, *Two Years on the Alabama,* 76.

tion as a commercial agent in South America, but to no avail.[8] In his letter to Kell, Semmes indicated that he would rely for his continued freedom on his military parole—even as he poured out his contempt for the government behind it:

> The Federal government, upon my surrender of my command, made a solemn convention with me that it would not molest me. Barbarous people keep such conventions as those and I presume even the Yankees will do as much. . . . I would not accept a pardon if it were freely tendered me as I might by this act imply that I had wronged in taking up arms against them.[9]

In time, Semmes would change his mind about a pardon. Although his bristling defiance at this time was not typical, many Southerners were unwilling to acknowledge the political consequences of military defeat. Required by the president to repudiate their acts of secession, several states of the former Confederacy repealed them in language that fell short of calling them null and void. Conventions called in the seceded states rejected Johnson's suggestion that the franchise be extended to educated blacks. In Alabama, veterans of the Confederate armed forces made up three quarters of the newly elected state legislature.[10] In returning to politics as usual, Southern traditionalists undercut those Northern moderates who, like Johnson and Seward, favored the return of the seceded states on easy terms. Gideon Welles complained in his diary, "The entire South seem to be stupid and vindictive."[11]

Semmes never recognized that, however correct his wartime behavior had been in his own eyes, his mere presence in the reconstituted United States was an affront to many Northerners. He was now about to become one of a few persons whose wartime activities were so controversial that the terms of their paroles were ignored.* Gideon Welles was no Radical Republican, but he sought now to bring the "pirate" Semmes to what he perceived as justice. On the night of December 15, 1865, a detachment of U.S. Marines surrounded The Anchorage. The officer in charge, Lieutenant Lyman P.

---

*The most notorious of these was probably Henry Wirz, commander of the Confederate prison at Andersonville, who, like Semmes, had been paroled with Johnston's army. Wirz was subsequently tried and convicted by a military commission and executed.

French, presented Semmes with an order for his arrest signed by Welles; the nominal charge was that Semmes had violated "the usages of war" by leaving the scene of his surrender to the *Kearsarge.*

French told his prisoner to prepare to go to Washington the following morning. According to Anne Semmes, the admiral promptly stretched out on a sofa and went to sleep. Mrs. Semmes had a reputation for excitability in her later years, and when she saw her husband—soon to be incarcerated in a Yankee dungeon—sleeping away his last hours of freedom, she awakened him. Semmes then assured his family—his daughters Katherine and Anne were also present—that there was no case against him, and rolled over, telling his family that he could sleep "though quite sure that I was to be hanged tomorrow."[12]

The next morning Semmes was taken to the headquarters of General Charles R. Woods, commander of the Federal troops in Mobile, where he drafted a protest against his arrest, charging that it was in violation of his parole. This protest was, of course, to no avail, and Semmes, accompanied by French and two noncommissioned officers, left Mobile for New Orleans on the steamer *Louise.* Aboard ship, Semmes met General Dabney Maury, a fellow passenger, to whom he suggested bitterly that the Yankees would doubtless flout all paroles. Maury was a friend of General Nathan Bedford Forrest, who was even more reviled in the North than Semmes; Maury hurried to Memphis to warn Forrest, but there was no cause for alarm. Only Semmes was the target of the administration's wrath.[13]

While on board the *Louise,* Semmes wrote to his acquaintance from Mexican War days, General Ulysses S. Grant, asking him for help in overturning his arrest.[14] When he landed at New Orleans, Semmes made a similar verbal appeal to the Federal district commander, General Canby. The prisoner received no satisfaction, but he and French were put up at the St. Charles Hotel, one of New Orleans's finest, where Semmes received a stream of sympathetic callers, including his son Oliver and generals Richard Taylor and Simon B. Buckner. While he waited for the steamer to take him north, Semmes wrote Pendleton Colston in Baltimore, asking him to retain a lawyer.

On the evening of December 20 Semmes and his escort waded through mud and climbed over cotton bales to board the steamer *Costa Rica,* destination New York. Semmes was treated with great courtesy by the captain and officers, but he also passed his fifth successive Christmas away from his family. The admiral kept a journal on board the *Costa Rica,* as he would subsequently do in prison.

"Passed the Tortuga light," he noted on December 23, perhaps recalling its technical characteristics from those easy years on the Lighthouse Board.

The *Costa Rica* reached New York City on December 28, and after a night at the Astor House, Semmes and his escort caught the train for Washington. There the prisoner was taken to the Navy Yard and initially lodged in the dispensary under close guard. After five days he was moved to a more spacious room in the attic, where his treatment improved. He was allowed a servant, writing materials, and meals from a local restaurant. In his diary Semmes described a typical day:

> I rise in the morning about 8:30, when the drum under my window beats the first call for morning inspection and parade; my attendant in the meantime has made me a fire. I proceed to wash and dress. I have plenty of water, soap and towels furnished me. . . .
>
> My newspaper and breakfast occupy me until 11:00 o'clock. I then rise and walk about in my room to stretch my cramped limbs and prevent the life current in my veins from actual stagnation. I walk and think until I am tired. I then sit down and read. I have some law books and histories with me by the thoughtful providence of friends. I have ever found when in trouble that the best remedy is to chain down the imagination in its flights and set reason at work. . . .
>
> I thus alternately walk and read, sometimes throwing myself on my sofa in my weariness and heartsickness, until the lock is heard to grate and turn in my door, and my guard re-enters with my dinner, my solitary dinner. It is now 3 o'clock in the afternoon. . . .
>
> The day now wanes, the sun is sinking over the hills of Virginia, the Navy Yard bell rings, and a stream of working-men comes out of the gates and is tramping up the avenue that leads by my prison. These men are going to their homes, to their firesides, to their little ones. Happy workingmen! . . . It is dark at 5:30 o'clock and I have five hours of candlelight before 10:30, bed-time, the hour of sweet oblivion.[15]

Although Semmes had kept logs and journals all his life, these had been required of him as a navy officer and were not political statements. His prison diary is a different matter. Semmes considered himself a political prisoner, consigned by a cruel fate to politicians whom he compared to the bloodthirsty radicals of the French Revolution.

Through his diary runs a strain of vengeful self-pity. He likened himself to a prisoner in the Bastille, to be held indefinitely without trial. But had he not struck at the very life of the American nation? Yes, Semmes admitted, "but I struck as the surgeon strikes, to save the life of the nation."[16]

When Pendleton Colston heard of his father-in-law's arrest, he hired the forty-two-year-old attorney James Hughes, a onetime Democratic congressman from Indiana who had switched his allegiance to the Republicans during the war. He was a personal friend of the president, and his access to Johnson made him an excellent choice. Ultimately, however, Semmes would be his own advocate. He wrote to President Johnson from prison, focusing on the illegality of his arrest. In his letter of January 15, 1866, Semmes first recapitulated the circumstances of his parole. He was to have been left undisturbed for as long as he observed its terms, and he had scrupulously done so. Not only had he been a law-abiding citizen in Mobile, he had passed up many opportunities to leave the country.

> The question for you to decide, Mr. President, is the legality of this arrest. Can I, in violation of the terms of the military convention already referred to . . . be held to answer for any act of war committed anterior to the date of that convention? I respectfully submit that I cannot be so held . . . without a flagrant violation of faith by the United States.[17]

The person behind Semmes's arrest was Father Neptune himself, Gideon Welles. The secretary considered Semmes one of the most disreputable of the Confederate leaders, in part because he was a native of Maryland, a person who did not have the excuse of following his own state into Confederate service. Welles complained in his diary that Semmes "made it his business to rob and destroy the ships and property of his unarmed countrymen engaged in peaceful commerce; when he finally fought and was conquered he practiced a fraud, and in violation of his surrender broke faith, and without ever being exchanged fought against the Union at Richmond."[18]

The only charge that Semmes knew to have been brought against him was that relating to his escape after the surrender of the *Alabama*. But this in no way invalidated the terms of his parole; if the government had wished to pursue this point, Semmes contended, he should have been excluded from the terms extended to Johnston's army. Attorney General James Speed had speculated about the possibility of trying some ex-Confederate leaders for treason, but Semmes had an answer here, too. Treason, according to the Constitution, consisted of levying war against the United States or giving aid and comfort to its enemies. These were wartime offenses, and whatever acts he may have committed during the war had been forgiven under the terms of his parole.[19] It was a good letter—respectful in tone, convincing in its logic. Johnson told Hughes that he had read it; to assure a wider audience, however, Hughes arranged to have it printed in *The New York Times*.

By now, Johnson and Welles probably wished that Semmes had escaped to Mexico or Brazil as other ex-rebels had done. The administration was already suspect in the eyes of some Radical Republicans for being soft on the South. To release the "pirate" Semmes would only lend credence to these doubts. But a conviction was growing that the government did not have a strong case. Attorney General Speed accepted part of Semmes's argument, telling Johnson that a person charged with treason should be tried in civil court, but that Semmes could not be tried because of the terms of his parole.[20]

To assess the situation and play for time, Johnson ordered an investigation by the navy's judge advocate, John A. Bolles. In late January, Bolles drew up a theoretical five-count indictment of Semmes:

1. That he had used false colors to deceive his foes;
2. That he had seized some of his prizes in neutral waters;
3. That his burning of prizes was illegal, because the ships in question had not been legally condemned;
4. That he was guilty of treason;
5. That he had violated the rules of war in escaping on the *Deerhound*.[21]

The first two charges were quickly dropped. The use of false colors was well established in international law, while violations of neutral waters were the concern of those countries whose waters had been violated. The question of Semmes's confiscation procedures was less clear, but ships of the U.S. Navy had condemned and burned prizes in both the Revolution and the War of 1812. As for treason, if Semmes was guilty, so were several thousand other Southerners who had left the Federal service for the Confederacy.

This left the charge that Semmes had violated the rules of war by escaping to England on the *Deerhound*; perhaps this one could be made to stick. On February 1, 1866, Bolles and Welles recommended to Johnson that Semmes be tried before a military commission made up of army and navy officers. Johnson said that he was opposed to a military trial but postponed any final decision.[22]

Meanwhile, Bolles explored a new tack: that Semmes was guilty of cruelty toward his prisoners. He placed advertisements in East Coast newspapers asking persons with evidence to present it, but the response was not what he and Welles had in mind. No one came forward with credible charges of cruelty, and George Fairchild, the U.S. diplomat who had been taken from the *Thomas B. Wales,* testified that he and his family had been treated with consideration.[23] Bolles reluctantly concluded that Semmes was "by no means the guilty monster" portrayed in the newspapers. In February, he became the first senior official involved in the case to recommend that Semmes be released.[24]

Semmes, of course, knew none of this, but the conditions of his confinement gradually improved. Anne came north to be nearby; she stayed with the Colstons in Baltimore and was allowed to visit her husband. Pendleton Colston was a frequent visitor, as was Judge Hughes, who thought the president friendly to Semmes's cause. On January 29, Horace Greeley's *New York Tribune* asked rhetorically why Semmes, who "shed no blood" during the war, should be tried for his life, while General Forrest, the "butcher of Fort Pillow," remained free.[25] Beginning on February 4 the prisoner was allowed to take daily exercise in the yard, accompanied by one or two Federal officers. Semmes enjoyed the companionship of the "clever young gentlemen," but there was no hard news about his future. "Fortunately," he wrote, "I have been bred in a good school of philosophy—the sea—where we are frequently called upon to restrain our impulses, curb our imaginations and practice self control and patience."[26]

On February 7 Bolles told Colston—on what basis is unclear—that his father-in-law would be tried by a military commission.[27] Semmes was extremely disturbed at this prospect, for while he was confident of acquittal on any charge of treason, he could not be sure what usages-of-war charge the government might trump up for a military commission. Gideon Welles, meanwhile, found the entire business perplexing. His favorite charge—that Semmes had violated the parole implicit in his surrender—was insubstantial, yet might be considered by a military commission. The remaining charges appeared more suitable for civil courts. President Johnson wished the entire matter would go away; he complained to Welles that he was tired of visits from Ann Semmes, "crying and taking on for her husband."[28]

On March 30 Welles raised the Semmes affair before the full cabinet, pointing out that the issue must be disposed of. In the discussion that followed, Attorney General Speed again urged a trial by military commission. Secretary of War Edwin M. Stanton concurred, adding that if a trial were to take place "he would wish . . . the extreme penalty of the law inflicted." Welles apparently responded that the Navy Department would not attempt to try Semmes on civil charges such as treason or piracy, but was prepared to try him on violations of the laws of war. The trouble was, the secretary conceded, that Semmes's alleged offenses "had been narrowed down and mitigated, so that I believe his offense was really less aggravated than had been charged and believed."[29]

Once again Johnson temporized. A few days later, however, Semmes's prospects improved as a result of developments not directly related to his case. First, President Johnson, on April 2, issued a proclamation that the war was over. Then, the following day, the Supreme Court issued its opinion in the celebrated case of *Ex parte Milligan*. Lambdin P. Milligan, a Confederate sympathizer living in Indiana, had been convicted of sedition by a military commission in 1864 and sentenced to be hanged. The Supreme Court, however, ruled on his appeal that military courts did not have jurisdiction where civil courts were available. With the war now officially over, the decision effectively precluded any trial of Semmes by a military commission.

On April 6, in cabinet meeting, Welles again asked what was to be done with his prisoner. Johnson replied that he was inclined to release him on parole, but Welles disagreed. If Semmes could not have a prompt trial, it would be better to release him unconditionally.[30] There was some inconclusive discussion as to what statement, if any, should accompany his release. Should it be tied to Johnson's proclamation ending the war or to the Supreme Court decision in *Milligan*? Ultimately, the president told Welles to prepare a memorandum recommending that Semmes be released. The secretary did so, Johnson approved the recommendation, and the following day Semmes was told that he was free to leave.

More than a decade later, John Bolles wrote of the Semmes case in *Harper's Weekly*. In his opinion, had Semmes been promptly tried after his arrest, he would have been convicted of treason and executed. But once the evidence was closely considered, his culpability was far less clear. Bolles concluded that Semmes was entitled as commander of a cruiser "to all the customary cheats, falsehoods, snares, decoys, false pretenses and swindles of civilized and Christian warfare" and that "the records of the United States Navy Department effectually silence all right to complain of Semmes for having imitated our example in obedience to orders from the Secretary of the Confederate Navy."[31]

Indeed, Bolles appears to have been impressed with Semmes. Writing in 1872, Bolles reflected on his orders to prey on Federal shipping. "Never in naval history," he wrote, "has such an order been so signally obeyed; never has there occurred so striking an example of the tremendous power of mischief possessed by a single cruiser." Semmes, with his "restless energy" and "untiring zeal," had found "no voyage too long, no movement too prompt . . . no danger too great, no labor too wearisome" in the accomplishment of his mission. Bolles refused to condemn Semmes because he had, "like our own Bainbridge, Morris, Porter and Stewart," carried out his orders to the letter.[32]

Far from feeling any gratitude at his release, Semmes treated the entire proceedings with lofty contempt. He returned to Mobile, where a cheering crowd greeted him at the waterfront. His imprisonment had added to his already considerable popularity, and friends in Mobile had delayed the election of a county probate judge until Semmes was free and available to run. Such a lucrative office could provide the Semmes family with the financial security that they had never enjoyed, and Semmes was eager to fill it. But he was an "unpardoned rebel," and when Judge Hughes attempted to sound out the president as to how the administration would view his election to a judgeship, Johnson had given him no encouragement.[33] Semmes, who could be quite obsequious when the situation so dictated, engaged in a bit of discreet politicking. At a dinner in his honor following his release he reportedly urged the people of the South to support President Johnson, calling him "our greatest friend among those in authority in the Government."[34]

On May 7, after two other candidates had withdrawn, Semmes was elected probate judge without opposition. Sure enough, General George H. Thomas, whose military district included Alabama, asked his superiors in Washington whether Semmes should be allowed to take the oath. In Mobile, four hundred "leading merchants and citizens" petitioned President Johnson to allow Semmes to serve. Stanton, however, replied by telegraph on May 15 that the issue had been raised with the president, who had decided that neither Semmes nor any other unpardoned rebel was eligible to hold civil office.[35]

To some extent, Semmes was a victim of poor timing. Just weeks earlier, a clash between black and white teamsters in Memphis, Tennessee, had triggered a riot in which city police and poor whites raided the black quarter of the city, killing and burning as they went. Most states of the old Confederacy were in the process of passing "Black Codes" aimed at disqualifying blacks from voting. In the North, even moderates were asking who had won the war.

At some time in May, Semmes appears to have applied to Johnson for a pardon, probably in the hope that his election might still be certified. The president's reply, passed to Semmes on June 2, was that the pardon requested could not be granted.[36] A person more sensitive than Semmes might have recognized the pressures on Johnson and settled for the right to earn a livelihood in the country that he had worked so hard to destroy. But forgiveness was not one of the admiral's more conspicuous virtues. Soon the kind words for Johnson as a friend of the South would be forgotten, and Semmes would dismiss the president as a "charlatan" and "a traitor to his state."[37]

Back in Mobile, Semmes seethed at his recent treatment and the voiding of his election. He continued to hope that some way would be found around his disqualification—a rather forlorn hope, for the Fourteenth Amendment included a section that disqualified Confederate military men who were former officers of the U.S. Army or the U.S. Navy from holding office, unless this disability were removed by a two-thirds vote of both houses.[38] Clearly, the "pirate" Semmes was unlikely to be the beneficiary of any such vote.

CHAPTER 21

Defiance

In Mobile, Semmes faced the discouraging prospect of building up a law practice sufficient to support his family in a city still recovering from the war. His recent martyrdom in Washington, however, was a factor in his favor. From London, Louisa Tremlett wrote Semmes to congratulate him on his escape "from the hands of those Yankee barbarians."[1] Closer to home, Southerners who might otherwise have been put off by the austere admiral considered his jailing to have been shameful.

One of many Southern educational institutions attempting to recover from the war at this time was the Louisiana State Seminary of Learning and Military Academy, today's Louisiana State University, in Alexandria. The seminary's last prewar president had been an eccentric Ohioan named William Tecumseh Sherman. Now, under a young Southern president, thirty-two-year-old David F. Boyd, the school was attempting a comeback. It had lost everything—faculty, students, resources—to the war; its only surviving assets were eighteen hundred pounds of cotton and its charter as a state institution. Boyd, however, was not intimidated. He secured some funds from the state and recruited a staff of young Southerners for his faculty. The college with the cumbersome name was back in business.

One faculty chair that remained unfilled in 1866 was that of moral philosophy and English literature, and Boyd obtained permission from his trustees to offer the post to Semmes. Although there is no evidence that the two men had ever met, the admiral had impeccable Confederate credentials and a reputation for erudition. That Semmes had never attended college did not matter; he was a scholar who had served The Cause, and Boyd made him a formal offer in October 1866. Semmes had misgivings about the salary—$3,000 a year would not go far—but he replied that he was honored by the offer and agreed to take up his duties at the beginning of the new year.[2]

Semmes traveled to Alexandria alone. He may have had doubts as to the length of his stay there, but his primary motive in leaving his family in Mobile was to maintain a legal residence in Alabama in hope of somehow gaining the judgeship that he regarded as his. At Alexandria, Semmes shared with another professor the house once occupied by Sherman. His fellow professors, virtually all of them in their thirties, were in awe of the legendary sea raider who so rarely discussed his wartime exploits. One of his colleagues recalled that Semmes hated condensed milk because he had had so much of it at sea. When fresh milk was not available at meals, he put butter in his coffee.[3]

Semmes invested long hours of research into his lectures. He wrote to Anne,

> I manage to occupy myself very well during the day. . . . It is at night-fall, when I am sitting by my lonely fireside, before lighting my lamp and commencing my *studies,* that I miss you all most. Only think of a man my age pursuing his studies, like a college boy! Such are the vicissitudes of life.[4]

Semmes had fifteen students in his class. Although the content of his course can only be inferred, he was well read in the writings of early American statesmen and of many British authors. Anne, who wanted him to work on his memoirs, twitted him about the time he devoted to his lectures. And lectures they were, for there was nothing egalitarian in the admiral's approach to education. As on the *Alabama,* he spoke and others listened. Semmes probably avoided commenting in class on controversial matters related to Reconstruction, lest he embarrass the seminary, but he pulled no punches in family correspondence. He wrote Pendleton Colston,

I am here at work playing school-master in my old age,
thanks to the bull-headed abortion who fills the President's
chair. I say bull-headed, but he is only bull-headed towards
his friends, or those of his enemies who are weak & power-
less to resist him. He is as timid as the coward that he is in the
presence of the strong. . . . Like a whipped hound he is afraid
even to bark in the presence of the radicals, who are kicking
and spurning him.[5]

Boyd may have erred in recruiting the controversial Semmes to his
staff. A radical newspaper in New Orleans attacked the seminary for
having on its faculty "no less than four rebel majors" plus Semmes,
who, "in derision of all decency," served as professor of moral philosophy.[6] Nevertheless, when Semmes left the seminary it was on his
own initiative. He had hardly begun his teaching when he received a
feeler from the *Memphis Bulletin* about its vacant editorship. Anne
thought a move to Memphis most promising, and she was certain
that the seminary trustees would not stand in his way:

Five thousand a year is quite a handsome salary & then there
are other inducements; if you do not finally get your
Judgeship, you can move to Memphis and establish yourself
with your sons in a law business. It would be a good opportunity for Raphael & a much better place for the girls; they
might have an opportunity of making an eligible marriage.[7]

Semmes decided that the offer was a serious one and in February
1867 went to Memphis to discuss it with the *Bulletin*'s owners. The
paper was a onetime Whig journal that in 1860 had supported the
third-party ticket of Bell and Everett. Semmes's talks with the owners, P. B. Wills and J. B. Bingham, apparently went well, for on March
2 he wrote to Boyd that, although he was sorry to leave the seminary,
he would be moving to Memphis.

Postwar Memphis was a shadow of the boomtown of the antebel-
lum years. The war had largely ended its cotton trade, and prolonged
occupation by Union forces had exacerbated political differences
among the residents. Tennessee had been the last state to join the
Confederacy, and its legislature had voted for secession over the
objections of representatives of the eastern counties. Now, however,
most residents hoped that the presence of a Tennessee man in the
White House would facilitate the state's return to the Union. When
the publishers of the *Bulletin* interviewed Semmes as their prospec-

tive editor, they probably didn't ask the right questions. Semmes had come to loathe Andrew Johnson, and if asked his opinion of the president, he would not have equivocated.

Semmes traveled to Memphis in March, once again leaving his family in Mobile. But he had friends in Memphis, including his foster brother, B. J. Semmes, and all went well for a time. In June 1867 he described his routine to Anne: "After [dinner] I retire to my room and read the newspapers, as we used to do at home . . . until 11 p.m. when I go to bed. I do all my writing in the morning from about 9 until 12 or half past, when I go down to the office."[8]

Semmes had accepted his position with the *Bulletin* in the belief that he would have full editorial control. Operating on this premise, he sought to make the *Bulletin* a states'-rights journal with a pronounced anti-Johnson tilt. Soon he was at odds with the publishers, who disapproved of his assaults on the president. Semmes probably could have remained at the *Bulletin* had he accommodated the views of the owners, but this was not his way. Calling the publishers "a set of political scoundrels," he resigned after only seven months.[9]*

The flinty Semmes was never an easy man to get along with. In any wartime command other than a cruiser at sea he would probably have proved as contentious as any of Jefferson Davis's generals. A life in the navy had steeped him in devotion to duty but had provided few opportunities for practicing conciliation and accommodation. Intellectual give-and-take was foreign to him. Perhaps Semmes's brief stint as an editor was doomed from the start, but his acrimonious departure from the *Bulletin* was a setback in that it removed him from the one field in which he might have had some influence in the postwar South. Henceforth he would live in the past, lecturing and writing on his wartime experiences.

Once again the admiral was looking for work. In June 1867 he had told Boyd not to keep the chair at the seminary open for him; four months later he regretted that move. Still, he had discovered in Memphis that there was considerable public interest in the story of the *Alabama*. After returning to Mobile he arranged a lecture tour of Kentucky and Tennessee for the first months of the new year, and he

---

*Spencer Semmes would later charge that partisans of President Johnson caused the *Bulletin* to be purchased by persons friendly to the administration, who proceeded to force Semmes out. The admiral's own correspondence indicates that his relations with the original proprietors were so strained that any change in ownership was incidental to his departure.

eventually spoke in some twenty towns. Among his subjects were
"Storms and Currents" and "Whales and Their Habits," but the lec-
tures that people came to hear were those relating to the war and the
Alabama.

An early arrival for one of Semmes's lectures, British traveler David
Macrae, found himself introduced to the speaker, whom he described
as "a small, dark-looking man; thin, wiry, weather-beaten in face,
with a fierce-looking moustache twisted outwards at the ends, and a
dangerous look about his . . . eyes." He thought Semmes uncomfortable as a speaker, for he appeared restless and was prone to twist his
mustache "with an abstracted air." Semmes asked "two or three gentlemen" if they wished to introduce him, but each respectfully
declined.[10]

At the appointed hour Semmes walked onto the stage and began
his talk without introduction. Macrae found the lecture, during
which Semmes compared the Confederate struggle against the North
to that of the American colonies against Britain, "exceedingly graphic
and interesting," but he was not impressed with the admiral as a
speaker. He thought Semmes's voice weak and noted his tendency to
smack his lips occasionally, as if his mouth were too dry:

> There were very few peculiarities in his speech, except his
> Cockney-like addition of "r" in "Alabamar" and "idear"; also
> his American pronunciation of "calmly" as if it were spelt
> "kemly," and of "u" as if it were "oo"—"We threw a shot
> astern which *indooced* the merchantman to heave to."[11]

Semmes alluded only briefly to the battle off Cherbourg, but said of
his beloved *Alabama,* "No enemy's foot ever polluted her deck. No
splinter of her hull, no shred of her flag, remains as a trophy in the
hands of the enemy!" This pronouncement, wrote Macrae, brought
down the house.[12]

Any lecture by Semmes included considerable bias and stereotyp-
ing. Referring on one occasion to the controversial burning of the
Martaban, Semmes noted some of the factors that made him suspect
that she was in fact American:

> One was that Samuel B. Pike, the master of the ship, had been
> cast by nature in that Down Easter mould that no amount of
> custom house paper . . . could [change]. There was no mistak-
> ing the nativity of that long, lank, angular frame, and peculiar
> physiognomy, even before he opened his mouth; but when he

spoke, you might have shut your eyes and sworn that he was from the State of Maine.

Did Semmes feel any regret about destroying vessels that were the sole livelihood of the hardworking sailors who manned them? He claimed to have felt sympathy:

> The spectacle of a burning ship was frequently a mournful one to me, & I always sympathized with the hard working sailor class, many of whom were completely ruined by the fortunes of war. When they would remonstrate with me, as they frequently did . . . I replied that I could make no discrimination; that they were bound by the acts of their own people, & that my orders required me to prey upon their commerce, so long as their armies remained south of the Potomac.

Semmes attempted to put the best gloss possible on his encounter with the *Kearsarge*. Sea lawyer that he was, he sought to equate the one-sided encounter off Cherbourg with the *Alabama*'s dispatching of the *Hatteras*:

> I consider that there was just about the same disparity between the *Alabama* and the *Hatteras* as there was between the *Kearsarge* and the *Alabama*—the disparity being in favor of the *Alabama* in the former case, & against her in the latter. Yet it took the *Kearsarge* an hour and five minutes to beat me.[13]

The lecture tour was a financial success, but Semmes was not eager to repeat it. He wrote to Anne from Selma, Alabama, that he did not mean to leave home again if he could help it. "We must try & see if we cannot scratch along, without the necessity of my running about & delivering lectures."[14] He again wrote to David Boyd, inquiring about the seminary, but his old chair had been filled and nothing else was available.

During his lecture tour Semmes dropped in on the Kell farm near Vinesville, Georgia. Greeting Blanche Kell, he congratulated her on "so safely anchoring" his first officer. After some general conversation, Blanche remarked that for all her husband's years at sea, he could not bring himself to discipline their three children. Nonsense, Semmes replied; her husband was a splendid disciplinarian, "and I could not have had the ship I did without him." Inevitably, politics intruded. Blanche spoke regretfully of her husband's "sectional pride." Her guest responded that he, Semmes, was at least fifteen years older than John Kell. "Give him that long to become reconciled to things as they are."[15]

In 1861 Semmes's zealous support for secession had set him apart from most army and navy officers. Now, he was one of a die-hard group who, while living in a restored Union, refused to acknowledge any need for accommodation with the victors. Not that the men who had led the South were united in their approaches to reconstruction. A few former Confederates, led by General James Longstreet, quickly came to terms with the Republicans and, as a result, became recipients of Federal patronage. At the other extreme were the "unreconstructed." This group was led by Jefferson Davis, who would devote his remaining years to defending the Confederate cause, and included generals like Jubal A. Early, who, at least initially, chose exile over submission.

Between these extremes were the many who chose to remain in the restored Union as long as they could earn a living. A few of these, like Robert E. Lee, were active in fields like education and sought to rebuild and regenerate the South. Others asked nothing more than to be able to support their families. Many went into insurance, railroads, and engineering.

Although Semmes was concerned about his livelihood, he was by no means prepared to put the war behind him. He was far closer to Jefferson Davis in his outlook than to Robert E. Lee. As he returned to Mobile to resume his unrewarding law practice, he turned his attention to a memoir of the war. He planned more than an account of his cruises with the *Sumter* and the *Alabama*; he had in mind a book that would justify the South's cause to future generations and stigmatize the victors as the bloodthirsty aggressors he believed them to be. Such a book would put the late war in perspective and perhaps prove financially rewarding as well.

By July 1868, seven of the eleven states of the former Confederacy, including Alabama, had been readmitted into the Union. While the rest of the country watched the impeachment proceedings against President Johnson, Alabama took the lead among Southern states seeking to keep the freedmen in something approaching slavery. In Alabama, "stubborn or refractory servants" or "servants who loiter away their time" were declared to be statutory vagrants subject to arrest. In Mobile, persons defined as vagrants—almost always blacks—were required to post security for their good behavior or risk jail.[16]

Semmes, meanwhile, devoted most of 1868 to his memoirs. He drew on the journals he had kept on board the *Sumter* and the *Alabama* and the speech drafts he had worked up for his lecture tour. He had in mind more than a narrative of his wartime cruises, but he did not contemplate a full autobiography. Readers of *Memoirs of Service Afloat During the War Between the States* were going to get a full exposition of the causes of the war and of Semmes's wartime cruises, but they would learn little of the author's personal life.

In part because so many of the Confederacy's prominent military leaders died during the war, Semmes's memoir was the first important Confederate retrospective. He took his responsibility seriously. As noted earlier, the first seven chapters constituted an eloquent defense of the right of secession, one that allowed Semmes to make full use of his readings in constitutional law. Decades later, historian Jonathan Dorris would call these chapters "as good a defense of the South as can be found anywhere."[17] Anyone who has struggled through the turgid prose of Jefferson Davis or Alexander H. Stephens may even feel that Dorris's praise is understated.

In his preface Semmes acknowledged that he was not attempting to write objective history. When one is struggling against barbarians, he suggested, it is not always possible to maintain an attitude of detachment. The author insisted, however, that although he had at times given vent to indignation, he had not written in malice. "If he has been occasionally plain-spoken, it is because he has used the English language, which calls a rogue a rogue, notwithstanding his disguises."

The narrative that follows is a rollicking account of the voyages of the *Sumter* and the *Alabama,* interspersed from time to time with Semmes's digressions on scientific and sociopolitical topics. When he turns his attention to nature, the result is some of his best writing, as in this description of South Africa's Saldanha Bay:

> The morning after our arrival—the 30th of July—was bright and beautiful, and I landed early to get sights for my chronometers. It was the first time I had ever set foot on the continent of Africa, and I looked forth, from the eminence on which I stood, upon a wild, desolate, yet picturesque scene. The ocean was slumbering in the distance, huge rocky precipices were around me, the newly risen sun was scatter-

ing the mists from the hills, and the only signs of life, save the *Alabama* at my feet, and the ox-team of a Boer which was creeping along the beach, were the screams of the sea-fowl as they whirled about me.[18]

These Thoreau-like passages stand in sharp contrast to Semmes's comments relating to the war. Avoiding the false humility and the evenhanded praise of friend and foe that mark many Civil War memoirs, Semmes portrays the war as a struggle between good and evil in which the South was clearly on the side of the angels. His lurid descriptions of burning ships suggest that he had long since overcome any aversion to destroying merchant vessels. And after a while the reader becomes conscious of the author's harsh unwillingness to credit his foes with any honorable qualities. The Federal consuls who harass him in foreign ports are beneath contempt—cowards, hypocrites, and prevaricators. A naval officer of Southern birth who remains in Federal service has clearly done so from the basest of motives.

Semmes views the war as a struggle between opposing cultures, and his views are unfailingly elitist: "When mobs rule, gentlemen must retire to private life."[19] He expresses contempt for the popular press in the North, only in part because of the aspersions cast on him and his ships. He admires Britain and its colonial empire; he sees the latter as improving the lot of native peoples without encouraging political democracy.

Semmes repeatedly compares the South's struggle for independence to the English civil war two centuries earlier. He likens the South to the king's Cavaliers, the North to the barbarous Roundheads. Describing one of his officers on the *Sumter*, Robert Chapman, Semmes notes that though Chapman wore his hair closely cropped, his behavior was "the very reverse of a round-head"—that is to say, it was chivalrous. Elsewhere, he describes actions of the Federal government toward John Maffitt as marked by "a vindictiveness and malignity peculiarly Puritan"—the most damning of all indictments in Semmes's eyes. The Yankees had fought the war as barbarians, but Semmes was prepared to be magnanimous. "We should rather pity than condemn men who have shown, both during and since the war, so little magnanimity as our late enemies have done. The savage is full of prejudices, because he is full of ignorance."[20]

As for slavery, Semmes could not conceive of the blacks' prospering in a situation where they were left to their own devices. Slavery had been abolished in Jamaica and other British colonies in the 1830s, and Semmes was not impressed with the result. Emancipation had all but ruined the sugar economy of the Caribbean, leading Semmes to conclude that Negroes were "nearly worthless" as free labor.[21] Like many Southerners of the period, Semmes is appalled by the thought of miscegenation. He comments of the people of the West Indies,

> Amalgamation, by slow but sure processes, will corrupt what little of European blood [that] remains in them, until every trace of the white man will disappear. The first process will be the mulatto; but the mulatto, as the name imports, is a mule, and must finally die out; and the mass of the population will become pure African.[22]

Semmes's knowledge of genetics left something to be desired, for, unlike mules, heterogeneous societies propagate freely and successfully. And while African-American communities would in time become dominant in many of the Caribbean islands, this development would owe much to the superior ability of Africans to adapt to the climate and working conditions of the Caribbean.

In places, Semmes indulges his romanticism. When he mentions his leave-taking from his family in 1861, he pulls out all the stops: "The heroism of woman! how infinitely it surpasses that of man." He finds symbolism in the burning woods through which he passed en route to Montgomery in 1861. He worships at the altar of Southern womanhood, as in his glowing description of the pilot's wife cheering the *Sumter*'s dash through the Mississippi passes. And though it was steam that had made Semmes's commerce raiding possible, he is unabashedly nostalgic for the world of sail:

> The sailing ship has a romance and a poetry about her which is thoroughly killed by steam. The sailor of the former loves, for its own sake, the howling of the gale, and there is no music so sweet to his ear as the shouting of orders through the trumpet of the officer of the deck, when he is poised upon the topsail-yard, of the rolling and tumbling ship.

One suspects that most sailors could find music sweeter than an officer's voice through the speaking trumpet, but Semmes continues:

Steam, practical, commonplace, hard-working steam, has well-nigh changed all this. . . . Seamanship, evolutions, invention, skill, and ready resource in times of difficulty and danger, have nearly all gone out of fashion, and instead of reefing the topsails, and club-hauling . . . some order is now sent to the engineer about regulating his fires and paying attention to his steam gauges.[23]

When he comes to the battle with the *Kearsarge,* Semmes is uncharacteristically brief. His description of the engagement requires only four of the book's more than eight hundred pages, although his comments and complaints cover quite a few more. Far from having reconciled himself to Winslow's use of protective chains, Semmes is more bitter than ever. He had thought that he might beat the *Kearsarge* in a fair fight, "But he did not show me a fair fight for, as it afterward turned out, his ship was iron-clad. It was the same thing as if two men were to go out to fight a duel, and one of them, unknown to the other, were to put on a shirt of mail under his outer garment."[24]

Nor had Semmes forgotten the defective shell from the *Alabama's* pivot that had found its way to the White House. As far as he was concerned, only the defective cap on this projectile had denied him the victory he deserved. He ignores the fact that this shell had reached the enemy's sternpost only on the ricochet; had it exploded on impact it would have inflicted only superficial damage. Writing of Winslow's delay in sending boats to the sinking *Alabama,* Semmes remarks, "What the war may have made of him, it is impossible to say. It has turned a great deal of the milk of human kindness to gall and wormwood."[25] Could he ever have considered that this comment might apply less to Winslow than himself?

For all their bias, Semmes's memoirs are generally accurate with respect to factual matters. Where it can be verified, his narrative is usually consistent with other accounts, including those of his victims. But there are interesting omissions. There is no mention of his own tendency toward seasickness. He does not deal with Captain Blake's charge that the *Alabama* was slow in sending help to the sinking *Hatteras*—to do so might detract from his similar complaint against Winslow. There is no mention of the feisty "stewardess" on the *Union Jack* who was doused with water for calling Semmes a pirate or of the occasional instances of severe punishment aboard his ships. He never mentions his discovery, well before the battle with the *Kearsarge,* that many of the *Alabama's* fuses were defective. He does not share with the reader his reasons for choosing Cherbourg as the *Alabama*'s port of call. And, in the face of considerable evidence to the contrary, he continues to deny any prior knowledge of the *Kearsarge*'s chains.

Were there other incidents in the *Alabama*'s cruise that Semmes chose not to mention? Two decades after Semmes's death, Lieutenant Richard Armstrong, then living in Canada, wrote a curious letter to Blanche Kell, who was helping her husband with his own memoirs:

> With regard to the little Malay pilot episode I have a perfect recollection of all the circumstances, but as these reflect discredit upon Captain Semmes I should strongly advise that no mention whatever be made of the affair."[26]

Indeed, no record of the episode survives.[27]

Semmes's memoirs may be unique in that they frequently put the author in a less favorable light than the circumstances warrant. Because Semmes cannot acknowledge that many Northerners were firmly convinced of the rightness of their cause, he comes through as a zealot. Instead of taking credit for the skill and daring with which he conducted his wartime cruises, Semmes goes out of his way to cite the ineptitude of the Federal response. Although he mentions the care accorded prisoners aboard his ships, his humanitarianism is largely obscured by his fulminations against Yankees as a class and by the relish with which he describes their burning ships.

One of his admirers who recognized this problem was Arthur Sinclair. In his own book about the *Alabama,* he sought to defend Semmes against his literary excesses:

> Semmes's verbal and written utterances manifest a bitterness of feeling toward his foes which are calculated to greatly mislead one respecting his real character. . . . He was uniformly just in his decisions. He respected private property and private feelings. And it was the rule, rather than the exception, that he provided in the best possible way for his prisoners. . . . It is by his acts rather than his utterances that a man like Semmes should be judged.[28]

Semmes worked on his memoirs through the hot summer of 1868, filling page after page of foolscap with material drawn from his journals and his memory. When Stephen Mallory suggested that he include anecdotes and vignettes of forecastle life, Semmes said that he would consider the suggestion, but that because he had been "more or less isolated socially from the rest of my officers," his supply of anecdotes was limited.[29] In July he wrote to Mrs. Clement Clay that the manuscript was two-thirds complete and asked whether she knew of a reliable person in the Huntsville area to act as his agent and to collect subscriptions for the book.[30]

Semmes's memoirs have a curious publishing history. In 1864 a two-volume work titled *The Cruise of the* Alabama *and the* Sumter was published in London and New York, claiming to have been drawn from Semmes's journals and other papers. In his preface to *Memoirs of Service Afloat,* Semmes acknowledged having lent his journals to the London house of Saunders, Otley & Company, but he disavowed the excerpts that they had seen fit to publish. Now he chose as his printer the Baltimore firm of Kelly, Piet & Company, which ran off its first printing in the final months of 1868.

No sales figures on *Service Afloat* are available, and the book's impact is difficult to judge. As a skillful presentation of the South's position on secession it doubtless gave satisfaction to unreconstructed rebels like its author. Other Southerners read with interest of a campaign in the late war about which they knew very little. Few copies of *Service Afloat* would have made their way north of the Mason-Dixon line, but navy professionals there were doubtless angered, as Admiral Porter was, by the author's lack of remorse for his destruction of Northern merchantmen.

Because the author had relatively few difficulties with his Confederate superiors, Semmes's book was not so controversial as were later memoirs by generals like Joseph E. Johnston, P. G. T. Beauregard, and James Longstreet. Its bellicose tone, however, made it analogous to the last shot in a war already lost; certainly, it was not a book designed to facilitate national reconciliation.

CHAPTER 22

Sunset

Semmes had just completed his memoirs when he received a warm, friendly letter from Louisa Tremlett, who asked a question: Did Semmes, four years after the war, still hate the Yankees? The admiral assured her that he did. "I hate the Yankee as cordially as ever—maybe even worse, if possible, as he has proven himself more of a *dog* since the war than during it." Part of this feeling, to be sure, grew out of slurs against himself in the Northern press, but its roots went deeper:

> I believe the Yankee, puritanical race of New England to be, taken all in all, the most unamiable and corrupt race of men that the sun shines upon—cowardly . . . treacherous and fanatical. I defy their venom and their hatred so far as directed toward me personally. I have never asked for amnesty and never will. Fortunately for my safety, the rascals made a bargain with me when I laid down my arms, which they find it impossible to get around.[1]

His memoirs now complete, Semmes devoted himself to the law practice that he shared with Oliver. He would have liked to hold public office, but in November 1870, because of his uncertain legal status, he withdrew his name as a candidate for mayor of Mobile.[2] A

261

few months later, however, he was appointed city attorney, a part-time job that nevertheless assured him a share of the city's legal business. It was hardly a windfall, but it reflected a determination on the part of Semmes's neighbors to honor their unreconstructed hero.

Nor did the city's largess end with the legal appointment. In 1871, a group of Mobile residents purchased for Semmes, by popular subscription, a two-story brick house on Government Street, one of the city's most gracious thoroughfares. Shaded by magnolia trees and adorned with the iron grillwork typical of the Gulf region, the house was grander than any of Semmes's previous homes. Apparently because of the admiral's uncertain legal status, the house was nominally presented to Anne Semmes.[3]

In Mobile, Semmes had close ties with Spring Hill College, the Jesuit institution from which Spencer had graduated before the war. When asked to deliver the commencement address there in 1871, Semmes accepted, realizing as he did so that he should avoid any remarks that might be provocative in terms of reconstruction politics. He chose as his topic the influence of Catholicism on America and in his remarks provided some insight into his own attitudes:

> With rare local exceptions, all the writers of our so-called American histories have been Protestants, and the readers of these histories would conclude that America was a Protestant country . . . and that our free institutions are due, solely and entirely, to Protestant brains and Protestant love of liberty.

Semmes, not surprisingly, disagreed. Columbus had been a Catholic, as had been explorers like La Salle and Father Marquette. The town of St. Augustine had been established by Spanish Catholics over half a century before the arrival of the *Mayflower*. Semmes went on to claim the Magna Carta—the basis of America's own liberties—as largely the work of British Catholics:

> The barons of England, who conceived and drew up this instrument, and forced its adoption upon a weak monarch, were good and loyal sons of old Mother Church . . . for up to this period no recusant son of hers had struck a blow at his Mother.
>
> Yet every Protestant boy who graduates at Yale, at [Harvard], at Princeton, or any other well-pronounced Protestant college, will swear to you by the beard of the Prophet that the Magna Charta is a genuine Protestant instru-

ment, and he will supplement this oath by declaiming to you, by the hour, of the tyranny and other abominations of the Catholic Church.[4]

Semmes lived in a world of villains. The values that he prized most were threatened not only by Yankees but by Protestants.

From Mobile, Semmes followed as closely as he could the remarkable negotiations between the United States and Britain aimed at resolving Washington's long-standing claim that Britain was responsible for the damage inflicted by the *Alabama* and other cruisers constructed in Britain during the war. While the war was in progress London had refused even to discuss the issue. Now, with the North victorious and Canada potentially at the mercy of a battle-tested U.S. Army, Britain could see advantages to removing the claims issue as an irritant in Anglo-American relations.

During 1867 and 1868 Secretary of State Seward had attempted to prod the British toward the conference table. In 1869 the two countries agreed that all outstanding claims between them, of which those for damages inflicted by Confederate cruisers were much the largest, would be submitted to arbitration. Semmes was outraged, for he regarded any aspersion on the legal status of the *Alabama* as a reflection on him. In his lectures he had reiterated his belief that no violation of international law had taken place in the Confederacy's acquisition of the *Alabama*. In his memoirs he went further, arguing that once a naval vessel was commissioned, no power could investigate its antecedents.[5]

Washington and London were less interested in the legalities than in improving Anglo-American relations. The negotiations were protracted and difficult. In January 1869 the Johnson-Clarendon Convention provided for a tribunal to arbitrate claims growing out of the war. Then Senator Charles Sumner of Massachusetts, chairman of the Foreign Relations Committee, interjected the volatile issue of "indirect damages"—costs arising from the prolongation of the war that might also be charged to Britain. Sumner maintained that Britain owed the United States half the total cost of the war, a figure that he estimated at $2.5 billion. Not that he expected John Bull to write a check for this amount; Sumner would settle for title to Canada, Newfoundland, Bermuda, and the British West Indies.[6]

Because Britain was not prepared even to discuss indirect damages, the Johnson-Clarendon Convention was overwhelmingly rejected by the Senate in April 1869. Negotiations were shortly reopened, however, and on May 8, 1871, British and U.S. representatives signed the Treaty of Washington. The treaty met most of the United States's long-standing demands: an expression of regret by Britain; recognition of the responsibilities of neutrals; and a promise of compensation for damage inflicted by Confederate cruisers. How Semmes must have writhed! The treaty not only repudiated the means by which the *Alabama* had been obtained by the Confederacy but promised compensation to its victims.

The treaty finessed the issue of indirect damages but created a tribunal composed of representatives of Britain, the United States, Italy, Switzerland, and Brazil to review claims for direct damages. Then came tedious months of analyzing the claims submitted to the tribunal. The United States did not immediately drop the question of indirect damages, and the negotiations came close to breaking down when U.S. representatives charged that the Confederacy was capable of offensive operations only at sea after July 1863, and that Britain was responsible for these operations.[7]

Ultimately, the tribunal determined that Britain had failed to exercise "due diligence" in the cases of the *Alabama,* the *Florida,* and the *Shenandoah*; it absolved Britain of blame in connection with the *Georgia* and several lesser vessels. On September 14, 1872, with only Britain dissenting, the tribunal awarded the sum of $15.5 million to the United States. Church bells rang in Geneva to mark the successful conclusion of the most important international arbitration up to that time. No bells rang in Mobile, Alabama, but Semmes may have felt a grudging satisfaction that the damages ascribed to the *Alabama*— $6.75 million—were by far the largest for any Confederate cruiser.[8]

Semmes's family was scattering. Spencer and his wife, Pauline, had left Alabama for Osceola, Arkansas, where he resumed his law practice. Osceola was only about sixty miles from Memphis, Tennessee, where the Semmes family remained well represented after the admiral's abrupt departure. B. J. Semmes, Raphael's foster brother, had moved to Memphis before the war and continued to live there afterward. Katherine Semmes had married a Memphis attorney, Luke Wright, who would gain a national reputation as governor general of the Philippines and later as secretary of war under Theodore Roosevelt. Young Raphael had moved to Memphis in about 1869 to work for the Memphis Street Railway.

In Mobile, the Semmeses were a close-knit family, their way of life frugal and private. The admiral enjoyed a game of whist, and many an evening was doubtless passed with friends over the card table. There were still three generations of Semmeses in the house on Government Street. Electra's husband, Pendleton Colston, had died after only three years of marriage, and Electra had returned with her two children to live with her parents. Anne, the youngest daughter, lived at home until her marriage in 1875 to another Memphis native, Charles B. Bryan. Oliver had his own home in Mobile, but his children spent much of their time at their grandparents' house.[9]

Semmes took a paternal interest in his godson, Raphael Semmes Kell. In a letter in 1872, Semmes admonished his six-year-old namesake to "do justice" to the two names he bore:

> There is more responsibility resting upon little boys who have our ancestors than upon those who have none; and some poor little boys, whose fathers and mothers are unknown in the world, can scarcely be said to have ancestors. . . . Give my true love to your papa, and mama, and tell them that I often think of them, & you, and wish you all the happiness that we poor mortals are permitted to enjoy in this world.[10]

Early in 1872 Semmes wrote Francis Tremlett to advise him of the latest developments among his Confederate navy friends. Matthew Maury, he wrote, had tentatively accepted the presidency of the University of Alabama but had subsequently returned to his professorship at the Virginia Military Institute. Semmes's own life was quiet. "The Yankees have, at last, ceased to abuse me, or even . . . to speak of me in print, except at very rare intervals. . . . When they do, they call me 'Admiral,' in quotation marks, instead of Pirate."[11]

In the summer of 1872 *Harper's Weekly* published two articles by John Bolles, the navy lawyer who had investigated Semmes's record in 1866 and concluded that Semmes was not such a bloodthirsty pirate after all. In a letter to the magazine, Semmes contended that Bolles's articles had done him "partial but not entire justice" and asked the magazine to publish a submission by him as well.[12] Perhaps he thought that a reflective article of his own might neutralize opposition to his holding office. No article appeared, however; the editors at *Harper's Weekly* may have felt that Bolles had done the admiral more than justice.

Meanwhile, Semmes made what proved to be his final attempt to remove the constitutional disqualification that had prevented his taking office as probate judge. The Fourteenth Amendment to the Constitution, adopted in 1868, provided that persons who had served the Confederacy despite having sworn an oath to defend the Constitution of the United States were barred from holding any federal or local office. Some had wanted such disqualification to be permanent, but the amendment as adopted included a clause that made the disability removable by a two-thirds vote in both houses of Congress.[13]

In 1873 Semmes attempted to regain his full political rights. His congressman, Frederick Bromberg, was a Harvard-educated Alabamian who had taught at his alma mater during the war and subsequently had been appointed treasurer of the city of Mobile by the local Federal commander. In November 1872 he had been elected to Congress as a Democrat. One year later Semmes asked Bromberg's assistance in having his political disabilities removed and, in writing him, took a far more conciliatory line than in his earlier correspondence with the Tremletts:

> It is now eight years and a half since the close of the late war between the States; and the defeated Section has submitted, and is submitting, in good faith to the decision of arms. That decision was, that henceforth . . . the people of the North and the people of the South should live together under the same federal government and have a common history.
>
> The feats of arms performed in that war are now the common property of our people. Have the terms "rebellion" and "rebel" any just application to such a war? Now that passions have cooled on both sides, is it generous in the stronger of the two Sections . . . to reproach the weaker? . . . No Southern man has any other country than that of his birth, or adoption, and if he is deprived of that, he is indeed a Pariah in this western world.[14]

In the first session of the Forty-third Congress the House passed a bill that removed the political disabilities of Semmes and others. In the Senate, however, there was reluctance to help ex-Confederates in states where resistance to Reconstruction was so strong that blacks rarely voted. Semmes wrote plaintively to Bromberg that the freedmen of Alabama, "far from being deprived of any of their civil rights, are masters of the situation."[15] Nevertheless, the relief bill failed to pass the Senate.

In the next session, Bromberg in the House and General John B. Gordon in the Senate each introduced a private bill designed to benefit Semmes. The House version passed on May 28, 1874, thanks in part to an unlikely supporter, General Benjamin F. Butler of Massachusetts, whose actions while commanding the Federal occupation of New Orleans during the war had caused him to be excoriated throughout the South. In one letter to Bromberg, Semmes called Butler "a distinguished leader of the Northern people"—a remark that he could hardly have conceived of making a few years before.[16] But all was for naught; the relief bill died in the Senate.

Was Semmes mellowing? In the spring of 1871, following the death of Robert E. Lee, Semmes joined a number of prominent ex-Confederates, including generals Braxton Bragg, John B. Gordon, and Nathan B. Forrest, in an appeal to all Americans on behalf of Washington and Lee College.[17] Three years later he was the principal speaker at the unveiling of a memorial to Confederate dead, held at the Magnolia Cemetery in Mobile. Such events were common in the post-war South, and as time went on, Union veterans were sometimes invited to participate. On this occasion a group of U.S. Army officers had brought a floral wreath, a fact that stirred the sentimental side of Raphael Semmes. One ex-Confederate who attended the ceremony recalled Semmes "with uncovered head, dressed in a plain black suit . . . erect, alert, and with all the fire of the old Admiral burning in his eyes."[18] Placing the wreath on the memorial Semmes told his audience,

> In the name of the people of the South here assembled, I accept with pleasure this offering of soldiers to the memory of departed soldiers. . . . It comes from the victor to the vanquished, in a spirit worthy of our age and our history. The perfume of these sweet flowers, Federal soldiers, is the more sweet, as coming from your hands.

Turning to the monument, the figure of a Confederate soldier, Semmes characterized the Civil War as a clash of principles deeply held on both sides: "The principle which [this monument] personifies, the principle of American liberty, as interpreted by the framers of the Federal and the Confederate Constitutions, will survive forever!"[19]

Semmes, in his midsixties, was the first citizen of Mobile. He was a familiar figure as he walked from his home to the single-story brick building on Conti Street that served as his and Oliver's law office. A fellow attorney recalled the admiral in his later years:

> While . . . not given to words, he was easy of approach, affable and pleasant in conversation, and kind and agreeable in his intercourse with his fellow men. . . . He had the esteem

and confidence of every one, and his practice was good considering the times, the scarcity of money [and the] unsettled conditions.[20]

Money was indeed scarce, and Semmes was never able to put much aside from his law practice. When William L. Maury, the former commander of the *Georgia,* inquired in 1876 about relocating to Mobile, Semmes gave him little encouragement, writing that new capital was a prerequisite to any economic recovery "in our stagnant old city of the Gulf."[21]

There was nothing stagnant about life at the Semmes home. There were regular visits from the Memphis Semmeses—Katherine and Anne with their spouses and children. Semmes enjoyed his grandchildren, but there were almost as many rules in the Semmes household as there had been on the *Alabama.* At the table, no child could have seconds until he or she had cleaned his plate. Frivolous conversation was discouraged, and good grammar was mandatory.[22] When friends came to dinner, however, the atmosphere was more relaxed. A grandson recalled one of the admiral's toasts,

> Here's to the ships of our navy,
> And here's to the ladies of our land;
> May the former be well rigged,
> And the latter—well manned.[23]

Toulmin Gaines, one of Oliver Semmes's stepsons, would testify that he was at first in awe of his grandfather, but soon found him "quiet and gentle." Why was he quiet? "He said his family never gave him a chance to talk, and I can well believe it. His wife was a very excitable, rapid talker, and the three daughters could keep pace with her."[24]

Gaines remembered the admiral most vividly as a woodsman. Semmes had built a cottage on Point Clear, across the bay from Mobile, and in the summer he would take groups of boys there for swimming and nature study. He once took days to whittle a toy boat from the limb of a tree, complete with a paddle at the stern powered by a rubber band. Oliver Semmes had asked his father to teach Gaines how to swim, and the boy was at first impressed that he was being carried into the water by the South's most famous sailor: "When he [then] put his hand on my head and shoved me under the water . . . I came up scared and angry. But [I] managed to struggle to where I could stand up. 'Now,' he said, 'you swam that far, all you need is confidence and practice.'"[25]

By 1877 Semmes had lived to see the end of Reconstruction and the withdrawal of Federal troops from the South. But his health was poor, apparently because of a chronic intestinal disorder. While at Point Clear in August 1877 he suffered an attack of food poisoning after a meal of seafood. Doctors were called, but Semmes's condition worsened. On August 29 he dictated his will, leaving all his property to Anne but adding a note for his children: "This is done not to disinherit any of my beloved children who are all equally dear to me, but because my estate is small and my children are in a better condition to support themselves than is their mother."[26]

That evening Semmes received the last sacrament of the Catholic church. He fell into fitful sleep, interspersed with memories of his youth. "How well I remember the night my father died," he murmured to Anne and young Raphael at his bedside.[27] His thoughts were on the distant past; there appear to have been no images of burning ships. Death came quietly at 7:30 A.M. on August 30, just days before Semmes would have turned sixty-eight.

The city of Mobile paid the highest tributes to its adopted son. On August 31, the day of his funeral, guns fired salutes from dawn until sunset. The city fathers declared a full day of mourning, and all businesses closed. After a service at the Cathedral of the Immaculate Conception, a hearse drawn by four white horses led the procession to the Catholic cemetery. A crowd of several hundred followed, oblivious to the downpour, which reminded some of a burial at sea.[28]

CHAPTER 23

Semmes of the *Alabama*

S emmes's death brought forth the eulogies that the South reserved for its heroes. The *New Orleans Delta* called him "one of the most chivalric leaders of the grand Confederate struggle for national supremacy." As a naval commander, he was "the Nelson of the Confederacy."[1] General Edward Alexander, who had worked closely with Semmes in the final months of the war, called him "the Stonewall Jackson of the sea."[2] The *Memphis Appeal* recalled Semmes's frequent visits to that city and sought to explain the enigma of his personality:

> His ardor, boldness and self-reliance often made him wear the aspect of dogmatism. But . . . he spoke from the mere honest frankness of an ardent nature; he practiced no reserve, used none of that cautious phraseology with which men control their feelings. . . . He was scrupulous in observing the rights of others.[3]

In Semmes's hometown the *Mobile Register* pulled out all the stops. In chronicling his career the *Register* focused not on the destruction he had wrought but on the underhanded way he had been provoked into fighting the *Kearsarge*, "cunningly turned into a real iron-clad." After the war, "the base, vindictive policy of the Federal Government" had caused the admiral to be snatched from the bosom of his family and incarcerated in a Northern dungeon. Denied the judicial office to which he had been elected by his fellow citizens, "the proud old hero manfully went to work" at the bar.[4]

The Northern press, predictably, was dry-eyed. The *Washington Star* reported Semmes's death briefly but factually, giving his rank as admiral without the detested quotation marks. *The New York Times,* however, ridiculed the obituary in the *Register,* calling it "a bit of Southern bathos."[5]

As time went on, naval professionals on both sides had opportunities to assess Semmes and his career. In 1883, James Bulloch published memoirs that detailed the Confederate effort to create a blue-water navy through purchases in Europe. Bulloch knew Semmes well, and his memoirs included a favorable if restrained portrait of the Confederate navy's most famous commander:

> As a mere sea-officer under the ordinary requirements of the naval profession, he was not especially distinguished. He had neither the physique nor the dashing manner which combine to make a . . . brilliant deck officer, and in the gift of handling a ship in fancy evolutions he had no special excellence. But in broad comprehensive knowledge of all the subjects embraced in a thorough naval education, in tact, judgment, acquaintance with diplomatic usage . . . and in the latent nerve and mental vigor necessary to impress his views upon those under him . . . he had few if any equals. . . . If circumstances had ever placed him at the head of a fleet, I feel sure that he would have achieved important and notable results.[6]

Three years later, Semmes's adversary in the Caribbean, Admiral Porter, published his *Naval History of the Civil War.* Porter tried to be fair toward Semmes, praising his escape from New Orleans in the *Sumter* and his destruction of the *Hatteras* within sight of a Federal flotilla. But he was sharply critical of Semmes's attempts to deny Winslow any credit for his defeat of the *Alabama,* and his general attitude was hostile:

> [Semmes] appears to have gloried in the burning of [merchant] ships, as if it was the greatest pleasure, instead of a disagreeable duty imposed upon him by the stern necessities of war; and it is not known that he ever experienced much regret for the burning of a beautiful ship, or sympathy for her master or crew.[7]

During his lifetime, Semmes was the South's most prominent naval figure, one whose fame—or notoriety—extended to the North and to foreign lands as well. As time went on, however, the *Alabama* came to be remembered better than her captain. Whereas the ship was a legend, celebrated by chroniclers of the Lost Cause, her commander was relegated to the back of the Confederate pantheon. Unlike other Confederate military heroes, Semmes had no constituency. He had no admiring legion to address at reunions; his crews had scattered to the four corners of the earth. His triumphs had been at sea, with no Little Round Top or "clump of trees" to mark them. Semmes was remembered best as a victim of Yankee duplicity: witness the chains that protected the *Kearsarge* and his incarceration after the war.

With Semmes's passing, John Kell, on his Georgia farm, became keeper of the flame. The first important book on Semmes and the *Alabama,* however, was published not by Kell but by Arthur Sinclair, who was attempting to earn a livelihood as a merchant in Baltimore. In places, Sinclair's narrative followed Semmes's so closely that Richard Armstrong dismissed his fellow officer as a plagiarist. What most bothered Kell, however, was Sinclair's insistence that Semmes had known about the *Kearsarge*'s chains. The two exchanged letters, but Sinclair would not back down. He spoke of Semmes as their "dear old leader" but insisted that he remembered seeing a French officer come on board and warn Semmes not to fight an armored vessel.[8]

Semmes had no more devoted admirer than John Kell, who called him "the most fearless man I ever knew."[9] In part to counter Sinclair, Kell, whose writing skills were modest, became a quasi-official spokesman for the famous raider. He wrote several articles, plus a memoir published in 1900, in all of which he insisted that Semmes had had no knowledge of the *Kearsarge*'s chains.

Shortly after Kell's death in 1900, Dr. Galt wrote to Blanche Kell that the officers of the *Alabama* had heard before the battle that the *Kearsarge* was "chain-clad." Blanche told her daughter that she had "suppressed" Galt's letter.[10] *Alabama* veterans closed ranks behind their captain and their ship, and it became increasingly difficult to separate fact from fiction. Richard Armstrong, in the letter to Blanche Kell in which he mentioned the affair of the Malay pilot, wrote,

I think we should not mention anything which would derogate from the fame of Semmes. . . . If I should ever write of . . .

my war service I feel now that to his faults I should be blind. Not perhaps that I love Semmes . . . but [that I love] the reputation of our ship the more.[11]

As time went on, the actual reasons for the defeat of the *Alabama*—defective ordnance and poor gunnery—were all but forgotten.

At a time when memories of the Civil War were giving way to more immediate issues in the United States, Raphael Semmes was well remembered by naval strategists in Europe. In 1894, Emperor Wilhelm II, destined to be the "Kaiser Bill" of World War I, was introduced to a U.S. diplomat, Frederick Opp. Learning that Opp was a native of Alabama, the kaiser—who was already contemplating a naval race with Britain—immediately associated his visitor with Raphael Semmes. "This meeting is indeed eventful for me," he said. "I reverence the name of Semmes. In my opinion, he was the greatest admiral of the nineteenth century. At every conference with my admirals I counsel them to read and study Semmes's *Memoirs of Service Afloat*."[12]

As well he might, for the sentiment to abolish commerce raiding—sentiment that had contributed to branding Semmes a pirate—never gained international acceptance. Two decades after the kaiser's praise for Semmes, a German submarine would torpedo the British liner *Lusitania* without warning, causing the loss of twelve hundred lives. A twentieth-century submarine thus inflicted twelve hundred more deaths in a single afternoon than had the *Alabama,* operating under very different rules, during its two-year cruise. The Germans proved adept students of Semmes; in World War I they emulated his practice of disguising his ships and refined the Confederate practice of supporting a cruiser with a tender.

With or without the kaiser's endorsement, Semmes's place in naval history is ensured. Of the two-hundred-odd Northern merchantmen destroyed by Confederate warships during the war, Semmes, in the *Sumter* and the *Alabama,* accounted for seventy-one, a figure that does not take into account ships he released on bond or prizes that otherwise found their way back to their owners. Hence he personally accounted for about 36 percent of the U.S. merchant ships destroyed by Confederate raiders. But his effectiveness is not to be measured entirely in terms of ships destroyed. His first year with the *Alabama* was so destructive that it precipitated the sale of many of the nearly five hundred American ships that changed flags in 1862 and 1863. In addition, the threat posed by the Confederate cruisers, and the resulting rise in insurance rates, immobilized many other vessels.

Semmes was not the first commerce raider of the nineteenth century; he was simply the best. He made full use of the archaic custom under which warships were allowed to display false colors before opening fire on an enemy. He skillfully threw off pursuit, sometimes by spreading false information in his ports of call, sometimes by passing his vessel off as a Federal warship. By using captured ships to dispose of his prisoners, he kept his raiders in the sea-lanes where fresh victims were to be found. He made effective use of such intelligence resources as were available to him and seems to have known almost instinctively how long he could operate in an area without running afoul of a more powerful enemy ship. He was able to keep two cruisers at sea for three years without once touching a home port. He was the only commander on either side to fight two battles at sea, and in defeating the *Hatteras* he became the only Confederate captain to sink an enemy warship.

In the United States there has been a curious tendency to credit Semmes excessively for certain aspects of his career, most notably the number of ships he captured and burned, while denying him credit in other areas. Although the total number of ships he destroyed is remarkable and could only have been achieved by a skillful navigator and seaman, Semmes operated at a time when victims were relatively plentiful. The tremendous advantage possessed by any steam-propelled raider when its quarry were dependent on sail has been noted earlier.

Because all except one of Semmes's victims were merchantmen, he has not always been given full credit for his initiative, pugnacity, and daring. The fact is that he operated in an environment of constant danger and in this environment was bold almost to a fault. His initial breakout from the Mississippi in the *Sumter,* pursued by the *Brooklyn,* required considerable courage. His winter crossing of the Atlantic in the leaky *Sumter* was an achievement in itself. His projected raid against New York City in the *Alabama,* although not carried out, was bold in conception. His attempt to disrupt enemy landings off Galveston resulted only in the sinking of the *Hatteras,* but it reflected his determination to get the maximum use out of the single vessel available to him. What Semmes would have undertaken if he had commanded more than a single ship can only be conjectured, but his initiative and resourcefulness would have made him a formidable antagonist indeed.

Just as Semmes has not always been given proper credit for his daring, he is sometimes faulted unduly for his decision to engage the *Kearsarge*. Having spent three years almost continuously at sea, Semmes knew little of the destructive potential of Winslow's eleven-inch guns. But could he have known that even a losing battle would win glory for the Confederacy and its navy? The clash off Cherbourg took place too late to influence the European powers, even if Semmes had been victorious, but the romance surrounding the *Alabama*'s last fight constituted a propaganda bonanza of sorts, one that Semmes exploited to the maximum.

Half of the U.S. merchant marine vanished during the Civil War. Some 110,000 tons were destroyed, and an additional 800,000 tons were sold.[13] Notwithstanding this remarkable record, the leaders of the Confederate navy have received comparatively little attention from historians, and that has not always been favorable. For instance, William M. Fowler Jr., in a study of the Civil War at sea, concludes that the Confederate attempt to carry the war to the enemy's merchant marine was unwise:

> Mallory's investment of scarce Confederate resources in building vessels abroad was a mistake. While the raiders did manage to take hundreds of Union merchantmen and whalers, their efforts had no demonstrable effect on the Union's ability to make war.[14]

To say that the Confederacy should not have undertaken its campaign against Northern commerce because it did not immediately affect the North's war potential is irrelevant. Because the South lacked the manpower and resources to compete with the North, the Confederacy's only hope of victory lay in inflicting such heavy punishment as to cause the North to quit—to accept disunion in preference to continued war. A campaign against Northern commerce was clearly one means of achieving this result, and the fact that the campaign failed does not mean that it should not have been undertaken.

Semmes's stated view was that the North did not at first recognize the threat posed by Confederate cruisers and, when the threat materialized, was "too heavily engaged" to heed it. This remark tells only part of the story, for the North's loss of much of its merchant marine in no sense crippled its foreign trade. In the words of one historian,

> Even if [Confederate] corsairs had driven Union shipping completely from the seas (as they very nearly did) and lured

many more blockaders away from their stations, would the result have differed? Probably not, for foreign shippers stood ready and eager to take up the slack in American trade.[15]

The war was a disaster for the North's merchant marine, but in aggregate economic terms the destruction of shipping by Confederate cruisers was more than compensated for by the industrial expansion that accompanied the war years.

What sort of man was the Raphael Semmes who blossomed into such a formidable warrior? He was, first and foremost, a product of nineteenth-century romanticism. He worshiped nature, spoke of his ship as his bride, and prized honor above all else. He knew enough of science to conclude that man, set against the immensities of the universe, was a puny, transitory being. He identified with the "gay and dashing cavaliers" of old England. A by-product of this romanticism was a strong sympathy for the underdog. He hated bullies and supported their victims, whether they were peons in Mexico or oppressed midshipmen like Francis Clarke or John Kell. It was this sympathy for the underdog that made him such a strong advocate of secession, for he saw the South as a victim of Yankee exploitation.

Over the years, Semmes's romanticism came to embrace the South and its way of life. He credited its elite with qualities that he himself admired—elegance, hospitality, and a disdain for mere money-grubbing. He had no interest in slavery as an institution but could not imagine how whites and blacks could coexist on any basis other than that of master and slave.

Semmes's romanticism was tempered by his naval service, with its emphasis on seamanship and discipline. His service in the prewar navy forced him to adapt his idealism to the realities of navy life, and over time he came to view discipline as a goal in its own right—a secular reflection of God's natural order. The fall of Richmond in 1865 was made more terrible for him by the collapse of discipline and order that accompanied it.

Semmes's legal training was important to him both during the war and afterward, but its effect was not altogether benign. The law seemed to narrow rather than to expand Semmes's horizons. He would develop a strong case in favor of a certain action, such as the South's right to secede, and seemingly block out all countervailing arguments. The result was a form of tunnel vision in which he dismissed all data opposed to a course he had chosen. After he had thrown in his lot with the South, Semmes decided that commerce raiding was the strategy that held the greatest promise for the fledgling Confederate navy. The fact that it was hardly heroic, and that even he had once favored its abolition, was swept aside; he rationalized the policy on legal grounds and by demonizing the Yankees as a class.

The zeal that Semmes brought to the Confederate cause had something to do with the timing of the war. In 1861 Semmes had passed his physical prime and had little to look forward to professionally except a succession of shore billets comparable to the Lighthouse Board. In personal terms the war was a godsend, for it gave Semmes an opportunity to display his skills and his daring on behalf of a cause to which he was totally committed.

If Semmes was not notable for his personal warmth, he nevertheless carried out his war on Northern commerce as humanely as possible. He estimated that five hundred seamen served as crewmen on the *Sumter* and the *Alabama,* and that he housed two thousand prisoners on his two raiders at one time or another.[16] His claim that he lost no one, either crewman or prisoner, to disease appears to be accurate and is remarkable considering that his ships were invariably crowded and were often storm-tossed. Semmes was a tough disciplinarian, but he took care of his men in mundane but critical matters such as clothing and diet.

Semmes was punctilious in all matters touching upon honor. The Yankee skipper who gave his word not to warn New England of the *Alabama*'s presence, and then proceeded to do so, earned his withering scorn. At Cherbourg, Semmes refused George Sinclair's offer to serve against the *Kearsarge* because he had given his word to the French port commander that he would not augment his complement. This preoccupation with honor helps explain his repeated protests about the *Kearsarge*'s chains, in the face of unanimous opinion from officers of both navies that Winslow was justified in protecting his ship. One did not undertake a duel with an unfair advantage, whatever others might say!

On occasion, Semmes's sense of honor took a strange turn. Another person might have dismissed Northern charges against "Semmes the pirate" as standard wartime propaganda; Semmes could not. His preoccupation in his postwar lectures with the *Alabama*'s provenance as a government cruiser rather than a privateer tried the patience of his listeners but was vintage Semmes: He could not permit the legend of the *Alabama* to be sullied by any hint of irregularity.

Like Nelson, Semmes regarded *duty* as the most sublime word in the English language. He carried out his duty even when it meant serving the U.S. government on the Lighthouse Board while Southern states were seceding. But his wartime ardor had a constricting effect, for it allowed little room for close friendship or for the "softer" virtues like tolerance and compassion. Indeed, Semmes the romantic seems to have feared any display of emotion. John Kell, an unqualified admirer, once testified that in three years together he had never heard Semmes laugh.[17] As a leader, he inspired confidence but rarely affection.

Semmes's commitment to the Confederacy helps explain, although it does not justify, one of his least attractive traits, an apparent unwillingness to credit his enemies with any decent impulse. Any officer who sided with the North did so out of some unworthy motive. Unlike Kell and Bulloch, Semmes could never bring himself to acknowledge that John Winslow had displayed a high level of professionalism in the clash off Cherbourg.

A descendant once called Semmes's foster brother, B. J. Semmes, "arrogant, as are all Semmeses."[18] Raphael Semmes's most visible flaw was indeed his pride. It had a positive side, including his fierce devotion to whatever cause he espoused, but often it manifested itself in arrogance and intolerance. Semmes rarely if ever acknowledged error, although he was wrong in 1861 regarding the likelihood of war, mistaken in burning the *Martaban,* and guilty at Cherbourg of underestimating his opponent. Semmes's pride contributed to a personal aloofness that, while understandable in the context of naval discipline, in time became an integral part of his character.

By the time of the Civil War the age of chivalry had long since been overtaken by the industrial revolution. In a conflict that has been called the first "modern" war, Semmes was an anachronism. But for all his faults, he deserves to be remembered as a man who had a code of conduct, one that he attempted to live by. He rescued Blake of the *Hatteras* and housed him in his own cabin. When the *Alabama* went down off Cherbourg, he looked after his wounded and was among the last to leave his ship. With the war clearly lost and his own status close to that of a war criminal, he made his way back to the Confederacy to face whatever the future held.

The historical marker outside the Semmes home in Mobile correctly calls Semmes's *Alabama* "the greatest sea raider of all time." The same words apply to her commander.

Epilogue

Anne Semmes continued to live in the house on Government Street until her death in 1892 at the age of seventy-seven. She was active in various charities associated with the war and founded one of a number of groups dedicated to decorating the graves of Confederate dead. Her sons probably provided her with financial assistance, but money was tight, and in 1884 she took out a $1,500 mortgage on her home.[1] When she died on March 7, 1892, the *Mobile Register* called her, with a bias that would have amused her husband, "a convert to the Catholic Church, but . . . a life-long Christian."[2]

Meanwhile, there was no lessening of popular interest in the exploits of the *Alabama*. The April 1886 issue of *Century Magazine* included no fewer than three articles on the *Alabama*. Two of them focused on the fight with the *Kearsarge,* but one purported to be a description of life on the *Alabama* by P. D. Haywood, said to be "one of the crew." His lurid descriptions of life on the raider, including many instances of insubordination, were hardly more damning than some of Semmes's own journal entries, but they were embarrassing to *Alabama* loyalists and they contained enough discrepancies to lead the *Alabama*'s surviving officers to charge that the narrative was fabricated. Sure enough, "Haywood" turned out to be a forger and swindler named James Young. He was eventually exposed by a reporter from the *Philadelphia Weekly Times,* but not before he had sold an expanded version of his story in book form to a prestigious publisher, Houghton Mifflin.[3]

As the *Alabama* became enshrined in Confederate lore, Semmes's admirers sought to memorialize her commander. They commissioned a bronze statue of the admiral by New York City sculptor Caspar Buberi, working with the advice of Electra Colston. Buberi depicted Semmes in Confederate uniform, stiff and erect, spyglass in hand, daring any Yankee to come within range. The statue, dedicated on June 27, 1900, was erected at the intersection of Royal and Government streets on the Mobile waterfront, where it stands today, an easy walk from the Admiral Semmes Hotel.

At one time it appeared that a remarkable relic of the *Alabama*— her bell—had somehow been recovered. During the 1930s, a British pub on the island of Guernsey used the bell, said to be that of the *Alabama,* to announce closing time. It was purchased by an American antiques dealer for $12,000 after World War II, and in December 1990 was consigned for sale to a New York City auction house. At this point the U.S. government stepped in and seized it as property of the United States. A court ruled in the government's favor, but subsequent testing of the bell cast doubt on its authenticity.[4]

In 1957 the original drawings for the *Alabama* were discovered in the Liverpool offices of the successor company to John Laird Sons, the firm that had built the *Alabama*. These were copied and three decades later were included in Charles G. Summersell's attractive book C.S.S. Alabama: *Builder, Captain and Plans.*

For more than 120 years the wreck of the *Alabama* lay undisturbed on the bottom of the English Channel at a depth of some 190 feet. Then, in October 1984, the French minesweeper *Circe* located, about seven miles offshore, a hull that appeared to be that of the Confederate raider. A few months later a French navy team led by Captain Max Guerout, a marine archeologist, examined film of the hulk. Although the floor of the Channel is littered with wrecks, this one was of wood construction, had a mechanical propulsion system, and mounted cannon of mid-nineteenth-century design. The decorations on two dishes of British manufacture confirmed that the wreck was the *Alabama*.

Exploration of the site began under the auspices of a nonprofit foundation, the C.S.S. *Alabama* Challenge. Captain Guerout retired from the French navy to devote his time to the exploration. The wreck was found to lie at a thirty-degree angle to starboard in an area of severe currents. The most readily identifiable portions of the ship were the funnel, the housing for the retractable screw, and several cannon.

The ship cannot be raised in any recognizable form. Large portions of the wooden hull have been destroyed by the current, and the decks have collapsed into the Channel floor. But among the artifacts that have been located and removed by the salvagers is the great steering wheel. The wooden spokes are long gone, but the metal rim still reads, "Aide-toi et Dieu t'aidera."

Appendix
Semmes's Victims

C.S.S. Sumter

Date Captured	Vessel	Disposition
3 July '61	*Golden Rocket*	Destroyed
4 July '61	*Cuba*	Recaptured
4 July '61	*Machias*	Freed by Spain
5 July '61	*Ben Dunning*	Freed by Spain
5 July '61	*Albert Adams*	Freed by Spain
6 July '61	*Naiad*	Freed by Spain
6 July '61	*Louisa Kilham*	Freed by Spain
6 July '61	*West Wind*	Freed by Spain
25 July '61	*Abby Bradford*	Recaptured
27 July '61	*Joseph Maxwell*	Freed by Spain
25 Sept. '61	*Joseph Park*	Destroyed
27 Oct. '61	*Daniel Trowbridge*	Destroyed
25 Nov. '61	*Montmorenci*	Bonded
26 Nov. '61	*Arcade*	Destroyed
3 Dec. '61	*Vigilant*	Destroyed
8 Dec. '61	*Eben Dodge*	Destroyed
18 Jan. '62	*Neapolitan*	Destroyed
18 Jan. '62	*Investigator*	Bonded

C.S.S. Alabama

Date Captured	Vessel	Disposition
5 Sept. '62	*Ocmulgee*	Destroyed
7 Sept. '62	*Starlight*	Destroyed
8 Sept. '62	*Ocean Rover*	Destroyed
9 Sept. '62	*Alert*	Destroyed

Date Captured	Vessel	Disposition
9 Sept. '62	Weathergauge	Destroyed
13 Sept. '62	Altamaha	Destroyed
14 Sept. '62	Benjamin Tucker	Destroyed
16 Sept. '62	Courser	Destroyed
17 Sept. '62	Virginia	Destroyed
18 Sept. '62	Elisha Dunbar	Destroyed
3 Oct. '62	Brilliant	Destroyed
3 Oct. '62	Emily Farnum	Bonded
7 Oct. '62	Wave Crest	Destroyed
7 Oct. '62	Dunkirk	Destroyed
9 Oct. '62	Tonawanda	Bonded
11 Oct. '62	Manchester	Destroyed
15 Oct. '62	Lamplighter	Destroyed
23 Oct. '62	Lafayette	Destroyed
26 Oct. '62	Crenshaw	Destroyed
28 Oct. '62	Lauretta	Destroyed
29 Oct. '62	Baron de Castine	Bonded
2 Nov. '62	Levi Starbuck	Destroyed
8 Nov. '62	Thomas B. Wales	Destroyed
30 Nov. '62	Parker Cook	Destroyed
5 Dec. '62	Union	Bonded
7 Dec. '62	Ariel	Bonded
11 Jan. '63	U.S.S. Hatteras	Sunk in battle
26 Jan. '63	Golden Rule	Destroyed
27 Jan. '63	Chastelaine	Destroyed
3 Feb. '63	Palmetto	Destroyed
21 Feb. '63	Olive Jane	Destroyed
21 Feb. '63	Golden Eagle	Destroyed
27 Feb. '63	Washington	Bonded
1 March '63	Bethiah Thayer	Bonded
2 March '63	John A. Parks	Destroyed
15 March '63	Punjaub	Bonded
23 March '63	Morning Star	Bonded
23 March '63	Kingfisher	Destroyed
25 March '63	Nora	Destroyed
25 March '63	Charles Hill	Destroyed
4 April '63	Louisa Hatch	Destroyed
15 April '63	Lafayette	Destroyed
15 April '63	Kate Cory	Destroyed

Date Captured	Vessel	Disposition
24 April '63	Nye	Destroyed
26 April '63	Dorcas Prince	Destroyed
3 May '63	Sea Lark	Destroyed
3 May '63	Union Jack	Destroyed
25 May '63	S. Gildersleeve	Destroyed
25 May '63	Justina	Bonded
29 May '63	Jabez Snow	Destroyed
2 June '63	Amazonian	Destroyed
5 June '63	Talisman	Destroyed
20 June '63	Conrad	Commissioned
2 July '63	Anna F. Schmidt	Destroyed
6 July '63	Express	Destroyed
5 Aug. '63	Sea Bride	Sold
6 Nov. '63	Amanda	Destroyed
10 Nov. '63	Winged Racer	Destroyed
11 Nov. '63	Contest	Destroyed
24 Dec. '63	Martaban	Destroyed
26 Dec. '63	Sonora	Destroyed
26 Dec. '63	Highlander	Destroyed
14 Jan. '64	Emma Jane	Destroyed
23 April '64	Rockingham	Destroyed
27 April '64	Tycoon	Destroyed

Notes

CHAPTER 1: "We Fired No Gun of Triumph"

1. James M. McPherson, *Battle Cry of Freedom* (New York: Oxford University Press, 1988), 314.

2. Chester G. Hearn, *Gray Raiders of the Sea* (Camden, Me.: International Marine Publishing, 1992), 2.

3. George W. Cable, "New Orleans Before the Capture," in R. U. Johnson, ed., *The Way to Appomattox: Battles and Leaders of the Civil War* (New York: Castle Books, 1959), 4 vols., vol. 1, 11.

4. Raphael Semmes, *Memoirs of Service Afloat During the War Between the States* (Baltimore, Md.: Kelly, Piet & Co., 1869), 97. Hereafter cited as Semmes, *Memoirs of Service Afloat.*

5. Charles G. Summersell, *The Cruise of the C.S.S. Sumter* (Tuscaloosa, Ala.: Confederate Publishing Co., 1965), 22.

6. Ibid., 96.

7. *Official Records, Navy* (hereafter cited as ORN), Series I, vol. 1, 691.

8. George W. Dalzell, *The Flight from the Flag* (Chapel Hill, N.C.: University of North Carolina Press, 1940), 34–35.

9. Semmes, *Memoirs of Service Afloat,* 104.

10. Semmes to Mallory, June 14, 1861. *ORN,* Series I, vol. 1, 615.

11. Ibid., 615–16.

12. Ibid., 616.

13. Charles G. Summersell, "The Career of Raphael Semmes Prior to the Cruise of the *Alabama*" (Ph.D. dissertation, Vanderbilt University, 1940), 157.

14. Richard S. West Jr., *The Second Admiral* (New York: Coward-McCann, 1937), 98–99.

15. *ORN,* Series I, vol. 1, 618.

16. Semmes, *Memoirs of Service Afloat,* 114.

17. Hearn, *Gray Raiders of the Sea,* 13.

18. Semmes, *Memoirs of Service Afloat,* 116.

19. Ibid.

20. Hearn, *Gray Raiders of the Sea,* 14.

21. Semmes, *Memoirs of Service Afloat,* 117.

22. David D. Porter, *Naval History of the Civil War* (New York: Sherman Publishing Co., 1886), 605–6.

23. Semmes, *Memoirs of Service Afloat,* 118.

24. *ORN,* Series I, vol. 1, 694.

CHAPTER 2: The Old Navy

1. Anderson Humphreys and Curt Guenther, *Semmes America* (Memphis, Tenn.: Humphreys, Ink, 1989), 298.

2. Ibid., 295–96.

3. Ibid., 296. Originally 38 First Street, the house received its present address during a renumbering of Georgetown houses in 1880.

4. Robert E. T. Pogue, *Yesterday in Old St. Mary's County* (New York: Carleton Press, 1968), 167.

5. Humphreys and Guenther, *Semmes America*, 331.

6. Leonard F. Guttridge and Jay D. Smith, *The Commodores* (New York: Harper & Row, 1969), 305.

7. Raphael Semmes, *Service Afloat and Ashore During the Mexican War* (Cincinnati: William H. Moore & Co., 1851), vi. Hereafter cited as Semmes, *Memoirs (Mexico)*.

8. James E. Valle, *Rocks & Shoals* (Annapolis, Md.: Naval Institute Press, 1980), 76.

9. Ibid., 30–31.

10. Dalzell, *The Flight from the Flag*, 28.

11. Edward Boykin, *Sea Devil of the Confederacy* (New York: Funk & Wagnalls, 1957), 28.

12. Raphael Semmes ZB File, Naval Historical Center, Washington, D.C.

13. William M. Fowler Jr., *Under Two Flags* (New York: W. W. Norton, 1990), 28.

14. Raphael Semmes ZB File, Naval Historical Center, Washington, D.C.

15. W. Adolphe Roberts, *Semmes of the* Alabama (New York: Bobbs-Merrill Co., 1938), 17.

16. Summersell, "The Career of Raphael Semmes," 10.

17. Ibid.

18. Ibid., 18.

19. Valle, *Rocks & Shoals*, 269.

20. Frances L. Williams, *Matthew Fontaine Maury* (New Brunswick, N.J.: Rutgers University Press, 1963), 129–30.

21. Semmes, *Memoirs (Mexico)*, 51.

22. Summersell, "The Career of Raphael Semmes," 20.

CHAPTER 3: Mexico

1. Kenneth J. Hagan, *This People's Navy* (New York: Free Press, 1991), 127.

2. Semmes, *Memoirs (Mexico)*, 76.

3. Summersell, "The Career of Raphael Semmes," 30–31. Semmes to Commodore David Conner, November 28, 1846, Gary Hendershott collection.

4. Semmes, *Memoirs of Service Afloat*, 276–77.

5. Ibid., 278.

6. Philip McFarland, *Sea Dangers* (New York: Schocken Books, 1985), 250.

7. Summersell, "The Career of Raphael Semmes," 37.

8. John M. Ellicott, *The Life of John Ancrum Winslow* (New York: G. P. Putnam's, 1902), 46.

9. Stephen Howarth, *To Shining Sea: A History of the United States Navy* (New York: Random House, 1991), 160.

10. Semmes, *Memoirs (Mexico)*, 137.

11. Byron Farwell, *Stonewall: A Biography of General Thomas J. Jackson* (New York: W. W. Norton, 1992), 45.

12. Howarth, *To Shining Sea*, 161.

13. Summersell, "The Career of Raphael Semmes," 48.

14. Semmes, *Memoirs (Mexico)*, 219–20.

15. Semmes to Winfield Scott, May 8, 1847. Semmes Letter Book, Acc. 2865, Library of Congress.

16. Winfield Scott to Semmes, May 9, 1847. Semmes Letter Book, Acc. 2865, Library of Congress.

17. Semmes, *Memoirs (Mexico)*, 212–13.

18. Ibid., 280.

19. Summersell, "The Career of Raphael Semmes," 84.

20. Semmes, *Memoirs (Mexico)*, 379.

21. Ibid., 419.

22. Colyer Meriwether, *Raphael Semmes* (Philadelphia: George W. Jacobs, 1913), 60.

23. Semmes, *Memoirs (Mexico)*, 17.

24. Ibid., 270–71.

25. Ibid., 271.

26. Semmes to Colonel ———, July 8, 1844, City Museum, Mobile, Ala.

27. Semmes, *Memoirs (Mexico),* 67.

28. Ibid., 478.

29. Ibid., 473.

30. Hagan, *This People's Navy,* 137–38.

CHAPTER 4: Through the Burning Woods

1. Semmes, *Electra* journal, City Museum, Mobile, Ala.

2. Valle, *Rocks & Shoals,* 79.

3. Semmes to ———, June 27, 1848, Semmes Letter Book, Acc. 2865, Library of Congress.

4. Norman C. Delaney, *John McIntosh Kell* (Birmingham, Ala.: University of Alabama Press, 1973), 54.

5. Semmes to Ballard Preston, March 9, 1849, Semmes Letter Book, Acc. 2865, Library of Congress.

6. Ibid.

7. Semmes, *Memoirs of Service Afloat,* 123.

8. These reviews were published as advertising material in various printings of Semmes's book.

9. Valle, *Rocks & Shoals,* 247–48.

10. Semmes to William B. Preston, August 15, 1850, Semmes Letter Book, Acc. 2865, Library of Congress.

11. Semmes to A. O. Dayton, February 1, 1852, Semmes Letter Book, Acc. 2865, Library of Congress.

12. Semmes to Franklin Pierce, June 21, 1853, Semmes Letter Book, Acc. 2865, Library of Congress.

13. Warren F. Spencer, "Raphael Semmes: Confederate Raider," *Captains of the Old Steam Navy* (Annapolis, Md.: Naval Institute Press, 1986), 199.

14. Semmes to J. C. Dobbin, July 16, 1856, Semmes Letter Book, Acc. 2865, Library of Congress.

15. J. C. Dobbin to Semmes, January 31, 1855, Semmes Letter Book, Acc. 2865, Library of Congress.

16. Francis R. Holland Jr., *America's Lighthouses* (New York: Dover Publications, 1972), 35–36.

17. Semmes to S. S. Semmes, May 30, 1859, Garnett Andrews Papers, University of North Carolina Library.

18. Constance Green, *Washington: Village and Capital* (Princeton, N.J.: Princeton University Press, 1962), 198.

19. Ibid., 186.

20. Harold D. Langley, *Social Reform in the United States Navy* (Urbana, Ill.: University of Illinois Press, 1967), 23.

21. District of Columbia Census, 1860, Ward 1, Martin Luther King, Jr., Library, Washington, D.C.

22. Semmes, *Memoirs of Service Afloat,* 40.

23. Ibid., 54.

24. Ibid., 55.

25. Ibid., 56.

26. McPherson, *Battle Cry of Freedom,* 197.

27. Ibid., 99.

28. Semmes, *Memoirs of Service Afloat,* 62.

29. Semmes to Wm. B. Harwood, February 18, 1859, collection of Lewis Leigh Jr.

30. Semmes to S. F. Baird, March 17, 1860, author's collection.

31. Norman C. Delaney, "Old Beeswax: Raphael Semmes of the *Alabama,*" *Civil War Times,* December 1973.

32. Edward M. Coffman, *The Old Army* (New York: Oxford University Press, 1986), 92.

33. Raphael Semmes to Samuel Semmes, August 12, 1865, *Mobile Daily Advertiser & Register,* January 16, 1866.

34. Ada Sterling, ed., *A Belle of the Fifties: Memories of Mrs. Clay of Alabama* (New York: De Capo Press, 1969), 144–45.

35. Charles G. Summersell, *The Cruise of the C.S.S.* Alabama (Tuscaloosa, Ala.: Confederate Publishing Co., 1965), 10.

36. Semmes, *Memoirs of Service Afloat,* 75.

37. Semmes, *Memoirs (Mexico),* 82.

38. Edward Boykin, *Ghost Ship of the Confederacy* (New York: Funk and Wagnalls, 1957), 26.

39. Semmes, *Memoirs of Service Afloat,* 82.

CHAPTER 5: "Give Me That Ship"

1. Bruce Catton, *The Coming Fury* (Garden City, N.Y.: Doubleday and Co., 1961), 204.

2. Pamphlet, "The First White House of the Confederacy," Montgomery, Ala., 1986.

3. Semmes, *Memoirs of Service Afloat,* 82.

4. *Official Records Army,* Series IV, vol. 1, 106–7.

5. Philip Van Doren Stern, *Secret Missions of the Civil War* (New York: Bonanza Books, 1959), 75.

6. Summersell, "The Career of Raphael Semmes," 135–36.

7. Semmes, *Memoirs of Service Afloat,* 87.

8. Semmes to Alexander H. Stephens, March 8, 1861, Woodruff Library, Emory University.

9. Semmes, *Memoirs of Service Afloat,* 86.

10. Roberts, *Semmes of the* Alabama, 39.

11. Semmes to Alexander H. Stephens, March 8, 1861, Woodruff Library, Emory University.

12. Semmes, *Memoirs of Service Afloat,* 89.

13. Ibid., 91.

14. Burton J. Hendrick, *Statesmen of the Lost Cause* (Boston: Little, Brown and Co., 1939), 366–67.

15. Joseph T. Durkin, *Stephen R. Mallory* (Chapel Hill, N.C.: University of North Carolina Press, 1954), 150.

16. Ibid., 64–65.

17. Hearn, *Gray Raiders of the Sea,* 2.

18. Frederick L. Schuman, *International Politics* (New York: McGraw-Hill, 1958), 131.

19. Fowler, *Under Two Flags,* 279.

20. Semmes, *Memoirs of Service Afloat,* 93–94.

CHAPTER 6: "Doing a Pretty Fair Business"

1. Semmes, *Memoirs of Service Afloat,* 127–28.

2. Ibid., 129.

3. Ibid., 131.

4. Ibid., 137.

5. *ORN,* Series I, vol. 1, 619–20.

6. Summersell, *The Cruise of the C.S.S. Sumter,* 68.

7. Hearn, *Gray Raiders of the Sea,* 19.

8. *ORN,* Series I, vol. 1, 696.

9. Semmes, *Memoirs of Service Afloat,* 154.

10. *ORN,* Series I, vol. 1, 623.

11. Summersell, *The Cruise of the C.S.S. Sumter,* 83–84.

12. *ORN,* Series I, vol. 1, 127.

13. Dalzell, *The Flight from the Flag,* 44.

CHAPTER 7: "Semmes Was Too Clever"

1. Semmes, *Memoirs of Service Afloat,* 173–74.

2. Summersell, *The Cruise of the C.S.S. Sumter,* 89.

3. J. G. Randall and David Donald, *The Civil War and Reconstruction* (Boston: D. C. Heath and Co., 1961), 449.

4. *ORN,* Series I, vol. 1, 633.

5. Semmes, *Memoirs of Service Afloat,* 184.

6. Ibid., 187.

7. Summersell, *The Cruise of the C.S.S. Sumter,* 91.

8. Semmes, *Memoirs of Service Afloat,* 190–91.

9. Hearn, *Gray Raiders of the Sea,* 25–26.

10. Boykin, *Ghost Ship of the Confederacy,* 112.

11. Delaney, *John McIntosh Kell,* 146.

12. Summersell, *The Cruise of the C.S.S. Sumter,* 104.

13. *ORN*, Series I, vol. 1, 634.
14. Summersell, *The Cruise of the C.S.S.* Sumter, 107–8.
15. Semmes, *Memoirs of Service Afloat*, 210.
16. Ibid., 213.
17. *ORN*, Series I, vol. 1, 635.
18. Boykin, *Ghost Ship of the Confederacy*, 116–17.
19. Summersell, *The Cruise of the C.S.S.* Sumter, 124.
20. *ORN*, Series I, vol. 1, 637.
21. Boykin, *Ghost Ship of the Confederacy*, 118. Semmes released the master of the ship the next day, following an apology.
22. *ORN*, Series I, vol. 1, 87–88.
23. Porter to Welles (August 1861), quoted in *ORN*, Series I, vol. 1, 83.
24. Guttridge and Smith, *The Commodores*, 200.
25. Hearn, *Gray Raiders of the Sea*, 28–29.
26. Roberts, *Semmes of the* Alabama, 67–68.
27. Summersell, *The Cruise of the C.S.S.* Sumter, 98.
28. Semmes, *Memoirs of Service Afloat*, 250.
29. *ORN*, Series I, vol. 1, 208–9.
30. Hearn, *Gray Raiders of the Sea*, 32.
31. Porter, *Naval History of the Civil War*, 617.
32. *ORN*, Series I, vol. 1, 213–14.

CHAPTER 8: Farewell to the *Sumter*

1. Hearn, *Gray Raiders of the Sea*, 33.
2. Semmes, *Memoirs of Service Afloat*, 270.
3. Summersell, *The Cruise of the C.S.S.* Sumter, 138–39.
4. *ORN*, Series I, vol. 1, 728.
5. Semmes, *Memoirs of Service Afloat*, 279.
6. *ORN*, Series I, vol. 1, 729.
7. Semmes, *Memoirs of Service Afloat*, 280–81.
8. *ORN*, Series I, vol. 1, 732.
9. James M. Morgan, *Recollections of a Rebel Reefer* (Boston: 1917), 129. Although Morgan did not serve on either the *Sumter* or the *Alabama*, and his comments are probably hearsay, they are consistent with statements by Semmes and others.
10. Delaney, *John McIntosh Kell*, 123.
11. Semmes, *Memoirs of Service Afloat*, 282–83.
12. *ORN*, Series I, vol. 1, 734.
13. Ibid., 736–37.
14. Semmes, *Memoirs of Service Afloat*, 308–9.
15. Delaney, *John McIntosh Kell*, 122.
16. Semmes, *Memoirs of Service Afloat*, 315.

17. Roberts, *Semmes of the* Alabama, 77.

18. *ORN,* Series II, vol. 2, 148–49.

19. Semmes, *Memoirs of Service Afloat,* 324–25.

20. *ORN,* Series I, vol. 1, 741.

21. Ibid., 641–42.

22. Ibid., 741.

23. Summersell, *The Cruise of the C.S.S.* Sumter, 161.

24. *ORN,* Series I, vol. 1, 310; Philip Van Doren Stern, *While the Guns Roared* (New York: Doubleday, 1965), 106.

25. Ibid.

26. *ORN,* Series I, vol. 1, 677–82.

27. Semmes, *Memoirs of Service Afloat,* 342.

28. John M. Kell, *Recollections of a Naval Life* (Washington, D.C.: Neale Co., 1900), 176.

29. Dalzell, *The Flight from the Flag,* 239.

30. Ibid., 245.

CHAPTER 9: The Mysterious *290*

1. Charles G. Summersell, *C.S.S.* Alabama (Birmingham, Ala.: University of Alabama Press, 1986), 4.

2. Hearn, *Gray Raiders of the Sea,* 53.

3. Ibid., 55.

4. William W. Wade, "The Man Who Stopped the Rams," *American Heritage,* April 1963.

5. Semmes, *Memoirs of Service Afloat,* 348.

6. Ibid.

7. Ibid., 352–53.

8. Ibid., 354–55.

9. Dalzell, *The Flight from the Flag,* 131.

10. James D. Bulloch, *The Secret Service of the Confederate States in Europe* (New York: Thomas Yoseloff, 1959), 2 vols., I, 238.

11. Summersell, *C.S.S. Alabama,* 14.

12. Bulloch, *The Secret Service of the Confederate States in Europe,* 240.

13. Dalzell, *The Flight from the Flag,* 134–35.

14. Semmes, *Memoirs of Service Afloat,* 404.

15. Summersell, *C.S.S. Alabama,* 12.

16. Semmes, *Memoirs of Service Afloat,* 402, 404.

17. Bulloch, *The Secret Service of the Confederate States in Europe,* 255.

18. Semmes, *Memoirs of Service Afloat,* 409.

19. Arthur Sinclair, *Two Years on the* Alabama (Annapolis, Md.: Naval Institute Press, 1989), 12–13.

20. Delaney, *John McIntosh Kell,* 130.

21. Semmes, *Memoirs of Service Afloat,* 412.

22. Ibid., 413.

CHAPTER 10: The Pirate Semmes

1. *ORN*, Series I, vol. 1, 786.
2. Semmes, *Memoirs of Service Afloat*, 423–24.
3. Ibid., 426.
4. Ibid., 430.
5. Ibid., 439.
6. Charles G. Summersell, ed., *The Journal of George Townley Fullam* (Birmingham, Ala.: University of Alabama Press, 1973), 24. Hereafter cited as Fullam, *Journal*.
7. Sinclair, *Two Years on the* Alabama, 22.
8. Semmes, *Memoirs of Service Afloat*, 441.
9. Sinclair, *Two Years on the* Alabama, 26–27.
10. *ORN*, Series I, vol. 1, 790.
11. Fullam, *Journal*, 26–27.
12. Semmes, *Memoirs of Service Afloat*, 444.
13. Fullam, *Journal*, 27.
14. *ORN*, Series I, vol. 1, 792–93.
15. Semmes, *Memoirs of Service Afloat*, 459.
16. Ibid., 446.
17. Fullam, *Journal*, 31.
18. Roberts, *Semmes of the* Alabama, 104.
19. Semmes, *Memoir (Mexico)*, 80.
20. Fullam, *Journal*, 39.
21. Semmes, *Memoirs of Service Afloat*, 453.
22. Summersell, *The Cruise of the C.S.S.* Sumter, 33.
23. Semmes, *Memoirs of Service Afloat*, 455.

CHAPTER 11: Off the Grand Banks

1. *ORN*, Series I, vol. 1, 490.
2. Hearn, *Gray Raiders of the Sea*, 176.
3. Fullam, *Journal*, 34.
4. *ORN*, Series I, vol. 1, 794–95.
5. Ibid., 793–94.
6. Semmes, *Memoirs of Service Afloat*, 247–48.
7. Ibid., 465.
8. Ibid., 418.
9. *ORN*, Series I, vol. 1, 795.
10. Semmes, *Memoirs of Service Afloat*, 467.
11. Fullam, *Journal*, 37.
12. Ibid., 37–38.
13. Semmes, *Memoirs of Service Afloat*, 477.
14. Kell, *Recollections of a Naval Life*, 193.

15. Semmes to Bulloch, November 19, 1862, Museum of the Confederacy, Richmond, Va.

16. Semmes, *Memoirs of Service Afloat,* 481.

17. Fullam, *Journal,* 41.

18. Ibid., 43–44.

19. Sinclair, *Two Years on the* Alabama, 37.

20. Semmes, *Memoirs of Service Afloat,* 492.

21. Dalzell, *The Flight from the Flag,* 242–43.

22. Summersell, *The Cruise of the C.S.S.* Sumter , 56.

23. Ibid., 43.

24. Ibid.

25. Semmes, *Memoirs of Service Afloat,* 495.

26. *ORN,* Series I, vol. 1, 804.

27. Roberts, *Semmes of the* Alabama, 118–19.

28. Kell, *Recollections of a Naval Life,* 197.

29. Ibid., 198.

30. *ORN,* Series I, vol. 1, 805.

31. Semmes, *Memoirs of Service Afloat,* 513.

32. Ibid., 515.

33. Fullam, *Journal,* 53.

34. Frank J. Merli, "Caribbean Confrontation," *Journal of Confederate History,* VI, 1990.

35. Fullam, *Journal,* 53.

36. *ORN,* Series I, vol. 1, 806.

CHAPTER 12: "Give It to the Rascals!"

1. Semmes, *Memoirs of Service Afloat,* 517.

2. Ibid., 518.

3. Hearn, *Gray Raiders of the Sea,* 183.

4. W. Stanley Hoole, ed., "Letters from a Georgia Midshipman on the C.S.S. *Alabama,*" manuscript in the University of Alabama library.

5. Fullam, *Journal,* 59.

6. Sinclair, *Two Years on the* Alabama, 50.

7. Semmes, *Memoirs of Service Afloat,* 530.

8. Ibid., 531.

9. Fullam, *Journal,* 63.

10. Semmes, *Memoirs of Service Afloat,* 534.

11. Kell, *Recollections of a Naval Life,* 205.

12. Gideon Welles, *Diary* (Boston: Houghton Mifflin, 1911), I, 207.

13. Semmes, *Memoirs of Service Afloat,* 536.

14. Ibid., 541.

15. *ORN,* Series I, vol. 2, 18.

16. Sinclair, *Two Years on the* Alabama, 62.
17. Fullam, *Journal,* 71–72.
18. Ibid., 77.
19. Roberts, *Semmes of the* Alabama, 137.
20. Norman C. Delaney, "At Semmes's Hand," *Civil War Times Illustrated,* June 1979.
21. Ibid., 26.
22. Accounts of the *Alabama-Hatteras* duel differ only in minor details. The account here draws upon the official reports of Semmes and Blake, as supplemented by accounts of Sinclair, Fullam, and Kell.
23. L. H. Partridge to D. G. Farragut, January 12, 1863. *ORN,* Series I, vol. 2, 21–22.
24. Porter, *Naval History of the Civil War,* 122.
25. *ORN,* Series I, vol. 2, 722.

CHAPTER 13: The Trail of Fire

1. Fullam, *Journal,* 79.
2. Kell, *Recollections of a Naval Life,* 209.
3. Sinclair, *Two Years on the* Alabama, 65–66.
4. Semmes, *Memoirs of Service Afloat,* 553.
5. Roberts, *Semmes of the* Alabama, 147.
6. Sinclair, *Two Years on the* Alabama, 67.
7. Ibid., 69.
8. Yonge subsequently defected to the Federals and became a paid informant of the U.S. embassy in London. He was the only one of Semmes's officers to desert or defect from either the *Sumter* or the *Alabama.*
9. Hearn, *Gray Raiders of the Sea,* 191.
10. Semmes, *Memoirs of Service Afloat,* 564–65.
11. Delaney, "Old Beeswax: Raphael Semmes of the *Alabama.*"
12. Boykin, *Ghost Ship of the Confederacy,* 224.
13. Sinclair, *Two Years on the* Alabama, 72.
14. Fullam, *Journal,* 89.
15. Sinclair, *Two Years on the* Alabama, 113.
16. Dalzell, *The Flight from the Flag,* 6.
17. Sinclair, *Two Years on the* Alabama, 75, 80.
18. *ORN,* Series I, vol. 2, 730.
19. Semmes, *Memoirs of Service Afloat,* 585.
20. *ORN,* Series I, vol. 2, 734.
21. Semmes, *Memoirs of Service Afloat,* 588.
22. Dalzell, *The Flight from the Flag,* 245.
23. Boykin, *Ghost Ship of the Confederacy,* 232.

24. Ibid., 297.
25. Clarence E. McCartney, *Mr. Lincoln's Admirals* (New York: Funk & Wagnalls, 1956), 222.
26. Fullam, *Journal*, 97–98.
27. Sinclair, *Two Years on the* Alabama, 85.

CHAPTER 14: Ruling the Waves
1. *ORN*, Series I, vol. 2, 736.
2. Ibid., 737. Semmes had probably been studying Psalms 8: 3–4, which reads, in the Revised Standard Version, "When I look at thy heavens, the work of thy fingers/the moon and the stars which thou hast established;/what is man that thou art mindful of him/and the son of man that thou dost care for him?"
3. Semmes, *Memoirs of Service Afloat,* 595.
4. Ibid., 599.
5. Ibid., 601.
6. Fullam, *Journal*, 105.
7. *ORN*, Series I, vol. 2, 740.
8. Hearn, *Gray Raiders of the Sea*, 81.
9. Semmes, *Memoirs of Service Afloat,* 611.
10. Ibid., 611.
11. *ORN*, Series I, vol. 2, 741–42.
12. Fullam, *Journal*, 110.
13. Ibid., 109–10.
14. Sinclair, *Two Years on the* Alabama, 102.
15. *ORN*, Series I, vol. 2, 687.
16. Ibid., 744.
17. Sinclair, *Two Years on the* Alabama, 108.
18. *ORN*, Series I, vol. 2, 813.
19. Ibid., 745.
20. Roberts, *Semmes of the* Alabama, 117.
21. *Official Records, Army,* Series II, vol. 2, 261.
22. Ibid., 252–53.
23. Katherine M. Jones, *Ladies of Richmond* (New York: Bobbs-Merrill Co., 1962), 188.
24. Humphreys and Guenther, *Semmes America*, 433.
25. Ibid., 426.
26. *ORN*, Series I, vol. 2, 745.
27. Welles, *Diary*, I, 316.
28. Semmes, *Memoirs of Service Afloat,* 629.
29. Ibid., 622.
30. *ORN*, Series I, vol. 2, 748.
31. Sinclair, *Two Years on the* Alabama, 115.

32. *ORN,* Series I, vol. 2, 751.

33. Hearn, *Gray Raiders of the Sea,* 312–13. Hearn lists 234 vessels captured by nine Confederate raiders. Of this total, which includes ships bonded or otherwise disposed of, fourteen were coastal fishing schooners and are not included in Confederate totals here considered.

34. John Niven, *Gideon Welles* (New York: Oxford University Press, 1973), 429.

35. John M. Taylor, *William Henry Seward: Lincoln's Right Hand* (New York: HarperCollins, 1991), 215–16.

CHAPTER 15: "Daar Kom die *Alabama*"

1. *ORN,* Series I, vol. 2, 749–50, 753.

2. Ibid., 752.

3. Fullam, *Journal,* 124.

4. Semmes, *Memoirs of Service Afloat,* 634.

5. John Thomas to Daniel Marcy, October 8, 1863, author's collection.

6. *ORN,* Series I, vol. 2, 757.

7. Ibid., 758.

8. Ibid.

9. Edna and Frank Bradlow, *Here Comes the* Alabama (Cape Town: A. A. Balkema, 1958), 56.

10. Sinclair, *Two Years on the* Alabama, 131.

11. Roberts, *Semmes of the* Alabama, 168.

12. *ORN,* Series I, vol. 2, 759.

13. Roberts, *Semmes of the* Alabama, 169–70.

14. Bradlow and Bradlow, *Here Comes the* Alabama, ii.

15. Semmes, *Memoirs of Service Afloat,* 652.

16. Bradlow and Bradlow, *Here Comes the* Alabama, 69.

17. Semmes, *Memoirs of Service Afloat,* 662.

18. *ORN,* Series I, vol. 2, 428.

19. Fullam, *Journal,* 140–41.

20. *ORN,* Series I, vol. 2, 764.

21. Semmes, *Memoirs of Service Afloat,* 666.

22. Hearn, *Gray Raiders of the Sea,* 209.

23. *ORN,* Series I, vol. 2, 765.

24. Kell, *Recollections of a Naval Life,* 230.

25. Dalzell, *The Flight from the Flag,* 150.

26. Roberts, *Semmes of the* Alabama, 175.

CHAPTER 16: In Asian Waters

1. *ORN,* Series I, vol. 2, 768.

2. Ibid., 777.

3. Harold S. Wilson, "The Cruise of the C.S.S. *Alabama* in Southeast Asian Waters," *Journal of Confederate History*, IV (*Special Commemorative Issue*, 1989), 34.

4. Semmes, *Memoirs of Service Afloat*, 689.

5. Ibid., 691.

6. *ORN*, Series I, vol. 2, 561.

7. Semmes, *Memoirs of Service Afloat*, 694.

8. Sinclair, *Two Years on the* Alabama, 162.

9. *ORN*, Series I, vol. 2, 781.

10. Ibid., 562.

11. Sinclair, *Two Years on the* Alabama, 165.

12. *ORN*, Series I, vol. 2, 785.

13. Ibid., 788.

14. Wilson, "The Cruise of the C.S.S. *Alabama* in Southeast Asian Waters," 45.

15. Semmes, *Memoirs of Service Afloat*, 712–13.

16. Sinclair, *Two Years on the* Alabama, 180.

17. Spencer, "Raphael Semmes," *Captains of the Old Steam Navy*, 207.

18. Stern, *While the Guns Roared*, 232.

19. Sinclair, *Two Years on the* Alabama, 189.

20. Lawrence Brown and Isaac Colby, "The *Sonora* and the *Alabama*," *Civil War Times*, October 1971.

21. Fullam, *Journal*, 172.

22. *ORN*, Series I, vol. 2, 794.

23. Sinclair, *Two Years on the* Alabama, 204.

24. Fullam, *Journal*, 177–78.

25. *ORN*, Series I, vol. 2, 800.

26. Semmes, *Memoirs of Service Afloat*, 740.

27. Hearn, *Gray Raiders of the Sea*, 219.

28. Semmes, *Memoirs of Service Afloat*, 745.

29. *ORN*, Series I, vol. 2, 807.

30. Semmes, *Memoirs of Service Afloat*, 745.

31. John Kell, manuscript report on the *Alabama*'s battle with the *Kearsage*, n.d., Gary Hendershott collection.

32. Sinclair, *Two Years on the* Alabama, 217.

33. Fullam, *Journal*, 183; Semmes, *Memoirs of Service Afloat*, 749.

34. Ellicott, *Life of John Ancrum Winslow*, 176.

35. Delaney, *John McIntosh Kell*, 157, 218.

36. *ORN*, Series I, vol. 3, 673–74.

37. Semmes, *Memoirs of Service Afloat*, 749–50.

CHAPTER 17: Showdown off Cherbourg

1. *ORN*, Series I, vol. 3, 652.

2. Ibid., 651.

3. John M. Browne, "The Duel Between the *Alabama* and the *Kearsarge*," in Johnson, ed., *The Way to Appomattox: Battles and Leaders of the Civil War*, IV, 624.

4. Ellicott, *John Ancrum Winslow*, 178.

5. Dalzell, *The Flight from the Flag*, 245.

6. Kell, *Recollections of a Naval Life*, 245.

7. Delaney, *John McIntosh Kell*, 159.

8. Ibid.

9. Dalzell, *The Flight from the Flag*, 161.

10. *ORN*, Series I, vol. 3, 677.

11. Ibid., 648.

12. McCartney, *Mr. Lincoln's Admirals*, 226.

13. Interview in the *New Orleans Picayune*, September 29, 1912.

14. Delaney, *John McIntosh Kell*, 160.

15. McCartney, *Mr. Lincoln's Admirals*, 228.

16. Roberts, *Semmes of the* Alabama, 228.

17. Browne, "The Duel Between the *Alabama* and the *Kearsarge*," in *The Way to Appomattox: Battles and Leaders of the Civil War*, IV, 615.

18. Summersell, *C.S.S.* Alabama, 76.

19. Delaney, *John McIntosh Kell*, 161.

20. Frank J. Merli, ed., "Letters on the *Alabama*," *Mariner's Mirror*, May 1972.

21. Semmes, *Memoirs of Service Afloat*, 756.

22. Philip Van Doren Stern, *The Confederate Navy* (New York: Doubleday, 1962), 190.

23. Browne, "The Duel Between the *Alabama* and the *Kearsarge*," in *The Way to Appomattox: Battles and Leaders of the Civil War*, IV, 623.

24. *ORN*, Series I, vol. 3, 650.

25. Delaney, *John McIntosh Kell*, 166.

26. Sinclair, *Two Years on the* Alabama, 240.

27. John M. Taylor, "The Fiery Trail of the *Alabama*," *Military History Quarterly*, Summer 1991.

28. John M. Taylor, "Showdown off Cherbourg," *Yankee*, July 1984.

29. Delaney, *John McIntosh Kell*, 170.

30. Bulloch, *The Secret Service of the Confederate States in Europe*, I, 286–87.

31. John M. Kell, "Cruise and Combats of the *Alabama*," in *The Way to Appomattox: Battles and Leaders of the Civil War*, IV, 610.

32. Sinclair, *Two Years on the* Alabama, 238–39.

33. Delaney, *John McIntosh Kell*, 174.

34. Semmes, *Memoirs of Service Afloat*, 763.

35. Kell, "Cruise and Combats of the *Alabama*," in *The Way to Appomattox: Battles and Leaders of the Civil War*, IV, 611.

36. Captain Evan P. Jones, quoted in Sinclair, *Two Years on the* Alabama, 248.

37. Ibid., 613.

38. Browne, "The Duel Between the *Alabama* and the *Kearsarge*," in *The Way to Appomattox: Battles and Leaders of the Civil War*, IV, 621.

39. Semmes, *Memoirs of Service Afloat*, 765.

CHAPTER 18: Defeated but Not Conquered

1. Delaney, *John McIntosh Kell*, 177.

2. Ibid.

3. *ORN*, Series I, vol. 3, 667.

4. Ibid., 79.

5. Ibid., 80.

6. Ibid.

7. Delaney, *John McIntosh Kell*, 179–80.

8. Roberts, *Semmes of the* Alabama, 213.

9. Ibid., 213.

10. Frank J. Merli, ed., "Letters on the *Alabama*," *Mariner's Mirror*, May 1972.

11. *ORN*, Series I, vol. 3, 649.

12. Ibid., 651.

13. Bulloch, *The Secret Service of the Confederate States in Europe*, I, 287.

14. William H. Parker, *Recollections of a Naval Officer* (New York: Charles Scribner's Sons, 1883), 341.

15. Norman C. Delaney, "Fight or Flee," *Journal of Confederate History*, IV (*Special Commemorative Issue*, 1989), 27.

16. Sinclair, *Two Years on the* Alabama, 223.

17. Delaney, "Fight or Flee," *Journal of Confederate History*, IV, 27.

18. *ORN*, Series I, vol. 3, 649–51.

19. Semmes to Samuel Barron, July 5, 1864, Swem Library, College of William and Mary.

20. Ibid.

21. Bulloch, *The Secret Service of the Confederate States in Europe*, I, 279.

22. *Frank Leslie's Illustrated Newspaper*, July 23, 1864.

23. *The New York Times*, July 6, 1864.

24. Charles L. Lewis, *David Glasgow Farragut* (Annapolis, Md.: Naval Institute Press, 1943), 255–56.

25. *ORN*, Series I, vol. 3, 74-75.

26. Quoted in Boykin, *Ghost Ship of the Confederacy*, 380.

27. C. Vann Woodward, ed., *Mary Chesnut's Civil War* (New Haven, Conn.: Yale University Press, 1981), 623.

28. Humphreys and Guenther, *Semmes America*, 325.

29. Quoted in Kell, *Recollections of a Naval Life*, 256–57.

30. Bulloch, *The Secret Service of the Confederate States in Europe*, I, 291.

31. Roberts, *Semmes of the* Alabama, 214–15.

32. *ORN*, Series I, vol. 3, 74–75.

33. John A. Winslow to S. McLochland, July 7, 1864, Christie's Catalogue 7814, December 1993.

34. Delaney, *John McIntosh Kell*, 179.

35. Semmes, *Memoirs of Service Afloat*, 763.

36. William J. Brinker, "Home Is the Sailor, Home from the Sea," *Journal of Confederate History*, IV (*Special Commemorative Edition*, 1989), 57.

37. Semmes, *Memoirs of Service Afloat*, 789–90.

38. Semmes to Louisa Tremlett, November 11, 1864, *Journal of Confederate History*, IV (*Special Commemorative Edition*, 1989), 58–59.

39. Semmes, *Memoirs of Service Afloat*, 794.

40. Ibid., 798.

41. Frederick W. Seward, *Seward at Washington* (New York: Derby and Miller, 1891), 228.

CHAPTER 19: "As Hard and Determined as Flint"

1. Semmes, *Memoirs of Service Afloat*, 801.

2. Ibid., 802.

3. Buchanan, the captain of the *Merrimack* in her battle with the *Monitor*, had been promoted to admiral on August 21, 1862.

4. Semmes, *Memoirs of Service Afloat*, 803.

5. Edward P. Alexander, *Fighting for the Confederacy* (Chapel Hill, N.C.: University of North Carolina Press, 1989), 506.

6. Semmes, *Memoirs of Service Afloat*, 804.

7. Ibid., 806.

8. Nelson D. Lankford, "Hard and Determined as Flint," *Journal of Confederate History*, IV (*Special Commemorative Issue*, 1989), 84.

9. J. Thomas Scharf, *History of the Confederate States Navy* (Baltimore: 1887), 746.

10. Semmes, *Memoirs of Service Afloat*, 812–13.

11. Burke Davis, *The Long Surrender* (New York: Random House, 1985), 34.

12. Semmes, *Memoirs of Service Afloat*, 814.

13. Ibid., 815.

14. Semmes Diary, *Alabama Review*, April 1975.

15. John M. Taylor, "The Second Surrender," *Military History Quarterly*, Spring 1991.

16. Semmes, *Memoirs of Service Afloat*, 817.

17. Ibid., 819.

18. Semmes, *Diary,* April 16, 1865.

19. George W. Brent to Raphael Semmes, April 16, 1865, Semmes Papers, Alabama Archives.

20. Semmes, *Diary,* April 16, 1865.

21. Ibid., April 18, 1865.

22. Semmes, *Memoirs of Service Afloat,* 821.

23. Semmes, *Diary,* May 1, 1865.

24. Ibid., May 9, 1865.

CHAPTER 20: "A Flagrant Violation of Faith"

1. Randall and Donald, *The Civil War and Reconstruction,* 519.

2. *Mobile Daily Advertiser & Register,* January 16, 1866.

3. Summersell, *C.S.S. Alabama,* 95.

4. Semmes to Pendleton Colston, December 5, 1865, Semmes Papers, Alabama Archives.

5. Quoted in *Mobile Daily Advertiser & Register,* January 16, 1866.

6. Semmes to Blanche Kell, November 28, 1865, Gary Hendershott collection.

7. Semmes to John Kell, November 28, 1865, Gary Hendershott collection.

8. The Semmes Papers in the Alabama Archives include a letter from the British banking firm of Fraser, Trenholm, which had paid Semmes for the chronometers, advising him in August 1865 that the company had no need of an agent in Rio.

9. Semmes to John Kell, November 28, 1865.

10. Randall and Donald, *The Civil War and Reconstruction,* 571.

11. Welles, *Diary,* II, 420.

12. Raphael Semmes III, quoted in *United Daughters of the Confederacy Magazine,* November 1958.

13. John A. Wyeth, *Life of General N. B. Forrest* (New York: 1899), 616–17.

14. In response to Semmes's letter, Grant told President Johnson, without enthusiasm, that he believed Semmes to be protected by the terms of his parole.

15. Semmes Prison Diary, Records Group 45, National Archives.

16. Ibid.

17. Semmes, *Memoirs of Service Afloat,* 827.

18. Welles, *Diary,* II, 404.

19. Semmes, *Memoirs of Service Afloat,* 830.

20. Jonathan T. Dorris, *Pardon and Amnesty Under Lincoln and Johnson* (Chapel Hill, N.C.: University of North Carolina, 1953), 181.

21. Summersell, *C.S.S. Alabama,* 98.

22. Welles, *Diary,* II, 423–24.

23. Roberts, *Semmes of the* Alabama, 250.

24. Summersell, *C.S.S.* Alabama, 250.

25. Jack Hurst, *Nathan Bedford Forrest* (New York: Alfred A. Knopf, 1993), 270.

26. Semmes, Prison Diary, January 28, 1866.

27. Pendleton Colston to James Hughes, February 7, 1866, published in "Raphael Semmes: Some Personal Correspondence" (Mobile Chamber of Commerce, 1977).

28. Welles, *Diary,* II, 474.

29. Ibid., 467.

30. Ibid., 476.

31. Dorris, *Pardon and Amnesty Under Lincoln and Johnson,* 183–84.

32. Humphreys and Guenther, *Semmes America,* 328–29.

33. Semmes to Pendleton Colston, May 9, 1866, Semmes Papers, Alabama Archives.

34. Undated press clipping in "Raphael Semmes: Some Personal Correspondence."

35. Edwin M. Stanton to General George H. Thomas, May 15, 1866, Lafayette McLaws Papers, University of North Carolina Library.

36. W. Cooper to Semmes, June 2, 1866, Semmes Papers, Alabama Archives.

37. Semmes, *Memoirs of Service Afloat,* 833.

38. Randall and Donald, *The Civil War and Reconstruction,* 584.

CHAPTER 21: Defiance

1. Louisa Tremlett to Semmes, May 14, 1866, Semmes Papers, Alabama Archives.

2. Semmes to David Boyd, November 19, 1866, *Alabama Review,* July 1952.

3. Roberts, *Semmes of the* Alabama, 252–53.

4. Semmes to Anne Semmes, February 3, 1867, Semmes Papers, Alabama Archives.

5. Semmes to Pendleton Colston, January 20, 1867, Semmes Papers, Alabama Archives.

6. Quoted in Roberts, *Semmes of the* Alabama, 253.

7. Anne Semmes to Semmes, January 27, 1867, Semmes Papers, Alabama Archives.

8. Semmes to Anne Semmes, June 1867, Semmes Papers, Alabama Archives.

9. Semmes to Louisa Tremlett, January 15, 1868, Museum of the Confederacy, Richmond, Virginia.

10. David Macrae, *The Americans at Home* (New York: E. P. Dutton, 1952), 379.

11. Ibid., 381.

12. Ibid., 382.

13. Semmes, Manuscript, "Second Cruise of the *Alabama*," Semmes Papers, Alabama Archives.

14. Semmes to Anne Semmes, March 9 [1868], Semmes Papers, Alabama Archives.

15. Delaney, *John McIntosh Kell*, 204.

16. James G. Blaine, *Twenty Years of Congress* (Norwich, Conn.: Henry Bill Co., 1886), II, 94–95.

17. Dorris, *Pardon and Amnesty Under Lincoln and Johnson*, 182.

18. Semmes, *Memoirs of Service Afloat*, 637.

19. Ibid., 233.

20. Ibid., 124, 355.

21. Ibid., 184.

22. Ibid., 189.

23. Ibid., 149.

24. Ibid., 753.

25. Ibid., 760.

26. Delaney, *John McIntosh Kell*, 219–20.

27. The only pertinent reference in either Semmes's journal or his memoirs is a journal note for December 21, 1863, in which he wrote, "Taking a Malay pilot anchored off Singapore at 5:30 p.m." *ORN*, Series I, vol. 2, 791.

28. Sinclair, *Two Years on the* Alabama, 255.

29. Semmes to Stephen Mallory, quoted in Durkin, *Stephen R. Mallory*, 410.

30. Semmes to Mrs. Clement Clay, July 6, 1868, Perkins Library, Duke University.

CHAPTER 22: Sunset

1. Semmes to Louisa Tremlett, January 15, 1868, Museum of the Confederacy, Richmond, Virginia.

2. *Mobile Daily Advertiser and Register*, November 19, 1870.

3. Personal communication from Charles Torrey, City Museum, Mobile, Alabama, to the author, June 1, 1993.

4. *Mobile Daily Advertiser and Register*, August 24, 1871.

5. Semmes, *Memoirs of Service Afloat*, 373.

6. Dalzell, *The Flight from the Flag*, 231.

7. Randall and Donald, *The Civil War and Reconstruction*, 676.

8. Roberts, *Semmes of the* Alabama, 279.

9. In 1874, in one more municipal tribute to the Semmes family, Oliver was elected judge of the city court, an office he would hold for forty-four years.

10. Semmes to Raphael Semmes Kell, October 26, 1872, Gary Hendershott collection.

11. Semmes to Francis Tremlett, January 5, 1872, Museum of the Confederacy, Richmond, Virginia.

12. Semmes to Jas. R. Osgood & Co., August 10, 1872, Perkins Library, Duke University.

13. Randall and Donald, *The Civil War and Reconstruction*, 584.

14. Semmes to Frederick G. Bromberg, November 6, 1873, Bromberg Papers, Library of Congress.

15. Semmes to Frederick G. Bromberg, December 17, 1873, Bromberg Papers, Library of Congress.

16. Semmes to Frederick G. Bromberg, June 1, 1874, Bromberg Papers, Library of Congress.

17. Hurst, *Nathan Bedford Forrest*, 337.

18. Saffold Berney, "Personal Recollections of Admiral Semmes," *Confederate Veteran*, September 1925.

19. Roberts, *Semmes of the* Alabama, 259–60.

20. Berney, "Personal Recollections of Admiral Semmes."

21. Semmes to William L. Maury, June 22, 1876, Philip H. Jones collection.

22. Roberts, *Semmes of the* Alabama, 261–62.

23. Raphael Semmes III, speech of January 1958, *United Daughters of the Confederacy Magazine*, November 1958.

24. Toulmin Gaines, "Childhood Recollections of 'The Admiral,'" *United Daughters of the Confederacy Magazine*, April 1947.

25. Ibid.

26. Raphael Semmes will, City Museum, Mobile, Alabama.

27. Roberts, *Semmes of the* Alabama, 263.

28. Ibid., 264.

CHAPTER 23: Semmes of the *Alabama*

1. Roberts, *Semmes of the* Alabama, 264.

2. Alexander, *Fighting for the Confederacy*, 79.

3. Humphreys and Guenther, *Semmes America*, 330.

4. *Mobile Register*, August 31, 1877.

5. *The New York Times*, September 6, 1877.

6. Bulloch, *The Secret Service of the Confederate States in Europe*, I, 289–90.

7. Porter, *Naval History of the Civil War*, 657.

8. Delaney, *John McIntosh Kell*, 218–19.

9. Ibid., 209.

10. Ibid., 220.

11. Ibid.

12. *Southern Historical Society Papers,* vol. 38, 24.
13. Dalzell, *The Flight from the Flag,* 247.
14. Fowler, *Under Two Flags,* 308.
15. Frank T. Merli, *Great Britain and the Confederate Navy* (Bloomington, Ind.: Indiana University Press, 1970), 251.
16. Semmes, *Memoirs of Service Afloat,* 751.
17. Delaney, "Old Beeswax: Raphael Semmes of the *Alabama,*" *Civil War Times,* December 1973.
18. Humphreys and Guenther, *Semmes America,* 364.

EPILOGUE

1. Personal communication from Charles Torrey, City Museum, Mobile, Alabama, to the author, June 1, 1993. Today the Semmes home is part of the First Baptist Church of Mobile. The facade is little changed from Semmes's day, but the interior has been radically altered to build a chapel in what was once Semmes's parlor and dining room.
2. *Mobile Register,* March 8, 1892.
3. Norman C. Delaney, "The Raider and the Rascal," *Civil War Times,* May 1973.
4. *Baltimore Sun,* May 14, 1991.

Index

Abby Bradford, 67, 68
Adams, Charles Francis, 103, 217
Agrippina
  description of, 103
  as tender of the *Alabama*, 129–30
Alabama
  Agrippina as tender of the, 129–30
  Alert capture by the, 111
  Altamaha capture by the, 112
  anchorage at Port Royal, 147–49
  Ariel capture by the, 138–40
  Baron de Castine capture by the, 127
  Benjamin Tucker capture by the, 112
  Brilliant capture by the, 114–15
  Charles Hill capture by the, 154
  Chastelain capture by the, 149
  christening of the, 106
  commercial impact of the, 128, 154
  complaint of marine insurance companies against the, 165
  condensing apparatus of the, 105
  consort to the, 168
  construction of the, 100
  cost of the, 105
  Courser capture by the, 112–13
  Crenshaw capture by the, 126
  crew regulations aboard the, 118–19
  description of the, 105
  Dunkirk capture by the, 122
  Elisha Dunbar capture by the, 113–14

escape from the *San Jacinto*, 132–34
first capture of the, 109
Golden Eagle capture by the, 151
Golden Rule capture by the, 149
Hatteras battle with the, 142–45
Kate Cory capture by the, 159–60
Kearsarge battle with the, 195–209,
  223, 258, 279
Kingfisher capture by the, 153
Lafayette capture by the, 125
Lauretta capture by the, 126–27
Levi Starbuck capture by the, 129
Louisa Hatch capture by the, 159–60
Manchester capture by the, 122
Morning Star capture by the, 153
mutiny aboard the, 131–32
Nora capture by the, 154
Ocean Rover capture by the, 111
Ocmulgee capture by the, 109–10
Olive Jane capture by the, 151
Parker Cook capture by the, 137
Sea Lark capture by the, 160–61
Semmes assumes command of the,
  101–2
sinking of the, 209
smuggling of liquor aboard the, 117
in South African waters, 175–80
Starlight capture by the, 110–11
surgeons aboard the, 88
Thomas B. Wales capture by the, 130

Alabama (cont.)
  Tonawanda capture by the, 122
  treatment of captives aboard the, 115,
    126
  Union capture by the, 137
  Union Jack capture by the, 160–61
  Virginia capture by the, 113
  Wave Crest capture by the, 122
  Weathergauge capture by the, 112
Albany, 37
Albert Adams, 61
Alert, 111, 112
Alexander, Edward P., 226, 270
Alsdorf, William, 206
Altamaha, 112
Amanda, 183
Amazonian, 166
Amelia Courthouse, 229
Anchorage, The, 236, 239
Angra Pequena, 176
Anne F. Schmidt, 171
Arcade, 85, 86
Ariel, 138–40
Armstrong, Richard F., 238, 272
  command of the *Sumter* by, 96
  defense of Semmes by, 259
  mention of the Malay pilot incident,
    259
  rank of, 117
  role in capture of the *Ariel*, 138–39
  role in capture of the *Ocmulgee*, 110
  turning over *Sumter* to, 96
  at the U.S. Naval Academy, 117
Articles of the Confederation, 44

Babcock, James, 185
Bahama, 99, 104, 106–8
Bahia, 161
Bailey, William, 60
Bainbridge, 149, 150
Baldwin, Charles, 178
Banks, Nathaniel P., 136
Baron de Castine, 127
Barron, Samuel, 195, 213, 214
Battle of Fredricksburg, 140
Battle of Manassas, 51
Beauregard, Pierre G. T., 54, 232, 260
Bell, Henry H., 142, 144

Ben Dunning, 61
Benjamin, Judah P., 231
Benjamin Tucker, 112
Berry, Marion Luckett, 220
Bethiah Thayer, 152
Bickford, John, 206
Bienville, 98
Bingham, J. B., 250
Blake, Homer, 142, 198
Bolles, John A., 243, 246, 265
Bonfils, M., 200
Bower, Bill, 149
Bowse, Tom, 149
Boyd, Bell, 164
Boyd, David F., 248
Bragg, Braxton, 267
Brilliant, 116
  Alabama capture of the, 114–15
  captain of the, 126
Britain, 193, 195, 263
  Confederate activities in, 102
Bromberg, Frederick, 266
Brooke, Philip, 217
Brooklyn, 144
  captain of the, 68
  search for the *Alabama* by the, 146
  Sumter escape from the, 6–10, 274
Brown, John, 42
Brown, Joseph T., 85
Brown, Lawrence, 188, 189
Bryan, Charles B., 265
Buchanan, Franklin, 225
Buchanan, James, 52
Bull, John, 263
Bulloch, James
  acquiring of the *Agrippina* by, 129
  on the *Alabama* and *Kearsarge* battle,
    213, 215
  description of, 98, 271
  desire to command the *Alabama*,
    101–2
  recruitment of John Low by, 167
  Semmes's correspondence with,
    125–26
  on the sinking of the *Alabama*, 213,
    215
Butcher, Matthew J., 103
Butler, Benjamin F., 267

Cable, George W., 3
Cadmus, 72
Call, Richard, 18
Campaign of General Scott in the Valley of Mexico, The (Semmes), 38
Canby, Edward R. S., 235
Cande, Maussion de, 80, 130, 133
Cape of Good Hope, 172
Cape Town, 177
Cayenne, 74
Chandler, Ralph, 132
Chapman, Robert, 63, 162, 256
Charles Hill, 154, 155, 156
Chase, Salmon P., 18
Chastelain, 149
Chesapeake, 217
Chesnut, Mary, 216
Circe, 280
Clara L. Sparks, 135
Clarke, Francis, 37, 38
Clay, Clement, 260
Clay, Clement C., 45
Clay, Henry, 42
Cobb, Howell, 50
Colston, Ann, 265
Colston, Pendleton, 242, 244, 249
  children of, 265
  death of, 265
  wife of, 236
Commerce raiding, 59, 71, 198
Compromise of 1850, 42
Confederate Lighthouse Bureau, 53
Conolly, Thomas, 226–27
Conrad, 167, 170, 193
Conrad, Charles M., 50
Constellation, 18, 19
Contest, 184, 185, 186
Cooper, Edward, 176
Cooper, John, 152
Costa Rica, 240, 241
Couronne, 202, 203
Courser, 113–14
Creesy, Josiah, 95
Crenshaw, 126
Creole, 24
Cruise of the Alabama and the Sumter, The, and disavowal by Semmes, 260
C.S.S. *Alabama* Challenge, 280

Cuba, 61, 64–65
Cummings, Simeon W., 173
Curaçao, 66, 67

Dacotah, 83, 102, 151
Daniel Trowbridge, 78
Dan River, 230
Davis, Jefferson, 224, 254, 255
  arrest of, 236
  attitude toward the Confederate navy, 55
  authorization of surrender by, 231
  capture of, 55, 234
  Confederate navy and, 55
  presidential oath of, 49
  Semmes congratulated by, 230
  valedictory speech of, 46
Dayton, William, 197
Declaration of Paris (1856), 56, 71
Deerhound, 202, 218
  rescue of Semmes by the, 208–9, 211
Dix, John A., 163
Dobbin, James C., 40
Dorris, Jonathan, 255
Douglas, Stephen A., 45
Drewry's Bluff, 226
Dudley, Thomas, 100
Dunkirk, 123
  Alabama capture of the, 122
Dunnington, James, 227
Du Pont, Samuel F., 168

Early, Jubal A., 254
Eben Dodge, 86
Edge, Frederick, 213
Egan, Robert, 118, 179
Electra, 35
Elisha Dunbar, 115, 116
  Alabama capture of the, 113–14
Elmstone, Thomas, 176
Emily Farnum, 115
Emma Jane, 190, 191
Enrica, 103–6
Essex, 59, 79
Evans, James, 126, 130, 188
Evans, William, 162
Ewell, Richard S., 228

Ex parte Milligan, 245
Express, 171, 172

Fairchild, George H., 130, 244
Farragut, David, 196, 216
Federal navy, 55
Fernando de Noronha, 157, 161, 165
Fingal, 167
Flirt, 39
Flores, 110
Florida, 160, 264
    escape of the, 102
    Maffitt's command of the, 153, 196
    purchase of the, 100
Forrest, George, 122, 136
Forrest, Nathan B., 240, 267
Fort-de-France, 80, 132, 133
Fort Sumter, 50
Fort Warren, 95
Fowler, William M., Jr., 275
France, 83, 195
Freeman, Miles, 83, 139, 202
Freemantle, Arthur, 93
French, Lyman, 239–40
Frost, William, 171
Fullam, George, 174, 187, 207
    account of battle of the *Alabama* and
        the *Hatteras*, 143
    journal of, 124, 132
    as principal boarding officer, 167

Gaines, Toulmin, 268, 269
Galt, Francis, 88, 123, 213
    in Brazil with Semmes, 158–59
    correspondence of, 272
    promotion to paymaster, 158
Georgia, 153, 196, 264
    Maury command of the, 162
    in South African waters, 178
Gibraltar, 97
Gifford, David R., 113
Gildersleeve, 164
Gladstone, William, 212
Gloire, 93
Godson, Henry, 189
Golden Eagle, 151, 152
Golden Rocket, 60, 62
    burning of, 129

Golden Rule, 149
Gordon, John B., 266, 267
Graham, Walter, 177
Grant, Ulyses S., 33, 227, 240
Grier, Robert, 71
Guerout, Max, 280–81

Hagar, George, 114–15, 116, 126
Harding, John, 104
Harpers Ferry, 42
Hartsuff, George L., 232–33
Hatteras, 253, 258, 274
    battle with the *Alabama*, 142–45
    Blake command of the, 142
    first officer of the, 147
Havana, 57
Henry, Patrick, 42
Hercules, 103
Highlander, 188
Hopkins, Charles, 37
Howell, Beckett, 225
Hudgins, A. G., 64
Hughes, James, 242

Illinois, 39
*Influence of Sea Power Upon History,
    The* (Mahan), 79
Ino, 95
Investigator, 92
Iroquois, 102
    captain of the, 198
    Sumter chase by the, 69, 79–81

Jabez Snow, 166
Jackson, Thomas J. ("Stonewall"), 26,
    161
James River Squadron, 140, 225
John A. Parks, 152, 153
John Laird Sons, 280
Johnson, Andrew, 254
    attitude toward secession, 237
    response to Semmes's plea for pardon,
        247
    Semmes's appeal to, 242–45
Johnson, Brent, 177
Johnston, Joseph E., 231, 260
Johnston-Clarendon Convention, 263
Jones, Albert J., 139

Jones, Evan P., 208, 210
Jones, John Paul, 59
Joseph Maxwell, 68, 71, 72
Joseph Park, 77, 78, 89
Justina, 165

Kate Cory, 159–60
Kearsarge, 96, 253, 270, 275
  at the Azores, 121
  Pickering command of the, 95
Kell, Blanche, 237, 253–54, 259
Kell, John McIntosh, 5, 100, 107
  abandoning the *Alabama*, 208–9
  on the *Alabama* mutiny, 131
  court-martial headed by, 122
  death of, 272
  description of, 74–75
  in the James River Squadron, 226
  praise for *Sumter* by, 97
  return to the Confederacy of, 219
  Semmes's correspondence with, 238
  Semmes's defense of, 37–38
  Semmes's reliance on, 63, 117
  Semmes's decision to fight the
    Kearsarge and, 198
  Semmes's visit to, 253–54
  son of, 237
  supervision of *Alabama* gunners by,
    206
  wife of, 237, 253–54, 259
Kell, Semmes Raphael, 265
Keystone State, 69, 79
Kingfisher, 153
Knox, William, 49, 234

Lafayette, 126, 159
  Alabama capture of the, 125
Lamplighter, 124
Lancaster, John, 202, 211, 217
Lauretta, 126–27
Lee, Robert E., 26, 30
  popular confidence in, 224
  Semmes's visit with, 225
  use of enemy journals by, 124
  victory at Fredericksburg of, 140
Levi Starbuck, 129, 130
  Alabama capture of the, 129
Lexington, 15

Lieutenant Izard, 18
Lighthouse Board, 40, 44
Lincoln, Abraham, 45, 140
  criticism of, 196
  inauguration of, 51
  interest in the Navy, 55
  praise for Winslow by, 223
  reelection of, 224
  Semmes's reaction to death of, 232
  Semmes versus, 51–52
Llewellyn, David, 207, 211
Longstreet, James, 45, 254, 260
Louisa Hatch, 157–60
  plundering of the, 161
Louise, 240
Low, John, 167, 177, 190
Lucas, Frederick J., 184
Lusitania, 273

Machias, 61
Macrae, David, 252
Maffitt, John, 102, 196, 256
Magnolia Cemetery, 267
Magruder, John B., 141
Mahan, Alfred T., 78
Mahoney, Michael, 179
Malay pilot incident, 259, 272
Mallory, Stephen R., 99, 126, 228
  appointment as Confederate navy sec-
    retary, 53–56
  arrest of, 236
  assessment of, 275
  directs Semmes to command the
    Alabama, 107
  Semmes's relationship with, 225
  valedictory speech of, 46
Manchester, 124
  Alabama capture of the, 122
Manet, Edouard, 202
Mars, Michael, 190, 205, 208
Martaban, 187, 252, 278
Martha Wenzell, 176
Mason, James, 94, 96, 100
Maury, Dabney H., 236, 240
Maury, Matthew, 20, 219, 265
Maury, William L., 162, 196, 268
Mayflower, 262
McDougal, David S., 182, 183, 185

Melita, 101
Memoirs of Service Afloat During the War Between the States (Semmes), 255, 260, 273
Memphis Bulletin, 250, 251
Mexican War, 42
Milligan, Lambdin P., 245
Minnesota, 6
Mississippi, 23
Mohican, 165, 183
Montgomery, Richard, 49
Montmorenci, 85, 86
Morning Star, 153
Muelnier, Maximilian von, 180
Myers, Henry, 95, 110

Napoleon, 203
Nashville, 87
Naval History of the Civil War (Porter), 271
Neapolitan, 91, 92, 93
  burning of the, 130
Niagara, 6, 79
Nora, 154, 155, 156
Nye, 160

O'Brien, Matthew, 184
Ocean Rover, 111
Ocmuglee, 109–10
Olive Jane, 151, 152
Oreto (see also *Florida*), 99, 101
Osborn, Abraham, 110

Pacific Mail Steamship Company, 79
Palmer, James, 81, 83, 198
Palmetto, 151
Paramaribo, 75
Parker, William, 213
Parker Cook, 137
Partridge, L. H., 144
Patrick Henry, 164, 226
Peerless, 234
Pendleton, George, 163
Perry, Matthew C., 24, 26
Petrel, 142
Pickering, Charles W., 95, 121
Pike, Samuel B., 187, 188, 252
Plover, 78

Point Clear, 268, 269
Poor, Charles, 68
Porpoise, 21
Porter, David D., 129, 144
  command of the *Powhatan* by, 68, 79
  criticism of Semmes by, 44, 260, 271–72
  father of, 79
  memoirs of, 83, 260, 271
  in the War of 1812, 59
Porter, Henry, 147
Port Royal, 147
Powhatan, 68–69, 79
Pozuela, José de la, 63
Princeton, 23
Privateers, 56, 169
Puerto Cabello, 67, 68
Pulo Condore, 185
Punjaub, 152
Pyrrho, Sebastiao José Basilio, 158

Q-ships, 78
Quang Tung, 191

Randolph, Victor, 37
Ranger, 59
Raritan, 23
Read, George, 138
Reconstruction, 266, 269
Rockingham, 191, 195, 199
Roe, Francis, 37
Ronckendorff, William, 132
Roosevelt, Theodore, 264
Rousseau, Lawrence, 50
Russell, John, 155

San Jacinto, 79, 80, 197
  Alabama escape from the, 132–34
São Luís, 75
Saunders, Otley & Company, 260
Savannah, 71, 126
Scott, Winfield, 22–30, 39
Sea Bride, 191, 193
  capture of the, 174–78
  sale of the, 178–79
Sea Lark, 160–61, 171
Semmes, Alexander, 3

Semmes, Anne Elizabeth (Spencer), 47, 236
  attitude toward secession, 3
  courtship of, 18
  death of, 279
  description of, 19
  marriage of, 19
  Mobile presents house to, 262
  move with children to Baltimore, 47
  parents of, 18
  personality of, 240
  Semmes's correspondence with, 120, 251
  Semmes's reunion with, 222
  visit to Semmes in confinement, 244–45
Semmes, Anne E. (daughter), 47, 240, 265, 268
Semmes, B. J., 264
  comments on loss of the *Alabama*, 217
  personality of, 278
  relationship to Semmes, 251
Semmes, Benedict, 12–13
Semmes, Catherine (Middleton)
  marriage of, 13
Semmes, Electra, 20, 47, 265
  children of, 265
  husband of, 236
Semmes, Katherine, 20, 47, 264
Semmes, Oliver, 221, 234
  capture of, 164
  Semmes's law practice with, 261
  stepson of, 268
  at West Point, 47, 53
Semmes, Pauline, 236
Semmes, Raphael
  abandoning the *Alabama*, 208–9, 219
  ancestors of, 12–13
  appointment as midshipman, 15
  arrest of, 240–46
  in Asian waters, 181–94
  assignment to Confederate Lighthouse Bureau, 53
  assignment to Lighthouse Service, 40
  assignment to the *Alabama*, 101–102
  assignment to the *Alabama* of, 57
  attitude toward blacks, 51, 257
  birth of, 13
  boyhood of, 14
  in Brazil, 76
  chauvinism of, 33
  children of, 20
  chronometer and flag collecting of, 89
  command of the *Sumter*, 4–11
  death of, 269
  decision to fight the *Kearsarge*, 196–200, 213–15
  description of, 2, 267–68
  as a disciplinarian, 88–90, 149–50, 177
  as editor of the *Memphis Bulletin*, 251
  effect of Civil War on family of, 3
  Emperor Wilhelm II's admiration for, 273
  in Europe following loss of the *Alabama*, 216–20
  family concerns of, 37
  father of, 13
  financial status of, 41
  foster brother of: *See* Semmes, B. J.
  godson of, 265
  identification of nationality of ships by, 126
  ill health of, 196
  James River Squadron command of, 225–30
  knowledge of international law, 134
  law practice of, 38–39
  on the lecture circuit, 251–53
  life after the Civil War, 236–37
  Lincoln versus, 51–52
  Mallory's relationship with, 225
  marriage of, 19
  meeting with John Maffitt, 101
  memoirs of, accuracy of, 258
  in the Mexican War, 22–33
  midshipman examination of, 17
  in Montgomery, 49–51
  mother of, 13
  nicknames of, 148
  officers' opinion of, 36
  personality of, 73, 88, 196
  philosophy of, 141
  physical description of, 14, 220
  politics of, 30–33, 44
  at Port Royal, 148–49

Semmes, Raphael (*cont.*)
  praise of Robert E. Lee, 30
  press criticism of, 115–16
  promotion to rear admiral of, 225
  Puritan hostility of, 122–23
  as Raymond Smith, 220
  reaction to Lincoln's death, 232
  record with the *Sumter*, 97
  recruiting techniques of, 107
  relationship with subordinates, 88–89,
    117–20, 150
  release from prison of, 246
  romanticism of, 257, 276
  secession and, 45
  in the Second Seminole War, 18
  service on the *Lexington*, 15–17
  slaves of, 43
  in South African waters, 170–80
  teaching career of, 249–50
  visit with General Lee, 225
Semmes, Raphael (son), 227, 264
  in Confederate service, 13
Semmes, Richard Thompson
  birth of, 13
  marriage of, 13
Semmes, Samuel, 236
  as a Unionist, 3
Semmes, Spencer, 39, 47, 264
  in First Regiment of Louisiana
    Infantry, 3
  marriage of, 236
  as a staff officer in Confederate army,
    164
Semmes, Thomas, 222, 224
*Service Afloat and Ashore During the
  Mexican War* (Semmes), 31, 38
Seward, William H., 155, 223, 263
Shenandoah, 225, 264
Shepherd Knapp, 69
Sheridan, Philip, 230
Sherman, William Tecumseh, 248
Simes, N. P., 115
Sinclair, Arthur, 112, 238, 272
  defense of Semmes by, 259
Sinclair, George T., 201, 202, 206
Slidell, John, 94, 200
Smith, Breedlove, 108, 124, 201

Smith, Edmund Kirby, 221
Smith, Raymond, 220
Solent, 220
Somers, 23–25, 233
Sonora, 188
Sparks, 136
Speed, James, 242, 245
Spencer, Electra, 18
Spencer, Oliver, 18
Sprague, Horatio, 95
Spring Hill College, 262
St. Louis, 197
Stanton, Edwin M., 245
Starlight, 110–11
States' rights doctrine, 42, 45
Stephens, Alexander H., 52, 255
Stone, Jabez, 188
Sumner, Charles, 263
Sumter
  Arcade capture by the, 85
  deficiencies of the, 60
  Eben Dodge capture of, 86
  en route to Brazil, 65–75
  escape from the *Iroquois*, 69, 79–81
  fire aboard the, 89
  Montmorenci capture by the, 85
  Neapolitan capture by the, 92
  regulations on the, 118–19
  sale of the, 97
  Semmes takes command of the, 57
  Vigilant capture by the, 85
Suriname, 74

Talisman, 166
Tasmanian, 220
Taylor, Richard, 164, 221
Taylor, Robert, 234
Texan Star, 188
Thomas, George T., 246
Thomas B. Wales, 244
  Alabama capture of the, 130
Thornton, James S., 196, 206, 210
Tilton, Shadrach R., 113, 115
Tonawanda, 123
  Alabama capture of the, 122
Toombs, Robert, 50
Toucey, Isaac, 46

Treaty of Washington, 264
Tredegar Iron Works, 51
Tremlett, Francis, 100, 148, 219
Tremlett, Louisa, 222
  gift to Semmes, 220
  Semmes correspondence with, 221,
    248, 261
Trent, 80, 92, 123
Tunsall, Tom, 93
Tuscaloosa, 171
  as escort of the Alabama, 168
  Low in command of the, 167–68
  seizure of the, 190–91, 193
Tuscarora, 95, 102, 121
Tycoon, 192, 195

Union, 137
Union Jack, 160–61, 258
Urania, 176

Vanderbilt, 165, 178, 179, 198
Vanderbilt, Cornelius, 139
Vigilant, 85, 86
Virginia
  Alabama capture of the, 113
  as part of the James River flotilla, 225,
    226, 227, 228
  prisoners from the, 115–16

Wachusett, 140
Walker, Baldwin, 179, 190
War of 1812, 40, 42
Warrior, 93
Washington, 152
Washington and Lee College, 267
Wave Crest, 122
Weathergauge, 112
Weaver, Charles P., 161
Welles, Gideon, 84, 154, 190
  charge against Semmes by, 244

complaints of insurance companies to,
    165
diary of, 140, 239
knowledge of naval matters, 68
reaction to commissioning privateers,
    169
Semmes's arrest and, 242
Semmes's criticism of, 170
on Semmes's escape from the
    Alabama, 216
Semmes's response to, 94
Whipple, George, 88, 95
White, David, 123, 211
Wilkes, Charles
  command of the San Jacinto by, 80,
    132
  expedition of, 40
  impetuosity of, 165
  Washington's repudiation of, 140
William C. Miller Company, 99
Wills, P. B., 250
Wilson, Joe, 117, 189, 226
  parole of, 234
  Semmes's farewell to, 234
Winged Racer, 183, 185
Winslow, John Ancrum, 196, 258, 271
  awards for, 223
  competency of, 198
  Semmes versus, 155, 201, 218
  treatment of prisoners by, 211
Woods, Charles R., 240
Wright, Horatio G., 163
Wright, Luke, 264
Wyoming, 184, 186, 198
  Semmes's desire to fight the, 182

Yancey, William L., 95
Yonge, Clarence, 107, 149

Zimmer, Louis, 51

About the Author

J OHN M. TAYLOR was born at West Point, New York, in 1930. He spent part of his early youth in Japan, where his father was attached to the U.S. embassy. He graduated from Williams College in 1952 with honors in history and earned a master's degree from George Washington University in 1954. From 1952 to 1987 he was employed by the U.S. government, including four foreign postings with the State Department and the Central Intelligence Agency.

Mr. Taylor is the author of five previous books, including a biography of his father, *General Maxwell Taylor: The Sword and the Pen* (1989), and *William Henry Seward: Lincoln's Right Hand* (1991). He is also a frequent contributor to *American Heritage*, *Military History Quarterly*, and *Civil War Times*, and he has written on more general subjects for the *Wall Street Journal* and the *Washington Post*. He and his wife, Priscilla, have three grown children and live in McLean, Virginia.